M000084309

OUR LATTER-DAY HYMNS

OUR LATTER-DAY HYMNS

THE STORIES AND THE MESSAGES

KAREN LYNN DAVIDSON

Deseret Book Company
Salt Lake City, Utah

First printing March 1988

Library of Congress Cataloging-in-Publication Data

Davidson, Karen Lynn.
Our Latter-day hymns : the stories and the messages / Karen Lynn Davidson.
p. cm.
Bibliography: p.
Includes index.
ISBN 0-87579-137-9
1. Hymns of The Church of Jesus Christ of Latter-day Saints, 1985. 2. Hymns, English—History and criticism. 3. Church of Jesus Christ of Latter-day Saints—Hymns. 4. Mormon Church—Hymns. I. Title.
BX420.H953D38 1988
264'.0933202—dc10 88-1067
CIP

Printed in the United States of America 18961

10

CONTENTS

PREFACE

Many of the readers who turn to *Our Latter-day Hymns: The Stories and the Messages* do so because they love the hymns and want to learn more about them. Others, who may hold music callings in the wards and stakes of The Church of Jesus Christ of Latter-day Saints, likely refer to this volume in order to be able to share with their group some interesting background about a hymn before teaching it or reviewing it.

Sometimes the story behind a hymn is dramatic and personal. In other cases, the author or composer noted that the hymn came into being under very ordinary circumstances. And in many instances, unfortunately, we have no information about the writing of a particular hymn.

But each hymn in our hymnbook has a message that justifies its inclusion, and the discussions in this book will at least help to establish the significance of each hymn's message. You will find something in each discussion that will help you and your group to become more sensitive to the beauty of the hymn and the importance of its message.

If you are turning to this book with a more scholarly purpose in mind, be assured that every effort has been made to give the important facts, so far as they are known, about the contributors and about the hymns that make up the 1985 hymnal. Stories and traditions that cannot be documented occasionally attach themselves to hymns and their writers; although I have referred to some of these traditions for the sake of completeness, I have endeavored not to repeat mere tradition as fact.

For some hymns, extensive information is available about the author, the composer, and the circumstances of the hymn's origin. Others still pose a question. Even some of our most popular hymns elude the efforts of researchers. For example, what is the source of the hymn tune we now associate with "The Spirit of God" (no. 2)? Who was James Lucas, the probable composer of the tune we use for "Come, Let Us Anew" (no. 217)? Somewhere, in family histories, journals, obscure hymnals, or little-known reference works, may be the answers to these and many other questions. I hope that anyone who has such information will forward it to the General Music Committee of the Church.

Other reference works have laid the groundwork for this volume. In particular, this book draws heavily on George D. Pyper's *Stories of Latter-day Saint Hymns* and on J. Spencer Cornwall's *Stories of Our Mormon Hymns*. For other important resources and scholarly volumes, please see Selected References, page 465.

The musical heritage of The Church of Jesus Christ of Latter-day Saints is a complex and fascinating field of study. A greater understanding of this heritage can deepen our commitment and our sensitivity as we seek to foster fine hymn singing among the Latter-day Saints.

ACKNOWLEDGMENTS

The contributions of hundreds of people have been essential to this book, and it is not possible even to begin to thank them all by name. Many of the authors and composers generously shared information concerning the background of the writing of their hymns. If a particular author or composer was no longer living, a relative came forward, in many instances, to provide vital information for this volume. Many people—genealogists, historians, the personnel of the Church Historical Department, my parents, "hymnology hobbyists," librarians, and musicians all over the Church—deserve sincere gratitude for their help. I especially wish to thank members of the General Music Committee of the Church for their willingness to read the manuscript and make countless valuable suggestions. In addition, I owe a great debt to two knowledgeable and skillful editors, Marvin K. Gardner and Suzanne Brady.

Four individuals have helped me in ways so significant and so long-term that it is only appropriate to thank them individually. Michael F. Moody, chairman of the General Church Music Committee, has been cheerfully ready at all times to assist in solving problems great and small. Two hymn scholars, G. William Richards and Bruce David Maxwell, have gone the second and even third mile in lending me the benefit of their knowledge. And finally, I would like to thank my husband, David A. Davidson; in his support of this work and in all other matters, he embodies the words of Charles Wesley: "the patience of hope, and the labor of love." (*Hymns*, 1985, no. 217.)

INTRODUCTION

In 1985, after years of preparation, The Church of Jesus Christ of Latter-day Saints published its first new hymnbook since 1950. The new hymnbook, titled *Hymns of The Church of Jesus Christ of Latter-day Saints, 1985,* has preserved most of the well-known hymns and songs from Latter-day Saint hymn tradition, while adding many new hymns and hymn tunes. Some of the new inclusions were recently composed; others were drawn from the hymnals of various Christian traditions.

The publication of a new hymnbook is an important event from many perspectives. The singing of hymns in private and public devotions can be traced far back into antiquity as an element of worship. From the texts of the hymns that have been preserved, we can discern the values, the collective wisdom, the beliefs, hopes, fears, and even something of the history of the people who wrote them.

A hymnbook is a testament to the unique qualities of a people. The book of Psalms, sometimes called Israel's hymnbook, reveals much about the faith and worship of the ancient Hebrews. And the fact that these "hymns" are now a part of the scriptural canon of both Christians and Jews says a great deal about the importance of any such collection in defining the character of a body of believers.

Similarly, a future scholar will be able to look back at the hymns chosen for the 1985 hymnal of The Church of Jesus Christ of Latter-day Saints and reach many conclusions about the Church in the late twentieth century. A comparison of the 1985 hymnbook with previous hymnbooks will show, for example, that we no longer expect all our converts to gather in Utah, that we no longer see the world around us as hostile, that our commitment to missionary work continues, and that we wish to emphasize our devotion to such important ideals as family, service, and obedience. These and many other characteristics and concerns will be evident simply from the hymns we have chosen to preserve or create.

Thus it is no small responsibility to assemble a group of hymns that will represent current realities, be "true to the faith" of past generations, and reflect the aspirations and commitments of those who sing. In creating

The book of Psalms, sometimes called the hymnbook of ancient Israel

a hymnbook and in using it so that it becomes part of our very nature, we build a record of ourselves, both as we are and as we hope to be. And we should not be surprised if, at some future time, our children's children look upon our hymns with much the same degree of reverence as we give to the biblical psalms.

The 1985 hymnbook was prepared by the General Music Committee of the Church under the direction of the First Presidency. A revised, updated hymnbook was desirable for many reasons. A new hymnbook can refine the previous hymnbook's collection by sifting out the little-used hymns and preserving those that represent the best spiritual and creative efforts of former generations; it can help members of the congregation give more careful attention to hymns and hymn singing; and it can offer new hymns that reflect current concerns. The 1985 hymnbook is the musical and poetic declaration of a new generation of Latter-day Saints, a generation that expresses its own vision and commitment while at the same time preserving and treasuring the unchanging truths of The Church of Jesus Christ of Latter-day Saints as they have been set forth by the finest authors and composers of the past.

The 1985 hymnbook differs from the 1950 hymnbook in several important respects. Each of these changes was intended to make the book more useful.

The most noticeable difference is the inclusion of seventy-nine new hymns, along with thirteen new hymn tunes that have been matched with texts from the previous hymnbook. (For a complete list of titles, see Hymns Newly Added, p. 18.) Approximately the same number of hymns was dropped, mostly from among those that were not often sung. (See Hymns Not Retained, p. 21.)

Many of the hymns that were retained have undergone some editing, both textual and musical. (For examples, see Hymnbook Trivia: Some Information for the Curious, p. 14.)

The preface to the 1985 hymnal, written by the First Presidency, encourages "an increase of hymn singing" and urges Church members to "use the hymns to invite the Spirit of the Lord into our congregations, our homes, and our personal lives. Let us memorize and ponder them, recite and sing them, and partake of their spiritual nourishment." Referring to the revelation given to Emma Smith when she was called in 1830 to compile the first Latter-day Saint hymnbook, the First Presidency concluded, "Know that the song of the righteous is a prayer unto our Father in Heaven, 'and it shall be answered with a blessing upon [your] heads.' "

Another feature of the 1985 hymnbook is an appendix entitled "Using the Hymnbook," which gives information useful to members who are called to serve in music positions in the Church. The inclusion of this section—along with brackets on each hymn suggesting suitable organ or piano introductions—is appropriate for the hymnbook of a church in which lay members, rather than paid professionals, fill both music and leadership roles.

The hymns were grouped according to subject matter, so that all the hymns on a specific topic—such as the Restoration, the sacrament, Christmas, missionary work, the temple, and the home—can be found in one section of the hymnal.

Seven indexes were included in the 1985 hymnal: an index of authors and composers, including the most recent research on attributions; an index of titles, tunes, and meters; an index of tune names; an index of meters; an index of the scripture references that accompany each hymn; a much-expanded topical index; and an index of first lines and titles.

Although the 1950 hymnbook had a separate section for choir hymns, the 1985 hymnbook does not; however, many of the hymns previously marked for choir use were retained and edited to make them suitable for congregational singing. The number of hymns for women's voices and for men's voices was reduced, and several children's songs were added.

How were hymns chosen for the 1985 hymnal? Approximately six thousand submissions—texts and tunes—were reviewed for possible inclusion. Names of authors and composers were removed from the hymns during the screening process so the hymns would be evaluated on their own merits rather than on the names or credentials of the originators. The Hymnbook Committee sought a balance of topics: hymns of general worship, sacrament hymns, hymns in honor of the gospel's restoration, hymns on specific gospel subjects such as fasting and family life, and many others.

Every hymn, whether already a part of Latter-day Saint tradition or a proposed new hymn, was carefully considered. The doctrine expressed in each hymn was of prime consideration. The musical and literary merit counted for a great deal; but if a hymn was widely loved, it did not run much risk of exclusion, even if it was not really a first-rate hymn by artistic standards. The Committee field-tested many of the new hymns in order to learn the preferences of the general membership.

In compiling the 1985 hymnal, the Hymnbook Committee sought to be sensitive to the wishes and needs of the members of the Church while maintaining high musical and literary standards whenever possible. Members of the Church love to sing old favorites; long tradition can add to the spiritual impact of a hymn, even if the hymn might not pass the editorial screening process if it were submitted as a new contribution. Thus the 1985 hymnal includes many popular hymns from the gospel-song tradition, more dignified favorites, and noteworthy new hymns, both borrowed and newly written.

In a review of the 1985 hymnal in *The Hymn*, the official journal of the Hymn Society of America, Hugh D. McKellar of the Centre for Religious Studies at the University of Toronto commented on the usefulness of the book:

"If a hymnbook is to be truly serviceable to the great majority of its projected users, should it seek, as this one frankly does, to reach them right where they are, and draw upon their judgment about which words and tunes have, in their experience, provided most spiritual sustenance? If hymns whose worst crime is their disregard for fashion can inspire rank-and-file Mormons to go out from worship week by week and put their faith into practice, might not editorial committees of other denominations profitably take note?" (*The Hymn*, Apr. 1986, p. 45.)

The present volume is intended as a companion to the 1985 hymnal and is in many ways the counterpart to similar hymnbook companions of the past, such as J. Spencer Cornwall, *Stories of Our Mormon Hymns* (Salt Lake City, Utah: Deseret Book Co., 1963) and George D. Pyper, *Stories of Latter-day Saint Hymns* (Salt Lake City, Utah: Deseret News Press, 1939)—invaluable sources for much of the information included here. In some cases, corrections or clarifications have been made to update the older information. And of course, this new companion includes background on the many hymns that are new to the 1985 hymnbook.

Hymn by hymn, this volume provides an overview of how each of our hymns came into being, so far as the story is known: the motives of the author and composer, the historical circumstances surrounding the hymn, and the subsequent changes that may have occurred in the words or the music. It is useful to realize that every hymn does have a history. Every hymn was once new, even our favorite "old standards"; each one had to be learned, appreciated, and assimilated before it could become a beloved part of Latter-day Saint tradition.

As the backgrounds unfold concerning the various hymns—some brand new, some hundreds of years old—readers will find that they are in for some surprises. Although many of us would like to believe that our favorite hymns were inspired by dramatic spiritual experiences, it is seldom true that the words or music of a hymn flashed unbidden, as a full-blown divine gift, into the mind of the author or composer. To be sure, some of the authors and composers describe such experiences. For example, refer to the commentary on "I Need Thee Every Hour" (no. 98). But even when the feeling of inspiration was very strong, most of the authors and composers reported that they had to meet this inspiration halfway and be willing to revise, discard, rewrite, and edit. Usually, the more experienced authors and composers were willing to discuss frankly the need for reconsideration and revision. As examples, see the commentary on "Let the Holy Spirit Guide" (no. 143) and "As Now We Take the Sacrament" (no. 169). Hymn 169 is an especially interesting example of how inspiration and revision are not mutually exclusive processes.

Sometimes, even if lightning did not flash, it is nevertheless true that a hymn grew out of intense personal experience, as we can see from the stories behind the hymn texts of "Lead, Kindly Light" (no. 97), "Thy Spirit, Lord, Has Stirred Our Souls" (no. 157), and "Ring Out, Wild Bells" (no. 215). But these writers didn't deal impulsively with these intense experiences, spilling out their emotions onto paper. They sought meaning in their experience, bringing to bear their creative talents and revising until they were satisfied that the words or music did justice to their feelings and made those feelings meaningful to others as well.

Sometimes a hymn was not tied to any immediate personal experience but was written in response to an assignment, as a job that needed to be done. For example, see the commentary on "We Meet, Dear Lord" (no. 151), "Carry On" (no. 255), and "Lord, Accept into Thy Kingdom" (no. 236).

A reading of some of the biographical entries will show that most of the contributors were experienced authors or composers; a first-rate hymn is seldom a first-time effort. While they did not always report a dramatic story of divine inspiration, these men and women prepared for the writing of these hymns through a lifetime of schooling, church activity, and sensitivity to spiritual matters.

One possible surprise, then, is how undramatic most of the background stories are. A second surprise for many readers will be the discovery that quite a few hymns have become so thoroughly assimilated into Latter-day Saint hymnody that we have almost lost sight of the fact that they were not originally our own. The music for "We Thank Thee, O God, for a Prophet" (no. 19) was originally written in honor of a fallen soldier by a woman who probably knew little or nothing at all of the Latter-day Saints. The words of "For the Strength of the Hills" (no. 35) seem to characterize perfectly the courage and vigor of the early Utah Saints, but in fact the hymn originally had nothing to do with them.

A third surprise, and an intriguing aspect of hymn scholarship, is how often a melody intended for a very different purpose has been adapted as a hymn tune. This practice was common among many Christian denominations. Sometimes a hymnbook editor would decide that a tune from a nonreligious source would make a suitable hymn tune, and other times the secular tune was more or less a popular choice. In earlier times, hymnbooks usually printed only the words of the hymn, and the congregation then chose from among tunes that were familiar to them. Although these tunes were sometimes secular in origin, they became so closely tied to a particular text that they were retained and printed in later hymnals. Examples of the many hymn tunes in our book that have a secular origin include the tunes associated with "O Ye Mountains High" (no. 34), "God, Our Father, Hear Us Pray" (no. 170), "Do What Is Right" (no. 237), and "The Time Is Far Spent" (no. 266).

A fourth surprise is not so much a surprise as it is a new way of thinking about hymns. We do not often concern ourselves with hymn *tunes* as a separate topic; we are not accustomed to thinking of a hymn tune as a distinct entity, with its own name, apart from any text. Occasionally a tune has been written for a specific text and is not interchanged with any other—such as LUX BENIGNA, the tune for "Lead, Kindly Light" (no. 97); EVENTIDE, the tune for "Abide with Me!" (no. 166); and SINE NOMINE, the tune for "For All the Saints" (no. 82). But usually the link is not so close. For example, FOREST GREEN, the tune for "I Saw a Mighty Angel Fly" (no. 15), could just as well be used for "O Little Town of Bethlehem" (no. 208), and other hymnals have in fact used it for this Christmas text.

During the decades when Latter-day Saint hymnals did not include tunes, the choice of a tune that would match the meter and mood of the hymn text was the responsibility of the music director; the congregation did not necessarily expect to pair the same tunes and words each time.

In this volume, the tune name is given in the conventional all-capital letters. Because there are no rules for the source of tune names, some may seem quite whimsical. But often the source is very straightforward: the tune name honors a family member, or the text that inspired the tune, or the composer's birthplace, or perhaps the place where the tune was written.

Knowing the name of a hymn tune is especially helpful to organists: arrangements of hymns are often listed by tune name only in collections of organ literature.

In the congregations of The Church of Jesus Christ of Latter-day Saints, members of diverse backgrounds meet together to form a devoted, effective unit. In the same way, each of the hymns of our 1985 hymnal, so diverse in age, origin, and message, can play a role in our individual and congregational worship.

LATTER-DAY SAINT HYMNBOOKS: A BRIEF HISTORY

The organization of The Church of Jesus Christ of Latter-day Saints took place in a log home in Fayette, New York, in 1830. The small group of original members was not just another Christian sect; they believed fervently, as members of the Church do today, that they were the heirs of the church Christ had established on the earth during his mortal ministry. Theirs was the true and original gospel message as it was taught by Jesus Christ, restored in modern times through the agency of the Prophet Joseph Smith.

It was natural for these first members of the Church to assume that hymn singing would be part of the Latter-day Saint pattern of worship. Hymn singing had always been an important part of Christian worship services in America. The Puritans brought their psalm collections to America, and the *Bay Psalm Book*, printed in Cambridge, Massachusetts, in 1640, was the first book of any kind printed in North America. Over the next two centuries, many immigrants were drawn to such populist sects as the Baptists, and they helped to spread a different type of hymn known as the gospel song, in the "singing-school" or "folk-hymn" tradition. During the nineteenth century, especially, authors and composers such as Lowell Mason, William B. Bradbury, and George F. Root wrote hymn texts and tunes that became popular in America among virtually every Christian denomination, and the Latter-day Saints were no exception. New converts loved to sing the hymns they already knew.

But even though many hymns and hymn traditions were available to them, the early Saints did not choose to adopt in its entirety any other church's hymn tradition. They felt the need for a distinctive hymn tradition that would reflect their unique theology. In July 1830, only three months after the organization of the Church, the Lord instructed Emma Smith, wife of the Prophet Joseph, as follows:

"It shall be given thee . . . to make a selection of sacred hymns, as

Latter-day Saint hymnody owes a great deal to many non–Latter-day Saint authors and composers, such as these: (left to right) George F. Root, Lowell Mason, and William B. Bradbury, about 1867

it shall be given thee, which is pleasing unto me, to be had in my church.

"For my soul delighteth in the song of the heart; yea, the song of the righteous is a prayer unto me, and it shall be answered with a blessing upon their heads." (Doctrine and Covenants 25:11–12.)

From the very beginning, the singing of hymns has been an essential part of the history and worship of The Church of Jesus Christ of Latter-

Emma Smith, about 1850. She had been called by the Lord in July 1830 to "make a selection of sacred hymns" (D&C 25:11). Her compilation, A Collection of Sacred Hymns, for the Church of the Latter Day Saints, *was published in 1835*

day Saints. Emma Smith's collection of hymns, edited and printed by William W. Phelps, appeared in book form in 1835 under the title *A Collection of Sacred Hymns, for the Church of the Latter Day Saints*. Its format was typical for the times: it was small enough to fit in a pocket, measuring only three inches by four and one-half inches; and it contained only the words—no tunes—for its ninety hymns. Between thirty and forty of these hymns appear to have been written by Latter-day Saints; the remainder were Protestant hymns.

Twenty-six of the hymns in Emma Smith's little volume were included in the 1985 hymnbook. The hymns that have been retained, listed by their original hymn number and original first line, are as follows, with the hymn number in the present hymnbook given in parentheses:

1 Know then that ev'ry soul is free (no. 240)
4 Glorious things of thee are spoken (no. 46)
6 Redeemer of Israel (no. 6)
10 He died! the great Redeemer died! (no. 192)
11 Earth with her ten thousand flowers (nos. 87; 313)
13 Guide us, O thou great Jehovah (no. 83)
14 We're not ashamed to own our Lord (no. 57)
15 Joy to the world! the Lord will come! (no. 201)
18 Now let us rejoice in the day of salvation (no. 3)
21 The happy day has rolled on (no. 32)
23 This earth was once a garden place (no. 49)
24 Gently raise the sacred strain (no. 146)
26 Now we'll sing with one accord (no. 25)
43 Come let us sing an evening hymn (no. 167)
46 Great God! to thee my evening song (no. 164)
54 Jesus, mighty King in Zion (no. 234)
57 O God th' eternal Father (no. 175)
65 Come all ye sons of Zion (no. 38)
66 Let Zion in her beauty rise (no. 41)
68 Come all ye saints, who dwell on earth (no. 65)
70 Great is the Lord: 'tis good to praise (no. 77)
74 From Greenland's icy mountains (no. 268)
79 I know that my Redeemer lives (no. 136)
82 How firm a foundation, ye saints of the Lord (no. 85)
86 O God! our help in ages past (no. 31)
90 The Spirit of God like a fire is burning (no. 2)

The preface to the 1835 hymnbook reflected the early Saints' feeling that they needed a collection entirely their own:

"In order to sing by the Spirit, and with the understanding, it is necessary that the church of the Latter Day Saints should have a collection of 'SACRED HYMNS,' adapted to their faith and belief in the gospel,

The Manchester Hymnal, first published in 1840

and, as far as can be, holding forth the promises made to the fathers who died in the precious faith of a glorious resurrection, and a thousand years' reign on earth with the Son of Man in his glory. Notwithstanding the church, as it were, is still in its infancy, yet, as the song of the righteous is a prayer unto God, it is sincerely hoped that the following collection, selected with an eye single to his glory, may answer every purpose till more are composed, or till we are blessed with a copious variety of the songs of Zion."

A second hymnal, expanded to 304 hymns—more than three times the length of the 1835 hymnal—was printed in Nauvoo in 1841.

A volume titled *A Collection of Sacred Hymns for the Church of Jesus Christ of Latter-day Saints in Europe* was printed in Manchester, England, in 1840 under the direction of Brigham Young, Parley P. Pratt, and John Taylor. It was thereafter known as the Manchester Hymnal. After the Saints' remarkable trek westward under the leadership of Brigham Young and during the succeeding decades of relative isolation in their new western home, new groups of converts from overseas brought with them copies of the Manchester Hymnal as they made the long journey to the Salt Lake Valley. It was similar to Emma Smith's hymnal in that it printed texts without music. New hymns were added with each new edition, most of them of American origin, but the Manchester Hymnal continued to be published in England until 1890.

In the history of early Latter-day Saint hymnals, many private individuals undertook at various times to print hymnbooks for the use of Latter-day Saints; the line between "official" and "unofficial" hymnbooks

The Latter-day Saints' Psalmody, *first published in 1889*

was sometimes a vague one. But the Manchester Hymnal clearly held the distinction of being the Church's official hymnbook for several decades, going through twenty-five editions by 1912.

In 1886 President John Taylor called a committee together to provide a musical supplement to the Manchester Hymnal. The result was the *Latter-day Saints' Psalmody*, which first appeared in 1889 and went through six more editions. The *Psalmody* emphasized "home composition," tunes by Latter-day Saint composers to suit the hymn texts of the Manchester Hymnal. Words, too, were included, but for some of the longer texts, only the first few verses were printed.

As the auxiliary organizations such as Sunday School and Primary took on greater importance, leaders of these groups began to feel a need for their own music. In 1873 the Sunday School began publishing Sunday School hymns—both words and music—in the magazine known as the *Juvenile Instructor*. In 1880, under the direction of Eliza R. Snow, the Primary published *The Children's Primary Hymn Book* and the *Tune Book for the Primary Association of the Children of Zion*. Four years later, the Sunday School published the *Deseret Sunday School Union Music Book*, which was replaced by the *Deseret Sunday School Song Book*. This book was in turn the predecessor of *Deseret Sunday School Songs*, which appeared in 1909; it continued in use for many years and is vividly remembered by many of today's Latter-day Saints.

The 1985 hymnal, Hymns of The Church of Jesus Christ of Latter-day Saints, 1985

One unofficial hymnbook, *Songs of Zion,* was phenomenally popular. Published by the Northern States Mission in Chicago, it went through eleven editions from 1908 to 1925. Its compiler, German Ellsworth, surveyed all the mission presidents then serving in the Church to find out their favorite hymns. Then he supplemented these choices with other selections, most of which appeared also in the 1909 *Deseret Sunday School Songs.*

Latter-day Saint Hymns, published in 1927, was intended to replace the Manchester Hymnal, the *Psalmody,* and the unofficial *Songs of Zion.* It was to be used in conjunction with *Deseret Sunday School Songs.* These two volumes represented two still-identifiable streams in Latter-day Saint hymn tradition: (1) the "true hymns," the more dignified and traditional sacred music from Latter-day Saint and non–Latter-day Saint sources, such as those compiled in *Latter-day Saint Hymns;* and (2) the gospel songs, characterized by energetic rhythms and exhortative texts, such as many of the hymns in *Deseret Sunday School Songs.*

In 1948 the Church published a volume titled *Hymns: Church of Jesus Christ of Latter-day Saints,* which was intended to replace both the 1927 hymnbook and *Deseret Sunday School Songs.* It incorporated many Sunday School and gospel songs as well as traditional hymns, including many standard Protestant hymns that had not previously been an official part of Latter-day Saint hymnody. This hymnal was replaced by a new edition in 1950, which dropped some of the borrowed hymns and added instead some of the best-known of the gospel songs that were not part of the 1948 hymnal.

Hymns of The Church of Jesus Christ of Latter-day Saints, 1985, the current hymnbook, was published in 1985, marking the 150th anniversary of Emma Smith's first hymnal. More than a generation had passed since the 1950 hymnal had been published, and the leading Brethren of the Church felt it was time to delete material no longer useful, replace outdated hymns with new material of high quality, and design a hymnbook that would reflect the growth and scope of the worldwide Church.

Saints in non–English-speaking countries have their own hymn traditions, of course; yet Latter-day Saint hymnody has been remarkably homogeneous. As missionaries and converts in other lands compiled hymn collections, they usually chose from hymns already established among English-speaking Saints. For future hymnbooks in other languages, the 1985 English-language hymnbook will offer a central group of familiar hymns that Saints can continue to share, whatever their language; this core group will be supplemented with choices and contributions from Latter-day Saints in those countries.

Singing the songs of Zion

HYMNBOOK TRIVIA: SOME INFORMATION FOR THE CURIOUS

Here are some random facts about the 1985 hymnal. They will be of interest to those who wish to know more about the format and history of this hymnbook.

From a total of 358 contributors, 168 are Latter-day Saints, and at least 67 are women. Several contributors have only a first initial, and no other information is known. More may be women.

The composer with the greatest number of hymn tunes to his credit in the 1985 hymnal is Evan Stephens, who wrote sixteen of the tunes. The author whose name is linked with the greatest number of texts is William W. Phelps: he wrote or adapted fifteen of the texts in the hymnal.

The total number of hymns is 341; however, the book actually contains 323 different hymn titles. Eighteen of the hymns are printed twice, seven in arrangements for women's voices as well as for congregation, eight in arrangements for men's voices as well as for congregation, one with two different settings for men's voices, and two with two different settings for congregation. As hymnals go, 341 hymns is not considered a large hymnal. Many of the standard Protestant hymnals have twice as many hymns.

Three hymns are for women's voices only and are not arranged as congregational hymns. Five hymns are for men's voices only, and six hymns are for men's choir only. No hymns in the 1985 hymnal are labeled as choir hymns; however, the First Presidency's preface encourages "choirs to use the hymnbook as their basic resource."

It is somewhat unusual for the principal hymnbook of a church to include children's hymns, because in many churches children do not attend the adult worship service. But Latter-day Saint families attend sacrament meeting together, and thus a group of favorite children's songs has been included in our hymnal.

From the 1950 hymnal, 249 hymns were retained in both words and

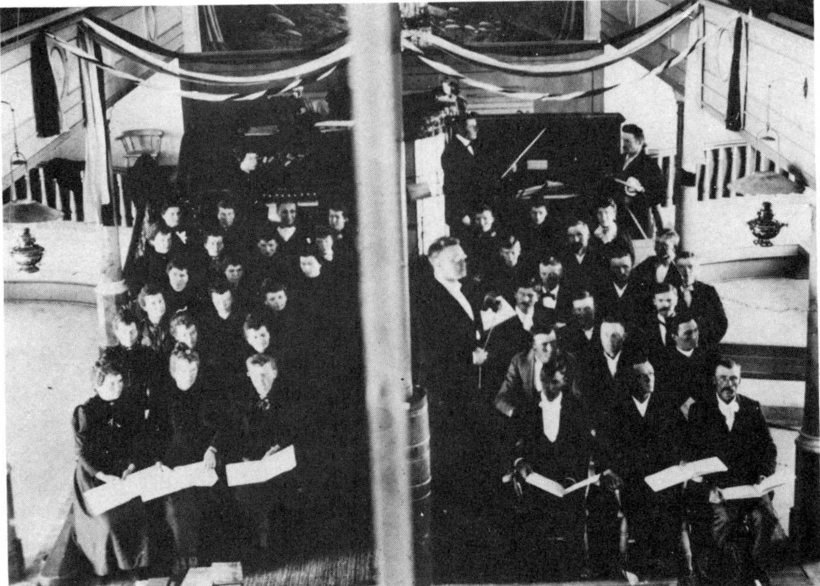

A Latter-day Saint ward choir in Ephraim, Utah, about 1900

music. Ninety-two hymns were newly created or newly borrowed for the 1985 hymnbook:

• Thirteen texts that were retained from the 1950 hymnal were paired with new tunes (newly composed or newly borrowed).

• Forty-four new compositions by Latter-day Saints, created since the publication of the last hymnbook, were added.

• Fourteen Latter-day Saint hymns and children's songs came from previous Latter-day Saint music publications.

• Five new Latter-day Saint texts were paired with newly borrowed non–Latter-day Saint tunes.

• Sixteen newly borrowed texts and tunes came from non–Latter-day Saint sources. (For a complete list of titles in each of these categories, see Hymns Newly Added, p. 18.)

Many of the hymns that were retained underwent some editing—in both text and music—for the 1985 hymnal. The Hymnbook Committee tried to avoid unnecessary tinkering; most of the changes are minor improvements and do not draw attention to themselves. Some, however, are more noticeable.

Of the musical changes perhaps the most noticeable is in key signatures. So that a worshiper who wished to sing the melody could reach the highest notes, 163 hymns were transposed to a lower key. Many of these lower keys have the additional advantage of being easier for the keyboard accompanist.

An early Church band in American Fork, Utah, about 1875

Time signatures were changed on twenty-three hymns. Most 12/8, 9/8, 4/2, and 3/2 hymns were changed to 4/4 and 3/4. Common time (𝄴) and cut time (𝄵) hymns were changed to 4/4 and 2/4.

Other examples of musical changes include the removal of rests at the ends of some phrases; the "beaming" of dotted rhythms rather than printing them as separate, unconnected notes with flags; and the occasional removal of duet passages in favor of four-part harmony.

Changes in the text were prompted by various motives. Many of the comments in this volume outline several kinds of changes and the reasons they were made. Examples of typical changes are as follows:

• Omission or revision of verses because they center too directly on North America at a time when we are becoming more conscious of ourselves as a worldwide church. For example, see the discussions of "Father, Thy Children to Thee Now Raise" (no. 91) and "Rejoice, Ye Saints of Latter Days" (no. 290).

• Changes because of awkwardness. For example, see the comments on the revision of "you who unto Jesus" in "How Firm a Foundation" (no. 85).

• Changes because a particular thought was expressed in a way that might be misunderstood. For example, see the discussions of "Have I Done Any Good?" (no. 223) and "Today While the Sun Shines" (no. 229).

• Changes because the hymn's language gave unnecessary emphasis to thoughts of violence or revenge. For example, see the discussion of "Up, Awake, Ye Defenders of Zion" (no. 248).

• Omission of a verse or verses to improve the effect and unity of a hymn. For example, see the commentary on "Ye Who Are Called to Labor" (no. 321).

• Changes in wording because a word or phrase in a hymn borrowed from another Christian denomination did not quite fit with Latter-day Saint belief. For example, see the discussion of "Our Father, by Whose Name" (no. 296).

• Alteration of titles, rather than using first lines as titles. Sometimes the first line did not really communicate the message of the hymn. For example, see the discussions of "Joseph's Smith's First Prayer" (no. 26) and "Scatter Sunshine" (no. 230). (A complete list is given in Hymns with New Titles, p. 24.)

Most hymnals of other denominations do not include metronome markings. But because music directors in Latter-day Saint congregations have varying degrees of musical training, some appreciate the specific metronome markings rather than just general indications of mood. The metronome markings in the 1985 hymnal show a range of tempos (♩ = 69–84, for example), rather than just a single metronome marking as in the 1950 hymnal.

HYMNS NEWLY ADDED

Ninety-two hymns are new, wholly or in part, to the 1985 hymnbook. Of that total, forty-four are new Latter-day Saint compositions, and fourteen others are Latter-day Saint hymns and songs previously published in Latter-day Saint music collections. Five are new Latter-day Saint texts paired with newly borrowed non–Latter-day Saint tunes, and sixteen are newly borrowed non–Latter-day Saint texts and tunes. Six are texts from the 1950 hymnbook paired with new Latter-day Saint tunes, and seven are texts from the 1950 hymnbook paired with newly borrowed non–Latter-day Saint tunes. The new hymns, listed by their 1985 number and title, are as follows:

New Latter-day Saint Compositions

8 Awake and Arise
22 We Listen to a Prophet's Voice
28 Saints, Behold How Great Jehovah
47 We Will Sing of Zion
71 With Songs of Praise
81 Press Forward, Saints
113 Our Savior's Love
123 Oh, May My Soul Commune with Thee
128 When Faith Endures
129 Where Can I Turn for Peace?
130 Be Thou Humble
134 I Believe in Christ
135 My Redeemer Lives
137 Testimony
138 Bless Our Fast, We Pray
139 In Fasting We Approach Thee
148 Sabbath Day
151 We Meet, Dear Lord
154 Father, This Hour Has Been One of Joy
155 We Have Partaken of Thy Love

168 As the Shadows Fall
169 As Now We Take the Sacrament
171 With Humble Heart
198 That Easter Morn
220 Lord, I Would Follow Thee
253 Like Ten Thousand Legions Marching
261 Thy Servants Are Prepared
263 Go Forth with Faith
277 As I Search the Holy Scriptures
279 Thy Holy Word
281 Help Me Teach with Inspiration
287 Rise, Ye Saints, and Temples Enter
290 Rejoice, Ye Saints of Latter Days
291 Turn Your Hearts
293 Each Life That Touches Ours for Good
295 O Love That Glorifies the Son
297 From Homes of Saints Glad Songs Arise
298 Home Can Be a Heaven on Earth
309 As Sisters in Zion
310 A Key Was Turned in Latter Days
311 We Meet Again As Sisters
320 The Priesthood of Our Lord
325 See the Mighty Priesthood Gathered
329 Thy Servants Are Prepared

Hymns and Songs Previously Published in Latter-day Saint Music Collections

64 On This Day of Joy and Gladness
176 'Tis Sweet to Sing the Matchless Love (MEREDITH)
249 Called to Serve
264 Hark, All Ye Nations!
300 Families Can Be Together Forever
301 I Am a Child of God
302 I Know My Father Lives
303 Keep the Commandments
304 Teach Me to Walk in the Light
305 The Light Divine
306 God's Daily Care
307 In Our Lovely Deseret
308 Love One Another
327 Go, Ye Messengers of Heaven

New Latter-day Saint Texts with Newly Borrowed Non–Latter-day Saint Tunes

12 'Twas Witnessed in the Morning Sky

143 Let the Holy Spirit Guide
197 O Savior, Thou Who Wearest a Crown
231 Father, Cheer Our Souls Tonight
256 As Zion's Youth in Latter Days

Newly Borrowed Non–Latter-day Saint Texts and Tunes

60 Battle Hymn of the Republic
69 All Glory, Laud, and Honor
82 For All the Saints
84 Faith of Our Fathers
86 How Great Thou Art
92 For the Beauty of the Earth
93 Prayer of Thanksgiving
124 Be Still, My Soul
203 Angels We Have Heard on High
205 Once in Royal David's City
206 Away in a Manger
219 Because I Have Been Given Much
265 Arise, O God, and Shine
296 Our Father, by Whose Name
299 Children of Our Heavenly Father

Texts from the 1950 Hymnbook with New Latter-day Saint Tunes

24 God Bless Our Prophet Dear (Our God, We Raise to Thee)
51 Sons of Michael, He Approaches
56 Softly Beams the Sacred Dawning
57 We're Not Ashamed to Own Our Lord
188 Thy Will, O Lord, Be Done (When in the Wondrous Realms Above)
240 Know This, That Every Soul Is Free

Texts from the 1950 Hymnbook with Newly Borrowed Non–Latter-day Saint Tunes

15 I Saw a Mighty Angel Fly
41 Let Zion in Her Beauty Rise
46 Glorious Things of Thee Are Spoken
48 Glorious Things Are Sung of Zion
54 Behold, the Mountain of the Lord
283 The Glorious Gospel Light Has Shone
284 If You Could Hie to Kolob
324 Rise Up, O Men of God (FESTAL SONG)

HYMNS NOT RETAINED

The following hymns, listed alphabetically by first line, were part of the 1950 hymnbook but were not retained in the 1985 hymnbook. All hymn numbers refer to the 1950 hymnbook unless stated otherwise.

All hail the glorious day (Choir), no. 223
Arise, my soul, arise (Choir), no. 227
As swiftly my days go out on the wing, no. 5
Author of faith, Eternal Word (Choir), no. 228
Awake! O ye people, the Savior is coming, no. 183
Beautiful Zion for me, no. 6
Blessed are they that have the faith (Choir), no. 233
Break forth, O beauteous heavenly light (Choir), no. 239
Bring, heavy heart, your grief to me (Women's Chorus), no. 349
Captain of Israel's host (Choir), no. 236; (Women's Chorus), no. 350
Come all ye saints and sing his praise, no. 11
Come, dearest Lord (Choir), no. 237
Come, go with me, beyond the sea, no. 15
Come, hail the cause of Zion's youth, no. 16
Come, lay his books and papers by (Men's Voices), no. 338
Come, thou Fount of every blessing, no. 70
Down by the river's verdant side, no. 55
Each cooing dove, no. 38
Farewell, all earthly honors, no. 35
For our devotions, Father, no. 107
Give us room that we may dwell (Choir), no. 256
Glory be to God in the highest (Women's Chorus), no. 359
God of our fathers, known of old, no. 76. The Leroy Robertson tune, ALICE, no. 77, was retained with this text.
Guide us, O Thou great Jehovah, no. 57. The tune CWM RHONDDA, no. 56, was retained with this text.
Hark, listen to the trumpeters (Choir), no. 253
Hark, ten thousand thousand voices (Choir), no. 249

Hushed was the evening hymn (Choir), no. 252
I'll praise my maker while I've breath (Choir), no. 254
Jesus, lover of my soul, no. 84. The tune REFUGE, no. 259, was retained with this text.
Land of the mountains high, no. 140
Let each man learn to know himself, no. 91
Lift thine eyes to the mountains (Women's Chorus), no. 370
Lo! on the water's brink we stand, no. 97
Lord imparted from above, The (Choir), no. 298
Lord of all being, throned afar (Choir), no. 287
Lord, thou wilt hear me when I pray (Choir), no. 265
M.I.A., we hail thee! no. 111
'Mid pleasures and palaces, no. 185; (Women's Voices), no. 372
Not now, but in the coming years (Choir), no. 267; (Male Chorus), no. 334; (Women's Chorus), no. 375
O awake! my slumbering minstrel (Choir), no. 268
O'er the gloomy hills of darkness, no. 127
O happy home! O blest abode! no. 133
O happy homes among the hills (Male Chorus), no. 337
Oh give me back my Prophet dear, no. 137
O my Father, no. 138. The tune MY REDEEMER, no. 139, was retained with this text.
One sweetly solemn thought (Choir), no. 272
On the mountain's top appearing (Choir), no. 273
Rejoice, ye saints of latter days, no. 207. A new hymn with this title, also written by Mabel Jones Gabbott, is no. 290 in the 1985 hymnal.
Rest, rest for the weary soul (Choir), no. 278
Sacred the place of prayer and song (Choir), no. 281
Savior, Redeemer of my soul (Choir), no. 282. The tune GLADYS, no. 155, was retained.
Seer, Joseph, the Seer, The (Choir), no. 296
Shall we meet beyond the river, no. 156
Sister, thou wast mild and lovely (Women's Voices), no. 381
Stars of morning, shout for joy, no. 164
Sweet is the hour when thus we meet, no. 12-A
Take courage, Saints, and faint not by the way, no. 167
There is a land whose sunny vales, no. 72
Think not when you gather to Zion, no. 21
Thou dost not weep to weep alone, no. 181
Though in the outward Church below, no. 102
Unanswered yet? The prayer your lips have pleaded (Choir), no. 286
Up! arouse thee, O beautiful Zion! (Choir), no. 283

We'll sing the songs of Zion, no. 205
What voice salutes the startled ear (Choir), no. 275
When Christ was born in Bethlehem (Choir), no. 295
When dark and drear the skies appear (Choir), no. 293
When first the glorious light of truth, no. 198
Ye children of our God (Choir), no. 288
Ye chosen Twelve, to you are given, no. 211

HYMNS WITH NEW TITLES

Twenty-seven hymns retained from the 1950 hymnbook were printed with new or altered titles in the 1985 hymnbook. These are the hymns, listed alphabetically by the former title:

Title and Hymn Number (1950)	*Title and Hymn Number (1985)*
Come, All Ye Sons of Zion (no. 303)	Come, All Ye Saints of Zion (no. 38)
Earth, With Her Ten Thousand Flowers (nos. 30; 354)	God Is Love (nos. 87; 313)
Ere You Left Your Room This Morning (no. 31)	Did You Think to Pray? (no. 140)
Firm as the Mountains Around Us (no. 42)	Carry On (no. 255)
From Greenland's Icy Mountains (no. 40)	Come, All Whose Souls Are Lighted (no. 268)
The Happy Day Has Rolled On (no. 250)	The Happy Day at Last Has Come (no. 32)
In a World Where Sorrow (no. 74)	Scatter Sunshine (no. 230)
It May Not Be on the Mountain Height (nos. 75; 318)	I'll Go Where You Want Me to Go (no. 270)
I Wander Through the Stilly Night (no. 294)	Come unto Him (no. 114)
Jesus, My Savior True (nos. 85; 309)	Guide Me to Thee (no. 101)
Now to Heaven Our Prayer (no. 171)	God Speed the Right (no. 106)

Title and Hymn Number (1950)	*Title and Hymn Number (1985)*
Oh Beautiful for Spacious Skies (nos. 126; 378)	America the Beautiful (no. 338)
Oh Hark! A Glorious Sound Is Heard (no. 134)	Rejoice! A Glorious Sound Is Heard (no. 257)
Oh, How Lovely Was the Morning (no. 136)	Joseph Smith's First Prayer (no. 26)
Oh Say, Can You See (no. 131)	The Star-Spangled Banner (no. 340)
O Sons of Zion (no. 152)	O Saints of Zion (no. 39)
Our God, We Raise to Thee (no. 144–A)	God Bless Our Prophet Dear (no. 24)
Shall the Youth of Zion Falter? (no. 157)	True to the Faith (no. 254)
There Is an Hour of Peace and Rest (no. 172)	Secret Prayer (no. 144)
There Is Beauty All Around (nos. 169; 383)	Love at Home (nos. 294; 318)
This Earth Was Once a Garden Place (no. 389)	Adam-Ondi-Ahman (no. 49)
To Nephi, Seer of Olden Time (no. 186)	The Iron Rod (no. 274)
A Voice Hath Spoken From the Dust (no. 291)	Men Are That They Might Have Joy (no. 275)
When in the Wondrous Realms Above (no. 199)	Thy Will, O Lord, Be Done (no. 188)
When the Rosy Light of Morning (no. 200)	Come Away to the Sunday School (no. 276)
When Upon Life's Billows (no. 202)	Count Your Blessings (no. 241)
The World Has Need of Willing Men (no. 206)	Put Your Shoulder to the Wheel (no. 252)

STORIES AND MESSAGES OF THE HYMNS

The Morning Breaks 1

Text: Parley P. Pratt (1807–1857; LDS)
Music: George Careless (1839–1932; LDS)
Tune name: HUDSON

In our 1985 hymnal, Parley P. Pratt's bold declaration of the restored gospel, "The Morning Breaks," resumes its traditional place as our premier hymn. As it has done in other Latter-day Saint hymnals, it sets an exciting, uniquely Latter-day Saint tone for the rest of the volume.

"The Morning Breaks, the Shadows Flee" was printed in the *Millennial Star* newspaper in 1840 and then appeared as the first hymn in the Manchester Hymnal, published in England that same year. Dr. Edward L. Hart, professor emeritus of English at Brigham Young University, pointed out that Parley P. Pratt apparently found the hymn's opening line in Charles Wesley's poem, "Wrestling Jacob," based on chapter 32 of Genesis. Jacob questions his heavenly visitor about his identity; finally, he exclaims: "The morning breaks, the shadows flee: / Pure universal Love Thou art!" (*Eighteenth Century Poetry and Prose,* ed. Louis I. Bredvold et al. [New York: Ronald Press Co., 1973], p. 693.)

Evidently Charles Wesley's line "The morning breaks, the shadows flee" stirred strong feelings in Parley P. Pratt. But these feelings took on a different emphasis: the glorious dawn that vanquished the shadows of darkness suggested to Elder Pratt the newly restored gospel of Jesus Christ. The rest of the text followed from this impulse. The gospel promises light to a world waiting in spiritual darkness, and the text makes special reference to the return of Israel to the promised land in fulfillment of prophecy.

The words have been sung to many different tunes, including DUKE STREET (the tune for "From All That Dwell below the Skies," no. 90). But the familiar George Careless tune now has a secure place in the hearts of Latter-day Saints as a fitting match for Elder Pratt's text. George D. Pyper gave this account of the tune's creation:

"Brother Careless set sail from England on the *Hudson* June 3, 1864. When the ship neared Castle Garden, New York, the captain came to George and said he had admired the singing of the Mormon group so much that he wanted one of the professor's hymn tunes.

" 'I am very sorry, captain, but my music is all packed up. I haven't even a bit of music paper, or I would write one for you.' The captain said he must have one. So young Careless took a piece of writing paper out of his pocket, drew a staff across it, then looked for a quiet place. On an empty barrel, in a corner of the vessel, he sat down and wrote the tune called 'Hudson' in honor of the boat upon which he had sailed and also of the Hudson River into which they were gliding. The tune he put to the words 'The Morning Breaks, the Shadows Flee.' After writing the music, Brother Careless assembled his choir and sang it for the captain, giving him the rough copy of the music, over which the captain seemed much delighted." (*Stories of Latter-day Saint Hymns*, pp. 41–42.)

The hymn tune was first published in 1876.

"The Morning Breaks" is one of only two hymns in the current hymnal with five verses included inside the music staff. (See also no. 214.) The 1985 Hymnbook Committee felt that none of the verses of this important hymn should be deleted or relegated to the bottom of the page.

The Spirit of God 2

Text: William W. Phelps (1792–1872; LDS)
Music: Anonymous (ca. 1844)
Tune name: ASSEMBLY

Because it is so closely tied with important events in Church history, and because it is part of such joyful occasions as temple dedications in our own day, "The Spirit of God" is one of the most significant and beloved hymns in Latter-day Saint hymn tradition. It truly affords an opportunity to sing and shout "with the armies of heaven."

For the Saints in Kirtland, Ohio, the year 1836 opened with hope and anticipation. Their brethren in Missouri were at peace, at least temporarily, with their Clay County neighbors. Joseph Smith had purchased ancient Egyptian artifacts and was preparing to translate the book of Abraham. During the previous year, Emma Smith had published a hymnbook for use throughout the Church. "The Spirit of God," already published in that hymnbook, was printed again in January 1836 in the newspaper called *The Messenger and Advocate.*

William W. Phelps's hymn text anticipated one of the most important milestones in Church history—the dedication of the Kirtland Temple on March 27, 1836. The minutes of that ceremony indicate that this hymn and "Now Let Us Rejoice" (no. 3) were sung to the same tune—HOSANNA—during that meeting. "The Spirit of God" was sung immediately following the dedicatory prayer, which is given in its entirety in section 109 of the Doctrine and Covenants.

The dedication of the Kirtland Temple was accompanied with remarkable manifestations of the Spirit. Joseph Smith reported: "A noise was heard like the sound of a rushing mighty wind, which filled the Temple, and all the congregation simultaneously arose, being moved upon by an invisible power; many began to speak in tongues and prophesy; others saw glorious visions; and I beheld the Temple was filled with angels. . . . The people of the neighborhood came running together (hearing an unusual sound within, and seeing a bright light like a pillar of fire resting upon the Temple), and were astonished at what was taking place." (*History of The Church of Jesus Christ of Latter-day Saints*, ed. B. H. Roberts [Salt Lake City, Utah: The Church of Jesus Christ of Latter-day Saints, 1948], 2:428.)

This Pentecost-like spirit is reflected in "The Spirit of God." The words of the traditional Hosanna Shout, in which the entire congregation participates during temple dedications, are repeated in the chorus, "Hosanna, hosanna to God and the Lamb!" The hymn is sung today at every temple dedication and is also frequently used in conferences and on other occasions that call for a strong expression of rejoicing.

Two verses found in Emma Smith's 1835 hymnbook have been omitted in our recent hymnals:

We'll wash, and be wash'd, and with oil be anointed
Withal not omitting the washing of feet:
For he that receiveth his PENNY appointed,
Must surely be clean at the harvest of wheat.

Old Israel that fled from the world for his freedom,
Must come with the cloud and the pillar, amain:
[And] Moses, and Aaron, and Joshua lead him,
And feed him on manna from heaven again.

The tune ASSEMBLY was first published in 1844 in a small hymnal designed for use by Latter-day Saint missionaries in New England. It may have been an already existing hymn tune; some believe it may even be HOSANNA, the tune used at the dedication of the Kirtland Temple. To this point, no researcher has uncovered the details of its origin.

Now Let Us Rejoice 3

Text: William W. Phelps (1792–1872; LDS)
Music: Henry Tucker (ca. 1863)
Tune name: LION OF JUDAH or PHELPS

The great promises of the restored gospel of Jesus Christ have sustained Church members in times of persecution. In this hymn, we have the privilege of repeating and reliving the commitment of the pioneer Saints.

The remarkable background of the writing of this hymn is a story that increases our admiration for the faith and courage of the early Saints.

William W. Phelps and his family were living in Jackson County, Missouri, where some twelve hundred Latter-day Saints had built homes and planted crops. Phelps was editor of the newspaper *The Evening and Morning Star*. "Presently, in 1833, a mob, plentifully armed and numbering between four and five hundred, came upon the settlement at Independence. They tore down the two-story brick building in which the press was housed and in the lower part of which the Phelps [family] lived; they destroyed the press, burned the books and papers, drove Mrs. Phelps and her baby out upon the street; . . . and they served warning on all the Saints living in the county not to do any more work or build or buy or sell in their settlements. Later, when the chill of November came, all the Saints were ejected from the county, and were not allowed to take with them any clothing or food. And later, more than two hundred houses in which they had lived were destroyed.

" 'Now Let Us Rejoice' came out of this situation. Defeat, frustration, homelessness, suffering, privation, hunger, even—these produced a hymn that still gives hope and sustenance to hundreds of thousands who live in better times. . . . It was the lily coming out of the ooze." (George D. Pyper, *Stories of Latter-day Saint Hymns*, p. 188. See B. H. Roberts, *A Comprehensive History of The Church of Jesus Christ of Latter-day Saints, Century One* [Salt Lake City, Utah: The Church of Jesus Christ of Latter-day Saints, 1930], 1:332–33; 343–44.)

In our day, it is not the "hundreds of thousands" noted by George D. Pyper but literally millions who derive strength from the words of this hymn. "Now Let Us Rejoice" recalls the amazing, resilient faith of our pioneers and helps us to strengthen our own. Even in the worst of times, we can still rejoice as we "watch for the day when the Savior will come."

Both "Now Let Us Rejoice" and "The Spirit of God" were sung at the dedication of the Kirtland Temple in 1836 to the same tune—HOSANNA. (See Joseph Smith, *History of The Church of Jesus Christ of Latter-day Saints*, ed. B. H. Roberts [Salt Lake City, Utah: The Church of Jesus Christ of Latter-day Saints, 1948], 2:416, 426.) This may be the tune that is used today for "The Spirit of God" (no. 2).

In "Source Book for *Hymns* (1950)," Bruce David Maxwell pointed out (pp. 42–43) that the tune PHELPS (the current setting for "Now Let Us Rejoice") is virtually the same as the tune known as LION OF JUDAH. It was first printed with the Phelps text in Eliza R. Snow's *Tune Book for the Primary Association* (1880). A non–Latter-day Saint gospel song collection called *Waters' Choral Harp*, published in 1863, credits Henry Tucker as the composer.

Truth Eternal 4

Text: Parley P. Pratt (1807–1857; LDS)
Music: Alexander Schreiner (1901–1987; LDS)
Tune name: MOORE

One of the first to learn and preach the truths of the newly restored gospel, Parley P. Pratt often spoke through poetry to convey his feelings about the gospel message. This hymn honors the power of truth. Truth will liberate, enlighten, and save.

As we can also see in "The Morning Breaks" (no. 1), Parley P. Pratt was fond of the image of the breaking of day as a symbol of the gospel's restoration. In this hymn, too, "Truth shall triumph as the light / Chases far the misty night."

We usually think of the gospel in two segments: the gospel of the former days, when Jesus was alive upon the earth, before apostasy occurred and priesthood powers were removed; and the restored gospel of the latter days, given again to the earth through the Prophet Joseph Smith. This hymn, however, emphasizes the eternal nature of the gospel. Although doctrinal truths and priesthood authority were taken from the earth for many centuries, they continued to exist in another sphere while awaiting the time of the Restoration. The priesthood holders of the latter days are "priests of heaven's royal line," and truth now encompasses all times and peoples as "endless ages own its sway."

Parley P. Pratt's devotion to the cause of truth literally knew no bounds. He pledged the ultimate commitment—that he would, if necessary, give his life for the cause of truth. In *Stories of Latter-day Saint Hymns,* George D. Pyper paid this tribute:

"Parley P. Pratt's life was full of trials and persecutions. He rarely found the peace his soul desired and finally gave up his life for the cause. That he had a premonition of his death is evidenced by a statement written by him in the preface to the second edition of the *Voice of Warning* printed in 1846, as follows: 'Should the author be called upon to sacrifice his life for the cause of truth, he will have the consolation that it will be said of him, as it was said of Abel, "He being dead yet speaketh." ' Not only will Parley P. Pratt, though dead, speak through his *Voice of Warning,* but even more powerfully will he be heard through the voice of song." (Pp. 185–86.)

The tune name, MOORE, honors Dr. Ernest Carroll Moore, formerly the president of the University of California at Los Angeles, where Alexander Schreiner served as organist and lecturer in music.

Both tune and text first appeared in *Latter-day Saint Hymns* (1927).

High on the Mountain Top 5; 333

Text: Joel H. Johnson (1802–1882; LDS)
Music: Ebenezer Beesley (1840–1906; LDS)
Tune name: DESERET

This hymn memorializes the faith of the Latter-day Saints in the universal blessing of the restored gospel. The strong, ringing melody captures the enthusiasm of the words. "High on the Mountain Top" is a wholehearted assertion of the glory of Zion and a fervent restatement of scriptural prophecy.

As is true of many of our finest hymn texts, this one is based closely on scripture. Joel H. Johnson's inspiration was Isaiah 2:2–3:

"And it shall come to pass in the last days, that the mountain of the Lord's house shall be established in the top of the mountains, and shall be exalted above the hills; and all nations shall flow unto it.

"And many people shall go and say, Come ye, and let us go up to the mountain of the Lord, to the house of the God of Jacob; and he will teach us of his ways, and we will walk in his paths: for out of Zion shall go forth the law, and the word of the Lord from Jerusalem."

In his brief autobiography, which he appended to his journal, Joel H. Johnson noted the following:

"After being baptized in 1831 I never lived but a short time in any one place on account of mob violence. And since I have been in Utah I have made eleven new places. Was never called on a mission without responding to the call and never asked to speak in public on the principles of religion when I excused myself. I have written nearly or quite one thousand spiritual hymns and sacred songs, now in a manuscript entitled, 'Zion's Songster, or the Songs of Joel.' " (Quoted in George D. Pyper, *Stories of Latter-day Saint Hymns,* p. 145.)

New members of the Church may be uncertain of the meaning of the word *Deseret,* in verse one. Elder Bruce R. McConkie explained: "*Deseret* is the Jaredite name for honey bee. (Ether 2:3.) Brigham Young and his followers first named their new intermountain empire the *territory of Deseret* after this unique Book of Mormon name." (*Mormon Doctrine,* 2d ed. [Salt Lake City, Utah: Bookcraft, 1966], p. 190.)

Two verses printed at the bottom of the page in the 1950 hymnal were not retained:

Then hail to Deseret! A refuge for the good,
And safety for the great, If they but understood
That God with plagues will shake the world
Till all its thrones shall down be hurled.

In Deseret doth truth Rear up its royal head;
Though nations may oppose, Still wider it shall spread;
Yes, truth and justice, love and grace,
In Deseret find ample place.

G. William Richards, who served as a member of the 1985 Hymnbook Executive Committee, noted in his research that the hymn tune DESERET bears a great similarity to an earlier tune by Lowell Mason called STOW.

The text first appeared in *The Western Standard* in 1856. The tune DESERET was published with this text in the 1889 *Latter-day Saints' Psalmody.*

Redeemer of Israel 6

Text: William W. Phelps (1792–1872; LDS);
adapted from Joseph Swain (1761–1796)
Music: Freeman Lewis (1780–1859)
Tune name: DULCIMER

The six verses of this hymn affirm many facets of the Savior's mission and personality. The vigorous words praise the Savior first as our invincible redeemer, then as our shepherd and protector, then as the millennial Messiah. The sixth verse is an ecstatic vision of his heavenly glory.

William W. Phelps was editor of *The Evening and Morning Star,* a newspaper in Jackson County, Missouri, when "Redeemer of Israel" was first published in that newspaper in 1832. It was included three years later in Emma Smith's hymnal.

William W. Phelps was a natural adapter and reviser. When he heard or read a hymn that caught his attention, his creative powers immediately began to work upon that text to give it a flavor and relevance that would express the feelings and doctrines of the Saints. This hymn is a case in point. He based his text on a hymn by an eighteenth-century Englishman, Joseph Swain. The two texts make an interesting comparison. Here is Joseph Swain's text, as printed by John Wyeth in the 1820 *Repository of Sacred Music*:

O thou in whose presence my soul takes delight,
On whom in afflictions I call,
My comfort by day and my song in the night,
My hope, my salvation, my all.

Where dost thou at noontide resort with thy sheep,
To feed on the pastures of love,
For, why in the valley of death should I weep,
Alone in the wilderness rove.

O why should I wander an alien from thee,
Or cry in the desert for bread,
My foes would rejoice when my sorrows they see,
And smile at the tears I have shed. . . .

He looks, and ten thousand of angels rejoice,
And myriads wait for his word,
He speaks, and eternity, fill'd with his voice,
Re-echoes the praise of her Lord.

The tune goes by several names: DULCIMER (Latin for "sweet song"), BELOVED, and MEDITATION. Other Christian hymnals usually pair it with Swain's text. Freeman Lewis, who is not known to have written any other tunes, apparently based this melody on an older tune called DAVIS.

Joseph Swain's text was first printed in 1791 in a collection of his verse and prose. The tune DULCIMER accompanied these words in an American hymn collection published in 1829. The first Latter-day Saint hymnbook to publish both tune and text was the 1889 *Latter-day Saints' Psalmody.*

Israel, Israel, God Is Calling — 7

Text: Richard Smyth (1838–1914; LDS)
Music: Charles C. Converse (1832–1918)
Tune name: ERIE

For us, the invitation to gather within "Zion's walls" is a symbolic invitation to repentance, truth, and happiness. To this hymn's author, it was also a literal invitation: forsake the temptations and errors of the world and join the Saints of the latter days in the peace and safety of their American settlement.

Richard Smyth served as a missionary three times in his life: once in Liverpool, just after his conversion to the Church, and then twice more, after he had settled in America, when he returned to his native Ireland to summon his countrymen to "Come to Zion!" During the nineteenth century, Latter-day Saint converts almost always planned to emigrate to America. The hymn compares this emigration to the gathering of the children of Israel from out of Babylon to the safety of the promised land. The Lord saved ancient Israel from destruction, both physical and spiritual, and the hymn's message is that he will do the same for his children in the latter days.

Few tunes have attained more popularity in the Christian world than ERIE by Charles C. Converse. Early Latter-day Saints were quick to make it one of their favorites. In *Stories of Our Mormon Hymns,* J. Spencer Cornwall reported (p. 94) that Saints in the earlier days of the Church sang it with the texts "O My Father" (no. 292) and "What Was Witnessed in the Heavens?" (no. 11). The tune was named after Erie, Pennsylvania, the home of the composer.

Most other denominations know ERIE as the setting for words by Joseph Scriven. The first verse of this popular text is as follows:

What a friend we have in Jesus,
All our sins and griefs to bear!
What a privilege to carry
Everything to God in prayer!
O what peace we often forfeit,
O what needless pain we bear,
All because we do not carry
Everything to God in prayer!

The first publication of the hymn tune ERIE was in an American hymn collection called *Silver Wings* (1870). Richard Smyth's words first appeared in the *Millennial Star* in 1861.

Awake and Arise — 8

Text: Theodore E. Curtis (1872–1957; LDS)
Music: Carolee Curtis Green (b. 1940; LDS)
Tune name: EMERSON

The gospel message carries with it the promise of hope and salvation for all. In this hymn, the gospel has burst forth "like a dawn," and those who will awaken to this light can leave forever the hopelessness and torpor of their long slumber.

The author of this hymn, the late Theodore E. Curtis, was the beloved grandfather of the hymn's composer. He wrote many volumes of poetry, some humorous, some sentimental, some spiritual. Three of his texts—"Come unto Him" ("I Wander Through the Stilly Night"), "Lean on My Ample Arm," and "Again, Our Dear Redeeming Lord"—were already part of the 1950 hymnal. Carolee Curtis Green had previously collected, typed, and duplicated her grandfather's poetry for family members, and when she read that Church members were invited to submit hymns for a new hymnal, she decided at once to compose music for one of his texts. She described herself as "teaming up with my dear grandfather, who might be noticing from heaven."

The hymn won first place in the 1984 *Ensign* hymn-writing contest, was printed in the *Ensign* in March of that year, and was then accepted for the 1985 hymnal. Carolee Curtis Green named her tune EMERSON, in honor of R. Emerson Curtis, son of the author and father of the composer, with whom Theodore E. Curtis lived for the last years of his life. She felt this name was particularly appropriate for the tune in light of the text for which it was written. In her words, R. Emerson Curtis is "like the message of the song: in all his teachings he is very earnest and exact, but very loving and kind; he is, indeed, a parent who wakes his child thoroughly when the time for slumber is past but wakes him benevolently."

The rhythmic pattern of the music, 𝅗𝅥 ♩ ♩ , is the basis for almost the entire melody. The melody's highest note, in the fourth line, coincides with "burst" in verse one and with equally triumphant words in verses two and three. The composer's goal was to convey "what a child and loving parent feel when the parent wakes the child from sleep to see or do something beautiful."

Come, Rejoice 9

Text and music: Tracy Y. Cannon (1879–1961; LDS); adapted
Tune name: HINCKLEY

Familiar to many Latter-day Saints as the first hymn of the 1950 hymnal, "Come, Rejoice" is a Christ-centered celebration of the restoration of the gospel. Jesus Christ, around whose life and teachings the early Church arose, has spoken again in latter days to gladden the hearts of his followers and gather them to him.

The lines "Shout hosanna to his name; / One and all his might proclaim" end all three verses of this hymn. The words "shout hosanna" bring to mind the familiar story of Christ's triumphal entry into Jerusalem, when his followers spread palm leaves in his path and welcomed him with cries of "Hosanna; Blessed is he that cometh in the name of the Lord." (Mark 11:9.) This glorious occasion was immediately followed by the events leading up to the Crucifixion.

In this hymn, we, too, welcome the Savior with our hosannas. It is not his physical presence we greet but his words of truth as he "speaks to earth again." His sacrifice, betrayal, and death are part of the past; now, the future promises joy and triumph. We, his followers, will spread his restored word: "Let all hear who live today! / This is life, the truth, the way."

Tracy Y. Cannon commented: "The reason for writing this hymn was that I desired to compose a hymn on the restoration of the gospel. It has always been easier for me to write music than words. The music of this hymn kept filling my mind and I, therefore, wrote words that seemed to me to suit the spirit of the music." (Quoted in J. Spencer Cornwall, *Stories of Our Mormon Hymns,* p. 4.)

"Come, Rejoice" was first published in *Hymns* (1948). It appears in the 1985 hymnal in an arrangement adapted for unison singing, with piano or organ accompaniment. The tune name honors the composer's wife, Carol Hinckley Cannon.

Come, Sing to the Lord 10

Text and music: Gerrit de Jong, Jr. (1892–1978; LDS)
Tune name: BELLE

There are many reasons to praise the Lord. In "Come, Sing to the Lord," we praise him for raising up prophets, both ancient and modern, to guide his people and for restoring priesthood authority in these latter days.

The first verse refers to Joseph Smith, the prophet raised up to restore "the blessed gospel." The second verse places this fact in the context of ancient prophecy: others who spoke in the name of the Lord foresaw the calling and mission of Joseph Smith. Latter-day Saint scripture is specific on this point:

"For Joseph [the Joseph who was sold into Egypt] truly testified, saying: A seer shall the Lord my God raise up, who shall be a choice seer unto the fruit of my loins.

"Yea, Joseph truly said: Thus saith the Lord unto me: . . .

" . . . And I will make him great in mine eyes; for he shall do my work. . . .

" . . . Behold, that seer will the Lord bless; and they that seek to destroy him shall be confounded. . . .

"And his name shall be called after me." (2 Nephi 3:6–8, 14–15.)

The third verse emphasizes the restoration of the "keys of the priesthood of our Lord." Following the Apostasy, many truths and partial truths remained on earth among the various religious denominations; truth did not disappear completely. But priesthood authority was taken away in its entirety. In our day, The Church of Jesus Christ of Latter-day Saints has been the means of restoring this authority to earth. Thus Gerrit de Jong chose to characterize the Restoration by devoting verse three entirely to the subject of priesthood restoration: "powers divine are manifest."

Concerning the background of this hymn, Gerrit de Jong said: "When an edition of hymns was going to be printed, Tracy Y. Cannon, chairman of the Church Music Committee, asked me to send him a congregational hymn. I wrote it in a few minutes after Sunday School and had a quartet sing it in Sacrament meeting that night in the Highland Park [Salt Lake]

Ward." (Quoted in J. Spencer Cornwall, *Stories of Our Mormon Hymns*, p. 39.)

The tune name honors the composer's daughter, Belle de Jong Van Wagenen. The hymn was first published in *Latter-day Saint Hymns* (1927).

What Was Witnessed in the Heavens? 11

Text: John S. Davis (1813–1882; LDS)
Music: Evan Stephens (1854–1930; LDS)
Tune name: JOYFUL SOUND

This unusual hymn has a question-and-answer format. It teaches the basic doctrine that the true gospel of former days was taken from the earth but now is restored.

The pattern of John Davis's hymn text resembles a *catechism*, a question-and-answer system of religious instruction used since the early days of Christianity to teach children and new converts. Some of the early Saints used the catechism method for a short while, with questions and answers designed to reflect basic Latter-day Saint beliefs that all members of the Church should understand clearly. Today we accomplish a similar purpose by requiring our Primary boys and girls to memorize the Articles of Faith to prepare for their advancement from Primary.

The music of Evan Stephens emphasizes the question-and-answer pattern of the words. The male voices alone sing the question; all voices together sing the answer. (In a very small congregation or in an all-female group, one possibility is to divide the group in half and ask all singers to sing in unison, with half the group singing the questions, half singing the answers, then joining together in the last half of the hymn.)

When someone learns for the first time that the gospel was taken from the earth for many centuries, an immediate question is likely to arise: "What became of those departed, / Knowing not the gospel plan?"

John Davis anticipated this question, and the hymn concludes with his reassuring answer: "In the spirit world they'll hear it; / God is just to ev'ry man."

The text first appeared in the *Millennial Star* in 1847, and text and tune were published together for the first time in the 1889 *Latter-day Saints' Psalmody*.

'Twas Witnessed in the Morning Sky 12

Text: G. William Richards (b. 1918; LDS)
Music: H. Walford Davies (1869–1941); altered
Tune name: SOLEMN MELODY

As congregations sing "'Twas Witnessed in the Morning Sky," new investigators can learn some of the important facts of the gospel restoration. And Latter-day Saints who already know and love this story can rejoice as they recall the angelic visitations that brought about the restoration of all "knowledge, gifts, and keys."

The author, G. William Richards, gave the following background of the hymn: "Since one of the topics to be emphasized in the new hymnbook was the Restoration, I submitted a text I had adapted in 1952 from the hymn 'What Was Witnessed in the Heavens?' I used the ideas and some of the actual phrases from the text by the original author, John S. Davis, for how else can one say something about the Restoration without using some of the same words he did? The third verse, however, is pretty much my own."

G. William Richards stated frankly that the question-and-answer format of "What Was Witnessed in the Heavens?" (no. 11) was not to his liking. As can be seen from comparing the two hymns (nos. 11 and 12 are on facing pages), G. William Richards changed the questions to assertions. In 1847, John S. Davis had written these words as the opening lines of his hymn:

What was witnessed in the heavens?
Why, an angel earthward bound.
Had he something with him bringing?
Yes, the gospel, joyful sound!

G. William Richards's version is this:

'Twas witnessed in the morning sky:
An angel earthward bound.
This messenger proclaimed anew
The gospel's joyful sound.

Many of the remaining lines of " 'Twas Witnessed in the Morning Sky" are entirely original, including, as the author stated above, all of verse three.

The word *morning* in the title and first line refers not to the morning of a specific day but rather to the dawning of the bright and happy era in the history of the world when the gospel was restored. Morning and dawn are frequently used as symbols of the Restoration.

G. William Richards, an organist and a hymn scholar as well as the author of this hymn text, said the music was his adaptation of a celebrated organ solo, "Solemn Melody," by Sir Walford Davies, an excellent composer of church music in England around the turn of the century. Both text and tune are new to the 1985 hymnbook.

The author stated: "I believe this hymn should be sung in a slow, solemn manner to be really beautiful. This concept may be an obstacle to the tune's acceptance and popularity, for many people think of the Restoration as bright and joyful. But truly, it is possible to be joyful in a solemn and dignified manner."

He noted also, "The four-part writing exceeds the reach of the hands, and therefore the organ pedal notes must be employed to encompass all the parts."

An Angel from on High 13; 328

Text: Parley P. Pratt (1807–1857; LDS)
Music: John E. Tullidge (1806–1873; LDS)
Tune name: CUMORAH

" 'An Angel from on High' belongs distinctively to Mormon hymnology. It is a song of the Restoration—a revelation of a divine truth of which Parley P. Pratt was an inspired torch-bearer." So stated George D. Pyper in *Stories of Latter-day Saint Hymns.* (P. 73.)

This hymn was not part of Emma Smith's first hymnal in 1835, but it appeared in the 1840 hymnal for which Parley P. Pratt was one of the editors. Its five stanzas tell briefly but effectively the story of the coming forth of the Book of Mormon and the purposes that these sacred writings are destined to fulfill. Hidden in Cumorah, as announced to Joseph Smith by the angel Moroni, these scriptures will bring to the world the fulness of the gospel and will prepare the peoples of the earth for the coming of Christ.

The hymn has been sung to many tunes, but Latter-day Saints today know and love the tune CUMORAH by John Tullidge, first printed in 1857. It is an unusual and effective setting, with the first two lines contrasting in mood and rhythm with lines three and four. A look at Parley P. Pratt's text will show why this musical contrast suits the words so well: in general, the first half of each stanza of the text is narrative and explanatory, whereas the last half is a declaration and a testimony. The matching of words and music is truly satisfying, since the 6/8 time signature of the first half is more tentative and tranquil, and the 4/4 time signature of the second half has a vigorous sense of arrival and declamation.

The 1985 hymnal included some new harmonization in lines one and two to make this former choir hymn more accessible to congregations.

Sweet Is the Peace the Gospel Brings 14

Text: Mary Ann Morton (1826–1897; LDS)
Music: Alfred M. Durham (1872–1957; LDS)
Tune name: CACHE

This hymn teaches a valuable truth in its title alone. The peace referred to is not an outward peace but a personal serenity that can transcend "wrangling sects" and the "tempter's power."

Latter-day Saints place great worth on the ideas expressed in this hymn text, and it fits naturally into our hymnal and into our thoughts. Not all Christian denominations would be comfortable with this hymn, however, because it places such a high value on reason; in fact, verse three equates gospel truth with reason. Human thought and effort are given a major role in the process of salvation.

Latter-day Saints understand the truth of this hymn's message. Without hesitation we welcome a hymn that exalts reason, thoughtful seeking, and the role of human beings in the divine plan; we have total trust in the intellectual completeness as well as the spiritual completeness of the gospel. Over the decades, among those who have found the reward of "the peace the gospel brings" have been fine thinkers, logicians, scientists, and philosophers. "Seeking minds" are blessings from our Father in Heaven, and Latter-day Saints welcome the exercise of this gift. We must, through our own study and efforts, work for knowledge of sacred truths.

Two words occurring in the text are somewhat unusual. One is *refulgent,* meaning "radiant" or "resplendent." Another is *lower,* a word rhyming with *power* (its rhyme-companion in the hymn), meaning "to frown; to be dark and threatening."

Verse three previously began with the line "Tradition flees before its power." The change in the 1985 hymnal to "Faithless tradition flees its power" improves the meter as well as the clarity of the line.

The tune name refers to Cache Valley, Utah, where the composer lived for many years. CACHE first appeared in *Hymns* (1948); the text has been part of Latter-day Saint tradition since it was first printed in the *Millennial Star* in 1852.

I Saw a Mighty Angel Fly 15

Text: Anonymous (ca. 1840)
Music: English melody; arranged by Ralph Vaughan Williams (1872–1958)
Tune name: FOREST GREEN

What people could sing with more enthusiasm and feeling than the Latter-day Saints about the "mighty angel" spoken of in the book of Revelation?

"And I saw another angel fly in the midst of heaven, having the everlasting gospel to preach unto them that dwell on the earth, and to every nation, and kindred, and tongue, and people.

"Saying with a loud voice, Fear God, and give glory to him; for the hour of his judgment is come: and worship him that made heaven, and earth, and the sea, and the fountains of waters." (Revelation 14:6–7.)

In Doctrine and Covenants 133:36, the Lord made known the identity and the purpose of this angel: he is the bearer of gospel tidings for the latter days, one who committed the "everlasting gospel" to Joseph Smith.

It is more than a little surprising that this hymn text, so relevant to our teachings, is not, in fact, of Latter-day Saint origin. It is an anonymous poetic rendering of the scripture in Revelation.

The hymn was included in the 1950 hymnal, but it was seldom sung. Because of the difficult George Careless tune, it was labeled as a choir hymn.

In an effort to make this fine text more widely known and sung, the popular hymn tune FOREST GREEN was chosen to accompany it in the 1985 hymnal. The hymn tune's name derives from the town in Surrey, England, where Ralph Vaughan Williams noted this tune in his studies of English folk songs. FOREST GREEN is often used in Protestant hymnals, sometimes as a tune for "O Little Town of Bethlehem."

But the new tune presented one problem. It was double the length of the previous tune. If the text had happened to have an even number of verses, then everything would have worked out nicely, because two short verses of text, combined into one new long one, would exactly fit FOREST GREEN. But there were originally *five* verses of text. That totaled two-and-a-half verses in the new format; the music for half of the last verse had no words.

The solution was to rewrite the last verse of the text to make it twice as long, still basing the words on the passage from Revelation.

Original last verse:

Fear God, and worship him who made
The heavens, earth, and sea.

Fear him on whom your sins were laid,
Who died to make you free.

New double-length last verse:

Fear God who made the water pure,
The heavens, sea, and land.
His judgment will be swift and sure;
The day is nigh at hand.
Then, all ye people, worship God;
Give glory to his name!
To spread these tidings far abroad
The holy angel came.

What Glorious Scenes Mine Eyes Behold 16

Text: Anonymous (ca. 1840)
Music: Ebenezer Beesley (1840–1906; LDS)
Tune name: ABRAM

Although we do not know the identity of this hymn's author, we can be certain of that author's response to the Book of Mormon. He or she studied it with not only the mind but also the heart and imagination on fire with "glorious scenes" and prophetic utterances.

Some knowledge of Latter-day Saint teachings is necessary to understand the significance of this hymn. The text does not mention the Book of Mormon by name but calls it "Ephraim's records." Elder Bruce R. McConkie explained, "The Book of Mormon is the *stick of Ephraim* in that it is a record of God's dealings with a people who were of the tribe of Ephraim." (*Mormon Doctrine,* 2d ed. [Salt Lake City, Utah: Bookcraft, 1966], p. 767.)

Verses three and four refer to the gathering of Israel. Prophecies of the gathering of Israel, both a spiritual and a temporal gathering, are important in Latter-day Saint belief. Joseph Smith recounted a vision in which Moses committed to him and Oliver Cowdery "the keys of the gathering of Israel from the four parts of the earth." (D&C 110:11.)

The tune first appeared in the 1889 *Latter-day Saints' Psalmody*. The text was in print by 1840.

Awake, Ye Saints of God, Awake! 17

Text: Eliza R. Snow (1804–1887; LDS)
Music: Evan Stephens (1854–1930; LDS)
Tune name: WILLARD

Eliza R. Snow's purpose in this hymn was to stir the Saints to call upon the Lord for protection from their foes. The words are a reminder that present fears and afflictions must be viewed in the perspective of the Lord's eternal purposes, for "his vengeance will not slumber long," and the day is coming when his followers will be vindicated and rewarded.

As is the case with several of our hymns (see the discussion of "Up, Awake, Ye Defenders of Zion," no. 248, for example), the sentiments that grew out of a time when the Saints were physically threatened and persecuted are not as relevant in a day when, in most places in the world, we take for granted the privilege of living as accepted members of the community. We live without fear, and a desire for vengeance is no longer one of the fuels that fire our determination. For this reason, and also because the 1985 Hymnbook Committee wished to avoid, when possible, the printing of extra verses at the bottom of the page, three verses of Eliza R. Snow's original text were omitted in the 1985 hymnal.

The omitted verses, originally numbers two, four, and six, give an insight into the desires and prayers of the early Saints who lived during times when persecution was a literal and a daily threat:

He will regard his people's cry,
The widow's tear, the orphan's moan.
The blood of those that slaughtered lie
Pleads not in vain before his throne.

Then let your souls be stayed on God,
A glorious scene is drawing nigh;
Though tempests gather like a flood,
The storm, though fierce, will soon pass by.

Our God in judgement will come near;
His mighty arm he will make bare.
For Zion's sake he will appear;
Then, O ye Saints, awake, prepare!

In addition, the term *fowler's snare* was changed to *tempter's snare* (verse one) in the 1985 hymnbook.

The tune name, WILLARD, honors the Utah town in which Evan Stephens settled as a twelve-year-old immigrant boy from Wales. The tune, paired with this text, was first printed in the *Utah Musical Times* in 1877. Eliza R. Snow's text had appeared in the *Times and Seasons* in 1841.

The Voice of God Again Is Heard 18

Text and music: Evan Stephens (1854–1930; LDS)
Tune name: REVELATION

"Generations have come and gone," said Brigham Young, "without the privilege of hearing the sound of the Gospel, which has come to you through Joseph Smith—that was revealed to him from heaven by angels and visions." (In *Journal of Discourses* [London: Latter-day Saints' Book Depot, 1860], 7:173.) Joyful gratitude for the privilege of being part of this restoration was the motive for "The Voice of God Again Is Heard."

This hymn was originally a part of *The Vision,* a cantata by Evan Stephens commissioned by the Church in 1920 to commemorate the centennial of Joseph Smith's first vision. It was also one of the Latter-day Saint hymns chosen for the Tabernacle Choir's 1955 European tour.

This hymn was part of the choir section of the 1950 hymnal. Two editorial changes in the music were intended to make it more inviting for congregational use. First, the time signature was changed to a more familiar 4/4 time. Second, the key of the hymn was transposed three notes lower so that the melody is now easier to read and sing.

Congregations and choirs who do not take the opportunity to sing this hymn are passing up a fine chance to affirm in song the message of the Restoration. The hymn's suitability for a meeting with a missionary theme is also evident from the message of the second verse: "O messengers of truth, go forth."

We Thank Thee, O God, for a Prophet 19

Text: William Fowler (1830–1865; LDS)
Music: Caroline Sheridan Norton (1808–1877)
Tune name: FOWLER

"It cannot be called the greatest hymn ever written by any of our authors. In fact, it does not compare in literary merit or poetic beauty with many of the other gems contained in our hymn books; but it has something different from our other hymns," stated George D. Pyper. It "is exclusively a Latter-day Saint hymn; a Mormon heart-throb; a song of the Restoration." (*Stories of Latter-day Saint Hymns,* pp. 45, 46.)

The author, Latter-day Saint convert William Fowler, served in England as a missionary for the Church before he emigrated to America. We do not know the date or circumstances of the hymn's writing, but George D. Pyper noted that "President Joseph F. Smith in his lifetime related that when he was in England Brother Fowler brought his new song to meeting where it was sung for the first time. As President Smith's mission was from 1860 to 1863, it was probably written somewhere between those dates. It was published in the 12th edition (1863) of the Latter-day Saint Hymn Book." (P. 48.)

The composer of the tune, Caroline Sheridan Norton, is remembered principally as a poet and pamphlet writer, but her musical instincts also served her well. When an acquaintance of hers, an English officer of high rank, was killed in the battle of Balaklava during the Crimean War (1853–1856), she wrote both words and music to "The Officer's Funeral March."

The first verse of the original song is as follows:

Hark to the shrill trumpet calling!
It pierces the soft summer air;
Tears from each comrade are falling,
The widow and orphan are there.
The bayonets earthward are turning,
And the drum's muffled breath rolls around;
Yet he heeds not the voice of their mourning,
Nor wakes to the bugle sound.

George D. Pyper gave two additional verses in *Stories of Latter-day Saint Hymns.* (See pp. 50–51.)

George D. Pyper continued: "Surely the old adage [that truth is stranger than fiction] has been exemplified in this case for William Fowler, a humble English elder searching for a tune to put to his hymn, found and adapted Mrs. Norton's composition to the present setting of 'We Thank Thee, O God, for a Prophet.'

"Could Mrs. Norton enter a Latter-day Saint chapel today she would be astonished to learn that the music which she dedicated to a fallen soldier of war is now frequently sung to a new song of praise in honor of a modern prophet of peace." (P. 51.)

An unusual editing change was made in this hymn's 1985 version: the melody line was changed at one point to conform to the way most members sing it. In verse one, note that the melody goes from A to B and back to A on the phrase "lighten our minds" (line 3). In previous editions, the melody remained on a constant note at that point. General practice seemed to dictate the change.

God of Power, God of Right 20

Text: Wallace F. Bennett (b. 1898; LDS)
Music: Tracy Y. Cannon (1879–1961; LDS)
Tune name: ELSIE

Writing in 1986, Wallace F. Bennett recalled his intention in writing this hymn text sixty years earlier: "Each verse relates two attributes of God to a desired human quality. First verse: God of power, God of right—priesthood might; second verse: God of wisdom, God of truth—shape our souls; third verse: God of mercy, God of love—touch, humble, bless."

At eighty-eight years of age, the author still remembered clearly how the hymn came to be written. "The committee that put out the previous hymnbook [1948/1950] met in our home. Someone suggested a lack of hymns especially suitable for priesthood meetings. Intrigued, I wrote this one, which was accepted and then set to music by Tracy Y. Cannon, chairman of the committee."

In the early 1960s Wallace F. Bennett provided some additional details to J. Spencer Cornwall: "I worked at [this hymn] casually. However, one Sunday morning, I woke up with the feeling that I could sit down and write the whole text. There was no set of words clearly in my mind, but rather a string of ideas. Within an hour, the text of this hymn was written, and I struggled only over one word. The word 'kindliness' at the end of the [third] verse is the one thing in the text with respect to which I still feel somewhat uncertain." In accordance with the author's wishes, this word became *holiness* in the 1985 hymnal.

The author continued, "I am not prepared to go so far as to say this was inspiration, but certainly the hymn almost wrote itself, and I didn't struggle over it as I have done over many of the other things I have written." (*Stories of Our Mormon Hymns,* p. 43.)

Wallace F. Bennett reported that each year, on the Sunday nearest his birthday, his ward in Salt Lake City has made a point of singing this hymn in his honor.

The tune name, ELSIE, honors the first wife of composer Tracy Y. Cannon.

Come, Listen to a Prophet's Voice 21

Text: Joseph S. Murdock (1822–1899; LDS);
verse four by Bruce R. McConkie (1915–1985; LDS)
Music: Joseph J. Daynes (1851–1920; LDS)
Tune name: CANNON

This hymn is a compelling invitation to follow in the ways of truth. It sets forth the determination of the Latter-day Saints to follow the head of their Church—Jesus Christ himself—by following the words of his mouthpiece here on earth, the prophet who stands at the head of the Church.

Verse one links the prophets of modern times with those who walked and talked with the Lord in biblical times: "We've found the way the prophets went / Who lived in days of yore." Verse two invokes a favorite image of Latter-day Saint hymn writers, that of the dawn bursting upon the earth as a symbol of the light of the gospel. Verse three sets the record straight for any who would mistake The Church of Jesus Christ of Latter-day Saints for the work of men: " 'Tis not in man they put their trust, / Nor on his arm rely." These words recall Nephi's observation: "I know that cursed is he that putteth his trust in the arm of flesh." (2 Nephi 4:34.)

The first three verses of this hymn appeared in *Times and Seasons* in 1843. The tune by Joseph J. Daynes appeared with these words in the 1889 *Latter-day Saints' Psalmody.*

Verse four is a modern addition by Elder Bruce R. McConkie. Amelia McConkie, widow of Elder McConkie, said that her husband "simply felt the three original verses left the thought incomplete, and so he wrote a fourth." The fourth verse adds to the hymn in two ways. First, it focuses our thoughts once again on the hymn's principal message: "Then heed the words of truth and light." And second, it admonishes us to the highest spiritual goals. The phrase "Till thine election's sure" has reference to a blessing that Elder McConkie himself explained in these words: "Those members of the Church who devote themselves wholly to righteousness, living by every word that proceedeth forth from the mouth of God, make their *calling and election sure*. That is, they receive the more sure word of prophecy, which means that the Lord seals their exaltation upon them while they are yet in this life." (*Mormon Doctrine,* 2d ed. [Salt Lake City, Utah: Bookcraft, 1966], p. 109.)

We Listen to a Prophet's Voice 22

Text: Marylou Cunningham Leavitt (b. 1928; LDS)
Music: Darwin K. Wolford (b. 1936; LDS)
Tune name: BRUCE

"My word shall not pass away, but shall all be fulfilled, whether by mine own voice or by the voice of my servants, it is the same." (D&C 1:38.) These words of the Lord himself, as preserved in holy scripture, are at the heart of this hymn.

Jerold Ottley, director of the Tabernacle Choir, asked Darwin K. Wolford to prepare an anthem based on "We Thank Thee, O God, for a Prophet" (no. 19). The anthem, entitled "Behold Thy Servant, Lord," features the melody of "We Thank Thee, O God, for a Prophet" woven into the organ accompaniment as the choir sings "We Listen to a Prophet's Voice." It was originally performed at general conference in October 1978 by the Tabernacle Choir.

Some revision was required before the hymn could be considered for congregational singing. Author Marylou Cunningham Leavitt recalled that "a sincere effort was made to indicate modern methods of communication—'How swiftly round the world his voice reveals the gospel word!'—without detracting from the sacred subject of revelation through the prophets."

"These words are my testimony," she said, adding that "as with every hymn text included in the Latter-day Saint hymnal, the words, when they are sung with heart, mind, and voice, are a testimony and a prayer unto the Lord, as he has stated." (See D&C 25:12.)

As director of organ studies at Ricks College in Rexburg, Idaho, Darwin K. Wolford felt a great sense of satisfaction and a strong emotional stake in that college's acquisition of a large Ruffatti organ, which was dedicated in November 1983. "Behold Thy Servant, Lord" was performed for that dedication ceremony. He said, "Because of his support in obtaining this fine organ and because of his pride in this and other musical achievements at Ricks College, Bruce Hafen, then president of Ricks, was the inspiration for the tune name BRUCE."

We Ever Pray for Thee — 23; 312

Text: Evan Stephens (1854–1930; LDS)
Music: Henry A. Tuckett (1852–1918; LDS); adapted by Evan Stephens
Tune name: SHADRACH

As a devoted Latter-day Saint, Evan Stephens was able to communicate in this beautiful hymn a feeling of reverence and love for the prophet who leads the Church. The words tell of the fervent, trusting prayers that are offered up on the prophet's behalf, and the tranquil harmonies of the musical setting enhance this prayerful mood.

Evan Stephens wrote the words for "We Ever Pray for Thee" as a trio for girls' voices in celebration of President Wilford Woodruff's ninetieth birthday in 1897. His music is an adaptation of a hymn tune by Henry A. Tuckett, "Our Loving Savior Dear." The arrangement for a trio of female voices was subsequently retained in Latter-day Saint hymnals.

The four-part congregational setting was arranged by Darwin Wolford for performance by the Mormon Youth Chorus and, via satellite, the Fayette New York Branch choir at the Sunday afternoon session of general conference on April 6, 1980. This conference commemorated the Church's sesquicentennial, or 150th anniversary.

It may seem odd to some people that our hymnal would include a text that refers to our prophet's advancing years and furrowed brow; however, the call to become prophet, seer, and revelator has invariably come after decades of devoted service; our prophets are men of seniority among the Lord's servants. We love them for their willingness to assume this responsibility at an age when most other men choose a tranquil retirement.

The reference to "children's prayer" in verse three is explained by the fact that a trio of girls' voices originally performed this hymn. The entire hymn has a reverent feeling, almost a mood of solemn wonder, reflecting the adoration of a child for a beloved prophet. Adults, too, can sing these words with feeling, because we wish to obey and sustain our prophet with childlike devotion.

God Bless Our Prophet Dear 24

Text: Bernard Snow (1822–1894; LDS); altered
Music: Harry A. Dean (1892–1987; LDS)
Tune name: EPHRAIM

If the words of our prophet are the center point from which our lives and aspirations grow, blessings and unity abound. The progression of thought in "God Bless Our Prophet Dear" teaches this vital truth.

First we invoke a blessing upon the prophet, praying for his health and comfort and asking that his words might be impressed upon the soul of each one who seeks righteousness. Then we sing of the results of obedience to his counsel: the gospel spreads "from sea to sea," and the Saints move as one body, without disagreement or distraction, toward divine and eternal goals.

The words of Bernard Snow have been altered somewhat from a poem that appeared first in the *Deseret News* in 1855 and has been part of Latter-day Saint hymnody since 1863. The hymn's title in the 1950 hymnal was "Our God, We Raise to Thee," and it was given as an alternative text to be used with the tune UTAH ("Our Mountain Home So Dear," no. 33). The hymn's original first verse, more appropriate to Utah Saints than to the worldwide Church, was omitted, thus making a new title necessary. The original first verse was as follows:

Our God, we raise to thee
Thanks for thy blessings free
We here enjoy.

In this far western land,
A true and chosen band,
Led hither by thy hand,
We sing for joy.

The remaining three verses were retained with minor changes. For example, the original second half of what is now the second verse used to read this way:

As one united whole
Truth burns in every soul,
While hastening to the goal
We long to see.

The editorial changes make these lines more singable and more grammatical:

Truth burns in ev'ry soul;
As one united whole,
We hasten to the goal
We long to see.

The name of the tune, EPHRAIM, honors Ephraim, Utah, where the composer lived. It was submitted for the 1948 hymnal but was not used until it was matched with the present text in the 1985 hymnal.

Now We'll Sing with One Accord 25

Text: William W. Phelps (1792–1872; LDS)
Music: Joseph J. Daynes (1851–1920; LDS)
Tune name: AZALIA

The events referred to in this hymn—the restoration of the gospel, the receiving of the priesthood, the translation of the Book of Mormon—were part of recent history for William W. Phelps when his hymn was first published in 1835. Joseph Smith, the prophet whom the hymn honors, was in daily contact with his followers, and their sense of these great blessings was immediate.

The age and historicity of this hymn become vivid when we realize that at the time it was first printed, the second half of verse two was in present tense:

Even Joseph he inspires;
Yea, his heart he truly fires,
With the light that he desires
For the work of righteousness.

The day of the Prophet's martyrdom would not come for nine more years. For us, these words, now in past tense, describe a historical happening; for the early Saints, the present-tense verbs described an ongoing, daily reality.

In addition to the change in verb tense, newer hymnals have altered the second half of verse three. These lines originally expressed their thought rather awkwardly:

The commandments to the church,
Which the saints will always search,
(Where the joys of heaven perch,)
Came through him from Jesus Christ.

The four long verses we have were originally eight short verses. For this reason, the second and fourth lines of the hymn in its modern version do not rhyme as we might expect them to. William W. Phelps's original verse pattern had three short rhyming lines and then a final line that stood alone, with no rhyme.

Joseph J. Daynes' tune, AZALIA, was first printed in the 1889 *Latter-day Saints' Psalmody.*

Joseph Smith's First Prayer 26

Text: George Manwaring (1854–1889; LDS)
Music: Sylvanus Billings Pond (1792–1871);
adapted by A. C. Smyth (1840–1909; LDS)
Tune name: DIVINITY

This hymn gives such a complete account of Joseph Smith's vision that even someone who knew nothing of that event could read or sing this hymn and know the essential facts.

Obviously, George Manwaring had read and been impressed by Joseph Smith—History 1:11–17. Joseph Smith's beautiful and moving account of the events leading up to and including the First Vision provide the visual details that find their way into the hymn text: "It was on the morning of a beautiful, clear day, early in the spring of eighteen hundred and twenty." (Joseph Smith–History 1:14.)

J. Spencer Cornwall told us further in *Stories of Our Mormon Hymns,* "Visual impression, however, increased the desire of George Manwaring to write the song, for he records that he was immediately inspired by a painting entitled 'The First Vision' executed by an artist named C. C. Christensen." (P. 140.)

Michael Hicks pointed out that the published version of this text may owe a great debt to the editors of the *Juvenile Instructor*. In George Manwaring's own notebook, the first stanza of this hymn is as follows:

'Twas on a lovely morn in spring
The sun was shining bright,
When Joseph saw the woodland shade
And humbly kneeling there he prayed
For wisdom and for light.

By the time it appeared in print for the first time in the *Juvenile Instructor* in 1878, it had taken on quite a different form to become the hymn we sing today.

The hymn's original title was restored in the 1985 hymnbook. "Joseph Smith's First Prayer" more clearly identifies the subject of the text than does the first line, "Oh, how lovely was the morning."

Though A. C. Smyth was given credit for this music in the 1950 hymnal, the third and fourth lines only are by him. The first two lines are by American composer Sylvanus Billings Pond, whose hymn tune, DIVINITY, was included in the 1889 *Latter-day Saints' Psalmody*. DIVINITY appeared at least as early as 1841 in Pond's collection, *United States Psalmody*, published in New York. (See William LeRoy Wilkes, "Borrowed Music in Mormon Hymnals" [Ph.D. dissertation, University of Southern California, 1957], p. 197.)

Praise to the Man 27

Text: William W. Phelps (1792–1872; LDS)
Music: Scottish folk song
Tune name: MARTYR

Soon after the death of the Prophet Joseph Smith, William W. Phelps, in an expression of grief and admiration for his close associate who had been so cruelly martyred, wrote "Praise to the Man." The words he penned as a personal tribute reflect the feelings of millions of Saints.

George D. Pyper remarked in *Stories of Latter-day Saint Hymns:* "What might be termed a joyful sadness runs through this song. It is an epitaphic eulogy of the divinely anointed Prophet and Seer raised up to establish the Last Dispensation and who will eventually be extolled by kings and revered by nations. It contains a cry unto heaven against his martyrdom; a panegyric concerning his Priesthood and endless glory, which will take him into God's kingdom with the prophets of old. . . .

"The refrain is a shout of exultation; a cry of satisfaction that traitors and tyrants will fight him now in vain; that his immortal soul, mingling with the highest, can plan for his Church and people, and that death will not again have power over him.

"Originally the first two lines of the second stanza read: 'Long may his blood, which was shed by assassins, / Stain Illinois while the earth lauds his fame.'

"When the Latter-day Saint Hymn Book was compiled in 1927, in order to be in harmony with the 'good neighbor' policy of the Church and nation, the second line quoted above was changed to 'Plead unto heav'n, while the earth lauds his fame.' " (Pp. 99–100.)

The text was first printed in *Times and Seasons* (1844). It appears, for the most part, to be an original creation of William W. Phelps; however, the opening lines of this hymn clearly owe a debt to a passage from Sir Walter Scott's *Lady of the Lake:*

Hail to the Chief who in triumph advances!
Honour'd and bless'd be the evergreen Pine!
Long may the tree, in his banner that glances,
Flourish, the shelter and grace of our line!

(Canto Second, XIX ["Boat Song"], *The Lady of the Lake and Other Poems* [New York: New American Library of World Literature, 1962], p. 56.)

J. Spencer Cornwall suggested that the American patriotic tune "Hail to the Chief" was most likely used for this hymn in its early days. (See *Stories of Our Mormon Hymns,* p. 164.) It was probably only after the Saints moved to Utah that the current tune, a variant of "Scotland, the Brave," was used for this hymn.

Saints, Behold How Great Jehovah 28

Text: Douglas W. Stott (b. 1925; LDS)
Music: A. Laurence Lyon (b. 1934; LDS)
Tune name: EDGAR

The Lord's kingdom will spread throughout the earth, moving forth in spite of all pessimism, obstacles, and opposition. Signs and prophecies point toward the day when "heaven's blessed King approaches." This hymn, new to the 1985 hymnal, exults in the thought of that welcome time and admonishes all Saints to "lift up Zion's standard."

Author Douglas W. Stott said that in 1972, while he was listening to "a particularly inspiring general conference address about the dramatic growth of the Church, its activities, and the miraculous ways in which seeming barriers to missionary work have dissolved," the words of this hymn began coming to his mind. Some fifteen years later, Douglas W. Stott was helping to establish Church programs in the West Indies, and thus he had a personal role in taking the gospel into areas that had seemed impossible to penetrate.

He noted further, "While on my mission I received a personal and very moving witness to the truthfulness of the Book of Mormon and have found that book to be not only the 'keystone of our religion,' as stated by Joseph Smith, but also a major key in unfolding for me significant insights into ancient biblical scripture." It is not surprising that his hymn incorporates Old Testament imagery into Latter-day Saint hymnody: the Saints are the New Jerusalem, lifting up the standard of Zion. All prophecies are brought together "into one" to foretell the great events to come.

Composer A. Laurence Lyon said, "I wanted to write a short, energetic piece not unlike the spirited pieces of English origin, such as 'For All the Saints' " (no. 82). The first two measures, with slight variation, constitute most of the hymn tune—six measures out of a total of eight. Because of this, congregations should feel secure when singing the melody for the first time.

The composer dedicated the tune to the memory of his father, T. Edgar Lyon, and named the tune EDGAR in his honor.

A Poor Wayfaring Man of Grief 29

Text: James Montgomery (1771–1854)
Music: George Coles (1792–1858); altered
Tune name: DUANE STREET

"Inasmuch as ye have done it unto one of the least of these my brethren, ye have done it unto me." (Matthew 25:40.) Jesus spoke these words after teaching his great lesson on charity. His message to his followers was that any act of generous compassion toward a person in need is counted as an act performed for the sake of the Savior himself.

"A Poor Wayfaring Man of Grief" is a narrative hymn that answers the question posed in Matthew 25:37–39:

"Then shall the righteous answer him, saying, Lord, when saw we thee an hungred, and fed thee? or thirsty, and gave thee drink?

"When saw we thee a stranger, and took thee in? or naked, and clothed thee?

"Or when saw we thee sick, or in prison, and came unto thee?"

The poem, originally titled "The Stranger," first appeared in an anthology of verse in 1834.

This hymn is especially loved among Latter-day Saints because of the role it played in the last hours before the martyrdom of Joseph and Hyrum Smith. On June 27, 1844, Joseph Smith was in jail in Carthage, Illinois, with his brother Hyrum, John Taylor, and Willard Richards.

Hostility was growing, mobs threatened violence, and the prisoners knew their lives were in danger.

John Taylor told of the scene in the jail cell: "All of us felt unusually . . . languid, with a remarkable depression of spirits. In consonance with those feelings I sang a song, that had lately been introduced into Nauvoo, entitled, 'A Poor Wayfaring Man of Grief.' . . . After a lapse of some time, Brother Hyrum requested me again to sing that song. I replied, 'Brother Hyrum, I do not feel like singing'; when he remarked, 'Oh, never mind; commence singing, and you will get the spirit of it.' At his request I did so." (*History of The Church of Jesus Christ of Latter-day Saints,* ed. B. H. Roberts [Salt Lake City, Utah: The Church of Jesus Christ of Latter-day Saints, 1932], 7:101–2.)

Not long after Elder Taylor sang the song the second time, the mob attacked the jail, murdering the Prophet and his brother.

The tune name DUANE STREET is taken from the Duane Street Church in New York City where, in 1839, the composer, the Reverend George Coles, preached a famous sermon in honor of the centennial of the Methodist Church. Our present tune is actually a rather elaborate variation of DUANE STREET.

Come, Come, Ye Saints — 30; 326

Text: William Clayton (1814–1879; LDS)
Music: English folk song
Tune name: ALL IS WELL

In the minds of many members of the Church, "Come, Come, Ye Saints" is the hymn that more than any other connotes the heritage and spirit of The Church of Jesus Christ of Latter-day Saints. The unforgettable words of this hymn allow us to pay tribute to the unflinching courage of the early Saints and to relate that commitment to our own lives.

William Clayton was a member of the first company of Mormon pioneers to face the westward trek to Utah. Forced to leave Nauvoo before the spring thaw, Clayton and his fellow exiles faced cold, mud, sickness, and hunger. News from loved ones left behind in Nauvoo was slow in coming. For two months William Clayton worried about his wife Diantha, who was still in Nauvoo, pregnant and unable to travel. On April 15, 1846, when word finally reached him of the birth of their son, he was ecstatic. "Truly I feel to rejoice at this intelligence," he wrote in his journal, "but feel sorry to hear of her [Diantha's] sickness." (She was soon to recover.) He then added, "This morning I composed a new song—'All is well.' " (*William Clayton's Journal* [Salt Lake City, Utah: Deseret News, 1921], p. 19.)

William Clayton had actually written new words to an older hymn, popular in his day, also titled "All Is Well." Published as early as 1838, it began –

What's this that steals (that steals) upon my frame –
Is it death? Is it death?
That soon will quench (will quench) this mortal flame –
Is it death? Is it death?
If this be death, I soon shall be
From every pain and sorrow free;
I shall the king of glory see –
All is well! All is well!

(Quoted in George D. Pyper, *Stories of Latter-day Saint Hymns*, p. 25.)

The new hymn, known today as "Come, Come, Ye Saints," quickly became a favorite among the Saints traveling west. A story became popular at a later time that Brigham Young had requested William Clayton to write the hymn, but William Clayton made no note of such a request in his journal, and we have no evidence that this story is true.

Oscar Winters, father-in-law of Heber J. Grant, related an incident that illustrates the significance of this hymn among the pioneers:

"One night, as we were making camp, we noticed one of our brethren had not arrived, and a volunteer party was immediately organized to return and see if anything had happened to him. Just as we were about to start, we saw the missing brother coming in the distance. When he arrived, he said he had been quite sick; so some of us unyoked his oxen and attended to his part of the camp duties. After supper, he sat down before the campfire on a large rock, and sang in a very faint but plaintive and sweet voice, the hymn 'Come, Come, Ye Saints.' It was a rule of the camp that whenever anybody started this hymn all in the camp should join, but for some reason this evening nobody joined him; he sang the hymn alone. When he had finished, I doubt if there was a single dry eye in the camp. The next morning we noticed that he was not yoking up his cattle. We went to his wagon and found that he had died during the night. We dug a shallow grave, and after we had covered his body with the earth we rolled the large stone to the head of the grave to mark it, the stone on which he had been sitting the night before when he sang: 'And should we die before our journey's through, Happy day! all is well!' ". (*Improvement Era*, June 1914, pp. 781–83.)

"Come, Come, Ye Saints" has appeared in every Latter-day Saint hymnbook since 1851. Many non–Latter-day Saints have learned to identify it with the Church through recordings, performances, and reprintings. It holds a special place in the hearts of all Latter-day Saints, since all members of the Church are the spiritual, if not the literal, descendants of the pioneers whose devotion is memorialized in the hymn.

O God, Our Help in Ages Past 31

Text: Isaac Watts (1674–1748)
Music: William Croft (1678–1727)
Tune name: ST. ANNE

No hymn stands as a greater monument to the genius of Isaac Watts than this one. It is as meaningful for occasions of sorrow as for occasions of rejoicing. As we sing "O God, Our Help in Ages Past," we proclaim our faith in the power of God and at the same time ask for his protective guidance to continue with us.

The original title of this hymn was "Man Frail, and God Eternal." God is the eternal ruler and sovereign, watching over his earth and his children throughout all time—"our help in ages past, our hope for years to come." This hymn has offered comfort to many Christians in difficult times. Because it has been used so often in war memorial services and for the dedication of war monuments, memories of such occasions add to the hymn's poignancy for many Saints in English-speaking countries.

Virtually all Christians find meaning in this hymn, and Emma Smith chose to include it in her 1835 hymnbook. One writer commented: "By universal consent this hymn is one of the grandest in the whole realm of English Hymnody. It is found in practically every hymnal. No other embraces in such moving language the whole scope of history, faith in a God who realizes His purposes through history, and the solidarity of a nation which in times of crisis places its hope in the Eternal." (Albert E. Bailey, *The Gospel in Hymns* [New York: Charles Scribner's Sons, 1950], p. 54.)

As he did for many of his hymns, Isaac Watts turned for inspiration to Psalms. Verse three, for example, is a verse rendering of Psalm 90:2: "Before the mountains were brought forth, or ever thou hadst formed the earth and the world, even from everlasting to everlasting, thou art God."

Three of the four phrases in verse four are identical with phrases in verse one; this repetition is a satisfying conclusion to the thoughts expressed in the hymn. In the 1950 hymnal, however, that concluding verse was rarely sung because it was an extra verse at the bottom of the page. Another extra verse, originally verse four, was not included in the 1985 hymnal:

A thousand ages in thy sight
Are like an evening gone;
Short as the watch that ends the night
Before the rising sun.

Although ST. ANNE was originally written as a musical setting for a version of Psalm 42 beginning "As pants the hart for cooling streams," it is almost impossible today to think of Isaac Watt's words without William Croft's appropriately vigorous tune. The tune name, ST. ANNE, is from St. Anne's Church, London, where Croft served as organist. Johann Sebastian Bach based his well-known "St. Anne Fugue" for organ on this tune.

The Happy Day at Last Has Come 32

Text: Philo Dibble (1806–1895; LDS)
Music: Ebenezer Beesley (1840–1906; LDS)
Tune name: ANIMATION

The feelings of the early Saints regarding the restoration of the gospel are still our feelings today. In 1833, only three years after the Church was organized, Philo Dibble's joyful text announcing the news of the Restoration appeared in the *Evening and Morning Star*. In 1835 it was included in Emma Smith's hymnal. The words show the optimism and excitement that filled the heart of one of Joseph Smith's close friends.

The text of this hymn shows some interesting revisions. Until the 1985 hymnal, the title and first line were "The happy day has rolled on." The 1985 Hymnbook Committee felt that a revised first line would be more clear and would have the advantage of doing away with the awkwardness of singing *rolled* as a two-syllable word.

The last line of verse three, "When God his strange work would perform," lost the word *strange* in favor of *great* in the present hymnal. The hymn's final line, "Come down to converse hold with men," was difficult to understand because of the split infinitive and unusual word order; in its 1985 revision it is "Come down to speak again with men."

Several lines had already been revised by the time of the 1950 hymnal. The original second line, "The glorious period now has come," had become "The truth restored is now made known," giving a better line and a closer rhyme. The original third line, "The angel sure has come again," had become "The promised angel's come again."

The tune ANIMATION was printed with this text in the 1889 *Latter-day Saints' Psalmody*.

Our Mountain Home So Dear 33

Text: Emmeline B. Wells (1828–1921; LDS)
Music: Evan Stephens (1854–1930; LDS)
Tune name: UTAH

Two of the finest talents of earlier days in Utah combined to produce this appealing song. The first two verses are a tribute to the natural beauty of the valleys and mountains of Utah, settled by the pioneer Saints at so great a cost. The third and fourth verses pay tribute to God as designer and giver of these splendid scenes.

To some Latter-day Saints, the actual locale described in this hymn is a beloved reality. To others, mountains and wildflowers may be known only through photographs. But all Saints can join together in singing our gratitude for the beauties of our world. "I, the Lord, stretched out the heavens," the Lord told the Prophet Joseph Smith, "and built the earth, my very handiwork. . . . For the earth is full, and there is enough and to spare." (D&C 104:14, 17.)

In *Stories of Latter-day Saint Hymns,* George D. Pyper told this story of the origin of "Our Mountain Home So Dear":

"One day 'Aunt Em' [Emmeline B. Wells], in conversation with Evan Stephens, whose genius she greatly admired, told him of [the words to] a love song in her possession that she would like to have set to music. He readily accepted an invitation for an evening at her home and after the reading of the poem mentioned, Evan said, 'Why don't you write the words for a song for me to set to music, Sister Wells?' She promised to think about it, and that same night, while others were sleeping, 'Aunt Em' wrote 'Our Mountain Home, So Dear.' The song, with Professor Stephens' lovely music, has an appealing charm and is very popular. He, himself, remarked when choosing the six songs for the Columbia records to be made for the Church in New York, that it was one of his favorites and that he preferred it to his own hymn [text] bearing a similar name. . . .

"When [Emmeline B. Wells] became acquainted with Evan Stephens, two kindred spirits met, both loving music, art, and God's beautiful outdoors. As a result of their common admiration for nature came this exquisite song. It tells its own story; it makes its own appeal. Read it for yourself; ponder every line and study it, for it is a literary gem." (Pp. 60–61.)

This hymn was first printed in the *Deseret Sunday School Union Music Book* in 1884.

O Ye Mountains High 34

Text: Charles W. Penrose (1832–1925; LDS)
Music: H. S. Thompson (ca. 1852)
Tune name: LILY DALE

A Latter-day Saint who lives in Hong Kong or Nebraska or Haiti probably will not think of the snow-capped mountains of Utah as "my own mountain home." But in fact, this hymn was written by a man who had seen Utah only in his imagination. And every member of the Church can respond to this hymn in its figurative meaning: the restored gospel grants to its followers a life of freedom, purity, and worship, far above the cares and errors of the world.

In *Stories of Latter-day Saint Hymns,* George D. Pyper quoted these words from Charles W. Penrose about the writing of the text of this hymn:

" 'O Ye Mountains High' was written somewhere along about 1854, published about 1856. I was walking on a dusty road in Essex [England]. My toes were blistered and my heels, too. I had been promised that if I would stay in the mission field another year I should be released. That was the cry every year: 'Brother Penrose, if you will stay and labor another year, we will see that you are released to go to Zion.' But it kept up for over ten years. Of course I had read about Zion and heard about the streets of Salt Lake City, with the clear streams of water on each side of the street, with shade trees, and so on. I could see it in my mind's eye, and so I composed that song as I was walking along the road, and set it to a tune—the Scotch ditty, 'O Minnie, O Minnie, Come o'er the Lea." . . . In Essex, we held a cottage meeting, and in that meeting I sang it for the first time it was ever sung. Of course the words were adapted to a person who had never been to Zion then, but it was afterwards changed in a very slight respect or two, to fit people who had gathered with the Saints." (P. 15.)

George D. Pyper commented further in his own words: "As the clouds of prejudice against the Mormon people disappeared and misunderstandings were cleared up it occurred to many of our own people that two lines in the third and fourth stanzas should be revised. They were, respectively—'On the necks of thy foes, thou shalt tread,' and 'The Gentiles shall bow 'neath Thy rod.' " (P. 17.) As a look at the 1950 and 1985 hymnals will show, this wish was carried out: those lines have become "Without fear of thy foes thou shalt tread" and "Thy land shall be freedom's abode."

The early Saints were always receptive to an engaging tune, whatever its source, and the popular song "Lily Dale" provided the melody to which we have sung these words for many decades. "Lily Dale," with words and music by H. S. Thompson, tells of a dying maiden who wishes to be buried "where the wild flowers grow." Our chorus of "O Zion!

dear Zion! land of the free" was originally "Oh, Lily, sweet Lily, dear Lily Dale." This tune was incorporated into the Oscar-winning musical score for the 1939 John Ford classic *Stagecoach,* a film set in the American West of the later nineteenth century.

The "Lily Dale" tune was originally published in 1852, and the hymn text was first published in the *Millennial Star* in 1856. The matching of hymn text and tune appeared for the first time in the *Tune Book for the Primary Association* (1880).

For the Strength of the Hills 35

Text: Felicia D. Hemans (1793–1835);
adapted by Edward L. Sloan (1830–1874; LDS)
Music: Evan Stephens (1854–1930; LDS)
Tune name: GRANTSVILLE

Though marked as a choir hymn in the 1950 hymnal, the appeal of "For the Strength of the Hills" is so great that it is beloved by congregations throughout the Church. This hymn reflects the Saints' gratitude for their refuge from persecution; it speaks of their faith in the guiding hand of a watchful and protective Father.

Latter-day Saints are so attuned to mountains as symbols of protection, strength, "Zion," and home that it is a surprise to most to learn that the "hills" originally referred to in this hymn were the Vaudois Mountains in Switzerland. Felicia Hemans had likely never heard of The Church of Jesus Christ of Latter-day Saints by the time of her death in 1835. Her poem, "Hymn of the Vaudois Mountaineers in Times of Persecution," naturally attracted the attention of Latter-day Saint adapter Edward L. Sloan.

The following verse was deleted from printings of the 1950 hymnal after 1965:

Here the wild bird swiftly darts on
His quarry from the heights,
And the red untutored Indian
Seeketh here his rude delights;
But the Saints for thy communion
Have sought the mountain sod. . . .

The 1985 hymnal added parts for tenors and basses in line three and deleted an additional verse:

For the shadow of thy presence,
Our camp of rocks o'erspread;
For the canyons' rugged defiles

And the beetling crags o'erhead;
For the snows and for the torrents,
And for our burial sod. . . .

In *Stories of Our Mormon Hymns,* J. Spencer Cornwall reprinted all four verses of Felicia Hemans' original poem. (See pp. 247–48.) Her first stanza is essentially the same as that in our hymnal, except for the lines (five and six) "Thou has fixed our ark of refuge / Where the spoilers ne'er trod." Her second stanza is almost identical with verse four in the 1985 hymnal. Her third stanza is as follows:

For the dark, resounding caverns,
Where thy still, small voice is heard;
For the strong pines of the forests,
That by thy breath are stirred;
For the storms, on whose free pinions
Thy spirit walks abroad. . . .

And her fourth stanza resembles the one quoted above that was not included in the 1950 hymnal, except, of course, that Switzerland had no Indians. Instead it reads, "And the stag that knows no master / Seeks there his wild delights."

J. Spencer Cornwall indicated that Evan Stephens patterned his hymn setting after C. Sylvester Horne's adaptation of "Hymn of the Vaudois Mountaineers": "The rhythm and many of the melodic phrases are similar." (*Stories of Our Mormon Hymns,* p. 248.)

The text and tune appeared together on Sunday School Music Card No. 38 and then in the *Juvenile Instructor* in April 1880.

They, the Builders of the Nation 36

Text: Ida R. Alldredge (1892–1943; LDS)
Music: Alfred M. Durham (1872–1957; LDS)
Tune name: BEAVER

Saints everywhere owe a debt to our Mormon pioneers, for without their sacrifice the Church organization would not have been preserved and the message of the gospel would not have been spread. In this hymn we pay them a tribute they earned at great cost.

This hymn highlights the role of the pioneers as an example and a model for those who followed them. Their deeds not only tamed the wilderness and built cities but also provided "stepping-stones for generations," a path for their children and grandchildren to admire and follow, an ideal by which all subsequent generations of Saints can measure their own dedication and courage.

In a conference address in April 1909, Elder David O. McKay spoke these words to the members of the Church assembled in the Salt Lake Tabernacle:

"On the 24th of July, 1847, they were here in this valley. What did they see? You try to picture what they saw. These words will call up the barren picture in the minds of pioneers who are with us today – God bless them and preserve them long with us for what they have done, that we might at least express our appreciation of their devotion to the truth. . . . There was nothing inviting; in fact, they had been warned that nothing would grow. . . . Yet, within a few feet of where we meet today, the prophet of the Lord said, 'Here we shall build a house to God.'

"Now what do we see? Just look at our city today, its climate modified, its fruit unexcelled, substantial and comfortable homes everywhere, towns and cities flourishing. To whom are we indebted for all this? The people of the Mormon Church, the pioneers of 1847 and of subsequent years. They were builders, colonizers, benefactors to our nation, benefactors to humanity." (*Gospel Ideals* [Salt Lake City, Utah: Improvement Era, 1953], p. 528.)

The tune name, BEAVER, is the name of the Utah town where Alfred M. Durham once served as head of the music department at Murdock Academy and as supervisor of music for Beaver City Schools. The hymn, both tune and text, first appeared in *Hymns* (1948).

The Wintry Day, Descending to Its Close 37

Text: Orson F. Whitney (1855–1931; LDS)
Music: Edward P. Kimball (1882–1937; LDS)
Tune name: ALEX

Why would a song of nostalgia and homesickness, penned by a man leaning on his windowsill, come to be so important in Latter-day Saint hymnody? The answer seems to be that for us, a poem of thankfulness for the peace and blessings of Deseret (home of the Utah pioneers) qualifies as a hymn, and "The Wintry Day, Descending to Its Close" is a great favorite with many Latter-day Saints.

Elder Boyd K. Packer referred to Orson F. Whitney as "a gifted and inspired poet whose work is virtually unknown in the Church." (*Ensign*, Aug. 1976, p. 64.) His contributions to our hymnal include this hymn and "Savior, Redeemer of My Soul" (no. 112). "The Wintry Day," originally a poem titled "A Voice from an Absent One," was first printed in the *Latter-day Saints' Southern Star* in 1899.

When we love something deeply—for instance, the landscape and the heritage of our home—distance can often lend greater idealism and enchantment to the scene than if we were actually present. First, the poet must set the scene that has moved him to such deep and sentimental thought: in some unknown place, far from home, an early winter darkness is settling over the snowy earth. Not until the beginning of verse three is the hymn's true subject introduced: the beauty and blessedness of Deseret, twice as dear because the poet is longing for those familiar comforts as his imagination reaches back through time and distance on this beautiful but lonely winter night.

The ingratiating musical setting by Edward P. Kimball no doubt accounts for much of this hymn's appeal. It was part of the choir section of the 1950 hymnal, but congregations will enjoy singing it, especially since the change to a 2/2 time signature makes it easier to read and the performance markings indicating changes in tempo have been removed. Textual editing in verse three changed the "savage" Indian band to a "fearless" one.

The tune name, ALEX, honors organist and composer Alexander Schreiner.

Come, All Ye Saints of Zion 38

Text: William W. Phelps (1792–1872; LDS)
Music: John E. Tullidge (1806–1873; LDS)
Tune name: TEASDALE

This hymn text, part of Latter-day Saint hymnody since Emma Smith's first hymnal in 1835, expresses the gratitude of the Lord's chosen people in these latter days and promises rich blessings to all who will hear his word and become one with the Saints. At that early point in the history of the Church, William W. Phelps foresaw a great movement of preaching, conversion, and gathering.

This hymn follows an interesting pattern. Verses one and four address those who have already heard the gospel message. As is true with so many of our early hymn texts, the author saw missionary work as not only a process of conversion but also a process of gathering—a literal coming together of all Saints into one location. The two verses that come between these messages of exhortation to the Saints are a call to the "dispersed of Judah," to those whose hearts are searching for the truth.

The terms *Judah* and *Israel* can have quite a general meaning in a context such as this, as Elder Bruce R. McConkie explained:

"Those who accept the gospel become of the *house of Israel* regardless of what their literal blood ancestry may have been. Because the blood of

Israel has been scattered among the Gentile nations, nearly all who come into the Church are in greater or lesser degree of the house of Israel literally. But if someone whose blood was wholly of Gentile lineage were converted, he would be adopted into the lineage of Abraham and Jacob and become of the house of Israel." (*Mormon Doctrine,* 2d ed. [Salt Lake City, Utah: Bookcraft, 1966], pp. 389–90.)

In this hymn, the house of Israel is gathered from its scattered state or released from bondage, just as in the time of the Babylonian captivity, so that these men and women may enjoy the blessings of righteousness in the promised land.

Originally titled "Come, All Ye Sons of Zion," the title and first line were changed to make the language more inclusive. It is now arranged as a congregational hymn instead of for men's voices, as in previous hymnals.

O Saints of Zion 39

Text: Ed M. Rowe (1878–1951; LDS)
Music: Robert P. Manookin (b. 1918; LDS)
Tune name: HAUGAN

"The words of this hymn are words of glory, praise, joy, and majesty," stated Robert P. Manookin, the composer of the hymn tune. "The attempt was made to provide a musical setting which would best clothe these inspiring thoughts and express their message. It is almost a 'march' of the [Saints] of Zion, glorious and triumphant." (Quoted in J. Spencer Cornwall, *Stories of Our Mormon Hymns,* p. 167.)

As the first verse exhorts us to prepare for the Savior's second coming, it refers to two relevant parables. The first is "the supper of the Lamb," found in Matthew 22:1–14. It tells of a king who prepares a marriage feast for his son. He sends his servants to invite many guests to the feast, but those who are invited refuse to come. The king punishes these unworthy people and invites a second set of guests, who come to the banquet to feast in honor of the king and his son. The final verse of this parable is the familiar warning, "For many are called, but few are chosen." John the Revelator referred to this parable: "Blessed are they which are called unto the marriage supper of the Lamb." (Revelation 19:9.)

The second parable alluded to in the first verse is the familiar story of the ten virgins, found in Matthew 25:1–13. When the bridegroom comes, five virgins are prepared for the wedding; their lamps are filled with oil. But five have empty lamps, and the door is shut against them. The parable concludes, "Watch therefore, for ye know neither the day nor the hour wherein the Son of man cometh." The hymn implies that the Savior's coming is near at hand: "Behold, the mighty Bridegroom comes / In majesty divine."

The second verse speaks of sacred keys that have been restored and of our responsibility to "declare the gospel plan."

The hymn's beautiful last line is a reminder that service should be motivated by gratitude, not by guilt, or obligation, or a desire for glory.

The hymn appeared in the 1950 hymnal under the title "O Sons of Zion." Robert Manookin noted: "Because over the years it was erroneously considered by many to be a priesthood hymn, it found less use than perhaps it would have done otherwise. For this reason, I suggested that its title and text be changed to 'O Saints of Zion.' "

The tune name honors Helene Haugan, wife of Robert P. Manookin.

Arise, O Glorious Zion 40

Text: William G. Mills (1822–1895; LDS)
Music: George Careless (1839–1932; LDS)
Tune name: VICTORY

To the early Saints, the community they had established was a fortress, offering safety and contentment. The light of Zion was a beacon to all the earth, and missionaries gathered the righteous out of many lands to come to "Zion's favored dwelling."

This hymn text echoes the spirit of many prophetic Old Testament scriptures, such as Isaiah 35:10: "And the ransomed of the Lord shall return, and come to Zion with songs and everlasting joy upon their heads: they shall obtain joy and gladness, and sorrow and sighing shall flee away." In fulfillment of this prophecy, Latter-day Saint missionaries went forth not only to convert the righteous everywhere but also to bring them back to Utah to build up the Lord's earthly kingdom. The time had come when, as had been foretold, Zion would "arise and shine in splendor."

The Saints had gone through many tribulations and uncertainties during the months and years before this hymn was written. Verse three honors the perseverance of the people and gives them some well-deserved recognition: "Through painful tribulation / We walk the narrow road." Then verse four, appropriately, gives final credit to the divine aid that has sustained the faithful through their sufferings: "To him be glory given, / Whose blood did us redeem."

When William G. Mills wrote this text, first published in 1849, the pioneers had been in the Salt Lake Valley for only two years. When he spoke of "Zion" and "the city of our Lord," he was, of course, referring to the new Zion and the new temple they were in the process of building in Utah. And he used the present tense: "Let faithful Saints be rearing /

The city of our Lord. / . . .The temple long expected / Shall stand on Zion's hill."

To make this hymn more applicable to today's Church—when the word *Zion* has worldwide rather than regional connotations—the 1985 Hymnbook Committee chose to delete three of the four verses that were included within the rows of music in the 1950 hymnbook. In their place were substituted three of the little-used "extra" verses printed below the hymn. Three-fourths of the text of this hymn, then, will be essentially new to our congregations. The message is now more central to the present-day Church.

The four verses included in the 1985 hymnal were originally verses one, five, seven, and eight. Verses two, three, four, and six of the original hymn are as follows:

2. *Let faithful Saints be rearing The city of our Lord,*
On mountain tops appearing, According to his word.
A sought-out habitation By men of truth and faith,
A covert of salvation From ignorance and death.

3. *The temple long expected Shall stand on Zion's hill,*
By willing hearts erected, Who love Jehovah's will.
Let earth, her wealth bestowing, Adorn his holy seat,
For nations great shall flow in To worship at his feet.

4. *What though the world in malice Despise these mighty things,*
We'll build the royal palace To serve the King of kings,
Where holy men anointed To know his sovereign will,
Each ordinance appointed To save us, will reveal.

6. *O hear the proclamation And fly as on the wind!*
For righteous indignation Shall desolate mankind!
Then, Zion, men shall prize thee And bow before thy shrine;
And they who now despise these Shall own thy light divine.

J. Spencer Cornwall felt that "if there are distinctive characteristics in Latter-day Saint hymns, 'Arise, O Glorious Zion' has all of them. It reflects the principles and teachings of the restored gospel. Also it has in it the hope and joy of latter-day truth." (*Stories of Our Mormon Hymns*, p. 237.)

Let Zion in Her Beauty Rise 41

Text: Edward Partridge (1793–1840; LDS)
Music: Anonymous (Württemberg, Germany, ca. 1784)
Tune name: ELLACOMBE

The vision of Zion, a beautiful, peaceful city, a place of refuge and righteousness, was a dream that sustained the early Saints during many years of struggle and conflict. When state governments and surrounding communities served them notice that they were not welcome, when neighbors rose up in arms, the Mormon people drew upon their faith in the Zion of the future, a city to be admired and envied by all.

Possibly no one in the history of the Church, except Joseph Smith himself, had a more concrete mental picture of what the earthly Zion was to be than did Edward Partridge. In 1831 Joseph Smith chose Edward Partridge to journey with him from Kirtland, Ohio, to Jackson County, Missouri, on the occasion of the Prophet's first visit there. At this time, Joseph Smith selected the site for the city that was to be named Zion, and in plans drawn up later he outlined how this ideal city was to be laid out. It was to be one mile square, and each ten-acre block would be divided into half-acre lots. Two city blocks would be devoted to a complex of temples. The Prophet chose Edward Partridge to stay in Missouri and supervise the temporal aspects of the building of Zion. In 1831, Edward Partridge was called as first Presiding Bishop of the Church. (See D&C 41:9–11.)

The anticipation of this beautiful city of the future, the city that was to prepare the Saints for the Messiah's return, was the inspiration for Edward Partridge's text, first printed in Emma Smith's 1835 hymnal. The first two verses of the original seven were essentially as we have them today. Verses three, four, and five, now omitted from the hymnbook, centered mainly on a somewhat frightening picture of the events that are to precede the Second Coming:

3. *But ere that great and solemn day,*
The stars from heav'n will fall,
The moon be turned into blood,
The waters into gall,
The sun with blackness will be cloth'd,
All nature look affright!
While men, rebellious wicked men,
Gaze heedless on the sight.

4. *The earth shall reel, the heavens shake,*
The sea move to the north,
The earth roll up like as a scroll,

When God's command goes forth;
The mountains sink the valleys rise,
And all become a plain,
The islands, and the continents
Will then unite again.

5. *Alas! the day will then arrive,*
When rebels to God's grace,
Will call for rocks to fall on them,
And hide them from his face:
Not so with those who keep his law,
They joy to meet their Lord
In clouds above, with them that slept
In Christ, their sure reward.

The sixth verse of the original is the same as our present third verse. In this verse, the worshiper asks the Lord to "prepare my heart" to stand with the blessed in the last days. The original final verse, omitted today, continues this prayer:

7. *Then when the thousand years are past,*
And Satan is unbound,
O Lord preserve us from his grasp,
By fire from heav'n sent down,
Until our great last change shall come,
T'immortalize this clay,
Then we in the celestial world,
Will spend eternal day.

Latter-day Saint hymnals until now paired these words with a hymn tune by Lewis D. Edwards. The 1985 hymnal used the tune ELLACOMBE for the first time.

Hail to the Brightness of Zion's Glad Morning! 42

Text: Thomas Hastings (1784–1872)
Music: Edwin F. Parry (1850–1935; LDS)
Tune name: BRIGHTNESS

J. Spencer Cornwall said of this hymn: "Usually the most telling line in a successful hymn text is the first one. 'Hail to the Brightness of Zion's Glad Morning' is a splendid example of this characteristic. After the exultant outburst, the entire hymn continues with exclamatory gladness." (*Stories of Our Mormon Hymns*, p. 199.)

Latter-day Saints are so accustomed to hymns that equate the restored gospel of Jesus Christ with the dawn of day (see "The Morning Breaks," no. 1, and "Softly Beams the Sacred Dawning," no. 56, as just two examples) that it is easy to assume that this text was written by a Latter-day Saint author, especially since verse three seems to describe the victory of the early Saints over the uncultivated terrains of the Territory of Deseret. But Thomas Hastings was not a member of the Church. He often used the image of the coming of day in his hymns; two other texts by him, not in our hymnal, begin "God of the morning ray" and "The rosy light is dawning." For this particular hymn, he may have drawn his inspiration from Isaiah: "Arise, shine; for thy light is come." (60:1.)

The original title of the text was "Missionary Success." It is essentially a vision of the spread of God's word throughout the world. Although Thomas Hastings did not think of his text in terms of the aspirations of the Latter-day Saints with regard to missionary work or the building of Zion, members of the Church recognized the sentiments of this hymn as something they could readily respond to.

The composer, Edwin F. Parry, was a Latter-day Saint, the same who wrote the music for "Oh, Holy Words of Truth and Love" (no. 271). The 1889 *Latter-day Saints' Psalmody* was the first hymnbook to publish both words and music of this hymn. The 1985 hymnal added tenor and bass notes on line three of the hymn.

Zion Stands with Hills Surrounded 43

Text: Thomas Kelly (1769–1854)
Music: A. C. Smyth (1840–1909; LDS)
Tune name: SAFETY

"They that trust in the Lord shall be as mount Zion, which cannot be removed, but abideth for ever.

". . . So the Lord is round about his people from henceforth even for ever." (Psalm 125:1–2.)

Latter-day Saints love this hymn and its promise of safety and security in "Zion, kept by power divine."

The scriptures frequently speak of "mount Zion," equating mountains with refuge and protection; the word of the Lord will go forth from the mountaintops, and nations will look toward an ensign unfurled on Zion's hill. Only when we remember how common such references are throughout the scriptures, especially as part of Old Testament prophecies, can we understand how a man who probably never heard of the Church during his lifetime could have written a hymn text so in tune with Latter-day Saint feelings.

George D. Pyper remarked: "What the author had in mind when he wrote his impressive lines is said to have been 'the safety of the church' [this was the hymn's original title], but he must have foreseen a condition that did not exist until seventy-seven years after he penned the lines, when the Saints established Zion, 'with hills surrounded.' He might have had in mind the City of David . . . , Jerusalem . . . , the Tribe of Judah . . . , or he might have envisioned the Latter-day 'Zion, the Pure in Heart,' spoken of in modern revelation (Doctrine and Covenants 97:19–21). In any case it was an inspired prophecy; for no Latter-day Saint could have more perfectly described the belief of the Mormon people than did Thomas Kelly back in the eighteenth century." (*Stories of Latter-day Saint Hymns*, pp. 173, 175.)

Latter-day Saint composer A. C. Smyth also wrote the music for "Come, Thou Glorious Day of Promise" (no. 50) and "Come Along, Come Along" (no. 244). He was the arranger/adapter of the music for "Joseph Smith's First Prayer" (no. 26). Words and music of "Zion Stands with Hills Surrounded" appeared together in *A Collection of Hymns and Anthems Set to Music by Home Composers* (1883).

Beautiful Zion, Built Above — 44

Text: George Gill (1820–1880)
Music: Joseph G. Fones (1828–1906; LDS)
Tune name: BARROW

In most of the "Zion" hymns in our book, the word *Zion* denotes an earthly city of righteous inhabitants working together to perfect themselves for the Savior's coming as they send forth the word of truth. This hymn describes a different Zion, a heavenly city of white-clad angels and celestial song.

The author of these words was not a Latter-day Saint. J. Spencer Cornwall informed us, "This familiar hymn was written by an Englishman, George Gill, . . . while he was laboring as a missionary on the island of Mangaia, Cook Islands." (*Stories of Our Mormon Hymns*, p. 92.) The vision of a heavenly reward was no doubt a sustaining thought for George Gill as he faced the hardships of missionary labors.

Joseph G. Fones, the composer, was a Latter-day Saint. The tune name, BARROW, can be accounted for by some information given by J. Spencer Cornwall: "Elder Fones was a self-taught musician. Soon after his conversion he organized a choir at Barrow in Furness, England. When they sang they drew large crowds." (*Stories of Our Mormon Hymns*, p. 92.)

The *Deseret Sunday School Union Music Book* first published the tune, BARROW, as an accompaniment to these words, which had first been published in 1864.

Lead Me into Life Eternal 45

Text: John A. Widtsoe (1872–1952; LDS)
Music: Alexander Schreiner (1901–1987; LDS)
Tune name: PARKER

A strong, dignified prayer for earthly guidance and eternal life finds expression in "Lead Me into Life Eternal." It is not a passive prayer, in which we promise nothing to the Lord in return; each singer wholeheartedly commits "all my heart" and "all my service."

Shortly before his death, composer Alexander Schreiner told this charming story concerning the musical setting and the editorial changes in the present hymn:

"This hymn, written by Elder John A. Widtsoe, was originally called 'Father! Lead Me Out of Darkness,' and the music was composed by Evan Stephens. It was in the 1927 hymnbook. When the time came to revise the book, the Church Music Committee suggested that this hymn be left out, since it wasn't ever sung. I objected. After all, these were words written by an Apostle of the Lord. It was decided that I should approach Elder Widtsoe, proposing to change the title, which seemed negative, and adjust a few of the words.

"Elder Widtsoe said, 'You don't understand, Brother Schreiner. It is being sung by a nonmember. I don't want anybody to change the words. Nonmembers *are* in darkness.'

" 'But Elder Widtsoe,' I responded, 'when you go to a stake conference and give an inspirational and enlightening message to the Saints, how would you feel if the stake president announced that the closing hymn will be "Father! Lead Me Out of Darkness" '?

"Elder Widtsoe could then see the point of giving this fine hymn a positive title, with only the rearrangement of a few words. The change in words made problems for the meter of the song, however, so Tracy Cannon asked me to write new music to suit the new meter."

Glorious Things of Thee Are Spoken 46

Text: John Newton (1725–1807)
Music: Franz Joseph Haydn (1732–1809)
Tune name: AUSTRIA

"Zion," originally a poetic name for Jerusalem, takes on a new, prophetic meaning in this hymn, a meaning with which Latter-day Saints can identify. Zion is the "city of our God," the city of safety, unity, and blessing, under the rulership of the Heavenly King. To sing this hymn is to remind ourselves of our most important hopes and goals.

The opening line of the hymn is from Psalm 87:3: "Glorious things are spoken of thee, O city of God." The text then goes on to mention aspects we would expect to find as part of any literal city of biblical times—the city's foundation, its walls, its rivers, its citizens, and its ruler. But each of these components takes on a glorious figurative meaning: the foundation is the Rock of Ages, the wall is the protective wall of salvation, the streams are "living waters," the inhabitants are "kings and priests" who have been "purchased by the Savior's blood," and the Heavenly King rules over all.

The celestial nature of this description is cast in even greater relief when life in such a "Zion" is compared with the early life of John Newton, author of this hymn. (See Biographies.) Only a sincere turning of his heart and life to new ways could have led him to such a vision of righteous blessedness. His hymn text was first published in 1779.

This text was included in Emma Smith's 1835 hymnal, with ten short verses. In the 1950 hymnbook, the number of verses was reduced to seven, and it was included as part of the choir section. Matched with a difficult hymn tune, however, it was not often sung. The 1985 hymnal combined six of the short verses into three longer ones and paired the text with its more widely used tune, AUSTRIA, one of the most elegant and uplifting hymn melodies in our book.

When Franz Joseph Haydn visited England and heard the English people sing "God Save the King," he felt the lack of a stirring national anthem for his own country, Austria. Probably basing his composition on a melodic suggestion from a folk song, he wrote "The Austrian Hymn" in honor of Emperor Franz. Haydn later used this melody for the beautiful second movement of his String Quartet opus 76 no. 3, known as the "Emperor Quartet" or "Kaiser Quartet."

We Will Sing of Zion 47

Text and music: Merrill Bradshaw (b. 1929; LDS)
Tune name: ZION

This hymn gives us an opportunity to contemplate in song the "kingdom of our God." It reminds us of qualities necessary to a Zion people: purity of heart; dedication to the example of the Savior, the words of the prophets, and divine law; and the attainment of peaceable and loving personal relationships. The Savior can come only when Zion is ready, and Zion can come only when her people are ready.

In 1979 Merrill Bradshaw was commissioned by the Church to write the music for the sesquicentennial pageant, *Zion*, which was to focus on one main idea: the task of Latter-day Saints to become a Zion people.

Merrill Bradshaw noted: "I came home looking for a text to capture this idea. After a couple of days of searching, it became obvious to me that if there were to be one, I would have to either write it or get someone else to do it. I set about writing one for a model and within just a few hours had not only the text but also the music." He wisely kept both words and music simple enough so that most congregations would be able to approach the hymn with confidence. His words are encouraging: "It is quite straightforward. Just sing it!"

The first line of this new hymn announces its topic: "We will sing of Zion, Kingdom of our God." That is exactly what the hymn invites us and allows us to do – sing of Zion. The second line refers to the scripture that was Merrill Bradshaw's principal source for this hymn:

"Therefore, verily, thus saith the Lord, let Zion rejoice, for this is Zion – THE PURE IN HEART; therefore, let Zion rejoice, while all the wicked shall mourn." (D&C 97:21.)

If purity of heart is the summing definition of Zion, then each description, reminder, and prediction that follows in this hymn can be a part of what will add up to that sum.

Glorious Things Are Sung of Zion 48

Text: William W. Phelps (1792–1872; LDS)
Music: Dutch melody (ca. 1710)
Tune name: IN BABILONE

Although the Bible gives us few details about Enoch, a fuller story of Enoch and his city is told in latter-day revelation. (See Moses 6–7.) That story is a witness of the blessings that may be obtained when an entire people commit themselves to live together in perfect unselfishness, obedience, and righteousness.

The first line of John Newton's "Glorious Things of Thee Are Spoken" (no. 46) may have suggested to William W. Phelps the first line of this hymn, but these two "Zion" texts are actually on different subjects. In this hymn, William W. Phelps praised the Zion that was the city of Enoch; the Lord himself gave the name *Zion* to the people of Enoch, "because they were of one heart and one mind, and dwelt in righteousness; and there was no poor among them." (Moses 7:18.) Enoch then built a city which he called "the City of Holiness, even ZION." (Moses 7:19.)

When William W. Phelps wrote that "the righteous . . . walked with God," and finally "the city went to heaven," he was not indulging in poetic exaggeration. These details are given in Moses 7:69:

"And Enoch and all his people walked with God, and he dwelt in the midst of Zion; and it came to pass that Zion was not, for God received it up into his own bosom; and from thence went forth the saying, ZION IS FLED."

Adam-ondi-Ahman, a word in verse two, was defined by Elder Bruce R. McConkie as "a name carried over from the pure Adamic language into English, . . . one for which we have not been given a revealed, literal translation. As near as we can judge—and this view comes down from the early brethren who associated with the Prophet Joseph Smith, who was the first one to use the name in this dispensation—*Adam-ondi-Ahman* means the place or land of God where Adam dwelt." (*Mormon Doctrine,* 2d ed. [Salt Lake City, Utah: Bookcraft, 1966], pp. 19–20.)

In the 1950 hymnal these words had a musical setting by Joseph J. Daynes that was marked for choir use. The 1985 hymnal provided a new musical setting that a congregation will be able to learn and sing more easily.

Adam-ondi-Ahman 49

Text: William W. Phelps (1792–1872; LDS)
Music: Anonymous, Southern Harmony, *1835*
Tune name: PROSPECT OF HEAVEN

So great was Elder Bruce R. McConkie's respect for this hymn and its message that he included all four of William W. Phelps's verses as part of his definition of *Adam-ondi-Ahman.* (See *Mormon Doctrine,* 2d ed. [Salt Lake City, Utah: Bookcraft, 1966], pp. 20–21.)

In his discussion, Elder McConkie said that the term means "the place or land of God where Adam dwelt." (P. 20.) He also provided the following additional information about the meaning of *Adam-ondi-Ahman,* with particular reference to Doctrine and Covenants 107:53–56:

"The early brethren of this dispensation taught that the Garden of Eden was located in what is known to us as the land of Zion, an area for which Jackson County, Missouri, is the center place. . . .

"One of the greatest spiritual gatherings of all the ages took place in the Valley of Adam-ondi-Ahman some 5,000 years ago. . . .

"At that great gathering Adam offered sacrifices on an altar built for the purpose. A remnant of that very altar remained on the spot down through the ages. On May 19, 1838, Joseph Smith and a number of his associates stood on the remainder of the pile of stones at a place called Spring Hill, Daviess County, Missouri. There the Prophet taught them that Adam again would visit the Valley of Adam-ondi-Ahman, holding a great council as a prelude to the great and dreadful day of the

Lord. . . . At this council, all who have held keys of authority will give an accounting of their stewardship to Adam. Christ will then come, receive back the keys, and thus take one of the final steps preparatory to reigning personally upon the earth." (Pp. 20–21.)

The hymn implies in verses two and three that this beautiful spot may also have been the location of the City of Enoch, called Zion. (See the discussion of "Glorious Things Are Sung of Zion," no. 48.) It is no wonder Adam-ondi-Ahman holds such an important place in the teachings of the Latter-day Saints, both for its past history and for the role it will one day play in the preparation for the second coming of the Messiah.

Three minor but interesting textual notes: this hymn was printed in our 1985 hymnal exactly as it was printed in Emma Smith's 1835 hymnal except that "old Israel's Canaan" was changed to "all Israel's Canaan," and the second line of our present last verse, "The Savior's second coming," was originally written "The Savior's second comin' " – Phelps's attempt to achieve a more exact rhyme with "Adam-ondi-Ahman." In addition, the current title, "Adam-ondi-Ahman," is more meaningful than the first line, which was used as a title in previous editions of the hymnbook.

This hymn was sung at the dedication of the Kirtland Temple in 1836, along with "The Spirit of God" (no. 2) and "Now Let Us Rejoice" (no. 3). (See Joseph Smith, *History of The Church of Jesus Christ of Latter-day Saints*, ed. B. H. Roberts [Salt Lake City, Utah: The Church of Jesus Christ of Latter-day Saints, 1948], 2:417.)

Come, Thou Glorious Day of Promise 50

Text: From Pratt's Collection, *ca. 1830; altered*
Music: A. C. Smyth (1840–1909; LDS)
Tune name: RUTH

George D. Pyper, writing in 1939, described this hymn as a prayer to the Lord to "redeem His ancient people, to end their unbelief and misery, and set them free." He continued, "If Alexander Neibaur were living today he could not write a hymn more applicable to the present sad condition of his [the Jewish] race than the one presented here." (*Stories of Latter-day Saint Hymns*, p. 180.)

For many years Alexander Neibaur was considered to be the author of this hymn text. It is a logical and pleasing assumption that this hymn would come from the pen of one of the most devoted and gifted of all the pioneer Saints, a man reported to be the first Jewish convert to Mormonism. (See Biographies; see also Pyper, *Stories of Latter-day Saint Hymns*, pp. 179–80.) In addition, the text seems to express the longing for "the day of promise" in words that seem especially appropriate to one of Jewish descent.

Nevertheless, even though Alexander Neibaur is no doubt responsible for the hymn's inclusion in Latter-day Saint hymnody, he is not the author. Hymn scholar Bruce David Maxwell noted that "Come, Thou Glorious Day of Promise" is "a slightly altered version of the hymn 'May the glorious day of promise,' which appeared in Mason and Greene's *Church Psalmody* (1831). . . . The early occurrences of this hymn in LDS periodicals carried the note, 'By a converted Jew.' To later editors this meant Alexander Neibaur. . . . The first occurrence of this hymn in an LDS publication, however, clarifies what was originally meant. The *LDS Millennial Star* I (1840) [p.] 216 published the hymn with the following note: 'The following hymn was composed by a Jew, and was sent to us for publication, by Bro. Neibaur, of Preston [England], who is himself a Jew.'

"Unfortunately, we do not know the name of the Jew who wrote this hymn. In Mason and Greene it is credited simply to *'Pratt's Collection'*; however, it is obvious that Alexander Neibaur was the original *contributor* of the hymn and not its author." ("Source Book for *Hymns* [1950]," p. 87.)

Sons of Michael, He Approaches 51

Text: Elias L. T. Harrison (1830–1900; LDS); altered
Music: Darwin K. Wolford (b. 1936; LDS)
Tune name: JULIE

In a uniquely Latter-day Saint picture of the events of the last days, this hymn calls upon us to hail the earthly parents of us all—Father Adam and Mother Eve. As we sing this hymn together, we sing *about* singing, particularly in verses two and four. We take our places as members of a triumphant chorus, participants in a great reunion.

The text is somewhat difficult to understand without some background. The name "Michael" and the phrase "ancient one" both refer to Father Adam. (See D&C 27:11; 138:38.) All human beings are descendants of Adam—"sons of Michael"—and therefore all people, from all times, are potentially part of this reunion. The chorus truly is made up of "voices million." Appropriately, Eve is at Michael's side. We welcome her with song and acclamation, and even dance in her honor!

The Prophet Joseph Smith spoke of a future glorious event when the sons and daughters of Adam and Eve will in fact come together to honor their ancient ancestor: "Daniel in his seventh chapter speaks of the Ancient of Days; he means the oldest man, our Father Adam, Michael, he will call his children together and hold a council with them to prepare them for the coming of the Son of Man. He (Adam) is the father of the human family, and presides over the spirits of all men, and all that have had the keys must stand before him in this grand council." The Prophet identified Adam-ondi-Ahman (see the discussion of no. 49) as "the place where Adam shall come to visit his people, or the Ancient of Days shall sit, as spoken of by Daniel the Prophet." (*Teachings of the Prophet Joseph Smith*, sel. Joseph Fielding Smith [Salt Lake City, Utah: Deseret Book, Co., 1979], pp. 157, 122.)

Some subtle changes made in this text for the 1985 hymnal emphasize the correct nature of Adam's role. Because he is the father of the human race, Adam deserves our love and respect; however, to distinguish this appropriate adoration from the worship we afford our Father in Heaven, references to Adam have not been capitalized in this hymn: *father, patriarch, head, lord, ancient one.* In addition, the phrase "his Paradise" has been changed to "his Father's house."

This imaginative, unusual text, first published in the *Millennial Star* in 1861, was part of the 1950 hymnal, but its musical setting was so difficult that only a choir could attempt it. In writing this new, more singable setting, Darwin Wolford admitted frankly that at first he did not find the text attractive. But he continued, "Since writing the music, I have come to love the fine poetry, strong imagery, and especially the solid doctrine regarding Father Adam, as well as the references to Eve, the mother of our generations, and to the events of the Second Coming."

Concerning the writing of the music, Darwin Wolford said: "As a composer, my first consideration was to make a melody that almost sings by itself. This hymn sounds wonderful with a choir or a congregation singing unison, with no accompaniment except perhaps the melody doubled in octaves. Unison singing really allows the singers to contemplate the meaning of the text. The music also sounds very good with the women singing in parts without the men (with or without the accompaniment)." He added, "As an organist, I wrote a setting that has a melodic bass line – one that feels good to the feet!"

The tune name, JULIE, honors the composer's wife.

The Day Dawn Is Breaking 52

Text: Joseph L. Townsend (1849–1942; LDS)
Music: William W. Clayson (1840–1887; LDS)
Tune name: MANCHESTER

When Latter-day Saint poets have sought a comparison to describe the coming of the gospel and the significance of this event for the world, the image of the breaking dawn has occurred to them repeatedly. And what comparison could be more appropriate? Like the gospel, dawn brings light; it is a new beginning; it is a signal to awaken, to arise and begin work; it dispels the clouds and darkness.

Though he often did not care for hymns in the less dignified gospel-song tradition, J. Spencer Cornwall had words of high praise for "The Day Dawn Is Breaking," calling it "distinct and interesting due to its chorus which is rhythmically different from the verse part, but beautifully co-ordinated with the tune and form of the verse. The symbolism of the first stanza taken from nature, together with the atmosphere of joyousness, created by the line 'Beautiful Day of Peace and Rest,' makes it a delight to sing." (*Stories of Our Mormon Hymns*, p. 197.) It was first published in the *Juvenile Instructor* in 1877.

When J. Spencer Cornwall asked Joseph L. Townsend about the origin of his hymn text "When Jesus Shall Come in His Glory" (in *Deseret Sunday School Songs*, 1909, no. 74), Brother Townsend responded by telling of a sacred personal experience which, because of its relevance also to "The Day Dawn Is Breaking," is given here:

"Since I became a member of our Church, in January, 1873, I have been instructed in my faith with many gifts of the Holy Spirit.

"It was after a wondrous vision of the advent of our Savior that I wrote ['When Jesus Shall Come in His Glory']. . . .

"The vision placed me on a wide open prairie with no buildings or improvements in view. The time seemed to be early summer, for the abundant flowers were in bloom. With me was a group of Church officers, all in the usual apparel of present fashions, and without banners, flags, or other insignia. Yet we were all aware of the great events soon to be displayed.

"A solemnity prevailed that hushed all conversation, and our group of brethren was intently gazing at the great masses of brilliant clouds approaching from the eastern horizon. When this wondrous pageant reached the zenith, our group of brethren saw angels and Saints within this glorious sheen of vapor, while it settled down till just above us.

"Then, one whom we recognized by his glorious and majestic appearance, descended and joined our group who were all officers of the Holy Priesthood.

"The long-expected King and Savior greeted us. He called by name and embraced and gave a holy kiss to the brow of each brother, while he gave to each the boon of the Comforter, the assurance of celestial glory.

"This was our reward of approval. My brethren were filled with an ecstasy of joy, and from the Heavenly Host above came the songs of joy that announced again, 'On earth peace, goodwill toward men.' " (Quoted in *Stories of Our Mormon Hymns*, pp. 75–76.)

Let Earth's Inhabitants Rejoice 53

Text: William Clegg (1823–1903; LDS)
Music: Leroy J. Robertson (1896–1971; LDS)
Tune name: PLEASANT GROVE

Convert, missionary, pioneer, lifelong devoted Latter-day Saint—the many roles and experiences that were part of the life of William Clegg seem to be brought together in the joyous declamation of "Let Earth's Inhabitants Rejoice."

It is an unselfish hymn, focusing not just on the future rewards of faithful Saints but also on all children of our Father in Heaven—"earth's inhabitants," excluding no one. The "glorious hour" mentioned in verse one is the hour of the restoration of the gospel, when the words of a prophet begin to prepare the Saints, and through them the peoples of the earth, for the "blissful time . . . by holy men foretold" spoken of in verse two. The blessings will touch everyone during the "long millennial day" of justice, freedom, and love.

Leroy J. Robertson's hymn tune is in the appealing and rhythmically simple style of a chorale. This tune "reflects in a joyous but noble manner," commented J. Spencer Cornwall, "the message of the words which describe the glories of the millennial day when peace shall reign upon the earth. The hymn's straightforward style makes it useful for any service or on any occasion where this subject is treated." (*Stories of Our Mormon Hymns*, p. 105.)

The town of Pleasant Grove, Utah, is the source of the tune name. Leroy J. Robertson lived in Pleasant Grove while attending high school, and he later met his wife there when both were teachers at Pleasant Grove High School. The tune was first published in *Hymns* (1948), accompanying a text that had first appeared in 1863.

Behold, the Mountain of the Lord 54

Text: Michael Bruce (1746–1767); adapted
Music: Leland B. Sateren (b. 1913)
Tune name: REGWAL

Christians never tire of contemplating the unfolding of the events of the last days. This hymn is a joyful restatement of the familiar but beautiful scriptural prophecies concerning Zion: a beacon on a hill will draw all nations to the mountain of the Lord, spreading peace and righteousness.

With its references to "the mountain of the Lord" and "Zion's hill," it holds immediate appeal for Latter-day Saints; however, it was not written by a member of the Church. The 1950 hymnal attributes the hymn to "Logan" (John Logan, 1748–1788). His name has been part of a long-standing debate among hymn scholars. Most now agree with the attribution to Michael Bruce, as given by our present hymnal. Apparently quite a few hymns claimed by Logan were actually written by Bruce, a young Scotsman, whose early death prevented him from establishing his claim to authorship when Logan printed the works under his own name.

A reading of Isaiah 2:2–5 will show why twentieth-century Latter-day Saints and an eighteenth-century Scottish Protestant would both find something familiar and meaningful in these images of Zion and her role in the last days. The entire hymn is based closely on these four familiar Old Testament verses. The repeated lines that constitute verse four are a paraphrase of Isaiah 2:5: "O house of Jacob, come ye, and let us walk in the light of the Lord."

The hymn text was first published in 1781, and it entered Latter-day Saint hymnody in 1841 with its inclusion in Emma Smith's second hymnal. The text of this hymn has been matched in Latter-day Saint hymnody with a musical setting by Joseph J. Daynes since 1889. But the ambitious musical setting was difficult even for choirs. The new tune by Leland J. Sateren, a present-day American composer and choir director, was discovered by the 1985 Hymnbook Committee in the Reorganized Latter-day Saint hymnal *Hymns of the Saints* (Independence, Mo.: Herald Publishing House, 1981). It was matched in that volume to a wonderful text by Frank von Christenson: "As Saints of old their first-fruits brought . . . / So we today first-fruits would bring." This hymn tune also happened to suit perfectly the text "Behold, the Mountain of the Lord." Notice the appropriate match of music and words in the last line of verse one, for example, when the melody rises to enhance the words "Up to the hill of God."

Lo, the Mighty God Appearing! 55

Text: William Goode (1762–1816)
Music: Evan Stephens (1854–1930; LDS)
Tune name: QUINCY

"Lo, the Mighty God Appearing!" is a graphic, awe-inspiring vision of the day of judgment. The nations of the earth hear the voice of Jehovah speaking like thunder. Fire, clouds, and tempests prepare his coming. The Saints claim their reward, but "sinners perish from before him."

This hymn was one of William Goode's many verse paraphrases of the psalms. A look at the first six verses of Psalm 50 will show that this

Old Testament passage is the source of most of the imagery of this fine hymn:

"The mighty God, even the Lord, hath spoken, and called the earth from the rising of the sun unto the going down thereof.

"Out of Zion, the perfection of beauty, God hath shined.

"Our God shall come, and shall not keep silence: a fire shall devour before him, and it shall be very tempestuous round about him.

"He shall call to the heavens from above, and to the earth, that he may judge his people.

"Gather my saints together unto me; those that have made a covenant with me by sacrifice.

"And the heavens shall declare his righteousness: for God is judge himself. Selah."

In the 1950 hymnal, "Lo, the Mighty God Appearing" was labeled as a choir hymn. Although it is not among our easiest hymns, it has been transposed into a lower register and soprano and alto parts have been added at the beginning of the last line to make it more manageable for congregations using the 1985 hymnal. The 1950 hymnal included one additional verse, in which William Goode gave a New Testament cast to the words of the psalm:

Gather first my Saints around me,
Those who to my covenants stood—
Those who humbly sought and found me
Through the dying Savior's blood.
Blest Redeemer,
Dearest Sacrifice to God.

Emma Smith included this hymn text in her 1841 hymnbook, and the 1889 *Latter-day Saints' Psalmody* printed the words with the present tune, QUINCY.

Softly Beams the Sacred Dawning 56

Text: John Jaques (1827–1900; LDS)
Music: J. Spencer Cornwall (1888–1983; LDS)
Tune name: PRAYER OF GRATITUDE

A beautiful, yearning vision of the Millennium emerges from the lines of "Softly Beams the Sacred Dawning." Rather than emphasizing the Second Coming as a time of reckoning and judgment, this serene hymn shows the Millennium through the eyes of the righteous: a time of peace, light, and blessing.

Verse four includes an unusual phrase: "the fair sabbatic era." This interesting comparison suggests that like the Sabbath day, which comes as the crown and reward after six days of labor, the millennium is the Sabbath of our earth's existence, "when the world will be at rest." The Second Coming is the triumph of light over darkness, the redemption of "nature's universal blackness," when all things are made holy.

In the 1950 hymnal, this text was paired with the tune SERENITY, which appeared in the 1985 hymnal as the tune for "O Thou Kind and Gracious Father" (no. 150). The tune with which the text was paired for the 1985 hymnbook was composed by J. Spencer Cornwall. He was the author of *Stories of Our Mormon Hymns*, the companion volume to the 1950 hymnal, but he was not represented in that hymnal as a composer. This tune is a fine addition to the 1985 hymnal. He wrote it at his home in Salt Lake City when he was ninety years old.

The 1950 hymnal included four additional verses that not only embellish the vision of the beautiful resurrection morning but also help us to realize that it was just such a vision that sustained the early Saints in times of trial:

Odors sweet the air perfuming,
Verdure of the purest green;
In primeval beauty beaming
Will our native earth be seen.

At the resurrection morning,
We shall all appear as one;
O what robes of bright adorning
Will the righteous then put on!

None have seen the untold treasures
Which the Father hath in store,
Teeming with surpassing pleasures,
Even life for evermore.

Mourn no longer, Saints beloved;
Brave the dangers, no retreat;
Neither let your hearts be moved;
Scorn the trials you may meet.

We're Not Ashamed to Own Our Lord 57

Text: William W. Phelps (1792–1872; LDS); altered
Music: John Longhurst (b. 1940; LDS)
Tune name: AUSTIN

"We're Not Ashamed to Own Our Lord" is a heartfelt, confident affirmation of faith. A committed follower of Jesus Christ, who at all times accepts and lives up to the role of disciple, can look forward with joy to a day of recognition, reward, and happiness in the New Jerusalem.

William W. Phelps was a close acquaintance and eager student of the Prophet Joseph Smith. He gave the Saints, very early in the history of the Church, many hymns that summarize the Prophet's teachings. This hymn, as J. Spencer Cornwall noted, "is one filled with restored gospel truths, notably its reference to the second coming of Christ." (*Stories of Our Mormon Hymns*, p. 261.)

This hymn appeared in Emma Smith's 1835 hymnal. William W. Phelps derived the hymn's first line from an Isaac Watts hymn beginning "I'm not ashamed to own my Lord." William W. Phelps' fourth verse also shows the influence of Isaac Watts.

Isaac Watts's words:

Then will he own my worthless name
Before his Father's face,
And in the New Jerusalem
Appoint my soul a place.

William W. Phelps's words, as originally written:

Then will he give us a new name
With robes of righteousness,
And in the New Jerusalem
Eternal happiness.

The first two lines of William W. Phelps's second verse were revised after the 1835 printing because they were awkward in the original: "When Jesus comes as flaming flame, / For to reward the just." Also, the original first line of verse three, now changed to a more easily understandable "When he comes down from heav'n to earth," was more cumbersome as William W. Phelps originally wrote it: "When he comes down in heav'n on earth." The implications of the original line are interesting, however. Its phrase "in heav'n on earth" conveys the truth communicated in the tenth article of faith: at the time of Christ's earthly reign, "the earth will be renewed and receive its paradisiacal glory." The righteous Saints truly will be blessed with a "heaven on earth."

These words were paired in the 1950 hymnal with a musical setting by Joseph J. Daynes. But that setting was so difficult that even choirs, in many cases, found it a struggle to sing the hymn, and only very experienced pianists or organists could play it.

Tabernacle organist John Longhurst was invited by the 1985 Hymnbook Committee to submit a new musical setting, one that congregations could sing and enjoy. A distinctive point concerning his hymn tune is that congregations must be prepared to move right on to the next phrase in the seventh measure, rather than dwelling on the word "earth" (verse one) as they might ordinarily expect to do. In the melody, the octave skip from the seventh to the eighth measure gives strong emotional emphasis to the words "We love."

The tune name, AUSTIN, is the brand name of one of the small pipe organs used by the Tabernacle organists in their preparation. John Longhurst said that he composed this hymn tune "seated one day at the Austin."

Come, Ye Children of the Lord 58

Text: James H. Wallis (1861–1940; LDS)
Music: Spanish melody; arranged by Benjamin Carr (1768–1831)
Tune name: SPANISH HYMN

This hymn is an exaltation of musical worship. When faithful Saints contemplate the events of the future—the Savior's second coming, the peaceable fellowship of the righteous—what wish could be more natural than to "sing with one accord"? What response other than song could so well reflect the emotions and gratitude of the followers of Jesus Christ?

Verse one is a joyous vision of the Second Coming. Latter-day Saints treasure in their hearts the anticipation of this day, and the hymn invites all to join together: "Let us raise a joyful strain." Verse two projects us forward to the day of the Savior's coming: "Oh, what songs we then will sing." In verse three, we cast ourselves in the role of those who shout and sing in celebration of the time of "love and beauty," when earth is cleansed from sin.

Though the words are of Latter-day Saint origin, the music of this hymn began as a Spanish folk melody, known popularly in the United States as a setting for a text beginning "Far, far o'er hill and dell." (In most versions of this melody, the dotted-quarter-plus-eighth-note rhythms are printed as half-notes.) In 1824, Benjamin Carr wrote a set of piano variations on the tune, and many Christian denominations incorporated the melody into their hymnals.

The tune was well known by the time James H. Wallis wrote the hymn text, first printed in the 1884 *Deseret Sunday School Union Music Book*. The hymn's subject possibly was suggested to him by a well-known set of words by Christian Henry Bateman (1813–1889), paired with this tune in other hymnals, beginning:

Come, Christians, join to sing
Alleluia! Amen!
Loud praise to Christ our King;
Alleluia! Amen!

Come, O Thou King of Kings 59; 332

Text: Parley P. Pratt (1807–1857; LDS)
Music: Anonymous (ca. 1889)
Tune name: SANFORD

Many of the hymn texts of the early Saints show how immediate and complete was their trust in the Savior and his promised coming. During trials it is hardly possible for us to imagine today, the pioneer Saints took comfort in the thought of a time when all would be made right and the just would be rewarded and protected. This favorite text by Parley P. Pratt is an example of just such a vigorous millennial hymn.

We do not know the exact circumstances under which Parley P. Pratt wrote this hymn, first printed in the *Millennial Star* in 1840, but George D. Pyper offered this conjecture:

"Parley P. Pratt and twelve hundred men, women and children had been driven from their homes in Jackson County, Missouri, in the autumn of 1833, by a murderous mob. Two hundred homes were burned and families separated. Many of the Saints were killed and others brutally flogged. Cattle were either shot or confiscated, hay and grain burned and the people forced across the river into Clay County [Missouri].

"It was amid such trying and perilous times, no doubt, that Parley P. Pratt wrote 'Come, O Thou King of Kings.' It was a fervent cry to the God of Israel to come and set His people free; an appeal to the mighty King of Kings to make an end of sin which was gripping the world, and to cleanse the world by fire; a prayer that the time might soon come when the Saints, in happier songs and rejoicings, might enjoy a reign of peace. The hymnist looked forward to the day when all the ransomed throng would join in singing a new triumphant song, filling the heavens with anthems from Zion's Hill. The hymn ends in a paean of praise to the Prince of Life and Peace, the Lord and Savior, before whom all nations shall bow the knee and every tongue give praise." (*Stories of Latter-day Saint Hymns*, p. 185.)

Because the hymn was not published until 1840, it may not have been actually written amid the events described above. But surely the memory of such trials strengthened Parley P. Pratt's longing for a day of peace and restitution.

The phrase "desire of nations" echoes many scriptural references to Jesus. See, for example, Haggai 2:7: "And I will shake all nations, and the desire of all nations shall come."

A welcome change in the 1985 hymnal is the inclusion of verses three and four within the music staff. In the 1950 edition, the last two verses of this favorite hymn were printed at the bottom of the page and were rarely sung. Now it is more likely that all four verses—the complete message of the hymn—will be sung.

Battle Hymn of the Republic 60

Text: Julia Ward Howe (1819–1910)
Music: Anonymous (ca. 1861)
Tune name: BATTLE HYMN

Who can resist the spiritual call to arms of this famous hymn? Its history ties it closely to the American Civil War, but its message is the spirit of Psalm 20:7: "Some trust in chariots, and some in horses: but we will remember the name of the Lord our God." Its words link patriotic heroism with the heroism of our Savior and Redeemer, Jesus Christ.

In 1861, the clouds of war began to gather over the United States. It was clear that the unthinkable was about to happen—a nation was to go to war against itself. Julia Ward Howe, a recent arrival in Washington, D.C., heard some soldiers on parade singing a marching ditty about John Brown, a martyr to the abolitionist cause: "John Brown's body lies a-mouldering in the grave; / His soul goes marching on." The familiar tune which the soldiers were singing had served for many sets of words, most of them comic or satirical.

A visiting friend from Boston, Julia Ward Howe's former pastor, James Freeman Clarke, challenged her to write some words that were more uplifting. She gave this background: "I awoke in the grey of the morning, and as I lay waiting for dawn, the long lines of the desired poem began to entwine themselves in my mind, and I said to myself, 'I must get up and write these verses, lest I fall asleep and forget them!' So I sprang out of bed and in the dimness found an old stump of a pen, which I remembered using the day before. I scrawled the verses almost without looking at the paper." (As quoted in Kenneth W. Osbeck, *101 Hymn Stories* [Grand Rapids, Mich.: Kregel Publications, 1982], p. 35.)

The poem was first published in *The Atlantic Monthly* in February 1862, and its popularity spread rapidly. Today, its meaning far transcends the original purpose indicated by the title—a battle hymn for the Northern Republic during the Civil War.

Some hymnals include two additional verses. The first of these evokes the Civil War background of the hymn; the second is a thrilling vision of the moment of the Second Coming:

I have seen him in the watchfires of a hundred circling camps;
They have builded him an altar in the evening dews and damps;

I can read his righteous sentence by the dim and flaring lamps;
His day is marching on.

He is coming like the glory of the morning on the wave;
He is wisdom to the mighty, he is honor to the brave;
So the world shall be his footstool, and the soul of wrong his slave.
Our God is marching on.

With the publication of the 1985 Latter-day Saint hymnbook, this hymn—which points toward a jubilant millennial return of the Lord Jesus Christ—again becomes a part of Latter-day Saint hymnody. It had earlier appeared in Latter-day Saint sources but was not included in the 1950 hymnal.

Raise Your Voices to the Lord — 61

Text and music: Evan Stephens (1854–1930; LDS)
Tune name: TOVEY

"Shout thanksgiving!" This exhortation occurs in both verses of this hymn text, written to close a meeting. This hymn expresses the hope that the fervent singing will prolong the spirit and conviction of the meeting throughout the coming week, "Until here we meet again / To renew the glad refrain."

A closing hymn such as "Raise Your Voices to the Lord" can serve an important symbolic purpose. During most of the meeting, the responsibility for what is occurring rests with one individual at a time. Various individual voices are heard in talks and prayers. Perhaps one member of the group performs a solo musical number. One person may be sustained in a new position, another given a new priesthood calling. A family may be welcomed into the ward or branch. But at the meeting's conclusion, all individuals join together in one expression of heartfelt praise. The final hymn brings the congregation together and makes them a whole. We express our praise *together*: "Let *our* song / Still our joy and praise prolong." (Italics added.)

The musical setting is in the style of a chorale, a simple hymn form dating back to early Protestantism. The half-note rhythms with which it was printed in the 1950 hymnal are more typical of chorale hymns, but the quarter-note rhythms of the 1985 hymnal are somewhat easier to read and are less likely to invite too slow a tempo.

This hymn first appeared in *Latter-day Saint Hymns* (1927).

All Creatures of Our God and King 62

Text: St. Francis of Assisi (1182–1226);
translated by William H. Draper, 1855–1933
Music: German melody; arranged by Ralph Vaughan Williams (1872–1958)
Tune name: LASST UNS ERFREUEN

St. Francis of Assisi, the gentle preacher who loved the birds and animals of the forest and every manifestation of the natural world, could have left no more fitting legacy than this great hymn to nature. It is a joyous inventory of the blessings heaped upon us by a loving Creator as each of His creations is urged to join in a chorus of praise.

Near the end of his life, St. Francis became increasingly weak, and periods of temporary blindness began to plague him often. As it became obvious to him that he would not live much longer, one of his last acts upon this earth was to compose a hymn declaring one final time his love for the simple things of nature and praising God for them. His feeling of unity with nature was all-inclusive and highly personal; the original version addresses the sun, wind, and fire as "brothers," the moon and water as "sisters," and the earth, as retained in our version, as "mother." As death came nearer, he added one final stanza, addressed to "our sister, the death of the body." Such were his feelings of peace as his life closed.

The original hymn is in the language spoken by the common people of the time of St. Francis, known as vulgar Latin. It marked a transitional point between classical Latin and modern Italian. Matthew Arnold's literal translation of the first stanza reads, "Praised be my Lord God with all his creatures, and specially our brother the sun, who brings us the day and who brings us the light; fair is he and shines with a very great splendor: O Lord, he signifies us to thee!" (Quoted in Albert Edward Bailey, *The Gospel in Hymns* [New York: Charles Scribner's Sons, 1950], p. 267.)

The translator of the well-known version in our hymnbook, William H. Draper, wrote his version for a schoolchildren's festival in England. He condensed the words of St. Francis and added the "Alleluias" that are part of our version.

The tune, first printed in Germany in 1623, received its title LASST UNS ERFREUEN (German for "Let us rejoice") from the opening words of the Easter text for which it was first the setting.

J. Spencer Cornwall offered the opinion that "this magnificent hymn, when sung by a congregation, should be performed in unison." (*Stories of Our Mormon Hymns*, p. 8.) A close adherence to tempo markings will help the congregation have adequate breath to sing the phrases exultantly, particularly the last "Alleluia!"

Great King of Heaven 63

Text: Carrie Stockdale Thomas (1848–1931; LDS)
Music: Leroy J. Robertson (1896–1971; LDS)
Tune name: JASPER

"Great King of Heaven" is a hymn of praise, with both words and music expressing the highest and most joyful gratitude. It unites two thoughts: first, our prayer of gratitude to our Father in Heaven, and second, our realization that the wonders of nature also declare their praise to the Lord "with one voice in one glad chord."

Psalm 145:10 states, "All thy works shall praise thee, O Lord." This hymn is a prayer that reflects a similar thought. Carrie Stockdale Thomas, the Latter-day Saint poet who wrote this hymn, must have loved the wonders of the natural world, for she conveyed in both verses her testimony of the Lord and her gratitude for his goodness that can be found within nature.

The hymn mentions four creations specifically: "vales," "hills," "earth," and "skies." The beautiful sentiment behind this hymn is the thought that the praises of the Saints, expressed in song, will awaken the vales and hills, so that all will sing together "with one voice." As the American philosopher Ralph Waldo Emerson stated in his book *Nature*: "Therefore is Nature ever the ally of Religion: lends all her pomp and riches to the religious sentiment. Prophet and priest, David, Jesus, Isaiah, have drawn deeply from this source." (*The Collected Works of Ralph Waldo Emerson*, ed. Alfred R. Ferguson [Cambridge, Mass.: Harvard University Press, 1971], p. 26.)

The word *myriad*, in the last line, means literally "ten thousand." It has taken on the meaning of "numberless." The phrase "myriad echoes" conveys the thought that the praise of God's creations will continue without ceasing.

The tune name, JASPER, honors Jasper H. Robertson, the father of the composer.

On This Day of Joy and Gladness 64

Text and music: Leroy J. Robertson (1896–1971; LDS)
Tune name: ALLELUIA

From the pen of Latter-day Saint composer Dr. Leroy J. Robertson came this fervent hymn of celebration and worship. New to Latter-day Saint hymnbooks, it is suitable for a special event, such as the dedication of a building. But since any meeting of the Saints is a "day of joy and gladness," it also serves as a general hymn of praise and exultation.

During the time Dr. Robertson was chairman of the General Church Music Committee, youth choruses were being encouraged throughout the Church. It was for these choruses that he wrote this number, originally an anthem entitled "Song of Praise." His daughter, Dr. Marian Robertson (Mrs. W. Keith Wilson), tells us that the anthem "sprang from the composer's ardent desire to bring music of great quality to the youth of the LDS Church." The version in our hymnal is abridged and adapted from the original anthem.

Although Leroy J. Robertson often set to music already existing texts, he was moved to write the words as well for "On This Day of Joy and Gladness." Marian Robertson Wilson noted: "My father always loved to set to music the Hebrew word *Alleluia*, probably because of its inherently beautiful sounds, its historical importance, and its meaning ('Praise Ye the Lord'); it is the key word to the entire text. This is a song of joy and promise, characteristic of his profound love of the gospel.

She continued: "This piece encompasses the three basic elements of a hymn as outlined in the ancient definition thereof: it is (1) a song (2) of praise (3) to the Lord. Verse one gives joyful praise to the Lord; verse two develops the idea of the blessings that flow to those who serve in the kingdom of God; verse three outlines the basic gospel doctrine of the true Church which brings the Saints to salvation. The music and words together present a message of joy and promise, characteristic of Leroy Robertson's profound love for the gospel."

Come, All Ye Saints Who Dwell on Earth 65

Text: William W. Phelps (1792–1872; LDS)
Music: William B. Bradbury (1816–1868)
Tune name: KEOKUK

Included in Emma Smith's first hymnal in 1835, this hymn served the early Saints as a call to worship. There is in it no mention of struggles or hardships. It is a hymn of simple praise and rejoicing: "The straight and narrow way we've found!"

This hymn text should have a particular appeal to all who love to sing hymns. The first verse is an invitation to join in hymns of praise; the expression "cheerful voices" sets the mood for the rest of this joyous hymn. The second verse centers on the theme of gratitude: "Shall we ungrateful be?" The third verse is one of exhortation and encouragement: "Then let us travel on." And finally, to round out the hymn in a satisfying way, the last verse again refers to worship through song. This time, however, the songs are those of a heavenly choir; we "sing his praise above."

Thus the hymn sets forth a beautiful thought (one that should warm the hearts of all ward music directors!): those who welcome the invitation to praise the Lord in song while on this earth, showing through their songs that they love him as their Savior and accept his precepts, will have the privilege of even more wonderful musical worship in the life to come. The words of this hymn are an excellent tonic for anyone who has fallen into the habit of half-hearted hymn-singing.

The interesting opening line of verse two – "His love is great; he died for us" – is the most concise and blunt expression possible of the paradox of the Savior's sacrifice. (For a discussion of paradox, see the comments on no. 196.) These eight one-syllable words are at the center of Christian thinking. The idea behind them has triggered millions upon millions of words of commentary, but in this hymn William W. Phelps made just this one brief allusion to the Atonement. He trusted that his fellow Saints, given only this small reminder, would bring to the hymn an understanding of the importance of the Atonement.

William B. Bradbury's tune has a rhythm termed "intriguing" by J. Spencer Cornwall. (*Stories of Our Mormon Hymns*, p. 16.) The first and fifth phrases are three measures long, rather than two measures long, as we would expect. It is interesting to hum the tune through, substituting ordinary rhythms by making each line (except for its final note) consist of quarter notes – in other words, by giving lines one and three the same rhythm as line two. It becomes clear that the unusual rhythm adds a great deal to the tune's appeal; J. Spencer Cornwall was probably right in saying that "the rhythm of this hymn tune is the musical reason for its inclusion." (P. 16.)

Rejoice, the Lord Is King! 66

Text: Charles Wesley (1707–1788)
Music: Horatio Parker (1863–1919)
Tune name: JUBILATE

"Rejoice in the Lord alway: and again I say, Rejoice." These exultant words from Philippians 4:4 were the germ of this fine hymn text, described by J. Spencer Cornwall as "heroic in character and . . . sequentially climactic." (*Stories of Our Mormon Hymns*, p. 166.)

Horatio Parker's tune was originally written in 1894 for the text of "Rejoice, the Lord is King"; the tune name, JUBILATE, is Latin for "rejoice." The tune is a wonderful complement for the words. In the chorus, particularly, each segment of the melody rises upwards; like the text, the music is "sequentially climactic."

Jesus has many names and aspects, and his followers can therefore praise him from many different points of view. This hymn triumphantly celebrates Jesus as King and Sovereign. He is Lord, King, God, Savior, Christ. "His kingdom cannot fail." Because of his power, because he controls the keys of death and hell, no one need any longer fear being a prisoner.

Many hymnals include an additional verse that looks forward to the glories and rewards of the Second Coming:

Rejoice in glorious hope!
Our Lord the Judge shall come,
And take his servants up
To their eternal home.

The repetition of *Rejoice* in the chorus grows to a triumphant swell. The words *lift up* are repeated four times in the chorus as the pattern of the tune rises to match the sense of the words. The word *again*—part of the verse from Philippians as well as of Charles Wesley's hymn text—implies that the rejoicing is never to cease.

The tune DARWALL (the musical setting for no. 265 in our hymnal) is the choice of many denominations as the tune for "Rejoice, the Lord Is King." When DARWALL is used, however, the text in verse one, line two, reads: "Rejoice [rather than "Mortals"], give thanks, and sing"—to preserve a proper match of syllables and notes. Like JUBILATE, DARWALL has an upward movement that makes it especially suitable for these words.

Glory to God on High 67

Text: James Allen (1734–1804); altered
Music: Felice de Giardini (1716–1796)
Tune name: ITALIAN HYMN

This dignified hymn draws all creatures, in heaven and earth, into one great moment of praise and adoration. Though it is a general hymn of praise and thanksgiving, behind this outpouring of praise and gratitude is a specific reason, as indicated in verse two: "Jesus, our Lord and God, / Bore sin's tremendous load."

The hymn unites the praises of heaven and earth. Its correlation with Revelation 5:9–13, the scripture reference given at the bottom of the page in the hymnal, is very close. John the Revelator sees and hears "a new song," the message of which is "thou [the Lamb] wast slain, and hast redeemed us to God by thy blood." This hymn of praise is sung by "the voice of many angels round about the throne . . . ;

"Saying with a loud voice, Worthy is the Lamb that was slain to receive power, and riches, and wisdom, and strength, and honour, and glory, and blessing."

Then other voices join those of the heavenly hosts: "And every creature which is in heaven, and on the earth, and under the earth, and such as are in the sea, and all that are in them, heard I saying, Blessing, and honour, and glory, and power, be unto him that sitteth upon the throne, and unto the Lamb for ever and ever."

In a beautiful poetic adaptation, this hymn greatly simplifies John's description, but both embody the same events: voices from heaven and earth unite to give thanks to Jesus Christ, the Lamb who was sacrificed for the sins of all. "Worthy the Lamb!"

The tune name, ITALIAN HYMN, honors the nationality of the composer. First published in 1761, the tune is included in most Christian hymnals, but the text is usually not the same one as in our hymnal. The more common hymn text is also a hymn of praise. Its first verse is as follows:

Come, thou almighty King,
Help us thy name to sing,
Help us to praise!
Father, all-glorious,
O'er all victorious,
Come, and reign over us,
Ancient of Days!

A Mighty Fortress Is Our God 68

Text: Martin Luther (1483–1546); adapted
Music: Attributed to Martin Luther
Tune name: EIN FESTE BURG

This beloved and historic hymn arose out of the struggle of the Protestant Reformation. Today, in Wittenberg, Germany, travelers may read on the tomb of Martin Luther the words "*Ein feste Burg ist unser Gott*": "A mighty fortress is our God."

The hymn, dating from 1529, is an extended figure of speech comparing our God to an unshakeable fortress that will protect us forever from the attacks of Satan. It takes its inspiration from Psalm 46, which begins, "God is our refuge and strength, a very present help in trouble." It has been translated innumerable times into English as well as dozens of other languages, and its popularity extends throughout the Christian world.

Martin Luther had an abiding conviction of the importance of musical worship, and he sought to establish congregational singing throughout the Protestant churches. He spoke of this conviction many times. Once he stated, "The devil, the originator of sorrowful anxieties and restless troubles, flees before the sound of music almost as much as before the Word of God." Another time he said: "If any man despises music, as all fanatics do, for him I have no liking; for music is a gift and grace of God, not an invention of men. Thus it drives out the devil and makes people cheerful. Then one forgets all wrath, impurity, and other devices." (Quoted in Kenneth W. Osbeck, *101 Hymn Stories* [Grand Rapids, Mich.: Kregel Publications, 1982], p. 14.)

Many writers throughout past centuries have paid tribute to Martin Luther's skill as a hymn-writer and to this great hymn in particular. Samuel Taylor Coleridge said that Luther "did as much for the Reformation by his hymns as he did by his translation of the Bible." The German poet Heinrich Heine called "A Mighty Fortress" the "*Marseillaise* of the Reformation." (Quoted in Charles S. Nutter and Wilbur F. Tillett, *The Hymns and Hymn Writers of the Church* [New York: Methodist Book Concern, 1911], p. 57.)

Most other hymnals include four verses. In a translation by Frederick H. Hedge (1805–1890), used in *The Methodist Hymnal*, the three additional verses read as follows:

Did we in our own strength confide,
Our striving would be losing,
Were not the right man on our side,
The man of God's own choosing:
Dost ask who that may be?
Christ Jesus, it is he;
Lord Sabaoth, his name,
From age to age the same,
And he must win the battle.

And though this world, with devils filled,
Should threaten to undo us,
We will not fear, for God hath willed
His truth to triumph through us:
The Prince of Darkness grim,
We tremble not for him;
His rage we can endure,
For lo, his doom is sure;
One little word shall fell him.

That word above all earthly powers,
No thanks to them, abideth;
The Spirit and the gifts are ours
Through him who with us sideth:
Let goods and kindred go,
This mortal life also;
The body they may kill:
God's truth abideth still;
His kingdom is forever.

All Glory, Laud, and Honor 69

Text: St. Theodulph of Orléans (ca. 760–821)
Music: Melchior Teschner (1584–1635)
Tune name: ST. THEODULPH

Only a few days before his crucifixion, Jesus entered Jerusalem in triumph, and the people "took branches of palm trees, and went forth to meet him, and cried, Hosanna: Blessed is the King of Israel that cometh in the name of the Lord." (John 12:13.) They welcomed him as the Messiah and shared testimony of the miracles he had performed. In this hymn we ask the Savior to accept our praises as he accepted theirs.

The story of Christ's triumphal welcome into Jerusalem should cause us to reflect: crowds of joyous followers were there to greet him at that happy moment. But a few days later, when Jesus had been arrested, their loyalty faded. Are we among those who will remain faithful to the Savior in times of persecution and hardship?

Originally a Latin hymn seventy-eight lines in length, "All Glory, Laud, and Honor" is more than eleven hundred years old. Theodulph, bishop of Orléans, wrote the hymn in 820 A.D. to be used as a processional hymn on Palm Sunday, the Sunday before Easter, when many denominations celebrate Christ's triumphal entry into Jerusalem.

The legend surrounding this hymn is familiar to students of hymn history. Theodulph had been imprisoned by the Emperor Louis, son of Charlemagne, because he suspected Theodulph of being in league with relatives who were fighting against him. The emperor was in Orléans on the Sunday before Easter. As the grand procession moved through the streets, it happened to stop under the tower where Theodulph was imprisoned. All at once the sound of a beautiful voice singing "All glory, laud, and honor" floated over the procession. When the emperor asked the name of the unseen singer, he learned that it was his own prisoner, Theodulph. The emperor was so moved by what he had heard that he immediately pardoned Theodulph and sent him back to his duties as bishop.

The story is undoubtedly a fabrication, but it shows the popularity of this hymn, which has endured more than a thousand years.

The English version in our present hymnal – the first Latter-day Saint hymnbook to include this hymn – is based on a translation by Englishman John M. Neale (1818–1866). One change in the standard text was made for our book: since we pray to the Father, rather than to the Son, we sing "Our praise and love [rather than *prayers*] and anthems" (verse 2, line 4), and "Accept the love [rather than *prayers*] we bring" (verse 3, line 3).

Melchior Teschner's hymn tune, which is always paired with this text, matches well the stately march of the words.

Sing Praise to Him 70

Text: Johann J. Schütz (1640–1690);
translated by Frances Elizabeth Cox (1812–1897)
Music: From Bohemian Brethren's Songbook, *1566; altered*
Tune name: MIT FREUDEN ZART

In joyous phrases, "Sing Praise to Him" catalogs the attributes of our Father in Heaven. Each verse reveals new mercies and new powers, and we praise him because we are the beneficiaries. Heart, soul, and body join together to worship him: "To him all praise and glory!"

The hymn text is based on comparisons that make vivid the strength and graciousness of our Father, and it is interesting to list the figures of speech the hymn-writer has chosen. God is a fount, a rock, an ever-watchful guardian and king – one whose tender care is like that of a mother. His blessings are a balm, a comfort, a "help and stay."

The author, Johann J. Schütz, was a member of the Pietists, a group that arose against the background of the German Reformation and stressed personal spiritual dedication, holy living, and dependence on the Lord. "Sing Praise to Him" is an example of the tendency of Pietist hymns to be more personal and subjective than previous Lutheran hymns had been.

The hymn tune name, MIT FREUDEN ZART, is German for "with tender gladness," the opening words of the German text originally associated with the tune.

A fifth verse included by many Christian hymnals invites all worshipers to join in praise of the only true God:

O ye who name Christ's holy name,
Give God all praise and glory;

All ye who own his power proclaim
Aloud the wondrous story!
Cast each false idol from his throne;
The Lord is God, and he alone:
To God all praise and glory!

With Songs of Praise 71

Text: Penelope Moody Allen (b. 1939; LDS)
Music: Newel Kay Brown (b. 1932; LDS)
Tune name: DENTON

This hymn gives thanks for the blessing of song itself. When words alone are not sufficient to celebrate, to thank, to worship, or to pray, the "heart too full to speak" can turn to music.

Penelope Moody Allen stated that she had little hope of being able to contribute something to the 1985 hymnal, because her poetic style was "generally too free for a musical setting." But when she decided to write a hymn text for women, it "poured out easily and surely," and she felt certain it would become a part of the new hymnal.

"But," she reported, "it was rejected. How could my inspired hymn be rejected? I have since realized that my experience was similar to many people's. Sometimes the Lord inspires us for our own edification and not for the edification of others."

She decided to try again. "I still had something to say," she said. "Through the years I had noted that some people never sang. Congregational singing invites the Spirit, unifies the separate people into a whole, praises the Lord, and is a means for conveying the joys of the gospel. I wanted to express how important hymns are, so I amassed all the ideas that I had had through the years and put them into the verses. How wonderful to realize that hymn singing is a permanent part of the gospel ['The Saints shall sing, when Christ shall come'] and was with us from early times ['In former days glad hymns were sung / By seed of Abraham'].

" 'With Songs of Praise' should be sung with fervor," she continued. "We have been commanded to *praise* the Lord." The opening notes of Mendelssohn's hymn tune for "O God, the Eternal Father" (no. 175) recalled to Newel Kay Brown "the strength of unison singing." As a result, he decided to begin the first two lines of the tune with three vigorous ascending unison notes. He suggested singing the entire hymn in unison initially, before singing the parts. It is useful for the congregation to note that the rhythm of the soprano line is slightly different from the more regular rhythm of the other three parts.

The tune name is for Denton, Texas, the composer's place of residence.

Praise to the Lord, the Almighty 72

Text: Joachim Neander (1650–1680);
translated by Catherine Winkworth (1829–1878)
Music: From Stralsund Gesangbuch, *1665;*
arranged by William S. Bennett (1816–1875) and
Otto Goldschmidt (1829–1907)
Tune name: LOBE DEN HERREN

"A magnificent hymn of praise to God, perhaps the finest production of its author, and of the first rank in its class." These are the words of renowned hymn scholar John Julian about "Praise to the Lord, the Almighty." (*Dictionary of Hymnology* [1892; reprint, New York: Dover Publications, 1957], p. 683.)

The word *praise* begins each verse of the hymn. It occurs a total of six times; the word *adore*, twice. The hymn's one purpose is to praise the Lord for his many blessings, too numerous and too great to name or describe adequately. Anyone familiar with the psalms will recognize that the spirit and imagery of the psalms permeate this hymn text. Rather than choosing just one psalm to paraphrase, Joachim Neander gathered many figures of speech and phrases that recall the attitude of the Psalmist and give the same reverent, joyful feeling as do the psalms of praise.

Each verse emphasizes a different aspect of the Father's character and mercy. Verse one emphasizes that he is the "King of creation"; initially we must praise him for our surroundings and for our very being. In verse two, he is the watchful caretaker who strengthens and sustains his Saints. This verse draws upon Isaiah 40:31: "They that wait upon the Lord shall renew their strength; they shall mount up with wings as eagles; they shall run, and not be weary; and they shall walk, and not faint." Verse three honors the Lord as protector and defender, with echoes of Psalm 23. Verse four is a final summons to praise. First the worshiper asks, "Let all that is in me adore him!" Then the invitation extends to all of Abraham's seed to join with "all that hath breath" for one final note of united praise.

Neander's original German text began with the words "Lobe den Herren" ("Praise the Lord"); hence the name of the hymn tune.

Praise the Lord with Heart and Voice 73

Text and music: Tracy Y. Cannon (1879–1961; LDS)
Tune name: ROSE ANN

We have many reasons to praise our Heavenly Father. We can praise him for the plan of salvation; for the sacrifice of his Son, our Savior Jesus Christ; for the teachings of the restored gospel; for the day when the Messiah will return; for the promise of heavenly reward. This hymn of praise glorifies our Father for his role as Creator.

Tracy Y. Cannon, who wrote both words and music for "Praise the Lord with Heart and Voice," said that he was drawn specifically toward this focus: "The music of this hymn came to me before I wrote the words. I was therefore under the necessity of writing words that would fit the music. As I wrote the words, I had a strong desire to make the hymn a song of 'Praise to my Creator.' " (Quoted in Spencer J. Cornwall, *Stories of Our Mormon Hymns*, p. 165.)

The hymn begins with the injunction to "Praise the Lord with heart and voice"; voice alone is not enough. We praise him for "life and light," not only for the light of the sun, moon, and stars that were part of the Creation but also for the gospel light of "truth revealed in splendor bright."

Verse three opens with two strong and effective lines:

Father, God, eternal Friend,
Thou art Life; there is no end.

The Lord is the source of life's creation. He is also the force that sustains life through one generation after another on earth and in an eternal sphere after life on earth: literally, "there is no end." All his works owe their existence to him, and his presence is made known through each of them:

All creation ev'rywhere
Lives in thee, for thou art there.

The last line of the hymn tune is similar to the first line. Tracy Y. Cannon wrote a text that correlates with this musical pattern, with each last line a repetition of that verse's opening line.

The tune name, ROSE ANN, honors the daughter of Tracy Y. Cannon. This hymn was first published in *Hymns* (1948).

Praise Ye the Lord 74

Text: Isaac Watts (1674–1748)
Music: Evan Stephens (1854–1930; LDS)
Tune name: ALBION

One of the great themes of the scriptures is the happiness and security that come to those who declare their faith in the Lord, praising him and trusting his name. In this noble hymn text, dating from almost three centuries ago, praise is not a duty; it is "work so pleasant, so divine."

Isaac Watts's great contribution to English hymnody was his poetic adaptation of the scriptures, particularly the psalms. In the seven verses of "Praise Ye the Lord," first printed in 1719, he restated Psalm 146 as a hymn. While meeting the formal requirements of rhythm and meter, he departed as little as possible from the original psalm. Thus, when we sing this hymn, we are actually singing scripture. Psalm 146 extols the mercy and power of the Lord and stresses that he is an eternal presence. The psalm text is as follows:

"Praise ye the Lord. Praise the Lord, O my soul.

"While I live will I praise the Lord: I will sing praises unto my God while I have any being.

"Put not your trust in princes, nor in the son of man, in whom there is no help.

"His breath goeth forth, he returneth to his earth; in that very day his thoughts perish.

"Happy is he that hath the God of Jacob for his help, whose hope is in the Lord his God:

"Which made heaven, and earth, the sea, and all that therein is: which keepeth truth for ever:

"Which executeth judgment for the oppressed: which giveth food to the hungry. The Lord looseth the prisoners:

"The Lord openeth the eyes of the blind: the Lord raiseth them that are bowed down: the Lord loveth the righteous:

"The Lord preserveth the strangers; he relieveth the fatherless and widow: but the way of the wicked he turneth upside down.

"The Lord shall reign for ever, even thy God, O Zion, unto all generations. Praise ye the Lord."

Evan Stephens was sufficiently moved by this text to write a musical setting for it, first published in the 1889 *Latter-day Saints' Psalmody*. Though the setting previously appeared in the choir section, it was included as a congregational hymn in the 1985 hymnal and should present no great difficulties for most congregations.

In Hymns of Praise 75

Text: Ada Blenkhorn
Music: Alfred Beirly
Tune name: OUR KING

"All things denote there is a God," declared Alma to Korihor, the unbeliever; "yea, even the earth, and all things that are upon the face of it, yea, and its motion, yea, and also all the planets which move in their regular form do witness that there is a Supreme Creator." (Alma 30:44.) Such sentiments have moved many speakers and writers, including the author of this hymn.

Alma's words are "the argument from design," an attempt to prove the existence of God based on his many creations. How, he asked Korihor, can you see the planets, the earth, the natural beauty of the earth, and not believe in the Creator of these marvels?

Ada Blenkhorn's hymn is almost a roll call of natural wonders, from the greatest to the least—from the planets that trace their ordered paths in the heavens, to the sparrow and the "little flower that lasts an hour." We need to realize this vast spectrum of creation: the planets, earth, seas, and skies teach us of the Creator's power, and the flower and the sparrow teach us of his love and care. No creation is too unimportant for his attention.

Spencer Kinard stated: "Who can look upon a tulip in bloom, a budding cherry blossom, who can smell a fresh lilac tree or the air after a gentle rain and not ponder the power that can compose and orchestrate the beautiful rebirth of an entire landscape? All of God's creations bear witness of his existence—including the earth, moon, and stars." (*A Time for Reflection* [Salt Lake City: Deseret Book Co., 1986], p. 135.)

And modern-day revelation has told us: "The earth rolls upon her wings, and the sun giveth his light by day, and the moon giveth her light by night, and the stars also give their light, as they roll upon their wings in their glory, in the midst of the power of God."

". . . any man who hath seen any or the least of these hath seen God moving in his majesty and power." (D&C 88:45, 47.)

God of Our Fathers, We Come unto Thee 76

Text: Charles W. Penrose (1832–1925; LDS)
Music: Ebenezer Beesley (1840–1906; LDS)
Tune name: WOOBURN GREEN

"God of Our Fathers, We Come unto Thee" is a prayer that sends forth praise and thanks to our Father in Heaven while asking for him to continue the blessings he has poured out in the past. It is a hymn of partnership: we ask him fervently to stay by us, and we promise, just as fervently, not to stray from him.

By the time Charles W. Penrose wrote "God of Our Fathers, We Come unto Thee," the Utah Saints were beginning to feel a sense of contentment and permanence in their mountain home. To describe the new civilization they had established in the wilderness, the author chose such words as *peace, bounty,* and *light*. Already, as the first two lines of the hymn show, the restored gospel was the heritage of more than one generation.

The background of this hymn involves a little-known chapter in the history of Latter-day Saint Sunday School music. The *Deseret Sunday School Union Music Book* was not published until 1884, but starting in 1877 the Sunday School printed individual hymns in a format called "music cards." In his "Source Book for *Hymns* (1950)," Bruce David Maxwell noted that the purpose of these cards was "to lessen the dependence of the Sunday School on non-LDS hymn books and replace them with 'home' materials." (P. 20.) This hymn, titled "Never from Thee," was published as Card No. 5.

Many hymns of praise involve thoughts and ideas similar to those in "God of Our Fathers, We Come unto Thee," but this text achieves the difficult task of recasting those ideas with some especially memorable wording, supported by an interesting and singable tune. The emphasis on the words *never* and *ever* in the chorus underlines the hymn's dual message of commitment (we will *never* stray) and praise (we will *ever* pray).

Great Is the Lord 77

Text: Eliza R. Snow (1804–1887; LDS)
Music: Ebenezer Beesley (1840–1906; LDS)
Tune name: EBENEZER

Throughout the world, through many centuries, devoted men and women have praised the name of God. Is it right that any people should outdo the Latter-day Saints in their praise and worship? The message of "Great Is the Lord" is that the most pure and fervent praises of all should arise from the Saints who are blessed to "live in this momentous age / And share the light of heaven."

Many of our hymns mention the first two members of the Godhead, but references to the Holy Ghost occur less often. The second verse of this hymn is particularly interesting in its statement that "the Comforter is sent again" to encourage and sustain the Saints until the second coming of Jesus Christ. These words still live for us today more than a century and a half after they were written.

The four verses printed in our hymnal are verses one, five, six, and two of Eliza R. Snow's original eight verses that formed part of Emma Smith's 1835 hymnal. The four omitted verses—three, four, seven, and eight—show the strong sense of "gathering" that was part of the outlook of the early Saints, and also their joy in their mission as the Lord's chosen people:

We'll praise him for our happy lot,
On this much favored land;
Where truth, and righteousness are taught,
By his divine command.

We'll praise him for more glorious things,
Than language can express,
The "everlasting gospel" brings,
The humble souls to bless.

Praise him, the time, the chosen time,
To favor Zion's come:
And all the saints, from ev'ry clime,
Will soon be gather'd home.

The op'ning seals announce the day,
By prophets long declar'd;
When all, in one triumphant lay,
Will join to praise the Lord.

Ebenezer Beesley's hymn tune was first published with Eliza R. Snow's text in the 1887 *Improvement Association Song Book.*

God of Our Fathers, Whose Almighty Hand 78

Text: Daniel C. Roberts (1841–1907)
Music: George W. Warren (1828–1902)
Tune name: NATIONAL HYMN

"God of Our Fathers, Whose Almighty Hand" offers us a chance to express our patriotic feelings in the form of a hymn. In its stirring phrases we praise the majesty of God and ask him to continue to guide our nation and protect its destiny in the future. We place our faith in God rather than in military might alone.

Though the hymn is suitable for a national occasion in any free country, it has its origins in the American Centennial of 1876. The author,

Daniel C. Roberts, wrote the text for a patriotic celebration in the small village of Brandon, Vermont. It was sung to a familiar hymn tune, RUSSIAN HYMN. J. Spencer Cornwall said that "after the first singing of the hymn, Mr. Roberts wrote, 'My little hymn had a very flattering official recognition, but that which would gladden my heart most is popular recognition which it has not received.' Little did Mr. Roberts know what the destiny of the hymn would be a decade later."(*Stories of Our Mormon Hymns*, p. 63.)

In 1892 this hymn text was published in the Episcopal hymnal with the tune George W. Warren had written for it. That tune, NATIONAL HYMN, includes the trumpet fanfares that awaken feelings of patriotism and praise. The hymn's popularity grew following its performance in 1894 for a celebration of the adoption of the United States Constitution.

The hymn's fourth verse is not printed in our hymnal:

Refresh thy people on their toilsome way,
Lead us from night to never-ending day;
Fill all our lives with love and grace divine,
And glory, laud, and praise be ever thine.

With All the Power of Heart and Tongue 79

Text: Isaac Watts (1674–1748)
Music: Lowell M. Durham (b. 1917; LDS)
Tune name: PRAISE

When we praise the Lord with "all the power of heart," as well as with our tongues, the angels themselves approve our hymn and join their voices with ours. So states this fine, psalmlike hymn text. The first verse declares our intention of singing with all our hearts a prayer of praise, and verses two and three carry out that pledge.

This text is based on Psalm 138. Many of the psalm paraphrases of Isaac Watts follow their original much more closely than this one does; for example, compare "Praise Ye the Lord" (no. 74) with Psalm 146. "With All the Power of Heart and Tongue" conveys the spirit, rather than the verse-by-verse message, of Psalm 138.

Some of the wording of verse two may be difficult to understand. Its meaning is more or less as follows: "Thy truth, thy mercy, and the wonders of thy word show thy power and glory even more than do thy works and names [titles of honor]." Verse three paraphrases Psalm 138:7: "Though I walk in the midst of trouble, thou wilt revive me: thou shalt stretch forth thine hand against the wrath of mine enemies, and thy right hand shall save me."

In 1944, when Lowell Durham was a graduate student in composition at the University of Iowa, he received a letter from Tracy Y. Cannon of the Church Music Committee soliciting hymn tunes for the new hymnal. This text was among those suggested, and it attracted Lowell Durham immediately. The tune and its creation are a good example of the way in which subconscious influences hover over the task of musical composition. After he had written it, the composer realized that the opening bars somewhat resembled both a Bach chorale and the United States Navy Hymn! "Any implied 'borrowing' was coincidental," he stated.

Writing in 1987, Lowell Durham called "With All the Power of Heart and Tongue" "one of the unfamiliar hymns that the Saints avoid." Many Latter-day Saints, however, including the compiler of this book, admire this stately and appealing setting of a classic Christian hymn text. As the 1985 hymnal brings a new open-mindedness with regard to hymns that are presently unfamiliar, perhaps more worshipers will take the opportunity to learn this exciting hymn and adopt it as one of their favorites.

God of Our Fathers, Known of Old 80

Text: Rudyard Kipling (1865–1936)
Music: Leroy J. Robertson (1896–1971; LDS)
Tune name: ALICE

During the near-century that has passed since this poem was written, our world has known wars of immense magnitude, and war's threat shows no signs of diminishing. Today, more than ever, we need to pray for faith in the arm of God alone, "lest we forget."

Rudyard Kipling left this account of the writing of this hymn:

"That poem gave me more trouble than anything I ever wrote. I had promised the [London] *Times* a poem on the Jubilee [the celebration of Victoria's sixty years as queen], and when it became due I had written nothing that had satisfied me. The *Times* began to want that poem badly, and sent letter after letter asking for it. I made many more attempts, but no further progress. Finally the *Times* began sending telegrams. So I shut myself in a room with the determination to stay there until I had written a Jubilee poem. Sitting down with all my previous attempts before me, I searched through those dozens of sketches till at last I found just one line I liked. That was: 'Lest we forget.' Round these words 'The Recessional' was written." (Quoted in Charles S. Nutter and Wilber F. Tillett, *The Hymns and Hymn Writers of the Church* [New York: Methodist Book Concern, 1911], p. 268.)

"The Recessional," Kipling's title for this poem, refers to the hymn sung in the Anglican Church as choir and clergy withdraw following the service. *Recessional* also has a more general meaning of departure or a withdrawal: Kipling foresaw the end of the British Empire's worldwide dominance. This meaning is even more clear in the two additional verses not printed in our hymnal:

If, drunk with sight of power, we loose
Wild tongues that have not thee in awe,
Such boastings as the Gentiles use,
Or lesser breeds without the law—
Lord God of Hosts, be with us yet,
Lest we forget—lest we forget!

For heathen heart that puts her trust
In reeking tube and iron shard;
All valiant dust that builds on dust,
And guarding, calls not thee to guard,
For frantic boast and foolish word—
Thy mercy on thy people, Lord!

The 1950 hymnal offered a choice of two musical settings. Only the dignified hymn tune of Leroy Robertson has been retained in the 1985 hymnal. The tune name ALICE honors Alice A. Adams Robertson, the composer's mother. It was first published in *Hymns* (1948).

Press Forward, Saints 81

Text: Marvin K. Gardner (b. 1952; LDS)
Music: Vanja Y. Watkins (b. 1938; LDS)
Tune name: EDGECOMBE

Nephi's thrilling admonition and promise in 2 Nephi 31:20 should have a place in the heart of every Latter-day Saint. "Press Forward, Saints" is a paraphrase of this Book of Mormon scripture: "Wherefore, ye must press forward with a steadfastness in Christ, having a perfect brightness of hope, and a love of God and of all men. Wherefore, if ye shall press forward, feasting upon the word of Christ, and endure to the end, behold, thus saith the Father: Ye shall have eternal life."

This verse of scripture was one of Marvin K. Gardner's favorites from his seminary and mission days. Then in 1984, when he heard a stake conference speaker quote it, he saw that Nephi's words fell naturally into a hymn format: line one on faith, line two on hope, line three on charity—with the second verse focusing on feasting on the words of Christ, and the third verse on enduring to the end. "The words of the scripture kept going through my mind well into the night and during the following weeks," he said. "Because I wanted the hymn to focus continually on the Father and the Son, I placed the words *God* and *Christ* at consistent points in all three verses. The repeated alleluias allow us to respond to Nephi's words and to express gratitude for the Savior's atonement."

Vanja Watkins knew that other musical settings were being considered for this text for the 1985 hymnbook, so, she reported, "I was puzzled to hear a tune to these words insistently going through my mind one evening. I wasn't home, and it was several hours before I could put the tune down on paper. Then I awoke several times during the night thinking of it and mentally harmonizing it. In the morning I wrote the harmony I had heard and continued to work with it for several days. Then, since I knew of no reason to submit it, I put it away in a drawer without mentioning it to anyone."

Later, after the Hymnbook Committee decided to look for a new musical setting for the hymn text, Vanja Watkins submitted her manuscript and it was accepted. "I knew it was through the Lord's inspiration that I was given the music to accompany these choice words," she says.

The optimism and encouragement of this hymn text are complemented by the tune's brisk tempo and emphatic melody line. The opening musical phrases in lines one and three are almost like a fanfare. And the alleluias in line four have a bold, refreshing sound that leads to a joyful expression of praise to the Lord.

The tune name, EDGECOMBE, is the name of the street in Salt Lake City where Vanja Watkins and her family live.

For All the Saints 82

Text: William Walsham How (1823–1897); altered
Music: Ralph Vaughan Williams (1872–1958)
Tune name: SINE NOMINE

Each of us likes to believe we would be valiant even if we were the only soldier left to fight on the side of righteousness. But how it lifts our spirits and gives us courage to know that we are *not* alone. Armies of righteous followers of Christ are ready to fight beside us, and with the Lord as "our captain," we will win the war that began long before our time.

This majestic hymn, new to Latter-day Saint hymnody, is loved today among many Christian denominations. When we sing it as Latter-day Saints, the history of the Church gives the words a special significance. The word *Saints* in the first line was not intended, of course, to refer to members of The Church of Jesus Christ of Latter-day Saints but to righteous men and women throughout all history. The giving of thanks for those who have sacrificed for their beliefs has immediate meaning for members of our Church. Our emphasis on keeping records of Church and family, our study of Church history, our hymns and holidays in honor of our pioneer forebears, our determination that our children will share in the pride of our heritage – all these show the importance we place on remembering the courageous acts and unselfish sacrifice of those who have preceded us. The wish to be worthy of what they have left us, to be equal to them in bravery and devotion, is the theme of this hymn. The memory of their triumphs strengthens us today. When we think about them and feel a fellowship with them, our "hearts are brave again, and [our] arms are strong."

In the 1985 hymnal, verses two and three of this hymn are in reverse order from How's original text. The 1985 Hymnbook Committee felt that by reversing the order of these verses, the new verse three would be an even stronger statement of the testimonies of *both* former-day and latter-day Saints. Instead of referring only to the faith of earlier Saints – "Thou wast *their* rock, *their* fortress, and *their* might, . . . *their* Captain, . . . the one true light" – we also include our own shared witness of Christ: "Thou art *our* rock, *our* fortress, and *our* might, . . . *our* Captain, . . . *our* one true light." (Italics added.) This shared testimony of the Savior draws us even closer to those earlier faithful Saints.

When the great English composer Ralph Vaughan Williams was an editor of *The English Hymnal*, he wrote this new tune for the words of William Walsham How. He marked it as "Anonymous" because he was reluctant to let it be known that he had included his own composition. Later it was established that he was the tune's composer. Since it originally appeared without the composer's name, the tune is known as SINE NOMINE, Latin for "without a name."

Note that verses one, two, and five are for unison singing, while verses three and four may include harmony. Organist and music director must be well rehearsed; otherwise the congregation may have difficulty understanding that they are not to enter until the second beat of each verse. The moving bass line played by the organ in verses one, two, and five evokes the steady forward movement of a determined army.

Guide Us, O Thou Great Jehovah 83

Text: William Williams (1717–1791);
verse one translated by Peter Williams (1722–1796)
Music: John Hughes (1873–1932)
Tune name: CWM RHONDDA

Like the children of Israel in the wilderness, we look to the Lord for guidance to our own "promised land." That guidance is always present for those who are worthy: "He took not away the pillar of the cloud by day, nor the pillar of fire by night, from before the people." (Exodus 13:22.)

Because he traveled almost one hundred thousand miles as a preacher in Wales, William Williams knew what it was to wander in hardship and to look forward to the "welcome day" when the journey would be over. One writer, Albert Edward Bailey, said: "It was a hard life that he entered. He was always in the open, soaked with rain, chilled by snow, bronzed by wind and sun, attacked by mobs. . . . Once . . . a crowd of ruffians carrying guns and cudgels fell upon him and beat him within an inch of his life." (*The Gospel in Hymns* [New York: Charles Scribner's Sons, 1950], p. 108.)

This popular hymn has been a part of Latter-day Saint hymnody since Emma Smith first chose it for her 1835 hymnal. Like all Williams's eight hundred or so hymns, it was originally written in Welsh. In 1771, verse one was translated into English by Peter Williams. William Williams himself wrote the English versions of verses two and three.

The 1950 hymnal included two musical settings for this hymn. The alternate tune, from the sentimental ballad "In the Gloaming" by Annie Fortescue Harrison, was omitted from the 1985 hymnal. Though some Church members may wish it had been retained, the vigor of Williams's text is far more suited to the melody by John Hughes. Its tune name, CWM RHONDDA, is pronounced approximately *koom RAWN tha*, with the meaning in Welsh of "valley" (CWM) and "river" (RHONDDA). It arises from the fact that the first formal performance of the hymn was at a Baptist hymn festival in Capel Rhondda, Wales.

J. Spencer Cornwall recorded the legend that Hughes wrote the tune on a piece of tarpaulin with chalk. At lunchtime, at the mine where he was working at the time, he called some of his fellow laborers together, and they sang the song for the first time. (See *Stories of Our Mormon Hymns*, p. 65.)

Faith of Our Fathers 84

Text: Frederick W. Faber (1814–1863)
Music: Henri F. Hemy (1818–1888) and James G. Walton (1821–1905)
Tune name: ST. CATHERINE

Because our Church has survived dramatic periods of persecution, the sentiments of this hymn should ring as true with Latter-day Saints as they do with any other Christians. The heritage of Latter-day Saint history belongs to every Church member, whether or not the Church is literally the faith of his fathers.

"Faith of Our Fathers" is a remarkable example of how a hymn written with a somewhat narrow purpose in mind can transcend the intentions of its author and attain universality. Frederick W. Faber was originally a clergyman of the Church of England, but he wrote this hymn after converting to Roman Catholicism. Thus, when he wrote about the "faith of our fathers," he meant the Roman Catholic Church. Frederick Faber's hope was that England might be restored to the Catholicism that had once been her religion. Two lines of the original four-verse hymn refer specifically to this goal: "Faith of our fathers! Mary's prayers / Shall win our country back to thee."

But today virtually all Protestant hymnals include this hymn—omitting the lines that are quoted above, of course—and it is a beautiful addition to the 1985 Latter-day Saint hymnal, ideally suited to our pride in our heritage and our missionary zeal. The sacrifices of faithful people in the past should inspire our determination today to "win all nations" to our faith, spreading the gospel through "kindly words and virtuous life."

The tune name, ST. CATHERINE, refers to the text originally sung to this melody. It began, "Sweet St. Catherine, maid most pure, / Teach us to meditate and pray."

The tune was first printed in 1864. Ten years later, when James Walton included it in a hymn collection he was editing, he added the last eight measures.

How Firm a Foundation 85

Text: Attributed to Robert Keen (ca. 1787)
Music: Attributed to J. Ellis (ca. 1889)
Tune name: FIDELITY

This hymn "becomes, indeed, a rod and a staff, to hold one in God's 'sovereign, eternal, unchangeable love,' " said George D. Pyper. " 'How Firm a Foundation' should be memorized by every Latter-day Saint." (*Stories of Latter-day Saint Hymns*, p. 31.)

This favorite hymn has been part of many Christian hymnals since its first publication in 1787 and part of Latter-day Saint hymn tradition since Emma Smith's first hymnal in 1835. Its vigor and conviction are irresistible. In the words of this hymn we express our absolute faith in the saving and protecting power of our Savior.

The author is not known for certain, though Robert Keen seems the most likely candidate. The first printing, in 1787, identified the author only as "K________," and three men whose last names begin with "K" have been suggested as author: Kirkham, Keith, and Keen.

Emma Smith's hymnal placed quotation marks around all verses except the first two. A careful look at the words of the hymn will show why this punctuation was logical: the hymn writer, in an unusual decision, wrote the last five verses as if they were spoken by Jesus himself to his faithful followers. The writer did not intend any presumption, because he was not really writing words in the Savior's behalf. The purpose of these verses is to convey in the boldest and most direct way how thorough, how all-encompassing, and how specific we know his promises to be. These verses are really just a poetic summary of the reassurances we find throughout scripture. The 1985 hymnal preserves all seven verses.

This hymn plays a role in a well-known story from Mormon history. In the dark days of 1838 in Missouri, a small group of persecuted Saints had gathered at Haun's Mill. The state militia attacked the defenseless group and killed seventeen Saints, including the husband and ten-year-old son of Amanda Smith. Another son, Alma, had been seriously wounded. Amanda Smith gathered with other bereaved women and children at the home of one of the Saints. "In our utter desolation," she wrote later, "what could we women do but pray?"

One day they received a message from the militia: the sound of their praying was hateful, and they would have to cease praying or be killed. They dared not pray aloud, but Amanda Smith stole out into a cornfield. "I prayed aloud and most fervently," she said.

"When I emerged from the corn a voice spoke to me. It was a voice as plain as I ever heard one. It was no silent, strong impression of the spirit, but a *voice*, repeating a verse of the Saints' hymn:

The soul that on Jesus hath leaned for repose,
I will not, I cannot, desert to his foes;
That soul, though all hell should endeavor to shake,
I'll never, no never, no never forsake!

"From that moment I had no more fear. I felt that nothing could hurt me." The attackers later shared some food with the Saints, and Amanda Smith remarked: "The Lord had kept his word. The soul who on Jesus had leaned for succor had not been forsaken even in this terrible hour of massacre." (Edward W. Tullidge, *The Women of Mormondom* [New York: Tullidge and Crandall, 1877], pp. 129–32.)

The last line of verse one was changed because of awkwardness: the words "you who unto Jesus" were changed to "who unto the Savior."

We would give a great deal to know the composer of the fine hymn tune that accompanies these words in our Latter-day Saint hymnal. Under the tune name MY JESUS, I LOVE THEE, it appears in the Salvation Army hymnal and is attributed to "J. Ellis." The tune's use among Latter-day Saints appears to date back to the early years of the Church; however, in the *Tune Book for the Primary Association* (1880), Eliza R. Snow used another tune often paired with these words, the melody known familiarly as "O Come, All Ye Faithful."

How Great Thou Art 86

Text: Stuart K. Hine (b. 1899)
Music: Swedish melody; arranged by Stuart K. Hine
Tune name: O STORE GUD

The Father speaks to us through his creations—this is the message that opens "How Great Thou Art." But even more than through his handiwork, the Father's goodness is shown through the sacrifice of his Son, our Savior, and through his desire to bless and reward those who are faithful. This hymn follows the thoughts of a devoted Christian as he meditates along these lines.

"How Great Thou Art" was popularized by the Billy Graham evangelism team in their tours of Britain and North America in the 1950s. By 1974 it had become, according to a poll among readers of the *Christian Herald* magazine, the most popular hymn in America.

Its history goes back a surprising number of years. In 1886, a Swedish minister, Reverend Carl Boberg, wrote a text beginning "O Mighty God" (in Swedish, "O Store Gud"—thus the hymn tune name). In 1907 the text was translated into German, and in 1912, a Russian clergyman, I. S. Prokhanov, made a Russian translation of this German version. In 1925 a clergyman in Chicago translated the Swedish text into English for the first time, but his translation, beginning "O Mighty God, when I behold the wonder," did not achieve wide popularity.

In 1923, the Reverend and Mrs. Stuart K. Hine, English missionaries, were preaching in Russia when they first heard this hymn. So impressed were they that it remained in their memories. They decided to write an English version, based partly on the Russian words they had heard and partly on the breathtaking scenery they had witnessed in their travels.

Thus were the first three verses born. The fourth verse was not written until after World War II. Reverend Hine stated that part of the inspiration for verse four was the question constantly on the lips of the eastern European refugees who had streamed into Britain: "When can we go home?" The joy of our heavenly home is at the center of this verse.

"How Great Thou Art" is new to the 1985 hymnbook. President Ezra Taft Benson often requested this hymn in meetings over which he presided.

God Is Love 87; 313

Text: Thomas R. Taylor (1807–1835); altered
Music: Thomas C. Griggs (1845–1903; LDS)
Tune name: TESTIMONY

Through the sights and sounds of nature, through the joy of everyday events and relationships, our Father communicates his boundless love to us at each moment. A hymn that reminds us of this often overlooked truth serves a beautiful and significant purpose.

This hymn's message is that the earth and its beauties and joys are a constant reminder of the goodness and love of the Creator. Elder Bruce R. McConkie emphasized that this thought is more than just a sentimental pleasantry:

"An all-wise Creator has structured all the creations of his hands in such a way, not only to call attention to himself as the Maker, Preserver, and Upholder of all things, but to bear record of the nature and kind of Being he is. . . . The voice of his creations declares his divinity. . . . If men fail to live that law which enables them to see the divine face and converse with their Creator in plain words, at least they are obligated to hear the voice of Nature, which is also the voice of God." (*The Promised Messiah* [Salt Lake City, Utah: Deseret Book Co., 1978], pp. 374–75.)

Because this hymn text appeared in 1832 in *The Evening and Morning Star*, of which William W. Phelps was the editor, it was for many decades misattributed to him. He may have been responsible for some of the slight changes in the words of Thomas R. Taylor, but in any case, the first two verses remain much as in the original. Verse three was altered more extensively from its original version:

All the hopes and fears that start
From the fountain of the heart;
All the quiet bliss that lies
In our human sympathies;
These are voices from above
Sweetly whispering, "God is love."

The tune TESTIMONY was first printed with Taylor's words in the 1883 *Collection of Hymns and Anthems Set to Music by Home Composers*.

The 1985 hymnbook restored the original title to this hymn. Perhaps the title "God Is Love"—which gives more of an indication of the subject than did the first line, "Earth, with her ten thousand flowers"—will encourage more frequent use of this fine hymn in years to come.

Great God, Attend While Zion Sings 88

Text: Isaac Watts (1674–1748)
Music: Joseph J. Daynes (1851–1920; LDS)
Tune name: KIMBALL

Worldly possessions and pleasures claim our attention daily. Their attraction is strong, and it is often easier to center our efforts on them than on righteous goals. This fine hymn text compares the glory of this world with the glory of God and reaffirms in the strongest terms our commitment to "our God, our King, whose sovereign sway / The glorious hosts of heaven obey."

Once again Isaac Watts has given us a poetic restatement of a psalm text, in this case, Psalm 84:9–12:

"Behold, O God our shield, and look upon the face of thine anointed.

"For a day in thy courts is better than a thousand. I had rather be a doorkeeper in the house of my God, than to dwell in the tents of wickedness.

"For the Lord God is a sun and shield: the Lord will give grace and glory: no good thing will he withhold from them that walk uprightly.

"O Lord of hosts, blessed is the man that trusteth in thee."

This hymn text was first printed in 1719. Nearly three centuries have passed since Isaac Watts wrote the text; three millennia, since the Psalmist wrote the words that inspired the hymn. Yet the lessons of the hymn have lost none of their relevance. The "tents of ease [and] thrones of power" are always with us, always beckoning with their superficial reward. But the rewards that God will bestow are far greater: "Blest is the man that trusts in thee!"

Of the musical setting by Joseph J. Daynes, J. Spencer Cornwall stated, "The main charm of the music of this choir hymn is in its unorthodox hymn form – a sustained melody in the soprano part with a chordal chant accompaniment in the alto, tenor, and bass parts." (*Stories of Our Mormon Hymns*, p. 253.) Though it is not the easiest of hymns, this hymn is intended in the 1985 hymnal for congregational use, and the "chordal chant accompaniment" has been simplified.

The Lord Is My Light 89

Text: James Nicholson (1828–1876)
Music: John R. Sweney (1837–1899)
Tune name: WANAMAKER

Taking its opening line from Psalm 27:1 – "The Lord is my light and my salvation; whom shall I fear?" – this energetic song communicates joy and reassurance. As we walk by faith, we depend on a divine, never-failing light to banish shadows and illuminate our path.

In our mortal lives, our sight is imperfect, as Paul phrased it in his letter to the Corinthians: "For now we see through a glass, darkly." (1 Corinthians 13:12.) Our understanding is limited, and we are at the mercy of influences that we perceive only vaguely and of events that lie in wait to surprise us.

We need something stronger than our mortal vision. The answer is that our Savior's vision is perfect: "There is in his sight no darkness at all." We can see him and come to know him, not through our human senses, but through "faith, stronger than sight," that "looks up through the skies."

As is the case with a number of the hymns in our hymnal, the value of "The Lord Is My Light" depends more on the significance of its message and the popularity it has attained among Latter-day Saints than on its musical worth. J. Spencer Cornwall commented in *Stories of Our Mormon Hymns*: "The third and sixth measures of the chorus of 'The Lord Is My Light' hint of coloratura style. Song styles which are foreign to the traditional hymn pattern are sometimes found in many of the hymns of lesser musical worthiness." (P. 115.)

This hymn was published in a book of evangelical gospel songs in 1885, and by 1892 it had found its way into a Latter-day Saint Sunday School song collection. In the 1985 hymnal, only Nicholson's four original verses and the chorus were retained; four additional verses added by compilers (but seldom sung) were deleted.

John Wanamaker, who is honored in the tune name, was Sunday School superintendent of Bethany Presbyterian Church in Philadelphia, Pennsylvania, where for many years John R. Sweney was in charge of music.

From All That Dwell below the Skies 90

Text: Isaac Watts (1674–1748)
Music: John Hatton (d. 1793)
Tune name: DUKE STREET

Gathering together for Sabbath worship brings us many blessings. One of the most important of these blessings is that as a community—as a group of his committed sons and daughters—we can sing our collective praises to the Lord. This majestic hymn perfectly reflects a spirit of joyful, reverent psalmlike praise.

One of Isaac Watts's outstanding contributions to Christian hymnody was *Psalms of David*, published in 1719. In this volume he included a version of each psalm adapted to the rhymed, metrical form of a traditional hymn text. Churchgoers of the time were accustomed to singing psalms as part of their services, but Isaac Watts provided a different emphasis for his psalm hymns. In accordance with his belief that followers of Jesus Christ should be able to sing about their Savior, he added a Christian flavor to many of the Old Testament psalms.

As an example of this practice, note the word *Redeemer* in verse one of "From All That Dwell below the Skies." Psalm 117, the basis of the verse, does not mention this word, but its addition gives the hymn greater meaning for Christians.

Verses one and four of this hymn are a wonderful instance of Isaac Watts's skill in the rewriting of psalm texts. Together these two verses are a restatement of an entire psalm, the brief Psalm 117:

"O praise the Lord, all ye nations: praise him, all ye people.

"For his merciful kindness is great toward us: and the truth of the Lord endureth for ever. Praise ye the Lord."

What about verses two and three? Though they are almost always included when this hymn is printed, they are in fact not by Isaac Watts. The author is unknown. But the writer showed considerable skill in matching the style and spirit of Isaac Watts's two original verses.

Little is known about composer John Hatton except his address—Duke Street, in the township of Windle, Lancaster, England—the source of the tune name.

Father, Thy Children to Thee Now Raise 91

Text and music: Evan Stephens (1854–1930; LDS)
Tune name: NINES

Some of our favorite Latter-day Saint hymns are those in which we exhort one another to good works. In others, we pray for the Lord's guidance or honor the deeds of the early Saints. But surely we would be remiss if we neglected to sing hymns that were simply an outpouring of joyful, heartfelt praise for our blessings. Such a hymn is "Father, Thy Children to Thee Now Raise."

This hymn shows many of the characteristics of the hymns of Evan Stephens. Its energetic mood is carried along by dotted rhythms and a text that expresses gratitude and faithfulness in every line. Its focus is on youth. Although as a lifelong bachelor he had no children of his own, Evan Stephens loved young people, and he loved to write hymns that would reflect the commitment of young Latter-day Saints and give a voice to their faith and enthusiasm.

Because the 1985 hymnal was to be used by English-speaking Latter-day Saints in many parts of the world, the Hymnbook Committee felt it preferable to avoid, whenever possible, references within the hymn texts that were too narrow in terms of geography or nationalistic sentiment. For this reason, the original second verse of "Father, Thy Children to Thee Now Raise" was not included. It could be restored for a particular occasion if a music director deemed it appropriate. The verse is as follows:

Thankful to thee that a pilgrim band
Brought us to dwell in this favored land,
Led o'er the deserts and plains by thee,
Here to a land of true liberty;
Thankful to thee for the mountains high,
The fresh'ning breeze and the clear, blue sky;
And for the fields covered o'er with corn,
Which now our loved mountain vales adorn.

The tune name, NINES, refers to the unusual meter of this hymn. It has eight lines of nine syllables each and is the only 9999D hymn (four lines of nine syllables, doubled) in our hymnbook. The hymn was first published in 1884 in the *Deseret Sunday School Union Music Book.*

For the Beauty of the Earth 92

Text: Folliott S. Pierpoint (1835–1917)
Music: Conrad Kocher (1786–1872)
Tune name: DIX

A hymn serves a valuable purpose if it can recall to our minds the importance of being attuned to the simple beauties of nature, family, and friendship. Such is the message of this hymn. It gives us a wonderful opportunity to refresh our appreciation for these day-to-day blessings and to offer thanks to the Lord at the conclusion of each verse.

The hymn names many sources of joy: the natural beauties of earth, including trees, flowers, hills, and vales; the wonders of the skies, including sun, moon, and stars; family members and friends; and "gentle thoughts."

One hymn scholar believed the scriptural inspiration for the hymn was James 1:17: "Every good gift and every perfect gift is from above." Another writer, Armin Hauessler, provided this account: "Folliott Sanford Pierpoint wrote this one day in late spring near his native city of Bath, England, when violets and primroses were in full bloom and all the earth seemed to rejoice. He climbed up a hill and sat down to rest and meditate. The panorama before him inspired him to write these beautiful lines." (*The Story of Our Hymns* [St. Louis, Mo.: Eden Publishing House, 1952],

p. 66.) The original hymn text includes additional stanzas giving thanks for the blessing of church and for God himself.

Although new to the 1985 hymnal, "For the Beauty of the Earth" appeared in previous Church music compilations, including the Primary songbooks *Sing With Me* (p. B-38) and *The Children Sing* (p. 25). Because of the directness of its message and the simple appeal of its melody, this hymn is popular with children as well as adults. The brief, uncomplicated references to the things we hold most dear evoke memories and emotions in almost everyone who sings it. We welcome the chance to pause for a moment and offer praise for blessings we so often just accept as our due.

The tune name, DIX, honors William C. Dix, who wrote the first English hymn text with which this tune was paired. Dix's text, a Christmas hymn widely used in Protestant hymnals, begins "As with gladness men of old / Did the guiding star behold." The refrain of Kocher's tune originally included two additional measures. William H. Monk, composer of "Abide with Me!" (no. 166), was the editor who created the shorter version used today.

Prayer of Thanksgiving 93

Text and music: Anonymous, from the Netherlands (early 17th century)
Tune name: KREMSER

When people who have endured long adversity offer thanks to the Lord, it is a two-fold thanks. First, they are grateful because the Lord has given them the strength to survive their trials; in the words of this hymn, "Thou, Lord, wast on our side." And second, they know that the most faithful are often "chosen . . . in the furnace of affliction." (Isaiah 48:10.)

In America, "Prayer of Thanksgiving" (often known by its first line, "We gather together to ask the Lord's blessing") is a traditional Thanksgiving hymn. Its strong statement of the sustaining power of faith in adversity makes it an appropriate hymn to mark the celebration of the Pilgrim harvest, and it was written only a few years after the Pilgrims held their historic feast. But neither the words nor the tune has any direct historical connection with these events in the New World. It is later tradition that has linked them.

Even though the historical circumstances that gave rise to the hymn are not the ones that immediately come to mind, they represent a dramatic chapter in the history of a people devoted to their faith. In 1625, approximately the year this hymn was written, the Netherlands had not yet thrown off the yoke of Spain. Hostilities had ceased, but it would be another two decades before the Protestant Netherlands regained their religious and political independence. The "wicked oppressing" had brought much suffering during the prolonged and bitter wars, but the faithful Protestants knew in their hearts, "from the beginning," that they would triumph.

Theodore Baker (1851–1934), an Englishman, gave the anonymous Dutch text its familiar English translation in 1894. The tune, apparently a Dutch folk melody, takes its name from a Viennese choirmaster named Edward Kremser, who published the melody in a collection of Dutch folk songs that he had arranged for male chorus.

Although "Prayer of Thanksgiving" previously appeared in Latter-day Saint publications, it is new to our hymnal.

Come, Ye Thankful People 94

Text: Henry Alford (1810–1871)
Music: George J. Elvey (1816–1893)
Tune name: ST. GEORGE'S WINDSOR

"Live in thanksgiving daily," exhorted the prophet Amulek. (Alma 34:38.) Especially during the Thanksgiving holiday season, the time when this hymn is usually sung, we should reflect even more thoughtfully and joyfully upon our blessings. This hymn gives us an opportunity to recognize and praise the generous goodness of our Heavenly Father.

Like "Prayer of Thanksgiving" (no. 93), this hymn, which Americans so automatically link with the Pilgrims and their first Thanksgiving feast, actually has no historical connection with these events. The author and composer both lived in England during the nineteenth century.

The hymn's original title was "After the Harvest." The first verse is a straightforward statement of rejoicing in a bounteous harvest. Because the grain has been safely gathered and stored "ere the winter storms begin," the "thankful people" know they are secure from want for another year, and a pause for praise, gratitude, and song is in order.

The thanks for the harvest leads naturally to the second verse's reference to the parable of the wheat and tares. Some of the words are based closely on the words of Jesus, as given in Mark: "For the earth bringeth forth fruit of herself; first the blade, then the ear, after that the full corn in the ear." (Mark 4:28.) The wholesome, desirable wheat grows side by side with the noxious and intrusive tares, as Matthew mentions in his account of this parable. (See Matthew 13:24–30.) Only at harvest time will the wheat finally be separated out and the tares burned.

The original four-stanza hymn concluded with these words, which complete and emphasize the thought that the righteous followers are the Lord's final harvest:

Then, thou Church triumphant come
Raise the song of harvest Home;
All are safely gathered in,
Free from sorrow, free from sin,
There for ever purified,
In God's garner to abide:
Come, ten thousand angels, come.
Raise the song of harvest-home.

(Quoted in Marilyn Kay Stulken, *Hymnal Companion to the Lutheran Book of Worship* [Philadelphia: Fortress Press, 1981], p. 444.)

The tune, ST. GEORGE'S WINDSOR, is named for the church where the composer, George J. Elvey, was organist for forty-seven years.

Now Thank We All Our God 95

Text: Martin Rinkhart (1586–1649);
translated by Catherine Winkworth (1829–1878)
Music: Johann Crüger (1598–1662)
Tune name: NUN DANKET

For more than four hundred years, Christians have turned to this stately and moving hymn to express their gratitude for the blessings and protection of their Father in Heaven. After the thanks of the first verse, the second asks for his continued presence and guidance.

This hymn text, dating from 1636, is based on some verses from the Apocrypha. Elder Bruce R. McConkie explained the Apocrypha in these words: "Scholars and Biblical students have grouped certain apparently scriptural Old Testament writings, which they deem to be of doubtful authenticity or of a spurious nature, under the title of the *Apocrypha*. . . . It is clear that the books of the Apocrypha were inspired writings in the first instance, but that subsequent interpolations and changes had perverted and twisted their original contexts so as to leave them with doubtful value." (*Mormon Doctrine*, 2d ed. [Salt Lake City, Utah: Bookcraft, 1966], pp. 41–42.) Section 91 of the Doctrine and Covenants explains further the status of the Apocrypha in the Latter-day Saint view.

Here are the apocryphal verses pertinent to this hymn:

"Now therefore bless ye the God of all, which only doeth wondrous things every where, which exalteth our days from the womb, and dealeth with us according to his mercy.

"He grants us joyfulness of heart, and that peace may be in our days in Israel for ever:

"That he would confirm his mercy with us, and deliver us at his time!" (Ecclesiasticus 50:22–24.)

The hymn was originally written as a grace to be said before meals—a time when our thoughts should turn to our blessings. In view of the events of Martin Rinkhart's life, these words represent a triumph of faith over unimaginable pestilence and suffering. (See Biographies.) Catherine Winkworth (1829–1878) was the translator of all but the last two lines of verse two.

This fine tune, first printed in 1647, has been incorporated by Johann Sebastian Bach and other composers into their works. The tune name comes from the first line of the original German text: "Nun danket alle Gott." The hymn is used in many countries to mark important national occasions and celebrations. It was sung, for example, in honor of Queen Victoria's Diamond Jubilee.

Dearest Children, God Is Near You 96

Text: Charles L. Walker (1832–1904; LDS)
Music: John Menzies Macfarlane (1833–1892; LDS)
Tune name: SINCLAIR

This hymn directed at children has a message for all who seek to do right: blessings, happiness, and the instructive companionship of the Holy Ghost come through doing what is right. The final words of verse two could be a motto for all, young and old alike: "Cherish virtue! God will bless the pure in heart."

The theme of this hymn text is accountability. Our actions have consequences, and children must begin to accept this truth from their earliest days. "Dearest Children, God Is Near You" presents this teaching in terms that children can understand. The "recording angel" concept on which verse two is based is an idea that can help them to understand their personal responsibility for their words and actions. This hymn reassures them (and us) that God is near them and desires to bless them. But it also cautions them that he can pour out the full measure of his blessings only if they are obedient and faithful.

The book *Yours Sincerely, John M. Macfarlane,* a volume printed privately by the descendants of the composer of this hymn tune, provides this information: "The story goes that a bored Charles L. Walker amused himself during a very long Sacrament Meeting by writing some lines which began, 'Dearest children, God is near you.' Shortly afterward the poem came to the attention of John M. Macfarlane, who set it to music. It was used locally in the Sunday Schools. This song appeared initially in the *Juvenile Instructor* on August 15, 1877. . . . In 1894, it was included in the

Deseret Sunday School Song Book, but under [the] title, 'God Will Bless the Pure in Heart.' . . . Soon after this, the song gained a permanent place in the L. D. S. Hymnal."

The tune name, SINCLAIR, honors John Macfarlane's mother, Annabella Sinclair Macfarlane.

Lead, Kindly Light 97

Text: John Henry Newman (1801–1890)
Music: John B. Dykes (1823–1876)
Tune name: LUX BENIGNA

The genius of one of the great English men of letters turned a moment of homesickness into a prayerful hymn of religious insight. In these moving words, beloved among Christians everywhere, we confess our weaknesses with humility and regret as we turn to the light of heavenly guidance.

In 1833, John Henry Newman had been traveling in Europe for his health. But he became ill in Sicily because of heat and poor living conditions. He recorded, "I sat sometimes by the bedside crying bitterly, and all I could say was that I was sure God had some work for me to do in England." (John Henry Cardinal Newman, *Apologia Pro Vita Sua* [New York: W. W. Norton and Co., 1968], p. 40.) He decided to sail for England, thinking that his chances of recovery would be better at home. But as he embarked on the first leg of his voyage, from Palermo to Marseilles, the breezes dropped, the fog closed in, and the ship was becalmed for a week. He was homesick and seasick, frustrated at the delay. And to make matters worse, he was seized by an attack of malaria.

These were the events that brought forth "Lead, Kindly Light." During this miserable week, his longing for England became associated in his mind with longing for heavenly light and comfort. In the past, pride and self-regard had destroyed his simple faith in divine guidance, but his hopes now rested in the Light, his secure protection until "the night is gone." (See Robert Guy McCutchan, *Our Hymnody: A Manual of the Methodist Hymnal* [New York: Abingdon Press, 1937], p. 495.)

In contrast to the solitary circumstances under which the text was written, John B. Dykes stated that the tune came into his head one day in August 1865 as he was walking in the Strand, one of London's busiest thoroughfares. He wrote the tune specifically for Newman's words: the tune name, LUX BENIGNA, is Latin for "kindly light."

The text originally appeared under the titles "The Pillar of the Cloud" and "Light in Darkness," but now it is almost always referred to by its first line. Latter-day Saints should not be too quick to equate the "angel faces" of verse three with loved ones at the time of a heavenly reunion. Cardinal Newman more likely was referring to the joys and hopes that are with us in times of faith.

I Need Thee Every Hour 98; 334

Text: Annie S. Hawkes (1835–1918)
Music: Robert Lowry (1826–1899)
Tune name: NEED

Though not of Latter-day Saint origin, this hymn strikes a meaningful chord among Latter-day Saints in its humble pleading for the constant presence of the Savior. In this hymn we petition him repeatedly to be with us, not just in our church meetings, not just in times of trial, not just on special spiritual occasions, but *every* hour.

Author Annie S. Hawkes was a member of the Park Avenue Baptist Church in Plainfield, New Jersey, where Robert Lowry was her pastor. She was a prolific writer, and he set many of her texts to music.

Both author and composer commented on the creative process behind the hymn. Annie S. Hawkes wrote: "I remember well the morning . . . when in the midst of the daily cares of my home . . . I was so filled with the sense of the nearness of the Master that, wondering how one could live without Him either in joy or pain, these words 'I need Thee every hour' were ushered into my mind. . . . It was wafted out to the world on the wings of love and joy, rather than under the stress of great personal sorrow. . . . It was not until long years after, when the shadow [of a great loss] fell over my way . . . that I understood something of the comforting in the words I had been permitted to write." Robert Lowry commented: "I have no method [of writing songs]. Sometimes the music comes and the words follow. . . . I watch my moods, and when anything strikes me, whether words or music, no matter where I am, at home, or on the street, I jot it down. . . . My brain is a sort of spinning-machine, I think, for there is music running through it all the time. I do not pick out my music on the keys of an instrument. The tunes of nearly all the hymns I have written have been completed on paper before I tried them on the organ." (Quoted in Phil Kerr, *Music in Evangelism* [Glendale, Calif.: Gospel Music Publishers, 1939], pp. 145, 223–24.)

The word *afford* in verse one may be confusing to some. It carries here the specialized meaning of "provide" or "make available."

Robert Lowry was coauthor of the text; he not only provided the music for the words of Annie S. Hawkes but also wrote the words of the refrain (last two lines of the hymn). The hymn was first published in 1873 in a collection he edited.

Nearer, Dear Savior, to Thee 99

Text: Joseph L. Townsend (1849–1942; LDS)
Music: William Clayson (1840–1887; LDS)
Tune name: LINDSAY

Joseph L. Townsend, the author of "Nearer, Dear Savior, to Thee," called this hymn his "heart song." (Quoted in J. Spencer Cornwall, *Stories of Our Mormon Hymns*, p. 74.) That is exactly what it is—the plea of a heart yearning to become more holy, more spiritual, and more refined by earthly experiences.

The central word of the text is *nearer*. As we sing this hymn, we express our prayerful desire to be nearer to Jesus Christ in two senses of the word. First, we wish to be nearer in terms of becoming perfected, more like him, closer to him in our thoughts, actions, and spiritual development. Second, especially in verse four, the word *nearer* takes on the sense of becoming *literally* closer to the Savior—actually being in his presence, sharing exaltation in his kingdom among his celestial associates.

The word *nearer* is repeated no fewer than twenty-one times in the four verses. But the repetition itself is significant. As we draw nearer to our Savior, is that process not a gradual one? If we sing this hymn with sincerity, each repetition should *bring* us nearer.

The text of this hymn emphasizes that the responsibility for this process is ours. In fact, a look at the third line of each verse will yield quite a list of the qualities of someone who is striving to become Christlike. That person is trustful, confiding, hopeful, humble, earnest, prayerful, loving, and obedient.

Elder Mark Lindsay baptized this hymn's composer, William Clayson, in England. The tune name, LINDSAY, honors that missionary. The hymn was first published in the *Juvenile Instructor* in 1882.

Nearer, My God, to Thee 100

Text: Sarah F. Adams (1805–1848)
Music: Lowell Mason (1792–1872)
Tune name: BETHANY

More than one-third of the words of this hymn consist of a repeated phrase of longing, stated in the title: "Nearer, my God, to thee." It is an emotional outpouring of a desire to be more closely united with the Father and his angelic hosts in both life and death.

It is not possible to understand this hymn fully without recalling the story of Jacob's dream-vision, as related in Genesis 28:10–22. Jacob, on a journey, falls asleep on a pillow of stones after sunset and dreams of a great ladder stretching to heaven, with angels ascending and descending. At the top of the ladder is the Lord God, who promises blessings to Jacob and his family and assures him, "I will not leave thee." (V. 15.) The astounded Jacob wakes the next morning and makes an altar from the stones he had used as a pillow, and he calls the place "Beth-el," meaning "God's house." He vows, "Then shall the Lord be my God." (V. 21.)

The imagery that relates specifically to this Old Testament passage begins in verse two: "Though like the wanderer, The sun gone down, / Darkness be over me, My rest a stone," compares our need and our longing to that of Jacob as he slept on his journey. The "steps" and "angels" of verse three parallel the ladder and heavenly visitors in Jacob's dream. The promise in verse four, "Bethel I'll raise," is that we will consecrate our lives—even our griefs—to the Lord, just as Jacob took the hard stones that had been his pillow and built an altar upon which to pour out an offering of oil to the Lord.

The hymn text dates from 1841, the hymn tune from 1859, and they were first printed together in 1869. Lowell Mason, who chose biblical names almost at random for his tunes, gave the name BETHANY to several of them. Jesus spent a great deal of time in Bethany, a village about two miles east of Jerusalem.

Musical editing of this hymn for the 1985 hymnbook omitted the dotted rhythms found in the first measure of each line in the 1950 hymnal, smoothing the flow of the music to the more traditional style found in most versions.

Guide Me to Thee 101

Text and music: Orson Pratt Huish (1851–1932; LDS)
Tune name: JAMES

The simple words of this hymn repeat an earnest plea: "Guide me to thee." As followers of Jesus Christ, we pray that we may be led, day by day, nearer to the presence of our Savior. The repeated supplications in this hymn are a prayer we would do well to carry constantly in our hearts.

Educators agree that repetition is the soul of learning. If we wish to engrave something upon our hearts, we must see it, hear it, repeat it many times. This truism has as much to do with spiritual learning as with any other kind of learning. Some denominations teach through repetition by means of catechism, which is a memorized series of answers to theological questions; by learning their catechism, children learn the basic doctrines of their particular religion. Many churches use what is known as a litany, a form of responsive worship in which a clergyman recites words of a prayer and the congregation together repeats certain set responses, such as "Hear us, we beseech thee, O Lord," at predetermined points during the prayer.

Latter-day Saints use neither catechism nor litany, but it would be incorrect to say that we do not use repetition to teach our truths. Through repeated singing of our beloved hymns, for instance, we learn and remember forever many important precepts and feelings. And through hymns we teach them to our children.

"Guide Me to Thee" is a perfect example of a hymn that serves a litany-like function. The plea "Guide me to thee" punctuates the hymn and controls the message it gives, and our prayer seems to gain strength with each repetition. Note that most of the rest of the hymn is negative: it speaks of strife, sin, darkness, crushed hopes, and death. It certainly does not try to sugarcoat the trials of human existence. But these negative references are completely offset by the beautiful, simple, positive prayer: "Guide me to thee." It can serve a beautiful, worshipful purpose not only for a congregation but also for an individual who wishes to recall a comforting hymn during a time of trial.

The hymn was first published in the *Deseret Sunday School Song Book* in 1892. The 1985 hymnal restored the hymn's original title, rather than using the first line, "Jesus, my Savior true."

Jesus, Lover of My Soul — 102

Text: Charles Wesley (1707–1788)
Music: Joseph P. Holbrook (1822–1888)
Tune name: REFUGE

When Christians of various denominations are surveyed concerning their favorite hymns, "Jesus, Lover of My Soul" usually ranks among the two or three that are named most often. This hymn is a tender acknowledgment of our dependence on the Savior, comparing him to a sheltered, safe harbor that promises refuge from the storms of life.

When a hymn is as popular as this one, many accounts of its origin inevitably spring up. People take great pleasure in the thought of an exciting or touching event that inspired the hymn's writing, and if such a story does not exist, one will soon be fabricated to fill the void. An often-told incident of a small bird, pursued by a hawk, flying into Charles Wesley's room through his window and taking refuge in his bosom is almost certainly fanciful. An additional story of how Wesley, during his days as a preacher, hid in a hedge to escape an angry mob is equally unlikely as the inspiration for the hymn.

But Charles Wesley's own journal documents an experience that certainly would have made the sea-imagery a vivid poetic possibility for him. In 1736, as he was sailing home to England after a short stay in America, the ship encountered a hurricane:

"Thurs. Oct. 28. The captain warned me of a storm approaching. In the evening at eight it came, and rose higher and higher. . . . There was so prodigious a sea that it quickly washed away our sheep and half our hogs, and drowned most of our fowl. . . . The sea streamed in at the sides so plentifully that it was as much as four men could do by continual pumping to keep her above water. . . . I prayed for . . . faith in Jesus Christ, continually repeating his name, till I felt the virtue of it at last, and knew that I abode under the shadow of the Almighty. . . .

"The captain, finding it otherwise impossible to save her from sinking, cut down the mizzen mast." (Quoted in Albert Edward Bailey, *The Gospel in Hymns* [New York: Charles Scribner's Sons, 1950], pp. 90–91.)

The famous preacher Henry Ward Beecher stated: "I would rather have written that hymn of Wesley's, 'Jesus, Lover of My Soul,' than to have the fame of all the kings that ever sat on the earth. It is more glorious. It has more power in it. That hymn will go on singing until the last trump brings forth the angel band; and then, I think, it will mount up on some lip to the very presence of God." (Quoted in Charles S. Nutter and Wilbur F. Tillett, *The Hymns and Hymn Writers of the Church* [New York: Methodist Book Concern, 1911], p. 245.)

The hymn text dates from 1756. In Latter-day Saint hymnals, the text has been printed at various times with the Thomas Hastings tune MARTYN as well as with the present tune, REFUGE. The first publication of this text with REFUGE in Latter-day Saint hymnody was in the privately printed *Songs of Zion* (1908).

Precious Savior, Dear Redeemer 103

Text and music: H. R. Palmer (1834–1907)
Tune name: PRECIOUS

With the singing of these words, we ask for the Spirit of Christ to "enter every timid heart." We ask to be blessed with the "sweet message" of the Savior so that temptation and sorrow may give way to "everlasting peace." It is a prayer for the companionship of the Spirit.

This hymn is not limited to any particular occasion, but it is especially suitable as an opening hymn. The first two lines ask for the message of the Spirit; without this blessing, the message of the speaker or lesson will not really enter our hearts. Conviction is a result of spiritual witness, not of rhetorical skill.

The Spirit of Christ—synonymous in many contexts with the Holy Ghost, according to Elder Bruce R. McConkie—is a powerful force. (See

Mormon Doctrine, 2d ed. [Salt Lake City, Utah: Bookcraft, 1966], p. 752.) It can accomplish many miraculous things. Moroni 10:9–17 lists divine gifts that may be given to the faithful here on earth, such as teaching, faith, healing, the working of miracles, prophecy, and tongues, and states that "all these gifts come by the Spirit of Christ." (V. 17.)

This hymn emphasizes three gifts of the Spirit of Christ. Verse one stresses that the Spirit will teach us, will leave with us a message if we are worthy. In verse two, we confess our weakness and vulnerability, and we praise the power of the Spirit to keep us from wrongdoing. In verse three, we ask for the Spirit of Christ to bless us at times when negative emotions, specifically sorrow and anger, threaten to take over our hearts.

This hymn is a succinct reminder of the many important roles the Spirit of Christ can play in our lives. It serves well in a meeting, when the gathering of Saints invokes the Spirit to be with them as a group. On an occasion when an individual might wish to repeat the words of this hymn-prayer, it would be useful to substitute *I* and *me* for the plural pronouns.

Jesus, Savior, Pilot Me 104

Text: Edward Hopper (1818–1888)
Music: John Edgar Gould (1822–1875)
Tune name: PILOT

Hymn-writers have used many different comparisons to evoke a deep feeling of trust in the care of a watchful Savior. This hymn, originally written for a congregation of sailors, is so powerful in its metaphor of seafaring that it has become popular with Christians everywhere.

Edward Hopper wrote this hymn in 1871 while he was pastor of the Mariner's Church at New York Harbor, known as "The Church of the Sea and Land." In his congregation were many sailors for whom the hymn's nautical imagery would have carried vivid meaning. Our life is a voyage, and we "near the shore" only as we near death. As long as we are at sea, the waters are often tempestuous and unfamiliar; we have no knowledge of where the dangers might be lurking—the rocks and shoals that would send us to sure destruction. Our only hope of safety is to turn to Jesus, the infallible pilot, who alone has the perfect "chart and compass."

Not only can Jesus pilot us safely through the storms; he can also still the waters with a word of command. The second verse moves logically from the sea metaphor of verse one into the familiar story of Jesus on the

Sea of Galilee, when the disciples feared for their lives because of the storm: "Master, carest thou not that we perish?

"And he arose, and rebuked the wind, and said unto the sea, Peace, be still. And the wind ceased, and there was a great calm." (Mark 4:38–39.)

The hymn contains no complicated theology. People young and old, of every level of education and experience, can respond to one simple idea—that a higher power knows the hidden dangers that threaten us and will guide us safely past them to the "peaceful rest."

J. Spencer Cornwall commented on the melody PILOT: "John Edgar Gould's lilting tune to 'Jesus, Savior, Pilot Me' with its repetitious phrases is rather charming. This fact has added much to preserve the hymn in popular favor." (*Stories of Our Mormon Hymns*, p. 126.)

Master, the Tempest Is Raging 105

Text: Mary Ann Baker (b. 1831)
Music: H. R. Palmer (1834–1907)
Tune name: PEACE, BE STILL

Since the beginning of Christian hymnody, poets have been moved by the dramatic incident on the Sea of Galilee when Jesus "rebuked the wind, and said unto the sea, Peace, be still." (Mark 4:39.) The disciples' doubts and fears, the Savior's dramatic and immediate miracle, and the amazed response of the disciples make this brief story an intriguing and colorful item on the list of Jesus' miracles.

This hymn, first printed in 1874, asks us to play several roles as we sing it. In the first verse, our words are those of a fearful disciple in that boat on the Sea of Galilee; our panic rises as a growing tempest threatens to capsize us at any moment. In the second verse, the fear and despair are just as great, but these are figurative storms, "torrents of sin and of anguish." The third verse recognizes the peace that comes after Jesus has calmed the storm, whether it is a storm on Galilee or a storm within the heart. The same chorus follows each verse, and here we speak words of faith in the Savior's ability to calm the storm. The hymn's central phrase and message, "Peace, be still," is repeated four times in this chorus.

The author, Mary Ann Baker, was left an orphan when her parents died of tuberculosis. She and her sister and brother lived together in Chicago. When her brother was stricken with the same disease that had killed their parents, the two sisters gathered together the little money they had and sent him to Florida to recover. But within a few weeks, he died, and the sisters did not have sufficient money to travel to Florida for his funeral nor to bring his body back to Chicago.

Mary Ann Baker wrote: "Although we mourned not as those without hope, and although I had believed on Christ in early childhood and had always desired to give the Master a consecrated and obedient life, I became wickedly rebellious at this dispensation of divine providence. I said in my heart that God did not care for me or mine. But the Master's own voice stilled the tempest in my unsanctified heart, and brought it to the calm of a deeper faith and a more perfect trust." (Quoted in Phil Kerr, *Music in Evangelism* [Glendale, Calif.: Gospel Music Publishers, 1939], pp. 167–68.)

God Speed the Right 106

Text: William E. Hickson (1803–1870)
Music: Ernst Moritz Arndt (1796–1860)
Tune name: SCHORITZ-RUGIN

"God Speed the Right" voices the feelings of loyal Christians who battle against great odds in the cause of righteousness. The rhythmic tune is strong and steady; it expresses well the patience, firmness, and perseverance which we claim as ours as we sing the hymn.

This hymn repeats twelve times a fervent, four-word prayer, "God speed the right." These words imply that the "right" has not yet arrived; we have not yet seen the day when the literal kingdom of Christ has been established on the earth, binding Satan and his powers. Thus the hymn is not about victory; it is about struggle and the attitudes we should bring to struggle. For the time being, at least, a proper attitude is the real victory.

By earthly standards, the life of Jesus was a failure. Most of his followers deserted him, and he was condemned and executed. Yet he foresaw the eventual rewards of this struggle, and every apparent failure was actually consecrated toward a holy cause.

Like our Savior, we will not win every battle in this life, even though we fight on the side of the right. But we carry on without discouragement; it is the struggle on the side of right that counts, not the outcome of a particular battle: "If we fail, we fail with glory."

As we sing the words of this hymn, we hope its words really do reflect our courageous resilience: we are "patient, firm, and persevering," fearless, unwearying, "ne'er despairing, though defeated," willing to continue the fight for as long as the Lord calls us to do so. Those who fight on the side of righteousness may often fail, but a failure does not undermine the cause or dampen the spirits. As many times as necessary, "Be that prayer again repeated, God speed the right."

A hymn collection published in 1862 by Lowell Mason and his brother

William was the first to print this hymn. In the 1950 Latter-day Saint hymnbook, this hymn carried its first line as the title: "Now to Heaven Our Prayer." The 1985 hymnal restored its original title. The tenor and bass parts at the beginning of line three have been reharmonized to avoid doubling the soprano and alto.

Lord, Accept Our True Devotion 107

Text: Richard Alldridge (1815–1896; LDS)
Music: Joseph J. Daynes (1851–1920; LDS)
Tune name: ELIZA

"Lord, Accept Our True Devotion" offers worshipful praise to the Lord and asks for his guidance in return. We express to him our desire for two blessings: the joy of obedience and righteousness in this life, and exaltation in the presence of our Heavenly Father in the next, "Ever praising, / Throughout all eternity."

This hymn has been a favorite among Latter-day Saints since it was first printed in the *Juvenile Instructor* in 1876. J. Spencer Cornwall made this comment: " 'Lord, Accept Our True Devotion' has in it the elements of popularity and longevity. The repetitive phrases 'Never leave us,' 'Ever guard us' and 'Ever praising' create an indelible impression on all who sing or hear this hymn." (*Stories of Our Mormon Hymns*, p. 114.)

Anyone who wishes to compare the 1950 hymnal will note that the 1985 hymnal made a significant change in the Joseph J. Daynes musical setting. Previously, the musical arrangement called for the women's voices alone to sing "Never leave us" in the chorus, to be answered each time by the men's voices singing the same words in antiphonal style. The new arrangement is simpler and more dignified, with men and women singing the words of the chorus at the same time rather than in response-fashion. It also lends itself more readily to unison singing.

Joseph J. Daynes is the composer of four other hymn tunes in our volume, including "As the Dew from Heaven Distilling" (no. 149). He named this tune ELIZA in honor of his mother, Eliza Miller Daynes.

The Lord Is My Shepherd 108; 316

Text: James Montgomery (1771–1854)
Music: Thomas Koschat (1845–1914)
Tune name: FORSAKEN or POLAND

Many hymn writers have undertaken the task of turning into verse one of the most beloved of all scriptural passages—the Twenty-third Psalm.

While giving it the rhyme and meter of a traditional hymn pattern, James Montgomery has retained the beauty and solace of this psalm. The comfort and reassurance of this psalm's message speak to us across thousands of years.

Like the words of the original psalm, James Montgomery's words first speak *about* the Lord, praising his watchful care: "He leadeth me beside the still waters" becomes "He leadeth my soul where the still waters flow," for example. Then the words are addressed *to* the Lord, thanking him directly: "Thou anointest my head with oil" becomes "With perfume and oil thou anointest my head." In both the psalm and the hymn, a grateful acknowledgment of the Lord's care leads naturally into a prayer of thanksgiving. This psalm paraphrase was first printed in 1822.

The comments of James E. Talmage about John 10:1–21 are relevant to the figure of speech that underlies this hymn: "Christ proclaimed: 'I am the good shepherd.' He then further showed, and with eloquent exactness, the difference between a shepherd and a hireling herder. The one has personal interest in and love for his flock, and knows each sheep by name, the other knows them only as a flock. . . . While the shepherd is ready to fight in defense of his own, and if necessary even imperil his life for his sheep, the hireling flees when the wolf approaches, leaving the way open for the ravening beast to scatter, rend, and kill." (*Jesus the Christ* [Salt Lake City, Utah: Deseret Book Co., 1969], p. 417.)

FORSAKEN may seem a strange name for a tune that is paired with the Twenty-third Psalm! The explanation for this tune name is that the original melody, composed or arranged by Thomas Koschat, first appeared in a volume of German folksongs (1879) for men's voices. The song began with the words "Verlassen, verlassen" ("Forsaken, forsaken"). This song achieved considerable popularity, but by the end of the nineteenth century many American Sunday School hymnals had adopted it as the tune for "The Lord Is My Shepherd." The tune is also known as POLAND.

James Montgomery is also the author of "A Poor Wayfaring Man of Grief" (no. 29) and "Prayer Is the Soul's Sincere Desire" (no. 145).

The Lord My Pasture Will Prepare 109

Text: Joseph Addison (1672–1719)
Music: Dmitri Bortniansky (1751–1825)
Tune name: ST. PETERSBURG

All of us depend for our safety and comfort on the Lord. But not often enough do we express our gratitude for his protection. Of "The Lord My Pasture Will Prepare," J. Spencer Cornwall stated, "Trust and confidence in the Lord are given poetic grace in the lovely lines of this hymn." (*Stories of Our Mormon Hymns*, p. 120.)

To give meaning and vividness to his message of comfort, poet Joseph Addison chose a comparison that is familiar from many scriptural passages, Psalm 23 in particular: the Lord's care for us is like the shepherd's care for his sheep. Just as the shepherd protects his trusting flock from hunger, predators, and heat, so the Lord guards his children from dangers that surround them. He is with them at every moment, whether it is noon or midnight. If, in spite of his watchfulness, one should wander into a place where danger threatens, he gently leads the way back to beautiful meadows and peaceful rivers. The poem first appeared in *The Spectator* in 1712.

Some of the words in the second verse of this hymn may be unfamiliar. A *glebe* is a field; thus a *sultry glebe* is a place too hot for the sheep. *Vale* and *mead* are simply poetic terms meaning "valley" and "meadow" respectively. *Verdant* means "green."

The soothing melody of this hymn tune, dating from 1825, speaks an equally peaceful message. When Dmitri Bortniansky wrote this tune, he was director of the Imperial Russian Choir in St. Petersburg (now Leningrad)—hence the tune name.

Cast Thy Burden upon the Lord 110

Text: Julius Schubring (1806–1889)
Music: Felix Mendelssohn (1809–1847)
Tune name: BIRMINGHAM

Every word and every note of "Cast Thy Burden upon the Lord" contributes to a mood of comfort and serenity. In times of stress, disappointment, or exhaustion, the message of this hymn, whether it is sung or merely recalled, can remind us that the Lord is at our side.

"Cast Thy Burden upon the Lord" was not originally written as a hymn. It is an excerpt from Felix Mendelssohn's oratorio *Elijah*. "Cast Thy Burden upon the Lord" occurs during a highly dramatic episode based on 1 Kings 18. Elijah and the priests of Baal are locked in a challenge: which god, Baal or the God of Israel, will send down fire from heaven to consume the sacrifice? The people watch as the priests of Baal call out to their god "and cut themselves after their manner with knives and lancets" (v. 28), but Baal is silent. Then Elijah steps forward, and the people gather to watch in excitement. He builds an altar to God and offers up his prayer: "Lord God of Abraham, Isaac, and of Israel, let it be known this day that thou art God in Israel." (V. 36.)

At this moment in the oratorio, the forward motion of the story pauses for a brief, peaceful contrast. A chorus of angels sings "Cast Thy Burden upon the Lord," and we are reminded of Elijah's perfect faith and trust. Then, after another brief prayer from Elijah, "the fire of the Lord fell, and consumed the burnt sacrifice." (V. 38.) Elijah's faith is vindicated before the people and before the false priests of Baal.

Felix Mendelssohn's librettist, Julius Schubring, assembled the words of this hymn from sections of four psalms: 55:22; 16:8; 108:4; and 25:3.

Elijah received its premiere in 1846 in Birmingham, England—thus the tune name—and was an immediate success. Prince Albert, husband of Queen Victoria, wrote words of high praise to Mendelssohn following this performance: "To the noble artist who, though encompassed by the Baal-worship of false art, by his genius has succeeded, like another Elijah, in faithfully preserving the worship of true art." (Quoted in Wilfrid Blunt, *On Wings of Song: A Biography of Felix Mendelssohn* [New York: Charles Scribner's Sons, 1974], p. 262.)

Rock of Ages 111

Text: Augustus M. Toplady (1740–1778)
Music: Thomas Hastings (1784–1872)
Tune name: TOPLADY

It is a temptation among some Latter-day Saints to focus more strongly on good works than on the atoning blood of Jesus as a means to salvation. But we do not believe in salvation by works alone. This hymn reminds us that no matter what we do or how faithful we are, the atoning sacrifice of Jesus is the bridge from death to salvation.

J. Spencer Cornwall believed that "Rock of Ages" is a hymn of "implicit faith in the saving power of a Divine Father." (*Stories of Our Mormon Hymns*, p. 294.) It is a highly personal hymn, using the pronouns *I* and *me* rather than the plural pronouns more common in hymns. This individual focus suits the topic well; though the Savior's sacrifice means resurrection for all, salvation is a highly individual matter, and each person must seek to understand and accept the full meaning of the Atonement for himself.

The use of a rock as a symbol of the strength and stability of Deity is common in both the Old and the New Testament. (See, for example, Deuteronomy 32; 2 Samuel 22:2–3, 32, 47; Psalm 18:31, 46; and 1 Corinthians 10:4.) The words of verse two—"Not the labors of my hands / Can fill all thy law's demands; . . . All for sin could not atone; / Thou must save, and thou alone"—echo 2 Nephi 25:23: "For we know that it is by grace that we are saved, after all we can do." And the hymn text also refers to the saving role of water and blood, as does Moses 6:59: "Ye must be born . . . of water, and of the Spirit, and be cleansed by blood, even the blood of mine Only Begotten: that ye might be sanctified from all sin."

One of the ironic facts of hymn history is that Augustus Toplady, throughout his life a bitter theological antagonist of Charles Wesley, based this hymn on a prose piece written by Wesley thirty years earlier, called *Hymns of the Lord's Supper*. In the preface, Charles Wesley quoted a few lines from Dr. Daniel Brevint: "O Rock of Israel, Rock of Salvation, Rock struck and cleft for me, let those two streams of Blood and Water, which once gushed out of Thy side, bring down pardon and holiness into my soul." (Quoted in Alice Loewen, Harold Moyer, and Mary Oyer, *Exploring the Mennonite Hymnal: Handbook* [Newton, Kans., 1983], p. 147.) And the title of another hymn in Charles Wesley's collection is "Rock of Israel, Cleft for Me."

Augustus Toplady's original title for this hymn was "A Living and Dying PRAYER, for the HOLIEST BELIEVER in the World." The title's implication is that even the holiest person must place his hope in the redeeming blood of Christ.

He first published his verse in 1776; not until 1832 did Thomas Hastings write the tune to which these words are always sung today.

The 1950 hymnal included a version of this hymn for women's voices only. The 1985 hymnbook included, instead, the standard four-part harmony for congregational use.

Savior, Redeemer of My Soul 112

Text: Orson F. Whitney (1855–1931; LDS)
Music: Harry A. Dean (1892-1987; LDS)
Tune name: GLADYS

The Savior has made possible for us the gift of redemption in the life to come. What could we possibly do to repay this blessing? We must be forever in his debt, since it is not in our power to do or say anything that even comes close to repayment. But in this hymn, we promise to do all that *is* in our power: we can love the Lord, we can love and proclaim his word, and we can serve him and live in harmony with his will.

Elder Boyd K. Packer called Elder Orson F. Whitney "a gifted and inspired poet whose work is virtually unknown in the Church." (*Ensign*, Aug. 1976, p. 64.)

Orson F. Whitney expressed a lofty vision of the future contributions of Latter-day Saint authors to world literature: "We shall yet have Miltons and Shakespeares of our own. God's ammunition is not exhausted. His highest spirits are held in reserve for the latter times. In God's name and by His help we will build up a literature whose tops will touch the heaven, though its foundation may now be low on the earth." (Quoted in Packer, *Ensign*, Aug. 1976, p. 61.)

In the 1950 hymnal, this hymn text appeared with two musical settings. One, a difficult choir setting by Evan Stephens, was not included in the 1985 hymnal. The hymn tune by Harry A. Dean beautifully complements the stately, worshipful movement of Orson F. Whitney's message. The tune name, GLADYS, honors his wife, Gladys Cutler.

Our Savior's Love 113

Text: Edward L. Hart (b. 1916; LDS)
Music: Crawford Gates (b. 1921; LDS)
Tune name: ETERNAL LIFE

The culmination of this quiet and elegant hymn is a reverent prayer to the Father. Verses one and two, as they unfold toward that prayer, speak of the gentle warmth of the Savior's guiding love and of the Holy Spirit's "voice of goodness."

The author, Edward L. Hart, stated that the whole hymn grew out of the initial figure of speech that compares the Savior's love to the light of the sun. It is interesting that this lofty comparison was suggested by everyday experience. "The simile goes back to seeing people in a fabric or clothing store take material outside and into the sunlight to test its color in the only true or 'perfect' source of light," he said. "In the same way, the only true test of love is the source, our Savior's love."

Though they are friends, the two creators of this hymn worked independently. The Church Music Committee sent Crawford Gates the text, inviting him to set it to music. "It was a text to which I could extend my full conviction for its message," Crawford Gates said. "For me, the simple melody does not seem to tire easily. I feel so blessed to be the channel by which it has come to be a part of the sacred hymnody of the Lord's kingdom." The hymn was first published in the *Ensign* in July 1977.

He further noted that as he heard several choirs and congregations rehearse and sing this hymn, it became obvious that the hymn "has a life and vitality of its own—that it has its own power apart from me, like a child which has grown up to be a self-sufficient and responsible adult."

Crawford Gates suggested that congregations "read, study, and ponder this beautiful and profound poem" before singing the hymn. Note the structure of the hymn: verse one speaks of the Son; verse two speaks of the Holy Ghost; verse three addresses the Father.

Come unto Him 114

Text: Theodore E. Curtis (1872–1957; LDS)
Music: Hugh W. Dougall (1872–1963; LDS)
Tune name: YOUNG

"Come unto Him" is a personal testimony of the power of prayer and trust. As we sing the words, we make the writer's feelings and experiences our own; along with him, we sense the enfolding presence of our Father in Heaven. His protection and help are at hand for all those who seek him.

This hymn is in reality a lyric poem that serves a hymnlike purpose. A chief characteristic of a lyric poem is that it reflects a personal experience, the emotions and responses of a single individual. "Come unto Him," with its singular first-person pronouns (*I, me*) and its retelling, in verse one, of an important private event, certainly fits this definition. But like all good lyric poets, Theodore E. Curtis sought the universal significance in his experience. Prayerful people can relate to his sense of God's presence, his impulse to kneel upon the grass and pray, and his sense of comfort and relief when he felt "an answer . . . without a voice."

The conclusion of verse three is a strong, direct invitation to identify with the hymn's message. The poet addressed three groups specifically, three categories of reluctant people who might hang back from the thought of leaning upon the Father's care and trusting his love and comfort: the "depressed," the "erring," and the "weary." A careful reading of the previous verses will show that the poet did not necessarily exclude himself from these groups; thus the hymn's promise of refuge and peace are doubly meaningful, and the writer's own experience validated the testimony he expressed in the hymn.

The hymn was listed by a first-line title, "I Wander Through the Stilly Night," in the 1950 hymnal, but the title "Come unto Him" gives a better idea of the hymn's message. Though originally written as a choir hymn, the appealing words and melody are within the capabilities of most congregations.

The tune name, YOUNG, honors Hugh W. Dougall's mother, Maria Young Dougall, who was a daughter of Brigham Young.

Come, Ye Disconsolate 115

Text: Thomas Moore (1779–1852);
verse three by Thomas Hastings (1784–1872)
Music: Samuel Webbe (1740–1816)
Tune name: CONSOLATION

Some hymns are prayers in and of themselves. "Come, Ye Disconsolate" is an invitation to prayer. Only the hardest heart could resist the gentle persuasion of the beautiful text and melody.

Although the Irish poet Thomas Moore (not to be confused with the famous Sir Thomas More, who lived three centuries earlier) is well remembered for his lyric verse, the only hymn among his works that survives today is "Come, Ye Disconsolate," written in 1816. He was not known as a man of strong religious feeling, but his poetry includes some thirty-two hymns. At least once in his life he turned his most sincere thoughts and best poetic gifts to the subject of prayer and the comfort it can bring.

The hymn stresses that the ones who will find the greatest comfort in prayer, the greatest release from sin and sorrow, are the truly repentant. The word *disconsolate* means "without consolation"—dejected, gloomy, and cheerless. Such phrases as "fervently kneel" and "bring your wounded hearts" convey the importance of a contrite spirit for one who seeks the healing consolation of heaven.

This hymn has an unusual rhythm for a hymn text. It is written in triple meter (one stressed syllable followed by two unstressed), a lively verse form that most poets would reserve for informal or humorous verse. But the galloping rhythm is smoothed out by Samuel Webbe's elegant tune, written twenty-four years before the text, with which it is always paired today.

Thomas Hastings is the author of the third stanza of our hymn. The original third stanza, less suitable to the spirit of the hymn even though by Thomas Moore himself, began with the words "Go ask the infidel what boon he brings us." The sense behind these words is that a pagan religion cannot offer the solace of Christian prayer.

Come, Follow Me 116

Text: John Nicholson (1839–1909; LDS)
Music: Samuel McBurney (b. 1847)
Tune name: INVITATION

The Savior's call, "Come, follow me," has inspired many Christian hymn texts. But this beautiful hymn has a distinctively Latter-day Saint emphasis: if we emulate the Savior throughout this earthly life, ours will be the opportunity to acquire even more of his attributes in the life to come.

This hymn cries out for all six verses to be sung. Verse six satisfies our wish for poetic completeness, since the three final words also begin the hymn and are the hymn's principal message: "Come, follow me." Even more important, the fourth verse begins a new point: that we must continue our discipleship of Jesus even in the next life. This point is rather inconclusive without the additional details of verses five and six, which state that "glory great and bliss are ours"—and, by implication, nothing less than godhood—if we are among the most faithful. This bold and compelling promise is unique to Latter-day Saint theology, and it is beautifully expressed in this Christ-centered hymn.

What are the "thrones, dominions, kingdoms, powers" alluded to in verse six? Elder Bruce R. McConkie explained, "In token of their kingship, sovereignty, and dominion, exalted beings shall sit on thrones in eternity." (*Mormon Doctrine*, 2d ed. [Salt Lake City, Utah: Bookcraft, 1966], p. 794.) He cited Doctrine and Covenants 121:29, the phrasing of which is reminiscent of the first words of verse six: "All thrones and dominions, principalities and powers, shall be revealed and set forth upon all who have endured valiantly for the gospel of Jesus Christ."

The text was first printed in the *Millennial Star* in 1871. The tune INVITATION was printed with the text in 1892 in the *Deseret Sunday School Song Book*.

Come unto Jesus 117

Text and music: Orson Pratt Huish (1851–1932; LDS)
Tune name: NIBLET

The Savior's love reaches every person, without exception. Even someone burdened with cares, or oppressed by sin, or in a distant and forgotten place—does that person, too, come within the compass of his love? This hymn answers that question with a quiet and unequivocal "yes."

It is too easy for us to discount our personal worth to such a degree that we feel we cannot approach the Savior, that we are not worthy of his love. This hymn comforts us with its calm reiteration of a truth we must never forget: the Savior's love is unconditional. His invitation, "Come unto me," not only included sinners but was often directed especially to them.

Spencer Kinard offered these comments in "The Spoken Word":

"One of the most frequent words in Christ's vocabulary was a small one—*come*. The gestures which we associate with him echo that same idea. Arms outstretched in welcome, his entire being said, 'Come.' This is not a restricted invitation for the few, for the elect, for those who somehow deserve it; he made it open and for all, no matter how weak or afraid or hesitant. . . . Come follow me, in fact, was the message of his life.

"*Come*. It is an immediate appeal, admitting no excuses. We who say to the Lord, 'I am too busy. I am too tired. I will work you in at another time,' have missed the point. There is not a mortal being who is not burdened with cares that threaten to absorb him altogether. All are preoccupied, all busy. . . .

"*Come*. It is without qualifications. Not come when we are perfect. Not come when we have no doubts or smudges, when life is uncontested and we have no problems. Nor is it an invitation to come only when life is at its darkest—only in time of dire need. It is a simple, 'Come now. Come as you are.' . . .

"He knows that if we will come to him in pain, we will leave in joy. If we come in confusion, we will leave in clarity. If we come in darkness, we will leave in light. So he offers the invitation and leaves it extended with a kind of divine hopefulness—until we respond." (*A Time for Reflection* [Salt Lake City, Utah: Deseret Book Co., 1986], pp. 113–14.)

The tune name honors Orson Pratt Huish's mother, Helen Niblet Huish. This hymn was first published in *Deseret Sunday School Songs* in 1909.

Ye Simple Souls Who Stray 118

Text: Charles Wesley (1707–1788); adapted
Music: Evan Stephens (1854–1930; LDS)
Tune name: MARTHA

Protestant hymn writer Charles Wesley here addressed one of the great paradoxes of human nature: when joy, peace of mind, and eternal reward are the result of righteousness, why do so many men and women scorn these blessings? The righteous who enjoy such happiness can only be puzzled and dismayed by the "simple souls who stray."

Originally titled "Expostulation with sinners," this 1747 text was given a beautiful musical setting by Evan Stephens. It is not an easy hymn to sing, but its flowing melodic line has great appeal.

The 1950 hymnal gave six verses for this hymn. In order to make the hymn more inviting for congregational use, the 1985 Hymnbook Committee decided to alter the text by "telescoping" the six verses into four. The first and final verses remain the same in both versions, but parts of verses two and three were combined into the new verse two, and parts of verses four and five were combined into the new verse three. In essence, four half-verses were omitted in the 1985 hymnal.

The second half of the original verse two is omitted:

As only born to grieve,
Beneath your feet we lie,
And utterly contemned we live
And unlamented die.

The first half of the original verse three is now omitted:

So wretched and obscure,
The man whom ye despise,
So foolish, impotent, and poor,
Above your scorn we rise.

The last half of the original verse four is now omitted:

The Spirit we receive
Of wisdom, grace, and power:
And though 'mid scenes of woe we live,
Rejoicing evermore.

And the final omission is the first half of the original verse five:

Angels our servants are
And keep in all our ways;
And in their watchful hands they bear
The sacred sons of grace.

Come, We That Love the Lord 119

Text: Isaac Watts (1674–1748)
Music: Aaron Williams (1731–1776)
Tune name: ST. THOMAS

This hymn declares the united gratitude of the worshipers for the Lord and his power. It summons all who love the Lord to make their feelings known through a song of praise, and it rebukes all who refuse to sing. The Lord's followers will be known because they "speak their joys abroad."

The original title of this hymn (1707) was "Heavenly Joy on Earth." Because it embodies so well the happiness and gratitude felt by faithful Christians, it holds a place in almost every Christian hymnal.

Modern preference is for hymns shorter than those sung in the days of Isaac Watts. We have verses one, three, four, and five of the original hymn, with verse three as altered by John Wesley. The verses omitted from our hymnal, together with the original third verse, appear below. Some are quite harmonious with Latter-day Saint thinking: verse two dismisses the gloomy connotations of religion, and verses seven and eight stress that for the righteous, joy is part of this earthly life, not just a reward for the hereafter.

2. *The sorrows of the mind*
Be banished from the place!
Religion never was designed
To make our pleasures less.

3. *The God that rules on high,*
And thunders when he please,
That rides upon the stormy sky,
And manages the seas.

6. *There we shall see his face,*
And never, never sin;
There, from the rivers of his grace,
Drink endless pleasures in.

7. *The men of grace have found*
Glory begun below;
Celestial fruit on earthly ground
From faith and hope may grow.

8. *The hill of Zion yields*
A thousand sacred sweets,
Before we reach the heavenly fields,
Or walk the golden streets.

9. *Then let our songs abound,*
And every tear be dry;
We're marching through Immanuel's ground
To fairer worlds on high.

The fine hymn tune by Aaron Williams was first printed in an English hymn collection in 1763.

Lean on My Ample Arm 120

Text: Theodore E. Curtis (1872–1957; LDS)
Music: Evan Stephens (1854–1930; LDS)
Tune name: ESTHER

Many times in the scriptures the Savior offered comfort and peace of mind to those who sorrowed. This hymn text is a poetic restatement that captures the essence of such scriptures. It promises rest and peace to all who lean upon the Savior.

In literary terms, "point of view" refers to the vantage point from which an author tells a poem or a story—the person the author chooses to serve as the mouthpiece for the message of the literary work. In "Lean on My Ample Arm," the message is expressed as if spoken by the Savior himself. This is not a common point of view for our hymns. (One other example is "Reverently and Meekly Now," no. 185.) But it is very effective in "Lean on My Ample Arm." What could be more persuasive than the words of the Savior himself? And because Jesus so many times called upon the suffering and the unfortunate to seek solace in him, it is not presumptuous on the part of the author to present this thought in verse form as if it were actually expressed by Jesus. A congregation can find great comfort in being reminded of the Savior's ever-present compassion and understanding.

J. Spencer Cornwall commented: "This choir hymn is almost of anthem proportions. It is somewhat dramatic in its harmonic content, reaching an imposing climax in the fourth line. The final measures which reiterate the first phrase are calm and impressively peaceful." (*Stories of Our Mormon Hymns*, p. 259.)

This hymn was labeled for choir use in the 1950 hymnal. The pitch was lowered for the 1985 hymnal, and the music is not too difficult for most congregations.

I'm a Pilgrim, I'm a Stranger 121

Text: Hans H. Petersen (1835–1909; LDS)
Music: Leroy J. Robertson (1896–1971; LDS)
Tune name: BOSTON

This plaintive hymn is an acknowledgment of dependence on our Heavenly Father. Most human beings, sooner or later, must endure a time of serious trial. Even if major misfortunes do not befall, our earthly lives are a time of uncertainty, and we may find ourselves longing for the security of the life to come.

The first two verses of this hymn paint a graphic picture of a forlorn outcast, marooned on a rocky shore, surrounded by vapors that overshadow the way to safety. Death seems imminent; this lonely exile fears becoming "the vulture's prey." In the third verse, the outcast turns to prayer, asking the Father for safety.

At first glance, it seems odd that a hymn devoted largely to such negative thinking would have a place in our hymnal. But an understanding of the extended figure of speech that underlies the hymn helps to illuminate its meaning. For many centuries, religious writers have expressed the idea that a true Christian must always be a stranger here on earth, because his true home is fixed in heaven.

In Hebrews 11:13–16, the scripture citation at the bottom of the hymn page, Paul expressed this thought: "[The faithful] confessed that they were strangers and pilgrims on the earth.

"For they that say such things declare plainly that they seek a country.

"And truly, if they had been mindful of that country from whence they came out, they might have had opportunity to have returned.

"But now they desire a better country, that is, an heavenly."

Leroy J. Robertson told J. Spencer Cornwall: "The music to this hymn was written to some other words as a class assignment when this composer was a student at the New England Conservatory of Music [in Boston—thus the tune name] in 1921. It was later adapted to the Petersen words for publication in the 1927 hymnal." (Quoted in *Stories of Our Mormon Hymns*, p. 259.)

Though Deepening Trials 122

Text: Eliza R. Snow (1804–1887; LDS)
Music: George Careless (1839–1932; LDS)
Tune name: RELIANCE

This hymn text, first published in January 1841, stands as a testimony to the strength and optimism of Eliza R. Snow. No one knew better than she the hardships and indignities suffered by the Saints at that time, and her words brought solace to her fellow Latter-day Saints. Almost a century and a half later, we draw courage from the same text.

The persecutions of Missouri and Nauvoo and the walk while driving an ox-team from Nauvoo to Winter Quarters took their toll on the health of Eliza R. Snow. Yet she was able to look beyond these sufferings to write hymns of hope and peace. Nothing could shake her faith in the eventual fulfillment of divine purposes: "This work is moving on apace, /And great events are rolling forth."

Because George D. Pyper was a personal friend of George Careless, his account of the tune's composition is particularly significant:

"George Careless composed the tune while under physical distress. He was very ill and needed encouragement—something to dispel his fears and raise him from the state of despondency into which he felt himself drifting. . . .

" 'Addie,' he called to his eleven-year-old daughter, 'bring me the hymn book.' She brought it to him. After scanning its pages for a few minutes he found what he was searching for—what his physical body as well as his spirit required. It was Eliza R. Snow's hymn, 'Though Deep'ning Trials Throng Your Way.' It gave him courage to fight his bodily ills and the faith that soon raised him from his bed of affliction. At the same time it inspired the muse that enabled him to pen one of the noblest of his compositions—one which, united with Eliza R. Snow's comforting poem, is among the most popular numbers in our Church hymnody.

"When George Careless recovered from his illness, he took his composition to Horace G. Whitney and asked him if he could suggest a title for it. Mr. Whitney, after looking it over, said 'Why not call it "Reliance," ' and as 'Reliance' it was published." (*Stories of Latter-day Saint Hymns,* pp. 139–41.)

The first hymn collection to publish this tune was the 1889 *Latter-day Saints' Psalmody*.

Oh, May My Soul Commune with Thee 123

Text and music: Lorin F. Wheelwright (1909–1987; LDS)
Tune name: STERLING

"True reverence comes from a humble heart seeking the Spirit of God," stated the author of this hymn in the July 1963 *Instructor*. "It is not mere compliance with external forms. . . . As we *feel* the presence of our Saviour, we *will* be reverent." (P. 252.) His hymn helps us carry out this resolution.

Lorin F. Wheelwright's note that he wrote this hymn in 1958 as a response to "years of playing preludes to the accompaniment of continuous conversations by leadership and members of the congregation" will bring a wry smile of sympathy to the face of many a ward organist or pianist. The author said frankly that his intention in this hymn was to change behavior and to convey "a deep love of reverence in worship. The value of this hymn lies in its simplicity and its direct petition for spiritual communion with the Spirit of God. My hope is that it may inspire an attitude of worship and reverence in our religious devotions."

As is the case with most of the hymns in our book, this hymn has evolved through several stages of revision. A comparison of the original text and the version published in the 1985 hymnal gives insight into the creative process by which a fine, distinctive hymn text emerges. The original lines are as follows:

Oh, may my soul commune with Thee
And find Thy holy peace;
From this harsh world of noise and sin,
Bring me sweet release.

Enfold me in Thy quiet hour,
Unbroken by intrusion,
Heal my heart with solitude,
Unmarred by crass confusion.

Bless them who serve to worship Thee,
Their tongues to keep in tune,
That I may hear Thy Still Small Voice,
And, Lord, with Thee commune.

Thrice blessed be these priestly men,
Who calmly guide my mind,
Who help me meditate on Thee,
And Thy sweet Spirit find.

Descend upon my troubled thought,
And let my turmoil cease.
Oh, may my soul commune with Thee,
And find Thy holy peace.

The tune name, STERLING, honors the author's brother, D. Sterling Wheelwright, who served as assistant director of the Tabernacle Choir from 1936 to 1937.

Be Still, My Soul 124

Text: Katharina von Schlegel (b. 1697);
translated by Jane Borthwick (1813–1897)
Music: Jean Sibelius (1865–1957)
Tune name: FINLANDIA

This hymn that frankly acknowledges the presence of grief and pain in our lives is a welcome addition to the 1985 Latter-day Saint hymnal. Because we know that we agreed to undergo a period of testing, to come to an earth where trials and misfortune were almost certain to be a part of our experience, we can overcome temporary discouragement and look to a future of "purest joys restored" with the same serenity as did the writer of this hymn almost four hundred years ago.

Katharina von Schlegel is a woman about whom little is known. She probably dedicated herself to a religious life in the Protestant equivalent of a convent setting. One fact is certain: she knew her scriptures well, both the Old and the New Testaments. In her hymn, she wove together in a creative and remarkable way a whole series of scriptural themes and references to biblical events.

The opening line of the hymn was suggested by Psalm 46:10: "Be still, and know that I am God."

"Bear thy cross of grief or pain" of course refers to the Savior's journey to Calvary, when he bore his cross. (See John 19:17.)

"Leave to thy God to order and provide" reflects the spirit of many scriptures, including Psalm 37:7: "Rest in the Lord, and wait patiently for him."

"All now mysterious shall be bright at last" relates to many biblical passages (1 Corinthians 2:7–16 is just one example) and also to Latter-day Saint scriptures such as 1 Nephi 10:19: "The mysteries of God shall be unfolded to them, by the power of the Holy Ghost."

"The waves and winds still know / His voice" recalls the story of Jesus stilling the waves on Galilee. (See Matthew 8:23–27.)

The spirit of the entire third verse may be compared with such scriptures as 1 Thessalonians 4:17: "Then we which are alive and remain shall be caught up together with them in the clouds, to meet the Lord in the air."

The tune, FINLANDIA, is named for the tone poem by Sibelius from which the melody is taken. "Finlandia" is familiar to many Latter-day Saints particularly because it has been performed and recorded many times by the Tabernacle Choir. The Choir's album on the Columbia label, *This Is My Country,* includes a performance of "Finlandia" with Eugene Ormandy and the Phildelphia Orchestra.

How Gentle God's Commands 125; 314

Text: Philip Doddridge (1702–1751)
Music: Hans G. Nägeli (1773–1836);
arranged by Lowell Mason (1792–1872)
Tune name: DENNIS

The words *command* and *commandment* usually carry stern connotations. But those who obey the Lord find their load lighter, not heavier. This is the paradox of obedience: if we seek obedience rather than happiness, the result is happiness after all. As we approach the Father's throne in a spirit of commitment, we can leave our "anxious load" and in its place "bear a song away."

The hymn's original title (1755), "God's Care a Remedy for Ours," echoes 1 Peter 5:7: "Casting all your care upon him; for he careth for you."

Under his entry for "Commandments" in *Mormon Doctrine,* Elder Bruce R. McConkie stated emphatically, "It is God's right to command; he is not restricted to sending requests or petitions." He then focused on the point made in our hymn, citing 1 John 5:3 and adding italics to the last phrase: "For this is the love of God, that we keep his commandments: and *his commandments are not grievous*." In Elder McConkie's words, "In his infinite wisdom he orders us to do what will further our interests and his." (2d ed. [Salt Lake City, Utah: Bookcraft, 1966], p. 149.) The security and joy described in the hymn text are the reward of obedience.

J. Spencer Cornwall commented concerning the tune, DENNIS, that "the undulating flowing melody of this tune is beautifully in harmony with the text, although the two were not associated when the composition was written." (*Stories of Our Mormon Hymns*, p. 81.) Most Protestant hymnals print DENNIS as the tune for the well-known John Fawcett text, "Blest Be the Tie That Binds."

How Long, O Lord Most Holy and True 126

Text: John A. Widtsoe (1872–1952; LDS)
Music: B. Cecil Gates (1887–1941; LDS)
Tune name: JACOB

This hymn is a prayer for release from the confusions and fetters of earthly life. It is a patient but urgent plea to the Lord, asking him to hasten the day when his kingdom will be established. By comparison with that future glorious day of truth and freedom, present life is a prison, dark and discouraging. Only the Lord himself can "swing wide the gates, and set us free!"

This is an unusual hymn in its message and tone. Some have suggested that the author, Elder John A. Widtsoe, also had in mind the postmortal state of the souls of men and women in spirit prison. In President Joseph F. Smith's vision of the redemption of the dead, souls were "awaiting the advent of the Son of God into the spirit world, to declare their redemption from the bands of death. . . .

"For the dead had looked upon the long absence of their spirits from their bodies as a bondage.

"These the Lord taught, and gave them power to come forth, after his resurrection from the dead, to enter into his Father's kingdom, there to be crowned with immortality and eternal life." (D&C 138:16, 50–51.)

Certainly the words of this hymn sustain that interpretation. But the hymn also has wider application. It can be seen as a dignified expression of the longing of a faithful Latter-day Saint for the order, enlightenment, and freedom that will come when the Lord will "speed on the day, redemption's hour." The faithful Saint who speaks these words has come to center his hopes and vision on that future time. Indeed, the Lord told the Prophet Joseph Smith: "He that feareth me shall be looking forth for the great day of the Lord to come." (D&C 45:39.)

Lamentations and plaintive cries are part of a distinct literary and scriptural tradition. The writings of the prophet Jeremiah are probably the best-known example. From ancient times, poets and prophets have cried out to the Lord in times of trial and discouragement, asking for his comfort and vindication.

Other hymns in our hymnal express the same longing. Examples are "Come, O Thou King of Kings" (no. 59) and "Come, Thou Glorious Day of Promise" (no. 50). (For other examples, see listings in the Topical Guide of the LDS edition of the King James Bible under "Jesus Christ—Second Coming" and "Millennium.") Just as our scriptures communicate expressions of longing and pleading as well as rejoicing and encouragement, so our hymns cover this same spectrum of emotion.

The moving hymn tune by B. Cecil Gates—named JACOB in honor of his father, Jacob F. Gates—is in a minor key, and it complements well the plaintive, longing message. This hymn was first printed in *Latter-day Saint Hymns* (1927).

Does the Journey Seem Long? 127

Text: Joseph Fielding Smith (1876–1972; LDS)
Music: George D. Pyper (1860–1943; LDS)
Tune name: FIELDING

Times of discouragement are part of everyone's lot in life, even for those who are certain that their commitment is wholehearted and their cause is righteous. "Does the Journey Seem Long?" is a hymn that can carry us through such moments—times of trial and weariness—when we should remember to "look upward in joy."

J. Spencer Cornwall noted of this hymn: "According to Elder Joseph Fielding Smith the words of this hymn were written while he was riding on a train to Arizona. When George D. Pyper saw the hymn, he asked for the privilege of writing the music for it." (*Stories of Our Mormon Hymns*, p. 250.) Elder Pyper named the tune FIELDING in honor of the author, and the hymn was first published in the 1927 Latter-day Saint hymnal.

Perhaps it was this train ride, as he saw miles of desert country passing by his window, that suggested to Joseph Fielding Smith the metaphor of the long journey. Or perhaps it was just that the train ride gave him some free time in his busy schedule to turn his thoughts to poetry.

The questions that form the first two verses show that Elder Smith had an intimate understanding of the burden of discouragement and sadness. Nevertheless, he took to heart throughout his life the admonitions that he expressed in this hymn. In 1970, more than forty years after he wrote these words, he was sustained as President of the Church. He was then ninety-three years old. His life validated the message of his hymn: do not give up the journey; do not yield to weariness; look toward the final goal and continue on.

The 1950 hymnal included one verse left out of the 1985 hymnal:

Are you weighed down with grief,
Is there pain in your breast,
As you wearily journey along?
Are you looking behind
To the valley below?
Do you wish you were back in the throng?

When Faith Endures 128

Text: Naomi W. Randall (b. 1908; LDS)
Music: Stephen M. Jones (b. 1960; LDS)
Tune name: WENDY

"When Faith Endures" is an unwavering statement of trust and assurance. As the scriptures repeatedly promise us, faith, prayers, and humility can cast out fear and anxiety. This truth receives a beautiful restatement in the hymn.

Author Naomi W. Randall told how the hymn came to be: "Through scripture study and discussion, I had been excited and lifted up in spirit with the statement made by Paul to Timothy in 2 Timothy 1:6–7: 'Stir up the gift of God, which is in thee. . . .

" 'For God hath not given us the spirit of fear; but of power, and of love, and of a sound mind.'

"A friend asked me to write a poem expressing my feelings and convictions. Immediately Paul's words came to my mind. So following some deep thought and sincere prayer during the summer of 1964, I penned my testimony. Through past experience I had come to know that fear does depart, and confidence, inner strength, and peace of mind come from love of God, genuine humility, and enduring faith!"

Composer Stephen Jones provided a detailed description of his hymn tune—a fascinating example of how a tune can underscore and emphasize the meaning of a text:

"The opening lines express faith and confidence in the Lord's love. Here the repeated, stable bass gives the music a solid, foundational beginning. The modulation in the second phrase lifts the music, depicting the 'inner strength and peace of mind' found through the Holy Ghost. The third phrase is the only one that does not begin with a solid, foundational bass. Here the bass and soprano move outward, opening the sound of the music and depicting the act of giving the Father our trust, prayers, and humility. The highest note in the melody occurs in this phrase, perhaps indicating a reaching out to God with the willingness spoken of in the text. The last phrase ends in long note values, suggesting the endurance we need to show in exercising our faith."

This text and tune were first printed in the 1985 hymnal.

Where Can I Turn for Peace? 129

Text: Emma Lou Thayne (b. 1924; LDS)
Music: Joleen G. Meredith (b. 1935; LDS)
Tune name: GRANT

"Who of us has not had Gethsemane times?" asked Emma Lou Thayne, author of this hymn. "And how often has each of us reached for the calm and the kindness that only the Savior can offer?" The honest and touching words of this hymn can help in difficult moments—first, because they help us realize that all men and women experience such moments, and second, because they remind us of the ultimate source of comfort and solace.

In 1971 the author and the composer, then members of the Young Women's Mutual Improvement Association General Board, were asked to write a musical number for a Laurel conference. Emma Lou Thayne telephoned Joleen Meredith to discuss the assignment.

Joleen Meredith continued the story: "I happened to be in the music room of our home at the time. Sister Thayne said she had been thinking of a message of hope and peace as the hymn's theme. As she began to relate some of the beginning lyrics, I stepped to the piano (I had a long telephone cord) and said, 'Sounds good—the music should go something like this . . .' She said 'good,' and gave me another line. I responded with additional measures of music. Before the conversation ended, we had mostly 'roughed in' the basic hymn. We have lovingly spoken of this number as the 'telephone hymn' throughout the years."

The text had a deep personal meaning for author Emma Lou Thayne.

"The words to the hymn came for me out of a troubled time for our family," she reported. "We had one daughter ill; I was facing a spinal fusion and interruption of teaching mid-quarter at the University of Utah; my husband was about to become bishop of a student ward; and four daughters were under the age of seventeen with busy lives. 'Pray at night, plan in the morning' had been the byword of our family; now it became 'Pray all the time.'

"It is ironic," she continued, "that the publishing and singing of this hymn happened in this particular year [1985] when hearing it and its long-ago but still-vital-to-me message has lent solace to a new time of personal trial. Five months ago a crowbar flew off the freeway and through my windshield to fracture eight bones in my face, barely missing my right eye. In this time, when reading and writing have not been part of my life, I have come to hear some inner music that is often prompted by the very searching that this hymn talks of. I am grateful for the unbelievably timely resurrection of the song that has helped so much in my own recent resurrection, a resurrection of what I might never have known without the trial and without the granted grace of the impulse to reach."

Joleen Meredith named the tune GRANT in honor of William Grant, her pioneer musician grandfather.

Be Thou Humble 130

Text and music: Grietje Terburg Rowley (b. 1927; LDS)
Tune name: BE THOU HUMBLE

The music and words of this tranquil hymn communicate beautifully the peace that comes with humble dependence on the Lord. What are the promised blessings if we are truly humble? Our prayers are answered; we enjoy peace of mind; we serve more effectively in our callings; and ultimately, we return to the Father who has led us, taught us, and blessed us.

Grietje Rowley said: "The words were written one wintry afternoon in 1981 when the house was quiet and still. Somehow they were put away and forgotten. Occasionally it would occur to me that I should find the words again and set them to music, but I just couldn't seem to get to it. Then late one night the first few measures came into my mind, unbidden, and I knew I would have to get them down on paper or they would be gone by morning. I worked late into the night until I had the basic melody written." This hymn was first printed in the 1985 hymnbook.

Grietje Rowley based her text directly on Doctrine and Covenants 112:10 and Ether 12:27. She noted: "I always pray for inspiration and guidance before I begin each composing session, and also many times during the process. I did so as I was working on this hymn, and each time a decision had to be made on a word or a note it seemed that the right choice was made clear to me. It was most reassuring."

Note the beautiful matching of tune and words, with the highest notes sung on the word *Lord* and all phrases resolved quietly and peacefully downward. It is also helpful to note the octave skip to the word *Lord* in the first line and the fact that the word *Lord* in the third line is one note higher than might be expected.

More Holiness Give Me 131

Text and music: Philip Paul Bliss (1838–1876)
Tune name: MY PRAYER

Influences of the world are always present to shape our character: the lure of wealth and power, the temptation of superficial pleasures. But Latter-day Saints choose not to be shaped by the world. This hymn is a prayer for Christlike qualities of character.

Philip Paul Bliss was a popular writer of gospel songs whose works became widely known in America near the end of the last century. Several of his hymns have been included in various Latter-day Saint collections. He wrote both words and music to "Brightly Beams Our Father's Mercy" (no. 335), and the tune to that hymn is also the setting for the text of "Should You Feel Inclined to Censure" (no. 235). "More Holiness Give Me" entered official Latter-day Saint hymnody when it was included in *Deseret Sunday School Songs*, 1909. In the 1985 hymnal, the time signature was changed from 12/8 to 4/4, making the music easier to read and direct.

This hymn text is a useful review of Christian qualities of character. The Savior himself is the source and example of these virtues, as indicated in the final line of the hymn: "More, Savior, like thee." After they are listed, one after the other, all of these qualities are finally summed up in this simple statement of the final goal—to be like Jesus Christ himself. As the Christian becomes more like the Savior, the "longing for home"—for a celestial life in the presence of the Savior—also increases.

God Is in His Holy Temple 132

*Text: Anonymous (*Hymns of the Spirit, *1864)*
Music: Frank W. Asper (1892–1973; LDS)
Tune name: WILSON

This unusual hymn text, though not by a Latter-day Saint author, will have particular significance for all Latter-day Saints who sing it. The presence of our Heavenly Father is always drawn to holy places, places that have been especially prepared for him. Each verse of this hymn uses the word *temple* to refer to such a place.

This hymn is a meditation upon Habbakuk 2:20: "But the Lord is in his holy temple: let all the earth keep silence before him."

To the mind of a Latter-day Saint, the word *temple* immediately suggests a building where faithful members of the Church meet to perform sacred ordinances, learn revealed truth, make eternal covenants, and dedicate themselves to the building up of the Lord's kingdom. The first verse of this hymn accords with this meaning of *temple.* A temple is a place where "with reverence we assemble / And before his presence bow." The holiness of the temple must be safeguarded, because the Lord has stated, "If it be defiled I will not come into it, and my glory shall not be there; for I will not come into unholy temples." (D&C 97:17.)

This citation from the Doctrine and Covenants is the first scriptural notation at the bottom of the hymn page. The second refers to the second meaning of *temple,* as it appears in verse two of this hymn. It is 1 Corinthians 3:16–17:

"Know ye not that ye are the temple of God, and that the Spirit of God dwelleth in you?

"If any man defile the temple of God, him shall God destroy; for the temple of God is holy, which temple ye are."

Just as the building known as the temple must be kept holy, so must the temple of our souls be free from defilement, so that the Lord's presence may dwell there, "In the reverent heart and simple, / In the soul from sin refined."

The tune name, WILSON, is the composer's middle name. The hymn was first published in *Latter-day Saint Hymns* (1927), but Frank W. Asper was not credited as composer.

Father in Heaven 133

Text: Angus S. Hibbard
Music: Friedrich F. Flemming (1778–1813);
arranged by Edwin Pond Parker (1836–1925)
Tune name: INTEGER VITAE or FLEMMING

Peace is the subject of the hymn "Father in Heaven." The first verse gives thanks for the peace we enjoy, the second asks for the heart of each worshiper to be filled with peace, and the third petitions the Lord to strengthen every nation of the world "in thy great peace where only is salvation."

The satisfying music of this hymn was originally written in 1811 for men's voices. Friedrich F. Flemming wrote many such songs, but only this one is often sung today; this tune alone earned him a place in *Grove's Dictionary of Music and Musicians*. The tune name, INTEGER VITAE, comes from the Latin text for which Flemming originally composed the music. That text is an ode by Horace that begins with the words, "*Integer vitae sclerisque purus,*" meaning "Blameless of life and free from guilt." The tune also goes by the name of FLEMMING, and it appears with various texts in other Christian hymnals.

Few hymns in our hymnal communicate such security and faith. The text features nouns that name positive emotions and feelings, such as *love, peace, joy,* and *trust*. Other important words, such as *abiding, firm,* and *enduring,* indicate that we know these feelings and emotions will be eternal, because of our faith in our Father in Heaven. Psalm 29:11, one of the scripture citations listed below the hymn, embodies the message of this confident, joyful hymn: "The Lord will give strength unto his people; the Lord will bless his people with peace."

I Believe in Christ 134

Text: Bruce R. McConkie (1915–1985; LDS)
Music: John Longhurst (b. 1940; LDS)
Tune name: WHITE CITY

Coming straight from the heart of a man who had devoted his life to studying about the Savior and serving him, the text of this hymn is truly a powerful declaration of faith in Jesus Christ, a definitive testimony of His divinity and mission.

The members of the Church first heard the words of this hymn when Elder Bruce R. McConkie, a member of the Quorum of the Twelve Apostles, delivered them as part of his general conference address in

April 1972. Elder McConkie's widow, Amelia S. McConkie, said that her husband "loved to express his love for the scriptures and Christ in poetry." The eight verses attracted considerable attention. They were first given an anthem setting by Latter-day Saint composer Rhea B. Allen and were performed by the Tabernacle Choir. The simpler hymn setting, created by John Longhurst for the 1985 hymnal, was introduced to the Church by the Tabernacle Choir at general conference in April 1985. John Longhurst noted, "This was Elder McConkie's last conference—the one in which he left his final testimony in a way that those who heard it shall never forget."

At that conference, Elder McConkie bore a powerful, moving witness of Jesus Christ: "I testify that he is the Son of the Living God and was crucified for the sins of the world. He is our Lord, our God, and our King. This I know of myself independent of any other person.

"I am one of his witnesses, and in a coming day I shall feel the nail marks in his hands and in his feet and shall wet his feet with my tears.

"But I shall not know any better then than I know now that he is God's Almighty Son, that he is our Savior and Redeemer, and that salvation comes in and through his atoning blood and in no other way." (*Ensign*, May 1985, p. 11.)

The words of this hymn are the words of a servant of the Lord who spent his life speaking and writing about the Savior. The text is a grand and sweeping testimony of Jesus Christ. Doubt and unhappiness disappear as faith in Jesus Christ dominates every thought and feeling.

The powerful musical setting in our hymnbook, as unwavering as the text, emphasizes the uplifting and positive nature of the words. As John Longhurst was working on the music, his first impulse was to cut the number of verses from eight to four, since he felt this length to be about right for current hymn usage. But Elder McConkie, whose health at that time did not permit extensive revision or collaboration with regard to this hymn, wished all eight verses of his testimony to be included. The solution was to create an eight-line hymn instead of a four-line hymn; each hymn verse actually includes two verses of the original poem. The first half of each verse is almost identical musically to the second half.

John Longhurst named the tune WHITE CITY because he began work on the tune while riding the White City bus in Salt Lake City.

My Redeemer Lives 135

Text: Gordon B. Hinckley (b. 1910; LDS)
Music: G. Homer Durham (1911–1985; LDS)
Tune name: EUDORA

President Gordon B. Hinckley, First Counselor in the First Presidency of The Church of Jesus Christ of Latter-day Saints, recorded in verse his testimony of the Savior. In the most unequivocal language, this hymn declares the divinity and mission of Jesus Christ. The images of light, faith, and security that are used so effectively in the text are familiar to every Latter-day Saint.

President Hinckley's poem first appeared in the *New Era* magazine in April 1983. Several composers submitted musical settings, one of which was to be chosen to be paired with the text in the 1985 hymnbook. President Hinckley himself expressed a preference for a simple setting. In his words, he wanted something he "could easily sing to the cows while milking them."

When President Hinckley first heard Elder G. Homer Durham's hymn tune, without knowing the name of the composer, he felt it was just the kind of direct, simple tune he had hoped for. When he learned the composer's identity, he was even more pleased. The two men had been lifelong friends, from grade school through college and mission days and beyond.

Beth S. Rasmussen, for eight years secretary to the hymn's composer, the late Elder G. Homer Durham, a member of the First Quorum of the Seventy, recorded her memories of Elder Durham's writing of the hymn tune. One weekend in March 1983, when Elder Durham traveled on assignment to a stake conference, he took with him a copy of the most recent *New Era* magazine, which included the poem, "My Redeemer Lives," by President Hinckley. By the time he returned home, he had sketched a hymn tune, which he said came quite easily to him as he read the poem. After he had written out the tune in final form, Beth Rasmussen suggested to him that they show it to Michael Moody, executive director of the Church Music Department. She reported, "Following a series of telephone calls a letter arrived in June 1984 which indicated Elder Durham's hymn tune had been selected for inclusion in the new hymnal. . . . After receiving a list of other suggested titles, Elder Durham wrote in bold, blue ink:

> 1st choice—'My Redeemer Lives'
> 2nd choice—'My Redeemer Lives'
> 3rd choice—'My Redeemer Lives'

He explained to me that although there are other well-known hymns with similar titles, he could not improve upon the title President Hinckley had given his own poem. I agreed wholeheartedly."

The tune name honors Eudora W. Durham, wife of the composer.

I Know That My Redeemer Lives 136

Text: Samuel Medley (1738–1799)
Music: Lewis D. Edwards (1858–1921; LDS)
Tune name: HE LIVES

Edward P. Kimball, composer and Tabernacle organist, had such a testimony of the power of this hymn that he offered this promise: "When doubt, discouragement, or any foe of the spirit of God manifests itself, pray and then sing or even play this truly inspired song and a new light to cheer and bless will kindle your soul." (Quoted in George D. Pyper, *Stories of Latter-day Saint Hymns*, p. 134.)

Samuel Medley, who wrote this text in 1775, was fond of alliteration and repetition in his hymns. Twenty-six of the thirty-two lines of "I Know That My Redeemer Lives" begin with the same two words: "He lives."

Repetition is not necessarily a fault in a hymn. Sometimes it is the very repetition that conveys the earnestness of the hymn's pleading or the conviction of its message. Consider, for example, "Nearer, My God, To Thee" (no. 100), "Count Your Blessings" (no. 241), "I Need Thee Every Hour" (no. 98), and "If You Could Hie to Kolob" (no. 284). Each of these hymns, too, is characterized by a key phrase repeated many times, and the repetition adds emphasis to the message.

The text of "I Know That My Redeemer Lives" appeared in Emma Smith's 1835 hymnal as seven short verses. When the short verses were combined to form long ones, the last verse needed to be repeated in order to fit the new musical format. But here again, repetition is a strength instead of a weakness; repeating the words in the last verse is like adding an additional witness or an extra "amen" to the testimony expressed in the hymn.

Two talented Latter-day Saints from among our early composers, George Careless and Edwin F. Parry, wrote musical settings for "I Know That My Redeemer Lives." But a melody by another Latter-day Saint, Lewis D. Edwards, published in 1901, has been the one to strike the right emotional chord among Latter-day Saints. Comments George D. Pyper, "If Samuel Medley had been here to direct he could not have suggested a tune more appropriate than this one, for Edwards caught Medley's style by giving accent to the key words which the hymnist loved to repeat in his refrains. As far as the Latter-day Saints are concerned, Edwards has linked his name with Medley's for all time." (*Stories of Latter-day Saint Hymns*, pp. 136-37.)

Writing in the 1920s, George D. Pyper noted a response to this hymn that continues today: "To hear this loved song rendered by an assembly of devoted Latter-day Saints is a spiritual baptism. It becomes a mass-testimony of many of the truths of the restored Gospel of Jesus Christ." (P. 135.)

Testimony 137

Text: Loren C. Dunn (b. 1930; LDS)
Music: Michael Finlinson Moody (b. 1941; LDS)
Tune name: TORONTO

In the memory of each Latter-day Saint are spiritual highlights to be treasured and recalled again and again. Often these sacred memories have to do with the sharing of testimonies. A testimony meeting was the inspiration for the words of this hymn.

In the early 1970s, Elder Loren C. Dunn, of the First Quorum of the Seventy, attended a seminar of Regional Representatives in Salt Lake City. Those in attendance bore such powerful testimonies that two of the General Authorities in attendance—Elder Dunn and Elder Bruce R. McConkie—were moved to jot down some lines of poetry before the meeting had finished. The lines by Elder Dunn became the first verse of "Testimony"; the rest of the poem came later.

Most Latter-day Saints will recognize the beautiful feelings expressed in these lines and will welcome a text that clothes these feelings in such expressive and accurate words. The love and faith shared by "those who know" has lifted the writer's spirit above the pain of day-to-day discouragement: "For one brief moment, heaven's view / Appears before my gaze."

Throughout his life Elder Dunn has expressed his feelings and insights through poetry; originally these lines were not intended as a hymn text. But later, when he shared his poem with Michael Moody, they discussed the possibility of a musical setting for four of the original six verses. Text and tune were first published together in *Hymns, 1985*.

"If those who sing this or any hymn will really think about the hymn's message, it should be an uplifting experience," said composer Michael Moody. "This is a simple hymn tune that came easily; I tried to achieve a quiet reflection of the words.

"I enjoy the process of composing music. My ideas don't usually come in brilliant flashes; more often it's a gentle, peaceful process. I think trying to create something under inspiration is often a matter of bringing long-range preparation and enlightenment to a particular opportunity."

He pointed out that the melody ends on the third note of the scale rather than on the keynote; his purpose was to create a "sense of continuation," since ideally the message and feelings of the hymn would carry on and on.

The tune is named for Maria Toronto, wife of Michael Moody.

Bless Our Fast, We Pray 138

Text: John Sears Tanner (b. 1950; LDS)
Music: James B. Welch (b. 1950; LDS)
Tune name: FASTING

What are the feelings and experiences of a meaningful Fast Sunday? Within the space of three short verses, this perceptive hymn provides an overview and a reminder. The congregation humbly seeks the Spirit of the Lord after having prepared for this blessing through the fast.

John Tanner and James Welch have been friends since they met as missionary companions in Brazil in 1970. "Bless Our Fast, We Pray" was a prizewinner in the *Ensign* hymn-writing contest in 1984. Though James Welch is a professional musician and John Tanner is a professional in the field of literature, this collaboration was the first hymn-writing experience for both.

John Tanner began the text on Fast Sunday in March 1983. "I remembered," he said, "that President Spencer W. Kimball said writing devotional poetry was an appropriate Sunday activity." After polishing the text during that month, he sent it to James Welch to be set to music. After the hymn was selected as a winner in the *Ensign* contest, however, it underwent considerable revision before appearing in the 1985 hymnal. James Welch gives credit to hard work and careful craftsmanship: "I just kept sitting at the piano and writing and erasing and writing."

Each verse of this hymn deals with a different aspect of the law of the fast: first, prayer; second, offerings; third, testimonies. After each statement of what *we* have done, the chorus asks the Lord for his presence in return. The chorus plays on the paradoxical similarity of the words *fast* and *feast*: we have gone without food, and yet we feast upon the Spirit of the Lord.

The hymn is a useful self-test: each member can ponder the question, "Can I honestly sing these words as a reflection of my Fast Sunday experience?"

In Fasting We Approach Thee 139

Text: Paul L. Anderson (b. 1946; LDS)
Music: Clay Christiansen (b. 1949; LDS)
Tune name: FRANCOM

What are the purposes of fasting? This hymn describes the spiritual growth and the distinctive blessings that come from a sincere, prayerful fast. Latter-day Saints will wish to set this text alongside their personal Fast Sunday experiences as a reminder of the potential blessings of the fast. The entire hymn is a prayer that our Father in Heaven will sanctify our fast.

Author Paul L. Anderson reported that he took a very practical approach when he decided to write a hymn text about Fast Sunday: because the 1950 hymnbook had no hymns about fasting, he felt that a text on this topic would stand a good chance of being accepted in the new hymnbook. His fine text eventually became one of two new hymns on this subject to be included in the 1985 hymnal.

But his motives were not entirely practical. "Several years ago, when I taught a Sunday School lesson on the subject of fasting, I had clarified in my own mind some thoughts about the blessings of the fast," he stated. "I felt that a text on this subject would meet a real need. I wanted to express the importance of fasting as a personal spiritual preparation, and verse one plays off the idea of being hungry against the idea of being filled at the same time. Verse two states that the hunger we feel when we fast reminds us of our dependence on the Lord for life and strength. Verse three focuses on another purpose of the fast: increased feelings of charity for those who are in need. And verse four is about the feelings of peace and joy that come from keeping the law of the fast."

Tabernacle organist Clay Christiansen described the feelings that brought forth his hymn tune: "Fasting is an act of humility done without show or fanfare. Such is the tune: humble, simple, without show or fanfare, but hopefully strong." The composer stated that his intention was to write a hymn that was "a worthy example of simplicity for congregation and organist alike. It should need very little—if any—teaching to a congregation beyond simply singing its stanzas a time or two."

He named the hymn tune FRANCOM in honor of his wife, Diane Francom.

Did You Think to Pray? 140

Text: Mary A. Pepper Kidder (1820–1905)
Music: William O. Perkins (1831–1902)
Tune name: STOCKBRIDGE

Most of us know from experience that even a few moments devoted to prayer in the morning can change our outlook for the better throughout the day. The greater the demands of the day, the greater seems to be our need for a private communication with the Lord. This hymn's message is a reminder of this important truth.

Each verse of this hymn expresses a distinct, important purpose for prayer. First, the "loving favor" of the Lord will serve as a protection during the day. The scripture citation at the end of the hymn (Psalm 5:3, 12) shows that this thought dates from Old Testament times:

"My voice shalt thou hear in the morning, O Lord; in the morning will I direct my prayer unto thee, and will look up. . . .

"For thou, Lord, wilt bless the righteous; with favour wilt thou compass him as with a shield."

Second, prayer will keep us from the destructive effects of anger. To extend forgiveness to another person is to be like the Lord, who in his patience forgives his children daily.

Third, prayer will ease our burden in times of sorrow and trial. Prayer will serve as "balm of Gilead." This expression is taken from Jeremiah 8:22: "Is there no balm in Gilead; is there no physician there?" When we are suffering from sorrow's wounds, we pray for an ointment to heal those wounds. The Bible Dictionary in the Latter-day Saint edition of the King James Bible explains that balm is "an aromatic gum or spice used for healing wounds. . . . A bush producing the resin from which the balm was made grew so plentifully in Gilead in O. T. times that the balm came to be known as the 'balm of Gilead.' " (P. 618, under "balm.") We can borrow this salve by means of our morning prayers "at the gates of day."

The tune name, STOCKBRIDGE, honors the composer's birthplace, Stockbridge, Vermont. The hymn entered Latter-day Saint hymnody in 1884 in the second edition of the *Deseret Sunday School Union Music Book*. The 1985 hymnal restored the more descriptive title to this hymn, "Did You Think to Pray?"

Jesus, the Very Thought of Thee 141; 315

Text: Attributed to St. Bernard of Clairvaux (ca. 1091–1153); translated by Edward Caswall (1814–1878)
Music: John B. Dykes (1823–1876)
Tune name: ST. AGNES

This renowned hymn text is not a hymn of doctrine or exhortation. It is simply a meditation upon the name and spirit of Jesus. St. Bernard was a man of intense and emotional faith, and the ecstatic phrases of his hymn help us to center our thoughts on the Savior and give utterance to our praise and gratitude.

St. Bernard's original Latin poem, written near the beginning of the twelfth century, is a joyous outpouring of feeling. It has sometimes been referred to as the "Rose Hymn" or "Rosy Hymn," or by its Latin title "*Jubilus rhythmicus de nomine Jesu*" ("Joyful rhythm on the name of Jesus"). In the original it is 192 lines long; the poem and many excerpts from it have been translated by both Catholic and Protestant writers over the centuries. The translator of the version in our hymnal was Edward Caswall, an Englishman who began as a clergyman in the Church of England but converted later to Roman Catholicism. In his translation, he wrote that it is "sweeter far" to see the face of Jesus and rest in his presence. It is interesting that the original Latin has a more tangible comparison: to see the face of Jesus is "sweeter than honey."

On many occasions, revelation and guidance have come to prophets and Church leaders as they meditated upon the scriptures or on other serious matters. Meditation on sacred subjects is perhaps something that happens too seldom among Latter-day Saints. The words of St. Bernard remind us how rich and significant such an experience can be. They are an actualization of the words of Psalm 104:34: "My meditation of him shall be sweet: I will be glad in the Lord."

The tune, written in 1866, was named after St. Agnes, in Catholic tradition a Christian maiden who lived in ancient Rome and at age thirteen was beheaded for her beliefs by the Emperor Diocletian. John B. Dykes, the composer, also wrote LUX BENIGNA, the tune for "Lead, Kindly Light" (no. 97).

Sweet Hour of Prayer 142

Text: Attributed to William W. Walford (1772–1850); altered
Music: William B. Bradbury (1816–1868); altered
Tune name: SWEET HOUR

Some hymns address the Father directly; in others, we exhort one another to good works or speak words of personal commitment. This hymn is unusual in that it is addressed to the "hour of prayer" itself. Speaking as if to a person, we express gratitude for the rest and comfort it provides amid the distractions and cares of daily life.

J. Spencer Cornwall observed that "this hymn is appealing to large numbers of people, due to its solemnity and its contemplative character." (*Stories of Our Mormon Hymns*, p. 184.) The text is said to have been written in 1842 by the Reverend William W. Walford, a blind English minister. The Reverend Thomas Salmon, pastor of the Congregational Church at Coleshill, England, wrote it down as Reverend Walford spoke the words; he had it published in the New York *Observer* in 1845.

The two verses in our hymnal are just as in Reverend Walford's original; however, the hymn originally had an additional verse that has been omitted in Latter-day Saint hymnals. As a matter of interest, the missing verse is given below; the phrase "God my Savior" is not consonant with Latter-day Saint belief in a three-member Godhead, and thus the verse is more suitable for a Protestant hymnal than for ours:

Sweet hour of prayer! sweet hour of prayer!
The joys I feel, the bliss I share
Of those whose anxious spirits burn
With strong desires for thy return!
With such I hasten to the place
Where God my Savior shows his face,
And gladly take my station there,
And wait for thee, sweet hour of prayer!

Editors of some modern hymnals shorten the tune to avoid the repetition of the last two lines. The omitted measures are those that appear as the next to last line of music in our hymnal.

Let the Holy Spirit Guide 143

Text: Penelope Moody Allen (b. 1939; LDS)
Music: Martin Shaw (1875–1958)
Tune name: GENTLE JESUS

What is the function of the Holy Spirit in our lives? This brief hymn is a wonderful teaching vehicle for adults and children. It is a tribute to the author's skill that within these three verses we have such a complete overview of the function of the Spirit: he will guide us, enlighten us, testify of Christ, protect us, and comfort us with his healing power.

Penelope Allen took the inspiration for her opening line from the title of an old hymn by Edwin F. Parry. "I was informed that my text had been accepted for the 1985 hymnbook," she reported, "and then the work began. The Hymnbook Committee liked the text in general, but we all had a belief that the hymn should relate as many functions of the Spirit as possible in its three short stanzas." Phone calls went back and forth, and she worked out several revisions for various lines of the text. In her words, "Every word was worked out painfully."

Then, the day before the hymn was to go to the printer, another call came from a Hymnbook Committee representative. Penelope Allen recalled the message: " 'Sister Allen, I almost didn't have the nerve to call you again, but we're still not completely satisfied with the last two lines. We feel we've been speaking of what the Spirit does for us, and now, at the end, we'd like to speak of what we can do to receive the Spirit. The line as it reads isn't quite as active as we'd like it.' "

She had made many alterations already, but she spent the evening seeking a different emphasis for the last line until, as she said, "the words blurred before my eyes. No changes would come to mind. Of course I prayed. But nothing came, and I went to bed with my evening prayers supplicating help.

"In the morning I awoke with a word in my mind: 'purity.' It was the key. I wrote 'May we purify our lives / To receive him hour by hour,' and I had the bedrock feeling that it was right."

Penelope Allen's text was paired with the tune that usually accompanies Charles Wesley's hymn for children beginning "Gentle Jesus, meek and mild"; thus the tune name.

Secret Prayer 144

Text and music: Hans Henry Petersen (1835–1909; LDS)
Tune name: SLAGELSE

Elder Bruce R. McConkie wrote, "Every good gift comes to those who through faith and prayer are enabled to abide the law upon which its receipt is predicated." (*Mormon Doctrine*, 2d ed. [Salt Lake City, Utah: Bookcraft, 1966], p. 587.) This important teaching is the basis for the hymn "Secret Prayer."

As we sing this hymn, we should try to enter into these sentiments with conviction, thus reinforcing our individual appreciation for the opportunity of private prayer and our commitment to seek out this "hour of peace and rest" more often. We repeat the first-person pronouns *I* and *my* some fifteen times. This personal focus in a hymn about prayer is an appropriately Latter-day Saint emphasis, since we believe strongly in direct personal prayers rather than the formal, set prayers used on occasion in other denominations.

The words and the music of this Latter-day Saint hymn were written by Hans Henry Petersen while he was director of the Hyrum Stake choir around the turn of the century. Though a native of Denmark, he quickly absorbed the tradition of the American gospel song. Characteristics of the gospel song, as shown in "Secret Prayer," are the verse-chorus division, the dotted rhythms, the tenor/bass "answering" harmony of the chorus, and a spirit of energetic exhortation. The hymn was first published in *Deseret Sunday School Song Book* in 1909.

Hans Henry Petersen wished to make vivid the problems and difficulties of life that can be solved by prayer, and to this end he chose two metaphors: in verse three life's trials are compared with a stormy sea beset with "billows of despair," and in verse four they are likened to a difficult journey along a pathway strewn with snares.

The tune name, SLAGELSE, honors the Danish village that was the birthplace of Hans Henry Petersen.

Prayer Is the Soul's Sincere Desire 145

Text: James Montgomery (1771–1854)
Music: George Careless (1839–1932; LDS)
Tune name: PRAYER

One writer said that this hymn is "a collection of beautiful metaphors that describe prayer: hidden fire, a sigh, a falling tear, an upward glance, vital breath. The plain prose of the first line is as good a definition of prayer as one can find in short compass." (Albert Edward Bailey, *The Gospel in Hymns* [New York: Charles Scribner's Sons, 1950], p. 161.)

This hymn and two other texts in our hymnal, "A Poor, Wayfaring Man of Grief" (no. 29) and "The Lord Is My Shepherd" (no. 108), show the remarkable range of subject matter to which James Montgomery turned his talents. In "Prayer Is the Soul's Sincere Desire" (1819), his entire focus was on prayer: what it is, what occasions bring it forth, and why it is essential to any follower of Jesus Christ.

In the editing of the 1985 hymnal, an effort was made to omit whenever possible any verses of a hymn that would not fit conveniently between the rows of music. The extra verses of many of these long hymns were seldom sung and made the page too crowded. But in some cases, such as this one, exceptions had to be made. Each verse of "Prayer Is the Soul's Sincere Desire" examines a different facet of prayer, just as light reflects from each of the facets that make up a beautiful diamond. All eight verses treat the same subject, yet there is no repetition; each makes a different point. Thus the decision was made not to omit any of the eight verses of this hymn.

Latter-day Saints are fortunate to have a tune from one of our own composers, George Careless, that suits very well the elegance and simplicity of this text. George D. Pyper called this tune "one of the most beautiful compositions of that gifted musician." (*Stories of Latter-day Saint Hymns*, p. 184.) The tune was first published in the *Utah Musical Times* in 1876, with the present text.

Gently Raise the Sacred Strain 146

Text: William W. Phelps (1792–1872; LDS)
Music: Thomas C. Griggs (1845–1903; LDS)
Tune name: URE

Known to millions as the hymn that begins each weekly broadcast of the Tabernacle Choir, "Gently Raise the Sacred Strain" is a tribute to the peace and blessings of the Sabbath. And what better theme song could be chosen for the broadcast? William W. Phelps and Thomas C. Griggs could not have guessed how well their hymn would echo the expectations of countless listeners who wait for the Tabernacle Choir to "raise the sacred strain" each Sunday.

In the words of George D. Pyper: "There is no dramatic story known concerning the origin of the hymn. It was no doubt written while Brother Phelps was under the spell of the Sabbath and the solemn Sacrament. It expresses gratitude for the return of the day of rest and its attendant blessings, thoughts on eternal life. . . . It sings of repentance and forgiveness." (*Stories of Latter-day Saint Hymns*, p. 129.)

The hymn text first appeared in Emma Smith's 1835 hymnal, and all six of the original verses were retained in the 1950 hymnal. The hymn as it appears in the 1985 hymnal omits two of the verses, however, since all six were seldom sung. The two omitted verses are numbers four and six of the original. The thought expressed in verse four is especially interesting, since here the peace and song of a Sabbath-day meeting are seen as a foretaste of the life that is our heavenly reward.

4. *Happy type of things to come,*
   When the saints are gather'd home,
   To praise the Lord,
   In eternity of bliss,
   All as one with one accord.

6. *Softly sing the joyful lay*
   For the saints to fast and pray,
   As God ordains,
   For his goodness and his love
   While the Sabbath day remains.

Especially significant in the "extra" verse (originally verse five) that was included as verse four in the 1985 hymnbook are these words: "Repent and live; / Though your sins be crimson red, / Oh, repent, and he'll forgive." These words are a beautiful extension of the sacramental image in verse three: "We bring our gifts . . . / Of broken hearts." These two verses enlarge the functions of this hymn about the Sabbath day: it becomes a meaningful sacrament hymn as well.

Thomas Griggs's beautiful hymn tune was first published, with these words, in the *Juvenile Instructor* in November 1883.

Sweet Is the Work 147; 317

Text: Isaac Watts (1674–1748)
Music: John J. McClellan (1874–1925; LDS)
Tune name: DOUGLASS

The work referred to in the title of this hymn is not manual labor. It is the work of the Sabbath: to sing praises to the Lord, to thank him, and to talk of his truths. As we sing the beautiful and confident sentiments of this hymn, we are in fact carrying out its message—doing the "sweet" work of the Sabbath by singing a hymn of praise.

Our present hymnal includes nine texts by Isaac Watts. His place in Latter-day Saint hymnody has always been an important one; in fact, out of ninety hymns in Emma Smith's 1835 hymnal, fifteen were by Isaac Watts! "Sweet Is the Work" was not part of that first Latter-day Saint hymnal, but today we can hardly imagine a Latter-day Saint hymn collection without this fine hymn, accompanied by the beautiful musical setting by former Tabernacle organist John J. McClellan.

The hymn's original title (1719) was "A Psalm for the Lord's Day." The word *psalm* in the title perfectly expresses the hymn's purpose: it is to praise the Lord and glorify the prospect of salvation in his presence. The hymn has fairly close parallels to one of the Old Testament psalms:

"It is a good thing to give thanks unto the Lord, and to sing praises unto thy name, O most High:

"To shew forth thy lovingkindness in the morning, and thy faithfulness every night." (Psalm 92:1-2.)

It gives us an insight into the creative process to note that the next verse of the psalm, "Upon an instrument of ten strings, and upon the psaltery; upon the harp with a solemn sound," set Isaac Watts's poetic imagination on a path that resulted in one of the most beautiful figures of speech in the hymn: "Oh, may my heart in tune be found, / Like David's harp of solemn sound!"

The tune name, DOUGLASS, is for John J. McClellan's wife, Mary

Douglass. The tune was first published in the 1892 *Deseret Sunday School Song Book.*

Sabbath Day 148

Text: Paul L. Anderson (b. 1946; LDS)
Music: Lynn R. Carson (b. 1942; LDS)
Tune name: CELESTIA

Worship is not limited to our church meetings; the Sabbath brings opportunities for other kinds of worship also, including family and private devotion. Each verse of this hymn ends with a prayer asking our Father in Heaven to bless us throughout the Sabbath day, as we worship him in these various settings.

Author Paul L. Anderson stated: "This is really a hymn about the consolidated meeting schedule. Many people were concerned about what would happen when Latter-day Saints were in Sunday meetings for only three hours. What would we do with the rest of the time? The first verse mentions gathering in the house of the Lord, and then verses two and three refer to other appropriate Sabbath activities—sharing time with friends and family 'in our homes,' and finding a 'quiet hour' for individual reading and contemplation." He noted further, "This was my first serious attempt at hymn-writing, and I was pleased when it won first place in the 1983 *Ensign* hymn-writing contest." It was first published in the *Ensign* in March of that year.

When composer Lynn Carson was traveling in South Africa in 1981 on assignment for the Church Genealogical Department, he composed a hymn tune in the form of "a nineteenth-century Anglican-style chant." When his friend and fellow ward member Paul Anderson showed him the "Sabbath Day" hymn text, he realized that his tune would need only slight modification to fit these words. Paul Anderson noted that the steady, marching, "heartbeat" rhythm of the bass line gives the music a dignity and quiet strength that makes it a satisfying match for the text. Text and tune became part of Latter-day Saint hymnody with the publication of the 1985 hymnbook.

As the Dew from Heaven Distilling 149

Text: Thomas Kelly (1769–1854)
Music: Joseph J. Daynes (1851–1920; LDS)
Tune name: BOUNTIFUL

The beautiful strains of this hymn tune are the traditional close of the Tabernacle Choir's weekly broadcast. Generations of Latter-day Saints as well as untold numbers of radio listeners and television viewers have come to love this peaceful, tender melody by former Tabernacle organist Joseph J. Daynes.

For many decades, Latter-day Saints have taken for granted the attribution of this hymn text to Parley P. Pratt; however, hymn researcher Bruce David Maxwell brought to light some new information about the hymn's origin. Parley P. Pratt, with his great love for truth and exactness, would no doubt be grateful to see the "clouds of error disappear." (See no. 1.)

Parley P. Pratt did not claim authorship of the hymn during his lifetime; his name was wrongly attached to the words after his death. As Bruce David Maxwell pointed out: "This hymn was virtually unknown in the United States outside the LDS tradition. For this reason later editors posthumously misattributed it to Parley Pratt. . . . The discovery of this hymn in a book of Thomas Kelly's hymnody published one year before Parley Pratt's birth merely corrects a long-standing error and in no way diminishes the LDS poet's accomplishment." ("Source Book for *Hymns* [1950]," p. 84.)

The hymn text is found in *Hymns on Various Passages of Scripture* (Dublin, 1806), a collection of texts by Thomas Kelly, who also wrote "Zion Stands with Hills Surrounded" (no. 43). The first Latter-day Saint source to print "As the Dew" was the 1840 *Collection of Sacred Hymns*, edited by Parley P. Pratt, Brigham Young, and John Taylor. The only words changed in our present hymnal from Thomas Kelly's original text are the words "*Thy sweet Spirit* shed around" in the fourth verse. Thomas Kelly wrote, "*Sweetest influence* shed around."

The metaphor in verses one and two—of doctrinal truths "descending from above" like "the dews from heaven"—is from an Old Testament verse:

"My doctrine shall drop as the rain, my speech shall distil as the dew, as the small rain upon the tender herb, and as the showers upon the grass." (Deuteronomy 32:2.)

It is not surprising that this hymn text would be loved by Latter-day Saints, who believe in continuing modern revelation.

We can be grateful that the record has at last been set straight, and that the Church has preserved this fine text as one of its most significant hymns. In the words of George D. Pyper, "When it is sung with the proper emotional feeling, a reverential seal is put upon the spoken word, through the power of music; and the congregation is guided into a spirit of adoration and confession and drawn one step nearer to the Infinite." (*Stories of Latter-day Saint Hymns*, p. 178.)

The tune, BOUNTIFUL, was first published in the 1889 *Latter-day Saints' Psalmody*, with the Thomas Kelly text.

O Thou Kind and Gracious Father 150

Text: Charles Denney, Jr. (1849–1937; LDS)
Music: George Careless (1839–1932; LDS)
Tune name: SERENITY

The words of this unassuming prayer are an excellent preparation for a Sabbath meeting. A congregation that sings these words with sincere attention will be in a reverent and teachable frame of mind. The love that is felt in the meeting and the truths that are shared can lead toward the final goal expressed in the hymn: "Help us all to gain salvation."

The fine, graceful tune by George Careless appeared twice in the 1950 hymnal. It served not only as the setting for "O Thou Kind and Gracious Father," but also for the John Jaques text "Softly Beams the Sacred Dawning." For many Latter-day Saints, however, the tune has remained a fairly unfamiliar one because both hymns were included as choir hymns rather than as part of the congregational section of the 1950 hymnal.

The tune was considered too difficult for congregational use for three reasons. First, the third and fourth phrases were written for women's voices alone, and it is not realistic to expect an entire congregation to follow such a sophisticated arrangement. Second, the melodic range of more than an octave is quite demanding. And third, the rapid movement of certain sections of the melodic line would be difficult even for a congregation familiar with the hymn.

But it was decided to include "O Thou Kind and Gracious Father," with the Careless setting, for congregational use in the 1985 hymnal. A new musical arrangement was made to include men's voices for the entire hymn. The key of the hymn was lowered, helping somewhat in the matter of the vocal range. It still remains a rather difficult hymn melody, but a congregation's patience with this hymn will be well repaid.

"Softly Beams the Sacred Dawning" (no. 56) was also retained in the 1985 hymnal but with a new musical setting.

We Meet, Dear Lord 151

Text: Vernald W. Johns (b. 1902; LDS)
Music: Laurence M. Yorgason (b. 1937; LDS)
Tune name: VERNALD

Faithful Latter-day Saints attend their church meetings week after week. What can we do so that this attendance does not become an unthinking routine? This hymn reminds us of the joy and blessings of gathering in our "Sabbath home." It offers praise to the Lord for blessings that come from meeting together: our Sabbath meetings are an opportunity to learn the gospel, feel the Lord's presence, associate with friends, pray together, and sing the praises of the Lord.

"A need for an expression in song of the particular blessings to be enjoyed from participating in our church services on the Sabbath led me to write the lines for 'We Meet, Dear Lord,' " reported Vernald W. Johns. The 1985 Hymnbook Committee sent the text to Laurence Yorgason and asked him for a musical setting. He noted, "The author is an uncle of mine, so I hoped that I would be able to write something that would enhance the text." He named the tune in his uncle's honor.

Among all the aspects of Sabbath meeting that are mentioned, one that receives special emphasis in verse two is the singing of hymns. When a congregation sings together, this act of collective worship and prayer helps to bring about many of the other blessings cited in the hymn—the pledging of faithfulness, the feeling of oneness, and the rejoicing in the Sabbath day. Vernald Johns commented, "As a song leader in the Church, I found it natural to think of joyfulness in terms of song."

God Be with You Till We Meet Again 152

Text: Jeremiah E. Rankin (1828–1904)
Music: William G. Tomer (1833–1896)
Tune name: GOD BE WITH YOU

Because of its connection with countless missionary farewells and other partings, "God Be with You Till We Meet Again" automatically strikes a sentimental chord in the hearts of most Latter-day Saints. It is a song wishing protection and safety for loved ones at the time of farewell.

The author, Jeremiah E. Rankin, explained that the text was "deliberately composed as a Christian hymn on the basis of the etymology of 'good-by,' which is 'God be with you.' " (Quoted in Charles S. Nutter and Wilbur F. Tillett, *The Hymns and Hymn Writers of the Church* [New York: Methodist Book Concern, 1911], p. 295.) This original form of the word *good-bye* constitutes most of the hymn text. In the three stanzas in the hymnbook, the phrase "God be with you" is sung nine times, and the phrase "till we meet" is sung twenty-four times.

The dotted rhythms and the verse/chorus structure mark this as a hymn in the gospel-song tradition. It was first published in 1883 in a collection titled *Gospel Bells.*

Even though the hymn is almost always used as a good-bye hymn, the chorus changes the meaning from a single farewell to a good-bye "till we meet" in heaven. When we bid good-bye, we do not usually plan to wait that long for a reunion; for this reason, many hymnals omit the chorus entirely.

A verse omitted from our hymnal is this one:

God be with you till we meet again;
Neath his wings securely hide you,
Daily manna still provide you:
God be with you till we meet again.

Lord, We Ask Thee Ere We Part 153

Text: George Manwaring (1854–1889; LDS)
Music: Benjamin Milgrove (1731–1810; LDS);
arranged by Ebenezer Beesley (1840–1906)
Tune name: HARTS

J. Spencer Cornwall called this hymn "well written, dignified, and enticingly singable." (*Stories of Our Mormon Hymns,* p. 125.) It is a prayer of benediction, asking that the teachings of the day take root in each member of the congregation so that all may grow in obedience, service, and holiness.

It is important to conclude a meeting reverently and meaningfully. If a *short* closing hymn can accomplish this purpose, then surely its brevity is an additional virtue. This hymn's efficiency is undoubtedly one of the reasons it is chosen so often as a closing hymn among Latter-day Saints; it closes the meeting quickly but without leaving anyone feeling short-changed. In only eight measures of music and twenty-eight syllables of text, each verse of this prayer makes a point that is straightforward, direct, and simple. Most congregations appreciate the strong but reverent rhythms that move efficiently toward the hymn's conclusion. It is a hymn that does not overstay its welcome, even when all four verses are sung.

The 1950 hymnal gave credit to Ebenezer Beesley for this hymn tune; however, more recent scholarship has shown that Beesley was the arranger of an already existing hymn tune written in 1769 by Benjamin

Milgrove. This tune, HARTS, was published in 1879 in the *Juvenile Instructor* to accompany the Manwaring text.

Father, This Hour Has Been One of Joy 154

Text: Nan Greene Hunter (b. 1938; LDS)
Music: Lynn R. Shurtleff (b. 1939; LDS)
Tune name: ALMA

"Father, This Hour Has Been One of Joy" is a simple, heartfelt expression of thanks at the conclusion of a meeting. It was inspired by the author's feelings at the conclusion of a sacrament meeting, but it is suitable for any meeting in which the hearts of the congregation have been touched and renewed by the Spirit of the Lord.

Lynn Shurtleff and Nan Greene Hunter collaborated on several hymns before they wrote "Father, This Hour Has Been One of Joy." Nan Hunter reported: "The Church needed closing hymns, and so when I sat down to write the words to this hymn, I thought of the feelings I have when I have been to sacrament meeting and how touched I am and how glad I am to have been there. I stated exactly how I feel (or as nearly as words can say) about the profound experience of partaking of the sacrament and meeting with the Saints of God."

Composer Lynn Shurtleff stressed that the hymn, though unusual in some respects, is not a difficult one for congregations to learn. "This is one of the few hymns in the 1985 hymnal that are in a minor mode," he stated. "This was a special problem because the hymn begins in minor and ends in major. For that reason a special introduction has been included that reminds the congregation of the tune and, at the same time, gives a proper starting note. The melody is simple and straightforward." He added, "Because the hymn is designed for the conclusion of a service, it is intentionally short."

Text and tune were published for the first time in the 1985 hymnal. The tune name, ALMA, honors the composer's wife, Alma Don McArthur.

We Have Partaken of Thy Love 155

Text: Mabel Jones Gabbott (b. 1910; LDS)
Music: Robert P. Manookin (b. 1918; LDS)
Tune name: BARBARA

For many Latter-day Saints, sacrament meeting is the oasis of the week. It is a time of refreshment after a week-long journey, a chance to feel restored and renewed. This beautiful closing hymn is a prayer of thanks for the blessings of sacrament meeting.

This hymn was written especially for the 1985 hymnal by two contributors whose names were already familiar to Latter-day Saints from previous hymnals. In the 1985 hymnal, four hymns owe their texts to Mabel Jones Gabbott, and Robert Manookin is responsible for six hymn tunes.

The simple, resolute hymn tune, with its reiteration of the final phrase, is a fine companion to the text. Each verse highlights a different blessing to be gained from sacrament meeting attendance: the taking of the sacrament is the focus of the first verse, the determination to live a better life is the focus of the second, and the third verse asks, in the name of the Son, a benediction from the Father.

Author Mabel Jones Gabbott reported: "I tried to express my personal gratitude for sacrament meeting—how we come together to feast on the goodness of the Lord, to partake of his love, to resolve to overcome the week's failures, and, strengthened by his cleansing power, to go forth to do his will and keep his word with his benediction until the next Sabbath." Each member of the congregation might ponder this question: do I derive all these blessings each week from sacrament meeting? If this description seems to be an idealized sacrament meeting experience rather than a real one, could I, myself, bring a more attentive, receptive spirit to the meeting?

The tune name, BARBARA, honors the composer's daughter, Barbara M. Hill.

Sing We Now at Parting 156

Text: George Manwaring (1854–1889; LDS)
Music: Ebenezer Beesley (1840–1906; LDS)
Tune name: PARTING

First published in 1880, this satisfying and appealing closing hymn has served Latter-day Saints for more than a century. It combines gratitude for our blessings with a petition for the Lord's companionship. As the meeting concludes, we return to our daily lives with a prayer that we may be more obedient and watchful.

"Sing We Now at Parting" puts a final "amen" on a sacrament meeting or other Sabbath gathering. We pause to thank our Father for his blessings, and then, in verse three, we pray directly for his guidance in the days to come. In the final two lines of verse three, we commit ourselves to thank him not only with our voices but also with our obedience and service.

J. Spencer Cornwall said: "This hymn will never become trite or worn out. It has a genteel loveliness about it which makes it beloved. It is beautifully written in both text and music." (*Stories of Our Mormon Hymns*, pp. 177–78.)

The eleven hymn tunes in the 1985 hymnal that were composed by Ebenezer Beesley are among the most popular in Latter-day Saint hymnody. They include the tunes for "High on the Mountain Top" (no. 5), "God of Our Fathers, We Come unto Thee" (no. 76), and "Let Us Oft Speak Kind Words" (no. 232). George Manwaring's talent is also well represented in our hymnal with five hymn texts, including "Joseph Smith's First Prayer" (no. 26) and " 'Tis Sweet to Sing the Matchless Love" (nos. 176; 177).

"Sing We Now at Parting" was published in 1880 by both the *Juvenile Instructor* and the *Tune Book for the Primary Association*.

Thy Spirit, Lord, Has Stirred Our Souls 157

Text: Frank I. Kooyman (1880–1963; LDS)
Music: Alexander Schreiner (1901–1987; LDS)
Tune name: BAVARIA

This closing prayer is as different as it can possibly be from a routine, formulaic prayer of dismissal. It is the perfect "amen" to a meeting in which hearts have truly been touched and eyes have truly been opened. The congregation acknowledges the solemnity of the moment and renews their commitment to the highest, most spiritual goals.

J. Spencer Cornwall discussed this hymn in *Stories of Our Mormon Hymns:*

"A spiritual experience such as this song mentions is a private possession, and when put into the words of a hymn, it becomes a personal testimony. . . . It may or may not strike a responsive chord in the hearts of others, but usually does. . . .

" 'Thy Spirit, Lord, Has Stirred Our Souls' was 'born' in a very spiritual meeting. We all, no doubt, have partaken in such gatherings when during a spirit-prompted address a profound silence falls upon the congregation, a hushing spell that is felt by all present. This song is intended to be a grateful closing hymn after a rich outpouring of the 'glowing power' of the Lord has moved the souls of the listeners and filled them with new determination to carry on, or newborn resolutions to do better." (P. 216.)

Two scripture references are crucial to an understanding of the text. The "burning bush near Sinai" refers to an incident recounted in the third chapter of Exodus. When Moses was leading a flock of sheep near Horeb

(Sinai), he saw a flame coming from a bush, but the bush continued to burn and was not consumed. "And when the Lord saw that he turned aside to see, God called unto him out of the midst of the bush, and said, Moses, Moses. And he said, Here am I." (Exodus 3:4.) The Lord spoke to Moses at some length, giving him instructions concerning his role as leader of the Israelites.

" 'Did not our hearts within us burn?' " is the question asked by the two disciples after Jesus, whose identity was unknown to them, had walked and talked with them on the road to Emmaus. After his departure, they realized that their companion had been the resurrected Lord himself. (See Luke 24:32.)

The common theme of these two scriptural events is that both times the Lord appeared under memorable and dramatic circumstances to communicate directly with his followers. This moving hymn implies that the congregation has had a comparable experience.

Before Thee, Lord, I Bow My Head 158

Text and music: Joseph H. Dean (1855–1947; LDS)
Tune name: SARAH

Sometimes at the conclusion of a meeting, emotions are so strong and hearts are so full that it is difficult to hold back tears. Each member of the congregation is moved to new resolution, and each is wishing to prolong the companionship of the Lord's Spirit and those tender feelings that motivate each worshiper toward higher spiritual goals. This hymn articulates such feelings.

After an intense spiritual experience, how do we keep a firm hold on the feelings and resolutions in our heart, so they do not dissipate within a few hours or days? How do we keep ourselves from sliding back into the day-to-day distractions of life? This hymn is a prayer that we may retain our high spiritual resolve: "Oh, help me, Lord, lest I forget." We pray that we may "break off the shackles of the earth"—that our hearts may be truly changed, forever, because of what we have just experienced.

Although this hymn was included in the choir section of the 1950 hymnal, it was popular with congregations as well. The 1985 hymnal lowered the pitch slightly, and congregations will not find it difficult to sing. Even the tenor and bass "answering measures" are not difficult once the congregation is familiar with the hymn. The phrase "My heart is broke" in verse two was revised: "My heart is full."

The tune name, SARAH, honors the wife of Joseph H. Dean.

Now the Day Is Over 159

Text: Sabine Baring-Gould (1834–1924)
Music: Joseph Barnby (1838–1896)
Tune name: MERRIAL

This short, evocative hymn is a perfect conclusion to a late afternoon or evening church service or family home evening. Originally written for children, the prayer for protection during the night is expressed in the simplest possible language. It has become a popular hymn among all age groups wherever Christian hymns are sung.

Sabine Baring-Gould wrote the words of this hymn in 1867 for the children of the parish over which he was minister. The Barnby tune was written a year later. The curious tune name has an interesting history. When Dr. Charles Robinson published this hymn in his *Laudes Domini* in 1884, he chose to name the tune after his daughter, Mary L. Robinson. The tune name later took the form MERRIAL (Mary L.).

The two verses in our hymnal form a sufficient and satisfying whole, but the original hymn actually has six additional verses. The four that are most frequently reprinted as part of the hymn are these:

Grant to little children / Visions bright of thee;
Guard the sailors tossing / On the deep, blue sea.

Comfort every sufferer / Watching late in pain;
Those who plan some evil, / From their sins restrain.

Through the long night watches, / May thine angels spread
Their white wings above me, / Watching round my bed.

When the morning wakens, / Then may I arise
Pure and fresh and sinless / In thy holy eyes.

J. Spencer Cornwall noted that when the Tabernacle Choir toured Europe in 1955, they concluded every concert by singing "Now the Day Is Over." (See *Stories of Our Mormon Hymns*, p. 127.)

Softly Now the Light of Day 160

Text: George W. Doane (1799–1859)
Music: Carl Maria von Weber (1786–1826);
arranged by Henry Greatorex (1813–1858)
Tune name: SEYMOUR

This hymn is often thought of as a song to be used at the close of a meeting. But it does not actually refer to parting or conclusion; it is a brief, personal prayer, a stated wish to commune with the Lord in the calm and meditative mood brought on by twilight.

Some hymnals print additional verses of George W. Doane's 1824 hymn text. Note that one of the subsequent verses draws a parallel between the closing of day and the closing of life.

Thou, whose all-pervading eye
Naught escapes, without, within,
Pardon each infirmity,
Open fault and secret sin.

When for me the light of day
Shall for ever pass away,
Then, from sin and sorrow free,
Take me, Lord, to dwell with thee.

The tune, SEYMOUR, was not originally written for a hymn. It is an extensively altered version of the opening chorus of Carl Maria von Weber's opera *Oberon* (1825–26).

The Lord Be with Us 161

Text: John Ellerton (1826–1893)
Music: Tracy Y. Cannon (1879–1961; LDS)
Tune name: FRANCES

As a congregation sings this hymn to close a meeting, the worshipers ask the Lord to continue to let his Spirit be with them as they leave the meeting and go to their homes. They ask him to abide in every heart and to protect each home throughout the night.

The verses of "The Lord Be with Us" move in sequence through the time period following a church meeting. The first verse asks for the Lord to be with us as we journey home. The second verse asks him to "be in every heart the light, / In every home the guest" as the evening turns to darkness. And verse three asks that he will ensure the safety of our homes and our sleep during the night.

The composer of the hymn tune, Tracy Y. Cannon, stated that he decided to provide a musical setting for this hymn text by John Ellerton because he "felt there was need for hymns suitable for use at the close of an evening sacrament meeting." (Quoted in J. Spencer Cornwall, *Stories of Our Mormon Hymns*, p. 37.)

Our hymn actually begins with the second verse of John Ellerton's text. The original first verse begins with a reference to the closing prayer of the Church meeting. It is as follows:

The Lord be with us as we bend
His blessing to receive,
His gift of peace upon us send
Before his courts we leave.

The tune name, FRANCES, honors the daughter of Tracy Y. Cannon. The tune was first published in the 1948 Latter-day Saint hymnal, matched with this text, which first appeared in an English hymn collection in 1871.

Lord, We Come Before Thee Now 162

Text: William Hammond (1719–1783)
Music: Harry A. Dean (1892–1987; LDS)
Tune name: LYNN

This hymn is a fervent, almost insistent pleading with the Lord for his Spirit and enlightenment. It is often used as the closing hymn of a meeting, but it need not be limited to that purpose.

The beseeching words of the hymn convey a tone of anxiety. It is a prayer of pleading rather than one of thanksgiving or rejoicing. The words are as insistent as those of Joseph after he wrestled with the angel: "I will not let thee go, except thou bless me." (Genesis 32:26.)

In a remarkable matching of the spirit of a text first published in 1745, Latter-day Saint composer Harry A. Dean wrote a pleading hymn tune in a minor key. The tune name, LYNN, honors Dr. Lynn C. Dean, the son of Harry A. Dean.

Lord, Dismiss Us with Thy Blessing 163

Text: John Fawcett (1740–1817)
Music: Jean Jacques Rousseau (1712–1778)
Tune name: GREENVILLE

This hymn is a prayer that we may make practical use of the gospel in our lives. We offer verbal thanks and adoration for the gospel, and we also ask the help of our Father in Heaven in rendering additional thanks through faithful and dedicated lives. The "joyful sound" of the gospel must manifest itself in our lives.

In Jean Jacques Rousseau's opera *Le Devin de Village* ("The Village Soothsayer"), one scene includes a melody, called the "Pantomime," for string instruments. The melody is often called "Rousseau's Dream," referring to a legend that the melody had come to Rousseau in a dream in which the heavenly hosts were singing this tune in honor of the Father. Under many titles, often with romantic words attached, the tune achieved considerable popularity in both France and England. It may have its origins in a French folk song.

Great God, to Thee My Evening Song 164

Text: Anne Steele (1716–1778)
Music: Edward P. Kimball (1882–1937; LDS)
Tune name: HAZEL

Traditionally, evening is a time for thoughtful reflection. The cares of the day are behind us, and perhaps for a few moments we turn our minds to spiritual matters. This hymn is an evening prayer of thanksgiving. As we sing it, we ask our Father in Heaven to accept our praise, to bless our sleep, and to preserve the gratitude we feel in our hearts.

This hymn text, first published in 1760, entered Latter-day Saint hymnody with Emma Smith's first hymnal in 1835. There it is included as one of six "Evening Hymns."

Emma Smith's hymnal included two additional verses that were omitted in later editions. These verses allude to the petitioner's weakness and vulnerability and to the need for forgiveness:

And yet this thoughtless, wretched heart,
Too oft regardless of thy love,
Ungrateful, can from thee depart,
And from the path of duty rove.

Seal my forgiveness in the blood
Of Christ, my Lord; his name alone
I plead for pardon, gracious God,
And kind acceptance at thy throne.

The tune name, HAZEL, honors the composer's wife.

Abide with Me; 'Tis Eventide 165

Text: Lowrie M. Hofford
Music: Harrison Millard (1830–1895)
Tune name: WELCOME GUEST

Darkness does not always bring peace and rest. Sometimes the night can bring a feeling of loneliness and even danger. But this hymn shows that the Savior's presence can turn night into a time of meditation and communion. It is a prayer for his continued companionship.

This hymn, like "Thy Spirit, Lord, Has Stirred Our Souls" (no. 157), takes as its point of departure the story of the walk to Emmaus, from the last chapter of Luke. Two of the disciples are on the road to the village of Emmaus when the resurrected Lord joins them and walks alongside them. But the disciples do not recognize the Savior. They tell him the news that is weighing on their hearts: Jesus of Nazareth has been crucified. Still without revealing his identity, Jesus explains the necessity of his sacrifice: "Ought not Christ to have suffered these things, and to enter into his glory?" (Luke 24: 26.) He then expounds the scriptures that prophesied his mission.

As he is about to depart, the disciples ask, "Abide with us: for it is toward evening, and the day is far spent." (Luke 24: 29.) They eat together, and just as the disciples realize who he is, he vanishes from their sight. Then they begin to comprehend the significance of their visitor and his message: "Did not our hearts burn within us, while he talked with us by the way, and while he opened to us the scriptures?" (Luke 24: 32.) Their visitor has been the resurrected Lord.

The hymn turns this dramatic New Testament story into a hymn of personal prayer. We compare ourselves to the disciples: as they did, we invite the Savior to remain with us as a welcome guest as the evening draws near. With us, too, he has walked and spoken, and our hearts burn within us. He is our light in a world where darkness always threatens.

Abide with Me! 166

Text: Henry F. Lyte (1793–1847)
Music: William H. Monk (1823–1889)
Tune name: EVENTIDE

"Abide with Me!" is one of the masterpieces of Christian hymn tradition. Although it is sometimes thought of as a hymn about the close of day, it is actually about the close of life. It is a solemn prayer for the Lord's presence at the moment of trial, particularly at the moment of death. It is also an affirmation of belief in an afterlife and in the Lord's power to sustain and bless.

On an anniversary of the death of Henry F. Lyte, an English newspaper printed these words about his beloved hymn:

"What is the secret of its healing power? Its divine simplicity. Its inspired truthfulness and sincerity. Every word is a cry from the human heart. Its rhythm is magically right because it follows the passion of the soul in wave after wave. It melts the human mind. It transfigures the human intellect. In sorrow and desolation it comforts and consoles. There is not a false note in its music. That is why it is the hymn of hymns." (Quoted in George D. Pyper, *Stories of Latter-day Saint Hymns*, p. 127.)

The hymn was written in circumstances of great personal sorrow. For twenty-four years, Henry F. Lyte had devoted his life and strength to serving as minister in a small English fishing village called Brixham. His love for his flock and his dedication to the Lord's service were exemplary. But during the last three years of his ministry, tuberculosis made him weaker and weaker. He traveled to France each winter in search of a more healthful climate. To his disappointment, he found each time he returned to Brixham that dissension and ill feelings were increasing among his congregation, and the choir he had labored so long to establish was not managing to carry on without him.

His health required that he retire from his post. In 1847, after he had preached his last Sunday sermon to the congregation that had been his for so long, he returned to his study and wrote "Abide with Me!"

The tune, composed about twelve years later by William H. Monk to be included in a hymn collection for which he was an editor, is now inseparably connected with this text.

The original hymn had eight stanzas, and many Protestant hymnals print four or five of them. In two of the stanzas not included in our hymnal, the Reverend Henry F. Lyte referred directly to the comfort of religious faith at the moment of death:

I fear no foe, with thee at hand to bless;
Ills have no weight, and tears no bitterness.
Where is death's sting? Where, grave, thy victory?
I triumph still, if thou abide with me.

Hold thou thy cross before my closing eyes;
Shine through the gloom and point me to the skies;
Heaven's morning breaks, and earth's vain shadows flee;
In life, in death, O Lord, abide with me!

Come, Let Us Sing an Evening Hymn 167

Text: William W. Phelps (1792–1872; LDS)
Music: Tracy Y. Cannon (1879–1961; LDS)
Tune name: LETTIE

This hymn of praise is a reverent and meditative conclusion to a church meeting. It can also serve as an individual or family hymn at the close of day, "to calm our minds for rest." As J. Spencer Cornwall commented, this hymn "suggests a very beautiful group or family custom." (*Stories of Our Mormon Hymns*, p. 245.)

This hymn text was included as one of six "Evening Hymns" that formed part of Emma Smith's first hymnal in 1835. The six original verses are all retained in our present hymnal, almost exactly as William W. Phelps wrote them. Countless Christian hymn writers have written evening hymns, but it is especially interesting to note the distinctive Latter-day Saint tone of this one. Writing in the very early years of the Church, William W. Phelps chose to center his gratitude on "grace and gifts / Renewed in latter days," and "every line we have received / To turn our hearts above." The Saints were the grateful possessors of truths that no other latter-day people possessed, and these were the thoughts of gratitude that the poet thought appropriate to express at close of day.

As do most evening hymns, this hymn prays that we may "wake in joy." But the final verse also alludes to another kind of awakening—that beyond the grave, after our final sleep. Followers of Jesus Christ rest in the assurance that death, too, will allow us to "wake in joy."

Though labeled as a choir hymn in the 1950 hymnal, this hymn is accessible to most congregations. Tracy Y. Cannon said about the writing of the hymn tune: "The words, written by W. W. Phelps, were assigned to me by Elder Melvin J. Ballard when the 1927 edition of the Latter-day Saint Hymnbook was being prepared. I immediately composed the music for these words and the hymn was first printed in the 1927 edition of the hymnbook." (Quoted in J. Spencer Cornwall, *Stories of Our Mormon Hymns*, p. 245.)

The tune name, LETTIE, honors the second wife of Tracy Y. Cannon.

As the Shadows Fall 168

Text: Lowell M. Durham, Jr. (b. 1943; LDS)
Music: Lowell M. Durham (b. 1917; LDS)
Tune name: SHADOWS

This serene evening prayer serves as a beautiful closing hymn or evening meditation. Though shadows in another context might symbolize threats or fears, the shadows in this hymn, because of its focus on the Savior and his protecting love, represent an enveloping comfort and security.

Lowell M. Durham reported: "In 1974, when President Spencer W. Kimball announced that a new hymnbook would be published, I took him at his word and phoned my son, Lowell Jr., to invite him to write some hymn texts that I could set to music. I immediately began composing the music to 'As The Shadows Fall,' which seemed to me to have the spirit of evening and contemplation.'' It was published in the *Ensign* in July 1977.

The composer advised: ''It should be sung softly. Perhaps the melody could be hummed the first time through.'' The added measure in the final phrase requires singers to prepare adequate breath in order to sing it smoothly.

As Now We Take the Sacrament 169

Text: Lee Tom Perry (b. 1951; LDS)
Music: Daniel Lyman Carter (b. 1955; LDS)
Tune name: SYLVIA'S HYMN

The author's thoughts about this hymn provide a fine introduction to its message: ''I tried to represent our stream of consciousness as we prepare to partake of the sacrament. I wanted the congregation to review the Savior's mission and some of its many implications for us. The language is neither flowery nor metaphorical. It is reflective and direct, focused on our gratitude to the Savior.''

Lee Perry wrote the text at the invitation of a friend who had written a hymn tune for a Brigham Young University composition class. The author related that the writing was not tied to any profound event but that it was ''a quiet, peaceful experience; there was a special calmness associated with the task, a feeling of being guided by the Spirit.'' He added, ''Mabel Jones Gabbott worked with me to improve several lines of the text. Her important contribution cannot go unrecognized.''

When the hymn was submitted for consideration for the 1985 hymnal, the text was accepted, but the Hymnbook Committee felt a different musical setting was needed. Daniel Lyman Carter was asked to take on this assignment, and it proved to be no easy task. The process he went through in writing this hymn tune shows once again that arduous work and divine inspiration are not mutually exclusive. Six musical settings were submitted and rejected. Then he finished the seventh. He continued: ''I played it for my mother-in-law, Sylvia Wood. Upon hearing it, she said, 'I believe this is the hymn that will be accepted.' The tune is called SYLVIA'S HYMN in her honor.''

When Daniel Carter heard a congregation sing the hymn for the first time, he was visiting his mother-in-law's ward in Alberta, Canada. Before the meeting, he had a sudden feeling of self-doubt when he saw it listed on the program. ''But,'' he reported, ''as the hymn was sung, I was overcome with peace, and I felt the same things I felt the night it was composed. There was no doubt whether the hymn was good enough to sing, because I felt it came from the Lord.''

Latter-day Saint congregations tend to sing old favorites among our sacrament hymns, because once a week our meeting format provides that we choose from the relatively short list of sacrament hymns. This hymn, with its references to forgiveness, grace, service, and gratitude, can give fresh, meaningful form to our thoughts as we prepare for this holy ordinance.

God, Our Father, Hear Us Pray 170

Text: Annie Pinnock Malin (1863–1935; LDS)
Music: Louis M. Gottschalk (1829–1869);
adapted by Edwin P. Parker (1836–1925)
Tune name: MERCY

Elder Bruce R. McConkie spoke of "the spirit of prayer, humility, and worship which attend sacramental administrations." (*Mormon Doctrine*, 2d ed. [Salt Lake City, Utah: Bookcraft, 1966], p. 661.) In a particular meeting, such a spirit may not be fully present at the time the ordinance of the sacrament is to begin. What better way to invoke this spirit and move ourselves toward a feeling of reverent, humble attentiveness than by singing a hymn?

The first verse of "God, Our Father, Hear us Pray" is the most general, praying for the Father to grant us his Spirit as we turn our thoughts to the emblems of the Savior's sacrifice. Verse two mentions the bread and asks for the Father's smile of approval as we participate in the ordinance. Verse three, with its mention of the water, concludes with a prayer for forgiveness and asks for a blessing on our continued efforts to be worthy partakers of the sacrament.

Louis Moreau Gottschalk was not a composer of hymn tunes; however, his composition "The Last Hope" (1854) is a graceful and appealing melody that has been used in many hymnals. (One hymnal gives it as a setting for the text "Softly Now the Light of Day," no. 160 in our book.) In its hymn-tune use it goes by the name MERCY because it was originally paired with a hymn by Charles Wesley:

Depth of mercy! can there be
Mercy still reserved for me?
Can my God his wrath forbear,
Me, the chief of sinners, spare?

Annie Pinnock Malin's text has been paired with this tune from the time of the text's first publication in the 1909 *Deseret Sunday School Songs*.

With Humble Heart 171

Text: Zara Sabin (1892–1980; LDS)
Music: Thomas L. Durham (b. 1950; LDS)
Tune name: WITH HUMBLE HEART

The familiar weekly ritual of partaking of the sacrament can become, unfortunately, a habit that may not carry a great deal of meaning. "With Humble Heart" reminds us that the sacrament offers an opportunity for profound insights and spiritual rededication.

Using the first person pronouns *I* and *we*, Zara Sabin describes an experience of being personally touched by the sacrament. In the first verse she alludes to the patterns and symbols that characterize any conscientious worshiper: she thinks of the Savior, taking the bread and water in his remembrance. But her thoughts then begin to reach for a deeper spiritual sense, one that moves beyond this outward ritual; her prayer is to "grow, dear Lord, to be like thee." These last four words kindle a spiritual high point, and they are immediately repeated as the opening of verse three: "To be like thee!" The possibility of becoming like the Savior—the meaning of this gift, this goal—causes her to lift her eyes from earth to heaven, and the hymn concludes with a prayer for "a change of heart, another birth," to make this possibility a reality.

The hymn tune was written in Salt Lake City in 1973. Composer Thomas L. Durham stated: "My father, Lowell M. Durham, who is also a contributor to the hymnbook, mentioned to me in 1973 that a new hymnal was being proposed. He handed me three or four different poems, and the one by Zara Sabin appealed to me because it was a sacrament hymn. It has always been my feeling that the sacrament hymns of the Church are the best—musically and spiritually. I sat right down at the piano, wrote out the melody, and the harmony followed immediately thereafter. The hymn nearly composed itself in the thirty to sixty minutes I was at the piano."

The text and tune appeared together for the first time in the 1985 hymnal.

In Humility, Our Savior 172

Text: Mabel Jones Gabbott (b. 1910; LDS)
Music: Rowland Hugh Prichard (1811–1887)
Tune name: HYFRYDOL

This reverent hymn emphasizes both the blessings and duties of the covenant of the sacrament. In the form of a prayer, the hymn asks the

Lord to bless us with sincere devotion and remembrance. It is also a gentle reminder that the Savior's sacrifice should call forth forgiveness and tolerance among his children.

The text was written in 1946. Mabel Jones Gabbott noted: "We were living [in the 1940s] in Salt Lake City, where my husband was bishop. We had two small children. As a poet, I was invited to a meeting at Church headquarters. There Alexander Schreiner, George D. Pyper, and others instructed us in the making of a hymn—line length, meters, regularity of accents, and quality of tone. A list of suggested subjects was given to each of us. I submitted some texts, including 'In Humility, Our Savior.' "

The tune HYFRYDOL (Welsh for "good cheer") is a perfect, peaceful musical pairing with Mabel Jones Gabbott's words. This well-known hymn tune appears in virtually every Protestant hymnal, often with William Chatterton Dix's text beginning "Alleluia! Sing to Jesus!"

While of These Emblems We Partake 173; 174

Text: John Nicholson (1839–1909; LDS)
Music (SAUL): Samuel McBurney (b. 1847)
Music (AEOLIAN): Alexander Schreiner (1901–1987; LDS)
Tune names: SAUL, AEOLIAN

J. Spencer Cornwall commented on this sacrament hymn: "The words are outstanding in poetic beauty. The contemplation of such thoughts is a religious duty asked of Latter-day Saints at the time of partaking of the emblems of the Lord's supper." (*Stories of Our Mormon Hymns*, p. 228.)

If a new convert to the Church were seeking to learn more about the meaning of the sacrament, John Nicholson's words would provide an excellent overview of the most basic truths of the Savior's sacrifice and of the ordinance carried out each week among Latter-day Saints in remembrance of that sacrifice. It is carefully instructive. Verse one: the purpose of the ordinance is to remember Jesus; we must make sure that we remain worthy to partake of the sacrament. Verse two: Jesus died for our sake. Verse three: his death paid our debt by satisfying the demands of justice, thus overcoming death. Verse four: because of the Atonement, all people can look forward to resurrection.

Our hymnbook offers a choice of two musical settings for this hymn text by John Nicholson. Both hymn tunes are masterful examples of the way in which the spiritual dimension of a text may be enhanced by just the right musical setting, and it would be a great loss to the hymnal if either were omitted. Both tunes are simple; both introduce a slight bit of harmonic tension in the middle of the tune and then settle back down into the serenity of the last phrase. With reference to the tune AEOLIAN (no. 174), J. Spencer Cornwall reported that "Mr. Schreiner advises that the hymn, 'While of These Emblems,' should begin quietly and devotionally, gradually rising in melody to the high point 'let us remember' and subsiding into devotional calm." (P. 228.)

The tune name AEOLIAN refers to the Aeolian-Skinner organ that Alexander Schreiner helped select for the Salt Lake Tabernacle in the 1940s. The tune name SAUL honors the father of Samuel McBurney.

While of These Emblems We Partake 174

See the discussion of hymn 173.

O God, the Eternal Father 175

Text: William W. Phelps (1792–1872; LDS)
Music: Felix Mendelssohn (1809–1847)
Tune name: ABSCHIED

From the earliest days of The Church of Jesus Christ of Latter-day Saints, members of the Church have prepared themselves to take the sacrament by singing these worshipful words. The first two verses are a poetic echo of the sacramental prayers themselves; by singing these words, we may remind ourselves of the covenants we are about to make.

Of the five sacrament hymns in Emma Smith's 1835 hymnal, only this one has survived in our hymnbook until the present day. William W. Phelps, the author of this hymn text, wrote or adapted twenty-nine hymns for the volume, and he also assisted Emma Smith in the task of editing. The first generation of Latter-day Saints probably sang this hymn to the tune printed in our present hymnbook with "Come, All Whose Souls Are Lighted" (no. 268).

Emma Smith's hymnbook included eight verses. Verses five through eight, omitted from our hymnal today, focus more on the prophesied Messiah than on Jesus the Redeemer. They are as follows:

'Twas done—all nature trembled!
Yet, by the pow'r of faith,
He rose as God triumphant,
And broke the bands of death:
And, rising conq'rer, "captive
He led captivity,"
And sat down with the Father
To fill eternity.

He is the true Messiah,
That died and lives again;
We look not for another,
He is the Lamb 'twas slain;
He is the Stone and Shepherd
Of Israel—scatter'd far;
The glorious Branch from Jesse:
The bright and Morning Star.

Again, he is that Prophet
That Moses said should come,
Being raised among his brethren,
To call the righteous home,
And all that will not hear him,
Shall feel his chast'ning rod,
Till wickedness is ended,
As saith the Lord our God.

He comes, he comes in glory,
(The [veil] has vanish'd too,)
With angels, yea our fathers,
To drink this cup anew—
And sing the songs of Zion
And shout—'Tis done, 'tis done!
While every son and daughter
Rejoices—we are one.

The tune name, ABSCHIED, German for "farewell," is applied to the beautiful Mendelssohn melody that originally was the setting for a poem titled "Farewell to the Forest."

'Tis Sweet to Sing the Matchless Love 176; 177

Text: George A. Manwaring (1854–1889; LDS)
Music (MEREDITH): Frank W. Asper 1892–1973; LDS)
Music (HANCOCK): Ebenezer Beesley (1840–1906; LDS)
Tune names: MEREDITH, HANCOCK

Because Latter-day Saints have the opportunity to partake of the sacrament each week, we can too easily lose sight of the importance of this privilege. This hymn honors the holy sacrifice that we commemorate through the sacrament, but it also gives thanks for the ceremony of the sacrament itself: "Oh, blessed hour! communion sweet!"

Our hymnal offers two settings for this 1878 hymn text. Latter-day Saints who have been members of the Church for some years will probably be familiar with both hymn tunes, MEREDITH by Frank W. Asper and HANCOCK by Ebenezer Beesley. Hymnals and Sunday School song books have vacillated between the two. The Asper tune, named MEREDITH for the middle name of his daughter Ellen, has greater dignity, and many Saints are fond of it; the Beesley tune, because of its gospel-song energy, also has great appeal.

The words that appear as the text for the chorus in HANCOCK are given as the fourth verse in MEREDITH.

The 1985 Hymnbook Committee decided that both tunes were worthy of inclusion. It is not unusual for Christian hymnals to offer a choice of as many as four or five hymn tunes for the same hymn text. In the 1985 Latter-day Saints hymnbook, two other texts besides " 'Tis Sweet to Sing the Matchless Love" are given with a choice of tunes: "While of These Emblems We Partake" (nos. 173; 174), and "Rise Up, O Men of God" (nos. 323; 324).

'Tis Sweet to Sing the Matchless Love 177

See the discussion of hymn 176.

O Lord of Hosts 178

Text: Andrew Dalrymple (b. 1817; LDS)
Music: George Careless (1839–1932; LDS)
Tune name: CHARITY

The Savior's example of compassion and forgiveness should be ever in our minds, to help us live with one another in love and union. Particularly as we prepare to take the sacrament—as we ask the Lord to cleanse our hearts and prepare our minds—we should feel at one with our brothers and sisters. Such is the message of this peaceful, elegant sacrament hymn.

This tune and text have been linked in Latter-day Saint hymnody since 1876, when they were first published together. The duet passage in the third phrase was the reason for its inclusion in the choir section rather than the congregational section of the 1950 hymnal. Many congregations chose to sing it anyway, and although the duet passage was retained in the 1985 hymnal, it presents no real difficulties as a congregational hymn.

This hymn and ten other sacrament hymns were in the choir section of the 1950 hymnal. A statement in a 1983 *Church Music Guide for Priesthood Leaders* read as follows: "Ward choirs . . . may sing after the sacrament or between speakers. They may also sing a prelude selection, or either the opening or closing hymn." By implication, the only hymn the choir could *not* appropriately sing was the sacrament hymn.

The wisdom behind the recommendation in the *Church Music Guide* is evident, since for most people, the opportunity to sing a sacrament hymn themselves is more meaningful in preparing to partake of the sacrament than listening to a hymn would be. But through the years, eleven sacrament hymns, some of them among the jewels of the hymnal, were not often sung. Being too difficult (at least theoretically) for congregations, they were relegated to use by choirs.

Now, because nine of the eleven sacrament hymns from the 1950 hymnal's choir section were retained in the 1985 hymnal and printed for congregational use, our choices for the sacrament hymn are greatly enriched.

Again, Our Dear Redeeming Lord 179

Text: Theodore E. Curtis (1872–1957; LDS)
Music: Alfred M. Durham (1872–1957; LDS)
Tune name: CAROLINE

As we sing this hymn, we present ourselves before the Lord as a congregation of his sons and daughters who are preparing to partake of the sacrament. A person in a truly penitent and worshipful frame of mind will find this hymn a beautiful reflection of his or her feelings in preparation for the taking of the sacrament.

"Again, Our Dear Redeeming Lord" describes the ideal attitude with which one partakes of the sacrament. It is in close parallel with the words of Elder Bruce R. McConkie: "Few ordinances or performances in the Church act as a greater incentive to personal righteousness than [the] worthy partaking of the sacrament. Those who partake of the sacramental emblems—having a comprehension of the covenant involved—are marking for themselves a course which will result in obedience, holiness, and sanctification." (*Mormon Doctrine*, 2d ed. [Salt Lake City, Utah: Bookcraft, 1966], p. 661.)

In the 1950 hymnal, this hymn was marked as a choir hymn. The 1985 hymnal included it for congregational use. It is not the easiest of sacrament hymns for a congregation to sing; but it has been transposed to a lower key, and the range of the melody is now more convenient for unison singing. Because of the relatively few sacrament hymns in the 1950 hymnal, and because a sacrament hymn is sung by a congregation almost every week, this and other sacrament hymns that expand the list of possibilities—both former "choir" hymns and newly created hymns—are welcome additions in the 1985 hymnal.

The tune name, CAROLINE, honors the mother of the composer.

Father in Heaven, We Do Believe 180

Text: Parley P. Pratt (1807–1857; LDS); altered
Music: Jane Romney Crawford (1883–1956; LDS)
Tune name: ROMNEY

In this sacrament hymn, we confidently pledge our worthiness to partake of the sacrament. It is a useful self-test; a worshiper who can sing these words with sincerity—who can, with an honest heart, say to the Lord, "I believe your promise, I repent, I choose the better part"—can partake of the sacrament with true peace of mind.

Now included among the sacrament hymns, this hymn was not listed as such in the 1950 hymnal: the central focus of Parley P. Pratt's original text was baptism and confirmation, not the sacrament. Yet the second verse particularly, with its reference to "broken heart" and "covenant," suggested to the 1985 Hymnbook Committee that with some alteration this little-used text would make an excellent sacrament hymn.

Thus the 1985 hymnal gives two versions of the original verse three. The original verse is included as verse five at the bottom of the page:

We will be buried in the stream
In Jesus' blessed name,
And rise, while light shall on us beam
The Spirit's heavenly flame.

This verse is, of course, suitable for singing at a baptismal service. When the hymn is used as a sacrament hymn, however, the note at the bottom of the page asks that the congregation sing the revised version, printed within the music staff as verse four:

Humbly we take the sacrament
In Jesus' blessed name;
Let us receive through covenant
The Spirit's heavenly flame.

The original fourth verse, rarely sung in the 1950 hymnal, became verse three in the 1985 version.

This double-duty use of the hymn has two significant advantages. First, we gain a strong sacrament hymn. Second, when we attend a baptismal service, which most of us do much less often than we attend sacrament meeting, we will be able to sing with confidence a baptismal hymn that we have become familiar with in another context.

This hymn text appeared for the first time in the 1840 hymnal of which Parley P. Pratt was one of the editors. Jane Romney Crawford wrote the musical setting of this text for the 1927 hymnal.

Jesus of Nazareth, Savior and King 181

Text and music: Hugh W. Dougall (1872–1963; LDS)
Tune name: BERNARD

Whatever the distractions of the week may have been, the ordinance of the sacrament brings with it a time to focus our thoughts upon the sacrifice and atonement of the Savior. The words of this sacrament hymn are a beautiful encouragement to sacred meditation.

Hugh W. Dougall's hymn text follows the thoughts and emotions of a worshipful congregation during the ordinance of the sacrament: first, we think of the Savior's sacrifice, the event commemorated through taking the sacrament; second, we eat the broken bread and think of the body of Christ, bruised and torn on the cross; and third, as we sip the sacramental water, we praise the Lord and ask to be led toward salvation.

The tune name, BERNARD, honors William Bernard Dougall, the father of the writer of this hymn. "Jesus of Nazareth, Savior and King" was first published in *Latter-day Saint Hymns* (1927).

We'll Sing All Hail to Jesus' Name 182

Text: Richard Alldridge (1815–1896; LDS)
Music: Joseph Coslett (1850–1910; LDS)
Tune name: EMMALINE

This hymn is an opportunity for members to offer their praises for the Atonement and to teach and exhort one another as they sing. Perhaps more beautifully than any other sacrament hymn, "We'll Sing All Hail to Jesus' Name" focuses on the Savior's triumph over sin and death.

One of the merits of this hymn is the meaningful sequence of its stanzas. Verse four, the one verse that refers directly to the sacrament, would not be nearly as effective if it came at the beginning. But before we get to it, the first three verses have carefully outlined the results of the Atonement: we are freed from the prison of the grave and the fetters of sin. Thus we are prepared, when we come to verse four, to have a new appreciation for the symbolism of the bread and water. And we are ready for the injunction to "partake and testify / Ye do remember him." For anyone singing the words thoughtfully, the impact should be significant.

J. Spencer Cornwall thought highly of this hymn: "It is an excellent hymn. The best principles of hymn composition such as interesting melodic line, integration of the various phrases, proper balance and emphasis, and simple but good harmonization, are in evidence throughout." (*Stories of Our Mormon Hymns*, p. 229.) He apparently would have voted against the omission of two seldom used verses, five and six, as happened in the 1985 hymnal: "All of the stanzas should be sung when it is used, to make the meaning complete." (Pp. 228–29.) As a matter of interest, here are the stanzas which he felt were required for completeness:

The sacrament the soul inspires
And calms the human breast,
Points to the time when faithful Saints
Shall enter into rest.

Then hail, all hail, to such a Prince
Who saves us by his blood!
He's marked the way and bids us tread
The path that leads to God.

The tune name, EMMALINE, honors Emmaline Haight, wife of composer Joseph Coslett. Tune and text were published together in the *Juvenile Instructor* in 1883, though the text alone had been published twelve years earlier in the *Millennial Star*.

In Remembrance of Thy Suffering 183

Text and music: Evan Stephens (1854–1930; LDS)
Tune name: REMEMBRANCE

In the words of J. Spencer Cornwall, "Evan Stephens shows his ability as a poet in this very lovely sacramental hymn. The rhythmical flow of the music in this hymn, induced by the ever-recurring triplets, makes it a likable song to sing as well as to hear." (*Stories of Our Mormon Hymns*, p. 258.)

In the 1950 hymnal, this sacrament hymn was marked for choir use. It was included for congregational use in the 1985 hymnal in the hope that congregations will be able to sing and enjoy it, even though it is among our more difficult hymns. Many syllables are sung on more than one note, and an additional difficulty is the omission of the bass line for three and one-half measures. But the key of the hymn has been lowered for easier unison singing, and most congregations, when they become thoroughly familiar with the melody, will enjoy this appealing sacrament hymn.

The hymn is unusual in its third verse, which focuses on the ordinance of the sacrament as an event marking the return of the Savior to this earth. Thus the weekly participation in the sacrament prefigures the time when we hope to share the sacramental bread and water with the Savior himself, as Saints who are spiritually prepared to meet with him at the time of his second coming.

This hymn was first published in 1884 in the *Deseret Sunday School Union Music Book*.

Upon the Cross of Calvary 184

Text: Vilate Raile (1890–1954; LDS)
Music: Leroy J. Robertson (1896–1971; LDS)
Tune name: MARIAN

Poetic and musical inspiration combine in this brief but memorable sacrament hymn. Three times the hymn invites us to envision the Savior "upon the cross," and each time that sacrifice is shown with a different emphasis: first, the blood that he shed for us; second, the overcoming of death; and third, the gift of "new birth" to all through the Savior's atonement.

J. Spencer Cornwall pointed out that although this hymn is a popular sacrament hymn, its text is at least as appropriate for Easter. (See *Stories of Our Mormon Hymns*, p. 232.)

The tune name, MARIAN, honors Dr. Marian Robertson (Mrs. W. Keith Wilson), daughter of the composer.

Reverently and Meekly Now 185

Text: Joseph L. Townsend (1849–1942; LDS)
Music: Ebenezer Beesley (1840–1906; LDS)
Tune name: MEEKNESS

This hymn should call forth special reverence from Latter-day Saints because in singing it we are singing words the poet imagined as those of the Savior himself. Instead of our petitioning him, he is pleading with us to remember his sacrifice, to be prayerful, and to be peaceable and forgiving toward one another.

It is the point of view of this hymn that is so startling and yet so effective. In simple terms, "point of view" means the vantage point from which a story or poem is given. It often involves the question of who the speaker or teller is assumed to be. This hymn is from the point of view of the Savior. Jesus is the speaker.

The writer, Joseph L. Townsend, wrote the words he imagined the Savior would say to us if he could speak to us directly just before the administration of the sacrament. In the hymn text, Jesus first describes the agony of his crucifixion. He then enjoins us to remember what the sacramental emblems stand for. Next, he asks for an end to strife and disagreement; the reward of forgiveness among us will be his "Spirit's grace." And finally, he tells us of his love for us and of his hope that we will choose to follow him in obedience.

This hymn was part of the choir section of the 1950 hymnal. In its original arrangement, men's voices alone sang the third line and the first half of line four. All four parts are now given in these measures, though in the last line the two measures for women's voices were retained as in the original arrangement. The key was lowered.

When Hugh D. McKeller of the University of Toronto reviewed the 1985 hymnal for the April 1986 issue of *The Hymn*, the journal of the Hymn Society of America, he singled out this hymn for special praise (p. 45): "A cameo like 'Reverently and Meekly Now' would enhance a communion [sacrament] service in any church."

The text of this hymn first appeared in 1891, and tune and text were published together in the 1896 *Latter-day Saints' Psalmody*.

Again We Meet Around the Board — 186

Text: Eliza R. Snow (1804–1887; LDS)
Music: George Careless (1839–1932; LDS)
Tune name: BETHLEHEM

After setting an appropriately reverent tone through meditation on the Savior's atoning sacrifice, this beautiful hymn moves into a solemn prayer, asking that we may realize the full significance of the Savior's gift, thereby making ourselves more worthy to partake of the sacrament. J. Spencer Cornwall notes that this hymn is "thoroughly Latter-day Saint in character." (*Stories of Our Mormon Hymns*, p. 249.)

"Again We Meet Around the Board" was one of the sacrament hymns marked for choir use in the 1950 hymnal. Although the key of the hymn has been lowered in the 1985 hymnal, the lovely four-measure soprano and alto duet—a more sophisticated feature than is usually found in a congregational hymn—has been retained. But this should not present a great difficulty for most congregations. With increased familiarity, most congregations should be able to find great uplift and enjoyment in this sacrament hymn.

Two verses of Eliza R. Snow's hymn that were printed in the 1950 hymnal were omitted in the 1985 version. Here are the omitted verses, the fourth and fifth:

We're his, who has the purchase made;
His life, his blood, the price he paid;
We're his, to do his sacred will,
And his requirements all fulfill.

Jesus, the great fac-simile
Of the Eternal Deity,
Has stooped to conquer, died to save
From sin and sorrow and the grave.

The original sixth verse is printed in the 1985 hymnal as verse four.

Eliza R. Snow's text was first printed in 1871 in the *Millennial Star,* and tune and text were published together in the *Utah Musical Times* in 1877.

God Loved Us, So He Sent His Son — 187

Text: Edward P. Kimball (1882–1937; LDS)
Music: Alexander Schreiner (1901–1987; LDS)
Tune name: MARGARET

If we had only the first line of this hymn, we would have an eloquent sermon on the meaning of the sacrament and the Atonement. It is a beautiful hymn on the significance of the Savior's life and death. First, the attention is on the Savior's mission—not only his mission of atonement but also that of teaching and showing an example. Then the focus turns to our responsibility: we must repay God's great love through bending our will to his.

J. Spencer Cornwall had words of high praise for "God Loved Us, So He Sent His Son": "It is a sacramental hymn, quiet, devotional, thought-provoking in quality both as to text and accompanying melody. . . . The doctrinal statements are couched in fervent, emotional expression. This quality is paralleled in the hymn melody and its poignant harmonies." (*Stories of Our Mormon Hymns,* pp. 196–97.)

Particularly when the hymn is used as a sacrament hymn, its message is more complete when all five verses are sung. The fifth verse is the only one referring specifically to the ordinance of the sacrament.

The tune name, MARGARET, honors Margaret Lyman Schreiner, wife of the composer.

Thy Will, O Lord, Be Done 188

Text: Frank I. Kooyman (1880–1963; LDS)
Music: Robert P. Manookin (b. 1918; LDS)
Tune name: HELENE

"Thy will, O Lord, be done": these words spoken by the Savior conclude each verse of this hymn. In verse one, these words take us back to the premortal council, when the Savior offered himself as a willing sacrifice for mankind. In verse two, these words reflect the Savior's life of service to his Father. In verse three, they remind us of the Redeemer's agony—and his obedience—in Gethsemane. But in verse four, it is the congregation that offers this sacred commitment. As we contemplate the Savior's sacrifice and prepare ourselves to take the bread and water that are its symbol, his words become our words.

The hymn offers a uniquely Latter-day Saint perspective on the Savior's sacrifice, focusing on the premortal selection of Jesus for this role. As J. Spencer Cornwall said of this hymn, "What a field for contemplation is opened here for heart and mind to enter while the sacred emblems of the body and blood of the Sinless One are being passed!" (*Stories of Our Mormon Hymns*, p. 213.)

The story of the hymn tune (named HELENE in honor of the wife of Robert P. Manookin) is an example of how some of our finest hymns—some of the most successful matchings of tune and text—come into being in a roundabout way. "Brother Michael Moody gave me the poem by President Gordon B. Hinckley, 'My Redeemer Lives,' and asked that I set it to music," related Robert Manookin. "Elder G. Homer Durham had also set the same poem to music, and his setting was chosen for publication [no. 135]. My setting of that poem accounts, in the last phrase, for the rise of a sixth in the melody to emphasize the words 'my King' in verse one. The music committee kindly made use of the music by matching it to the words of Brother Kooyman. The final phrase also fits well with his words."

Under the title "When in the Wondrous Realms Above," and with a different hymn tune, Frank I. Kooyman's words were part of the 1950 hymnal.

O Thou, Before the World Began 189

Text: William H. Turton (1856–1938; LDS)
Music: Frank W. Asper (1892–1973; LDS)
Tune name: NOALL

Latter-day Saints have a unique perception of the atoning mission of Jesus Christ. He was not sent as a last-minute emergency remedy to save an erring world. His mission, as this hymn so beautifully relates, was part of an eternal plan, established before our earth was created, to ensure the resurrection and redemption of mankind.

This belief is central to the Latter-day Saint perception of the Savior's mission. Elder James E. Talmage described the premortal existence and foreordination of Christ in these words:

"We affirm, on the authority of Holy Scripture, that the Being who is known among men as Jesus of Nazareth, and by all who acknowledge His Godhood as Jesus the Christ, existed with the Father prior to birth in the flesh; and that in the preexistent state He was chosen and ordained to be the one and only Savior and Redeemer of the human race." (*Jesus the Christ* [Salt Lake City, Utah: Deseret Book Co., 1969], p. 6.)

The Savior's sacrifice "continues new"; it is efficacious for all time. The last verse of this dramatic hymn asks us to move our vision back across "the years between" and view the moment of the Crucifixion: "My Lord, my God, who dies for me."

Like several other sacrament hymns, "O Thou, Before the World Began" was included as a choir hymn in the 1950 hymnal but was adapted for congregational use in the 1985 hymnbook. (See no. 178.)

The tune name, NOALL, honors the family of the composer's mother.

In Memory of the Crucified 190

Text: Frank I. Kooyman (1880–1963; LDS)
Music: Alexander Schreiner (1901–1987; LDS)
Tune name: GAILEY

In this hymn, we address the Father directly. Our purpose, as stated in verses one and four, is two-fold: to ask for his Spirit to abide with us, and to ask him to sanctify the sacrament we are about to partake of. The two verses that come between speak first of the Savior's bitter cup in Gethsemane and then of the bread and cup we are about to take in remembrance of his sacrifice.

J. Spencer Cornwall wrote the following in *Stories of Our Mormon Hymns*:

"According to the composer of this hymn, it is a sacramental hymn, directing us to the emblems, and thoughts which should be in our meditations at that time. Calm, not rousing to action, but rather inviting to contemplation of divine qualities. This hymn melody is written in the style of the old German chorale.

"It is unusually sacred in its expression, being clearly directed to our Heavenly Father with these words: 'May thy sweet Spirit here abide, that all may feel its glowing power.' And the purpose of this hymn is clear, also: 'to prepare our minds and hearts for the partaking, worthily, of the emblems of the Sacrament.'

"[Brother] Kooyman's old-world religious experience[,] the limited administration of the Lord's Supper there – only a few times a year – may have had a tendency to make him more appreciative of its constant use in the restored Church. Be that as it may, he feels that with the coming of the true gospel . . . into his life, there also came a better understanding, a fundamental change in his valuation of the Sacrament." (P. 112.)

The tune name, GAILEY, honors Elder William E. Gailey, who baptized Alexander Schreiner in Nurnberg, Germany, in 1909.

Behold the Great Redeemer Die 191

Text: Eliza R. Snow (1804–1887; LDS)
Music: George Careless (1839–1932; LDS)
Tune name: SACRAMENT

The first word of this hymn, *Behold,* takes us to Calvary as eyewitnesses to the Savior's crucifixion. We see his suffering and hear his words as if we were there. In verse six, our hymnic vision brings us to renewed commitment as we partake of the sacrament in remembrance of what we have just witnessed.

Only a very absent-minded singer can fail to be moved by the words of Eliza R. Snow. Her purpose was to help us bring all our attention to bear on the suffering of Christ and the meaning of his sacrifice. The hymn takes us through the experience of the Crucifixion, event by event: the piercing of his hands, feet, and side; the insults; the crown of thorns; Christ's willingness to proceed with the will of his Father; the darkness and earthquake that followed his death. After the sorrow and grief of Christ's death, the final verse of the hymn states simply and joyfully, "He lives – he lives."

The hymn was printed for choir use in the 1950 hymnal. Now in a lower key, it otherwise retains the same arrangement, with a soprano and alto duet in measures nine through twelve.

The tune SACRAMENT and this hymn text were first published together in the *Utah Musical Times* in 1877.

He Died! The Great Redeemer Died 192

Text: Isaac Watts (1674–1748); altered
Music: George Careless (1839–1932; LDS)
Tune name: OFFERING

This powerful sacrament hymn juxtaposes the two emotions we feel as we contemplate the Savior's sacrifice: on the one hand, grief that it was necessary for him to suffer torture and humiliation; on the other hand, joy at the miracle of his resurrection. The tears of verse one give way to "sudden joys" and the triumphant, welcoming shouts of angels.

The original Isaac Watts text began "He dies! the Heavenly Lover dies." It became a well-known hymn in an altered version by Martin Madan (1726–1790), an Englishman who was editor of an important hymn collection. Madan's version began "He dies! the Friend of Sinners dies! / Lo! Salem's daughters weep around!"

It was a variant of this hymn—Madan's modification of Watts—that appeared in Emma Smith's 1835 hymnal. This 1835 adaptation was probably by William W. Phelps. Here are verses five and six from that hymnal, verses not retained in our present-day collection:

Wipe off your tears, ye saints and tell
How high your great deliv'rer reigns:
Sing how he triumph'd over hell,
And how he'll bind your foe in chains.

Say, "Live forever wond'rous King!
Born to redeem and strong to save!"
Then ask the monster—"Where's thy sting?
And where's thy vict'ry, boasting grave?"

I Stand All Amazed 193

Text and music: Charles H. Gabriel (1856–1932)
Tune name: GABRIEL

Many people are quick to condemn themselves because of their own unworthiness. Yet the Savior's atonement extends to everyone. As we sing this hymn, we express our gratitude for the great gift of the Atonement, which far exceeds anything we can do to deserve it. We acknowledge our weakness and at the same time pledge our faith and everlasting gratitude.

This popular sacrament hymn entered Latter-day Saint hymnody in *Deseret Sunday School Songs* in 1909, only ten years after its first publication in a gospel-song collection. It has gone through three stages of musical revision. In the 1909 printing, the melody of the verse was given to the tenors, with the altos (or all the women's voices) singing a harmony part. J. Spencer Cornwall called this arrangement "a musical effect which was very pleasing and unusual in hymn writing." (*Stories of Our Mormon Hymns*, p. 94.) In addition, in the chorus the women's voices alone sang the words "that He should care for me, / Enough to die for me!" while the men's voices repeated the words "wonderful! wonderful!" in harmony with the words "care for me" and "die for me."

In the 1950 hymnal, the arrangement of the chorus remained the same, but sopranos and altos carried the duet of the verse.

In the 1985 hymnal, the soprano/alto duet remains, but all four voice parts sing the same words in the chorus; the men's response of "wonderful! wonderful!" has been omitted. Each step of this musical revision has made the hymn easier to sing, although some Latter-day Saints, in agreement with J. Spencer Cornwall, may miss the more colorful effects of the original arrangement.

There Is a Green Hill Far Away 194

Text: Cecil Frances Alexander (1818–1895)
Music: John H. Gower (1855–1922)
Tune name: MEDITATION

This hymn is a gentle and beautiful preparation for the sacrament. Rather than emphasizing the details of Christ's suffering, it reminds us that the Savior's love for us motivated his sacrifice; in return, our love for him should motivate us as we reaffirm our commitment of obedience and service.

The Christian education of children was one of Cecil Frances Alexander's lifelong priorities, and she wrote this hymn and many others, such as "He Is Risen!" (no. 199) and "Once in Royal David's City" (no. 205), to help her Sunday School class learn important Christian truths. The hymn is a commentary on the most basic doctrines of the Atonement: that the sacrifice of Jesus was for our salvation, that he was the only one qualified to fill the requirements of the Atonement, that his sacrifice "unlock[s] the gate / Of heaven," that in return we should trust and serve him.

Mrs. Alexander did not ever travel in the Holy Land. Those who have been to Judea will have noted the absence of anything like the "green hill" of the hymn's first line; such hills are more typical of Mrs. Alexander's native Ireland. But the doctrinal truths of the hymn are more important than its correlation with geographical reality. The simple assertions of the four short verses have made it a favorite with both children and adults in many Christian denominations.

It should be noted that the phrase "without a city wall" means "outside a city wall." This use of *without*, no longer common today, is simply the opposite of *within*.

J. Spencer Cornwall noted: "Many tunes are extant for 'There Is a Green Hill.' In a previous volume of Latter-day Saint Hymns, this hymn was given the old ballad tune of 'Drink to Me Only with Thine Eyes.' This kind of combination of music and words can hardly be condoned. The setting . . . by John H. Gower is very appropriate and lovely—especially so in the third phrase." (*Stories of Our Mormon Hymns*, p. 214.)

How Great the Wisdom and the Love 195

Text: Eliza R. Snow (1804–1887; LDS)
Music: Thomas McIntyre (1833–1914; LDS)
Tune name: MORMON

This beautiful sacrament hymn has a distinctly Latter-day Saint emphasis in the way it presents the Atonement. The first and sixth verses place the Savior's sacrifice in the context of a great plan established from the foundations of the earth. Our vision of the Atonement, our sense of its significance, grows more complete as we sing of the eternal plan of which this event was a part.

Of all the hymn texts by Eliza R. Snow, "How Great the Wisdom and the Love" may be the most often sung. In dignified and memorable phrases, the hymn tells the story of the sacrificial offering of Jesus Christ. Because of the exceptional beauty of this text, all six verses were retained in the 1985 hymnbook.

The hymn opens with a reference to Christ's ordination in the premortal life as the one who would redeem mankind from sin. Verses two and three then tell of his earthly mission, referring to the blood of his sacrifice and to his triumph through "strict obedience" to the will of his Father. Jesus was the first who "marked the path and led the way" toward the vision of the promised resurrection, as unfolded in verse four. Verses five and six (now in reverse order from the way they were printed in the 1950 hymnbook, because the original verse five is actually a more satisfying conclusion) highlight the meaning of Christ's mission in our own lives.

It is possible that Eliza R. Snow derived the suggestion for this hymn's opening line from an 1817 hymn by Benjamin Beddome, beginning "How great the wisdom, power, and grace," but no other lines are similar. Eliza R. Snow's text first appeared in *Sacred Hymns and Spiritual Songs* in 1871. The tune, MORMON, first appeared with this text in the *Juvenile Instructor* in January 1879.

Jesus, Once of Humble Birth 196

Text: Parley P. Pratt (1807–1857; LDS)
Music: Giacomo Meyerbeer (1791–1864); adapted
Tune name: DELIVERANCE

A paradox is a seeming contradiction—an apparent impossibility or lack of logic—that turns out to be harmonious when it is understood more fully. Christ's teachings are full of paradox; Matthew 23:11, "He that is greatest among you shall be your servant," is just one example. This hymn is a triumphant meditation on the paradoxes of the Savior's life and ministry.

By setting up a repeated "Once . . . , Now . . ." sequence, Elder Parley P. Pratt structured a series of poetic contrasts. On the one hand are the poverty, pain, and submissiveness of the Savior's life; on the other hand are his sovereignty and power, the miracle of his atonement and resurrection.

The events of Jesus' earthly life were often painful or humiliating. He was born in a stable; he submitted to torture and mockery, a sham trial and conviction, and an agonizing death. But in his divinity and his mission, he is King of both heaven and earth.

The words of this hymn allow us to dwell upon and revel in these contrasts. What joy this meditation brings to our hearts! Whatever his struggle, whatever his trials, Jesus triumphed over all in the fulfillment of his mission.

J. Spencer Cornwall observed of this hymn: "The dynamic markings found in the earlier editions of the hymnal are omitted in the 1950 edition. It is my opinion after hearing it sung by congregations both ways, that the loud and soft variations enhance the interest in this hymn." (*Stories of Our Mormon Hymns*, p. 101.)

Latter-day Saints whose experience in the Church goes back several decades will remember that for "Jesus, Once of Humble Birth," most congregations made use of vocal dynamics in a way that was not true of any other hymn. The earlier hymnals referred to by Brother Cornwall marked the first four measures *piano* (soft), measures five through eight *forte* (loud), measures nine through twelve *piano*, measures thirteen through sixteen *forte*, and the last four *piano*. Thus, through the volume of its singing, the congregation was able to emphasize the paradoxes presented in the text.

The tune, DELIVERANCE, is from a little-known opera by Meyerbeer titled *Il Crociato in Egitto* (*The Crusader in Egypt*).

O Savior, Thou Who Wearest a Crown 197

Text: Karen Lynn Davidson (b. 1943; LDS)
Music: Hans Leo Hassler (1564–1612); adapted by J. S. Bach (1685–1750)
Tune name: PASSION CHORALE

For Easter season, or in preparation for the sacrament, this hymn gives us an opportunity to meditate upon the suffering and sacrifice of the Savior. Even those who betrayed and tortured Jesus at his crucifixion are still within the embrace of his atonement.

The author of this hymn text is also the author of this book. I was thrilled to learn that the 1985 hymnal was to include PASSION CHORALE, a hymn melody that Christians have sung for almost four hundred years. J. S. Bach incorporated this chorale in the *St. Matthew Passion*, the *Christmas Oratorio*, and five cantatas.

The actual text had not been decided upon, but the subject of the text was a foregone conclusion, since the tune has almost always been paired with a crucifixion text. (The word *passion* refers to the Savior's suffering from Gethsemane until his death.) The melody suits this serious subject in a powerful way; many Protestant hymnals contain a version beginning "O sacred head, now wounded."

My goal in this text was three-fold: to write a text that did not flinch from the details of the Crucifixion; to show that Christ's agony and death were the paradoxical source of healing and release for his children; and to provide a text that could serve a Latter-day Saint congregation as both a sacrament hymn and an Easter hymn.

My first efforts were, in part, an amalgamation of existing English-language versions of the traditional text, in the hope that a text already in print might be suitable for the Latter-day Saint hymnal. But the Hymnbook Committee sent my efforts back, suggesting further work. I had tried, it hadn't worked out, and it appeared that someone else would have to furnish the words for PASSION CHORALE.

Then I attended the 1984 meeting of the Hymn Society of America in Chicago. The guest of honor, a well-known British hymn writer, spoke of the need for any hymn-text author to be willing to revise again and again: false pride should have no role.

His words hit home; it was time for another attempt. What topic, after all, is more worthy of prayerful and painstaking attention than the Savior's atonement? It required many hours and dozens of rewrites, but the final "click" when the words fell into place was as satisfying as finally seizing upon the solution to a complex puzzle or math problem.

This hymn tune works so well as prelude music that the congregation could become familiar with it before singing it by hearing it over several weeks. It is easy to sing because of the mostly stepwise movement of the melody and because the first two lines are identical in all voice parts. The tune echoes perfectly the gravity of the words. It is a hymn of serious thought and contemplation.

That Easter Morn 198

Text: Marion D. Hanks (b. 1921; LDS)
Music: Robert Cundick (b. 1926; LDS)
Tune name: EASTER MORN

The joyful message of Easter is that Christ has conquered death in our behalf. Anxieties concerning death, extinction, oblivion, or separation need have no place in our thoughts. Because of the resurrection of our Lord Jesus Christ on that first Easter morning long ago, we may truly "conquer fear."

During sacrament meeting on Easter Sunday in 1970, Elder Marion D. Hanks of the First Quorum of the Seventy wrote a poem—"That Easter Morn"—on the back of a ward bulletin. Later, when Tabernacle organist Robert Cundick asked Maxine Hanks to suggest one of her husband's poems for him to set to music, she chose "That Easter Morn." This hymn is new to the 1985 hymnal.

Most hymn texts follow a strict form, as decided upon by the author. Each line must have a certain number of syllables, and rhymes must occur at certain points. In "That Easter Morn," Elder Hanks set himself an impressively demanding poetic task. Consider what must happen in the last two lines of each verse: the lines must rhyme with each other, they must include a form of the verb *conquer*, and they must advance the hymn's message in a natural way—all this in the space of only four syllables per line! Because of the poet's technical skill, the poem's beautiful message emerges in a fresh and significant form.

The phrase "first and last," an expression of the everlasting nature of Deity, occurs many times in the scriptures. A comparable phrase is "alpha and omega"; alpha and omega are the first and last letters of the Greek alphabet. (See their use as a title for Christ in D&C 19:1.) When the Lord appeared to Joseph Smith and Oliver Cowdery, as described in Doctrine and Covenants 110, he introduced himself with these words: "I am the first and the last; I am he who liveth, I am he who was slain; I am your advocate with the Father." (V. 4.)

Elder Hanks's reversal of this phrase, "Last and First," works especially well in an Easter hymn, since Jesus was the last to die before resurrection was made a reality, and the first to be resurrected.

The congregation will not find this hymn tune particularly difficult if the music director and organist have rehearsed carefully, so that the fermata (hold) and the distinctive instrumental passages sound natural and convincing.

He Is Risen! 199

Text: Cecil Frances Alexander (1818–1895)
Music: Joachim Neander (1650–1680)
Tune name: NEANDER

In terms both children and adults can understand, this joyful hymn is an Easter proclamation, announcing to the world that Jesus Christ has risen. This miracle embraces all mankind. As the hymn states, "Death is conquered, man is free. / Christ has won the victory."

Cecil Frances Alexander's most popular hymns were written for children. This text and the text "There Is a Green Hill Far Away" (no. 194) and "Once in Royal David's City" (no. 205) were part of a series of religious verses that she wrote to instruct children in the meaning of various parts of the Apostles' Creed, which is a statement of belief recited by the congregation in some Christian denominations as part of a worship service. The hymn text "He Is Risen!" (1846) relates to the lines of the Apostles' Creed that state, "The third day he rose again from the dead; He ascended into Heaven."

Even when a particular Easter morning happens to be dark and rainy, we can still understand the figurative meaning of this hymn's statement that "Not one darksome cloud is dimming / Yonder glorious morning ray." Because Jesus has triumphed, once and for all, over death—"sin's dark prison"—the "Easter beam" of the Resurrection is always with us. The resurrection that occurred on the first Easter morning sends forth a ray of light that symbolizes the resurrection of all mankind.

This much-loved hymn tune was first published in 1680, almost two hundred years before the text was written.

Christ the Lord Is Risen Today 200

Text: Charles Wesley (1707–1788)
Music: Anonymous, Lyra Davidica *(1708)*
Tune name: EASTER HYMN

One of the best-loved of all Easter hymns, "Christ the Lord Is Risen Today" proclaims the great, central miracle of Christianity: that Jesus Christ, though dead, arose from the tomb, and that through this resurrection he conquered death on behalf of all mankind.

The original hymn text, published in 1739, had no "alleluias"; they were added later with the use of this tune, EASTER HYMN. *Alleluia,* a transcription of a Hebrew word meaning "praise ye the Lord," or "praise ye Jehovah," is a joyful exclamation that is clearly appropriate to the triumphant message of this hymn.

The original hymn was eleven stanzas long. Lines three and four of the second verse, as printed in our hymnal, are altered from Charles Wesley's original lines: "Lo! the sun's eclipse is o'er; / Lo! he sets in blood no more."

Other verses sometimes included in Christian hymnals include these:

Vain the stone, the watch, the seal,
Christ hath burst the gates of hell:
Death in vain forbids his rise;
Christ hath opened paradise.

Soar we now where Christ has led,
Following our exalted Head;
Made like him, like him we rise,
Ours the cross, the grave, the skies!

"Christ the Lord Is Risen Today" is probably the most popular of all Easter hymns among Latter-day Saints. It is interesting to note that although Emma Smith included this text in her 1841 hymnal, for some reason it was dropped from Latter-day Saint hymnody until the 1948 hymnbook.

Joy to the World 201

Text: Isaac Watts (1674–1748);
altered by William W. Phelps (1792–1872; LDS)
Music: George F. Handel (1685–1759);
arranged by Lowell Mason (1792–1872)
Tune name: ANTIOCH

Ever since Emma Smith included it in her hymnal of 1835, this energetic and dignified hymn has been a favorite among Latter-day Saints. Today we follow the practice of the rest of the Christian world in using it mainly as a Christmas carol.

But this hymn has also served a second purpose: it is clear that William W. Phelps's intention was to adapt it as a millennial hymn. The early Saints loved to sing of the millennium, and with some changes in verb tense—such as "The Lord *will* come" (rather than *is* come)—and a few other alterations, William W. Phelps made it suitable for that purpose. It is interesting that Isaac Watts's original title for the hymn suggests this millennial spirit: "The Messiah's Coming and Kingdom."

The 1985 hymnal returned to the traditional verb tense in the opening line—"the Lord is come"—preserving the more common Christmas message. Other changes made by William W. Phelps have been retained, however, such as the line popular among members of the Church: "And Saints and angels sing" (rather than "heaven and nature").

George F. Handel and Lowell Mason share credit for the remarkable melody. (Note how the first phrase is nothing more than a descending major scale!) How Lowell Mason arrived at the tune is not perfectly clear, but it is possible that he brought together two melodic suggestions from Handel's *Messiah.* First was the opening of "Lift Up Your Heads":

mf
Lift up your heads, O ye__gates,

This phrase suggested the first measures of "Joy to the World." And the first measures of the accompaniment to the tenor aria "Comfort Ye My People"

became a later passage in "Joy to the World":

And Saints and an-gels sing, And Saints and an-gels sing, And Saints,

Lowell Mason himself gave principal credit to George F. Handel; when he published "Joy to the World" in *Occasional Psalms* (1836), he marked it "Arr. from Handel." We do not know for sure why he named the tune ANTIOCH; he took Bible names almost at random for his tunes.

Oh, Come, All Ye Faithful 202

Text and music: Attributed to John Francis Wade (ca. 1711–1786)
Tune name: ADESTE FIDELES or PORTUGUESE HYMN

This regal and dignified carol is a summons to join the faithful who are thronging toward Bethlehem to see the newly born King, the long-awaited Savior. Repeatedly, we urge one another, "let us adore him"—adore him as an infant in the manger, and, by implication, as our guide and Redeemer.

"Oh, Come, All Ye Faithful" is one of the most popular of all our carols, but decades of research by Christian scholars have failed to resolve the question of its origins. Seven manuscripts from the eighteenth century include this hymn, and it has not been found in any earlier sources. Since the seven manuscripts in which it appears were all the work of the same copyist—John F. Wade—a strong possibility exists that he was the author as well as the copyist. At no time did Wade claim authorship, however, and scholars continue to suggest alternative sources.

The original language of the hymn was Latin. Though Frederick Oakeley is credited with our hymnal's translation, his version has been altered; his original first line was "Ye faithful, approach ye." The tune title, ADESTE FIDELES, meaning "Be present [draw near], ye faithful," comes from the first words of the original Latin hymn.

PORTUGUESE HYMN, an alternate tune name, has its origins in the fact that the Duke of Leeds first heard this hymn in the Portuguese Chapel in London about 1785. He had charge of a concert series called Concerts of Ancient Music, and when he introduced the hymn on one of his programs he referred to it as the "Portuguese Hymn."

Angels We Have Heard on High 203

Text: French carol (ca. 1862)
Music: French carol
Tune name: GLORIA

"Angels We Have Heard on High," a traditional French Christmas carol, is new to the 1985 hymnal. It tells the story of the angels' appearance to the shepherds in the fields of Bethlehem. So many Latter-day Saints had already been charmed by this delightful carol that it was a welcome addition to the hymnbook.

The note at the bottom of the hymn gives the approximate date of the text as 1862. This is the year the carol first appeared in print; its origins may in fact date back a hundred or more years before that time. No one knows the date of the carol's origin, its author, its composer, or the translator of our English version.

The carol can be read as a question-and-answer encounter between the excited shepherds and a stranger who does not know about the miraculous event that has just taken place. In verse one, the shepherds exclaim over the angelic chorus they have just heard. Naturally, in verse two, the stranger wants to know more: Why are you so joyful? What are the tidings that inspire this celebration? In verse three, the shepherds answer: "Come to Bethlehem and see . . . Christ the Lord, the newborn King."

In the chorus, we sing the Latin translation of the words of the angel chorus: "Gloria in excelsis Deo" (*ex CHEL sis DAY o*) means "Glory to God in the highest."

Other Christian hymnals sometimes include a fourth verse that continues the narrative and takes the scene to the stable itself:

See him in a manger laid,
Whom the choirs of angels praise;
Mary, Joseph, lend your aid,
While our hearts in love we raise.

Silent Night 204

Text: Joseph Mohr (1792–1848);
translated by John F. Young (1820–1885)
Music: Franz Gruber (1787–1863)
Tune name: STILLE NACHT

The holy child and his mother, the shepherds, the angelic hosts—the scenes from the scriptural account of the Nativity are referred to only in the briefest way in this beloved Christmas hymn. Yet the peaceful, familiar melody evokes the entire scene. As we sing, our hearts and memories fill in what is missing, and our sense of that sacred night is complete.

It is amazing to realize that this best-known of all Christmas carols was virtually an "instant hymn." The words were written, set to music, and first performed all in a single day. Though fanciful stories often spring up over the years about popular hymns, the account that is often told of the writing of "Silent Night" can in fact be documented as historical. This carol was written in an attempt to make the best of a musical emergency when the organ of a small Austrian church broke down on the morning of Christmas Eve.

On December 24, 1818, Father Joseph Mohr, the assistant parish priest at the St. Nikolaus Catholic Church in Oberndorf, Austria, decided to write a new hymn for the evening service. Because the church organ could not be repaired in time, he needed a Christmas hymn that the organist, Franz Gruber, could accompany on his guitar. He took the words to Franz Gruber, who wrote the music, and the two of them sang the hymn at the evening service, with the choir joining in on the last two lines.

The carol's fame spread far faster than that of its creators. Traveling musicians soon popularized it throughout Europe and the United States, and the tune was attributed to many different composers, including Mozart! But in 1854, Franz Gruber wrote a public letter setting the record straight and establishing proper credit for himself and Father Joseph Mohr.

The original hymn text was quite a bit longer; today English-speaking congregations use the first, sixth, and second verses of the original. The translator was John Freeman Young (1820–1885), an American Episcopal bishop. The tune, also, has been changed somewhat from Franz Gruber's original melody.

The tune name, STILLE NACHT, is from the first two words of the original German hymn, meaning "quiet night."

Once in Royal David's City 205

Text: Cecil Frances Alexander (1818–1895)
Music: Henry J. Gauntlett (1805–1876)
Tune name: IRBY

This popular children's carol, new to the 1985 hymnal, can be enjoyed by both children and adults. It not only tells of the birth of Christ but also looks toward the events that will follow and bears testimony of the Savior's mission.

Two other hymn texts in our hymnbook are by Cecil Frances Alexander: "There Is a Green Hill Far Away" (no. 194) and "He Is Risen!" (no. 199). Her purpose in writing "Once in Royal David's City" was the same as in writing the other two hymns: she wished to make it easier for children to understand the meaning of different parts of the Apostles' Creed, a statement of belief recited by the congregation during worship services in some Christian denominations. "Once in Royal David's City" tells of the events that surround the section of the creed that states: "Who was conceived by the Holy Ghost, Born of the Virgin Mary." All three of these hymns first appeared in *Hymns for Little Children,* published in 1848.

Mrs. Alexander had a great gift for expressing Christian truths in language that even a child could understand. "Once in Royal David's

City" tells the Christmas story in such simple terms that even someone who knew nothing of the events of Jesus' birth could begin with this hymn to learn the answers to some essential questions: Where did it take place? What was the setting? What were the names of the mother and child? What made this child different from any other child ever to be born upon the earth? Why are his life and mission significant to all people everywhere?

The tune name, IRBY, refers to a town in Lincolnshire, England.

Away in a Manger 206

Text: Anonymous (ca. 1883, Philadelphia, Pennsylvania)
Music: William J. Kirkpatrick (1838–1921);
harmonized by Rosalee Elser (b. 1925)
Tune name: CRADLE SONG

This famous Christmas carol is clearly intended to be sung by children. But it has become so popular with adults as well that many Christian hymnals—including the 1985 Latter-day Saint hymnal—include it among the Christmas carols.

A well-known story says that Martin Luther was the author of this hymn. In fact, it is sometimes called "Luther's Cradle Hymn," and the story has been elaborated to state that Martin Luther sang his own children to sleep with this carol of his own composition. But this charming story has no basis in fact. The text first appeared not in Germany but in the United States. We do not know the author's name, but the text was written in America in the 1880s and first published by the American Lutheran Church.

Many composers have been attracted by these simple, appealing words, and the text has been sung to various folk melodies as well. The hymn tune CRADLE SONG by William J. Kirkpatrick was chosen for our hymnal because of its dignity and simplicity.

The second verse seems to make quite an abrupt shift from the scene at the manger to a prayer to Lord Jesus to "look down from the sky / And stay by my cradle. . . ." But this verse is actually quite skillful in representing the thoughts of a child. The first half of verse two tells of Jesus being roused by the lowing of the cattle and awaking in darkness, and this reference might bring thoughts of anxious, wakeful nighttime hours to many children. So the request to Jesus, "stay by my cradle till morning is nigh" does not really represent a leap in logic—at least not from the point of view of a child.

It Came upon the Midnight Clear 207

Text: Edmund H. Sears (1810–1876)
Music: Richard S. Willis (1819–1900)
Tune name: CAROL

When the angels appeared to the shepherds to announce the birth of the infant Jesus, their message was significant to the entire human race. From that birth began a series of changes and miracles, foretold by prophets, that would teach and redeem the people of the world. This hymn sings of the angels' message and its implications.

Edmund H. Sears, a Unitarian minister who wrote this popular carol in 1849, was naturally concerned with the social changes that would, or should, result from the Savior's birth and ministry. His hymn text is concerned with the angels' message not just as a one-time event but as an announcement that continues today to float "o'er all the weary world," heralding a new age of peace and happiness.

The author's social concerns are even more evident when we read two verses not included in our hymnal:

Yet with the woes of sin and strife
The world has suffered long;
Beneath the angel strain have rolled
Two thousand years of wrong;
And man, at war with man, hears not
The love song which they bring:
O hush the noise, ye men of strife,
And hear the angels sing!

And ye, beneath life's crushing load,
Whose forms are bending low,
Who toil along the climbing way
With painful steps and slow,
Look now! for glad and golden hours
Come swiftly on the wing:
O rest beside the weary road,
And hear the angels sing!

The clergyman who was editor of the volume that first printed this hymn remarked, "I always feel that, however poor my Christmas sermon may be, the reading and singing of this hymn are enough to make up for all deficiencies." (Quoted in Charles S. Nutter and Wilbur F. Tillett, *The Hymns and Hymn Writers of the Church* [New York: Methodist Book Concern, 1911], p. 63.) The poem, written in 1849, originally bore the title "Peace on Earth."

The tune that today seems so inseparable from these words was not originally written for them. Composed in 1850, it served as the melody for two other Christmas carols, "See Israel's gentle shepherds stand" and "While shepherds watched their flocks by night," before it was linked so successfully with "It Came upon a Midnight Clear."

O Little Town of Bethlehem 208

Text: Phillips Brooks (1835–1893)
Music: Lewis H. Redner (1831–1908)
Tune name: ST. LOUIS

This carol takes us back two thousand years—to the "little town of Bethlehem," where a miraculous gift has just been given to the world. A casual observer would at first sense nothing out of the ordinary. But as Christians, we look back on that night in awe and expectation.

The hymn's author, Phillips Brooks, was a Harvard-trained minister whose dynamic and Christ-centered sermons brought him great popularity. He traveled widely during his lifetime, and he based his Christmas hymn and its picture of Bethlehem on memories of an 1865 visit to the Holy Land. During these travels he arranged to spend Christmas in Bethlehem. On Christmas Eve, he visited the field where according to tradition the shepherds heard the angelic proclamation. He then attended services in the Church of the Nativity. Afterwards he wrote a letter to the children of his Sunday School in Philadelphia, to whom he was exceptionally devoted, telling them of "standing in the old church in Bethlehem, close to the spot where Jesus was born, when the whole church was ringing hour after hour with the splendid hymns of praise to God."

These vivid memories remained with Phillips Brooks. In 1868 he wrote this hymn text that embodies his lifelong devotion to the divine sonship of Jesus Christ. Lewis H. Redner, the superintendent of Reverend Brooks's Sunday School and also the church organist, set the text to music. An editor later named the tune ST. LOUIS, deriving this name from the composer's first name.

Our hymnal prints the first three verses of the carol. Originally it had two more, though Phillips Brooks himself later withdrew the fourth. Many hymnals include the fifth verse today, printing it as verse four. These are the original verses four and five:

Where children, pure and happy,
Pray to the Blessed Child;
Where misery cries out to thee,
Son of the Mother mild;
Where charity stands watching,

And faith holds wide the door,
The dark night wakes, the glory breaks,
And Christmas comes once more.

O holy Child of Bethlehem!
Descend to us, we pray;
Cast out our sin, and enter in,
Be born in us to-day.
We hear the Christmas angels
The great glad tidings tell;
O come to us, abide with us,
Our Lord Emmanuel.

Hark! the Herald Angels Sing 209

Text: Charles Wesley (1707–1788)
Music: Felix Mendelssohn (1809–1847)
Tune name: MENDELSSOHN

This favorite Christmas carol is an invitation to all people to join with the angels in their joyous song: Glory to the newborn King! Because all people, through this Savior, will have a "second birth," all may appropriately "join the triumph of the skies" in gratitude.

Most hymn scholars regard this hymn as among the finest in English hymnody. Since 1739, when the text was first published, many editors have made small changes in Charles Wesley's original words. The beginning and final lines of verse one were originally as follows:

Hark, how all the welkin [sky] rings!
Glory to the King of Kings; . . .
Universal nature say,
"Christ the Lord is born today."

Two of Charles Wesley's verses are not as consonant with Latter-day Saint beliefs and terminology and are not included in our hymnal:

Christ, by highest heaven adored,
Christ, the everlasting Lord:
Late in time, behold him come,
Offspring of a virgin's womb.
Veiled in flesh the Godhead see,
Hail th' incarnate Deity!
Pleased as man with men to dwell,
Jesus, our Immanuel.

Come, Desire of nations, come!
Fix in us thy humble home:
Rise, the woman's conquering seed,
Bruise in us the serpent's head;
Adam's likeness, Lord, efface,
Stamp thine image in its place:
Second Adam from above,
Reinstate us in thy love.

Felix Mendelssohn's fine melody is taken from a cantata that he wrote in 1840 in honor of the four hundredth anniversary of the invention of printing. Felix Mendelssohn himself expressed doubt that this tune could ever serve as a musical setting for a sacred text, but time has proved him wrong.

With Wondering Awe 210

*Text and music: Anonymous (*Laudis Corona, *Boston, 1885)*
Tune name: LAUDIS CORONA

In this appealing carol, the Christmas star becomes a symbol of peace throughout the world. Its rays are known everywhere. As Christians remember the Christmas story and the message of the angels, their hearts are turned toward the Christ child. Like the wise men, they wish to seek him.

The author and composer of this carol are not known. The first Latter-day Saint hymn collection in which it appeared was the *Deseret Sunday School Union Music Book* in 1884. It is likely that the carol was borrowed from an earlier non–Latter-day Saint source that has not yet been identified. The tune name, LAUDIS CORONA, is the name of a hymn collection published in Boston in which the tune appeared in 1885.

The scriptural accounts of the wise men say they followed a star; no mention is made there that the wise men "heard the angels singing," as the hymn states. Clearly, "With Wondering Awe" is an interesting example of how much we take for granted the text of a familiar hymn, without stopping to consider what might be a point of confusion in its details. In any case, the hymn's message of Christmas peace and joy is one we can accept without reservation, and concern over what the wise men saw or heard need not interfere with our enjoyment.

While Shepherds Watched Their Flocks 211

Text: Nahum Tate (1652–1715)
Music: Yorkshire carol (ca. 1800)
Tune name: YORKSHIRE MELODY

A part of the Christmas story loved by child and adult alike is the narration concerning the humble shepherds who were the first to hear the announcement of the Christ child's birth. We love to think of their amazement and delight, and we love to think on the nature of a Father who would choose lowly shepherds to receive this announcement.

Nahum Tate and his friend Nicholas Brady are known in the history of English hymns for their collaboration on a new metrical version of the psalms. It appeared in 1696 and soon supplanted the older hymnals of the Church of England.

By 1700, Nahum Tate and Nicholas Brady had published a supplement to their psalm volume that included sixteen new hymn texts based on other scriptural passages, including "While Shepherds Watched Their Flocks." That hymn text is a poetic rendering of the visit of the angels to the shepherds as told in Luke 2:8–14, and is by Nahum Tate alone, without the help of his collaborator. Emma Smith included a version of this carol in her 1841 hymnal.

Today, the text is popular throughout the English-speaking world and is paired in various hymnals with several different tunes, of which YORKSHIRE MELODY is one of the most familiar.

Far, Far Away on Judea's Plains 212

Text and music: John Menzies Macfarlane (1833–1892; LDS)
Tune name: CHATTERLEY

Most Latter-day Saints could not imagine a Christmas without the opportunity to sing this favorite carol. We can be proud of this Latter-day Saint contribution to the music of Christmas.

In a biography called *Yours Sincerely, John M. Macfarlane,* written and privately printed by his descendant L. W. Macfarlane, we learn the family tradition surrounding the writing of this carol. John Macfarlane was a choir director in St. George, Utah. "As involved as he was in music," the biography tells us, "John M. Macfarlane even dreamed music, and more than once, it is said, he would spring from his bed in the middle of the night to jot down a melody, lest the light of morning should erase it from his memory."

In the preholiday season of 1869, he decided his choir needed a new carol for their Christmas program. At his request, his friend Charles L. Walker provided a suitable text. But John Macfarlane labored in vain for a suitable melody; the music just would not come.

The biography continues: "Then one night it came, suddenly, in a dream. John was awake instantly. He shook Ann [his wife] into wakefulness, crying out, 'Ann, Ann, I have the words for a song, and I think I have the music too!' "

He found the next morning that the words he had written were in fact quite different from Charles L. Walker's text. Even so, he urged Charles Walker to put his name down as author, but the biography gives this as Walker's reply: "These are not my words, John. I have never seen them before. These are your words. You have written both the words and music yourself, and you must take the full credit."

We have no record of Walker's original words, and no way of knowing how close to our present text were the lines that served as a catalyst for Macfarlane. He wrote no other hymn texts—music was his talent. The tune name honors Macfarlane's wife, Ann Chatterley.

Visitors to the Holy Land know that Judea's shepherds herded their sheep on rocky hills rather than on plains. But this error in topography, made by one who had never traveled to Bethlehem, certainly does nothing to diminish the significance of this Latter-day Saint hymn.

"Far, Far Away on Judea's Plains" was first published in the *Juvenile Instructor* on December 15, 1889, twenty years after it was written.

John Macfarlane and Charles L. Walker collaborated on other hymns, of which "Dearest Children, God Is Near You" (no. 96) is still in our hymnal today.

The First Noel 213

Text and music: Traditional English carol (ca. 17th century)
Tune name: THE FIRST NOEL

This Christmas carol celebrates one of the best-loved incidents of the Christmas story: how the simple shepherds in the fields outside Bethlehem were the first ones ever to receive a Christmas greeting, when the angels appeared to them and "said" the first Noel.

The word *noel,* a French word sometimes used among English-speaking people as a Christmas greeting, is related to the Latin *natalis,* meaning "birthday." "The First Noel" is loved for its simplicity; it is not a sophisticated rendering of biblical events. Though Luke ties the Christmas star to the wise men, in this carol the shepherds, also, see the star.

When "The First Noel" was first printed in 1833, it had nine stanzas. The two printed in our hymnal do not carry the narrative beyond the appearance of the star. Various Christian hymnals choose different stanzas. Three that are often included change the focus from the shepherds to the wise men:

And by the light of that same star
Three wise men came from country far;
To seek a King was their intent,
And to follow the star wherever it went.

This star drew nigh to the northwest,
O'er Bethlehem it took its rest,
And there it did both stop and stay,
Right over the place where Jesus lay.

Then entered in those wise men three,
Full reverently upon the knee,
And offered there, in his presence,
Their gold and myrrh and frankincense.

I Heard the Bells on Christmas Day 214

Text: Henry Wadsworth Longfellow (1807–1882)
Music: John Baptiste Calkin (1827–1905)
Tune name: WALTHAM

As Christmas bells peal their traditional carols, a moment of despair overcomes one who hears them. With such hate and conflict in the world, how can this listener trust the message of "Peace on earth, good will to men"? But the song of hope and promise swells even louder: "the wrong shall fail, the right prevail, with peace on earth, good will to men."

Henry Wadsworth Longfellow's original poem, published in 1867, was seven stanzas long. The Christmas carol version omits the original verses four and five, which show his grief and frustration over the American Civil War. These omitted verses describe how the the awful sounds of war overpower the song of the Christmas bells:

Then from each black, accursed mouth
The cannon thundered in the South,
And with the sound
The carols drowned
Of peace on earth, good will to men.

It was as if an earthquake rent
The hearthstones of a continent,
And made forlorn

The households born
Of peace on earth, good will to men.

Verse three of the original poem has been made the final verse of the carol, so that two positive verses conclude the carol and leave us with a feeling of faith and optimism.

Ring Out, Wild Bells 215

Text: Alfred Tennyson (1809–1892)
Music: Crawford Gates (b. 1921; LDS)
Tune name: MARSDEN

In this hymn written to mark the joy and resolve of a new year, faith and optimism are triumphant. The false makes way for the true; the darkness makes way for "the Christ that is to be." It is a strong statement of hope in the future and in the divine destiny of mankind.

Tragedy came into the life of Alfred Tennyson when his closest friend, the gifted Arthur H. Hallam, died at age twenty-two. Over the next fourteen years, Tennyson worked through his grief in a long poem (actually a series of 131 shorter poems), which he called *In Memoriam.* He sometimes referred to *In Memoriam* by the subtitle, "The Progress of the Soul," because it describes the steps by which his intense personal grief finally brought him to greater compassion and spiritual sensitivity. "Ring Out, Wild Bells," one of the poems from this long work, shows Tennyson's determination to leave behind the disappointment and narrow vision of the past and reach out toward "the larger heart, the kindlier hand."

The composition of the tune involves an equally dramatic story. Crawford Gates had loved "Ring Out, Wild Bells" since he was a child, when his aunt Lucile Gates read to him from the poems of Tennyson. He had always considered it "a poetic encouragement to real repentance. The final line, 'Ring in the Christ that is to be,' asks us to rise to the full stature of Christ within ourselves."

In 1945, as a young officer of the United States Navy, Crawford Gates had been in Hawaii awaiting orders to participate in one of the Pacific invasions of World War II. He reported, "The dreaded assignment never came." At the war's end, when others were celebrating with cheers and revelry, he felt only one impulse: "to drop on my knees in the middle of my barracks and thank my Heavenly Father that the killing had stopped."

A few days later, in the Oahu Stake tabernacle, he set "Ring Out, Wild Bells" to music. The first to hear and learn this new hymn was Marsden Durham, a beloved former missionary companion of Crawford

Gates. Marsden Durham had been wounded while serving as an army chaplain in Okinawa and had been sent to Hawaii to recover. The two friends sang the new hymn together many times, and Marsden Durham departed for the island of Hawaii for further recuperation.

But two days later he was dead, killed in an accident when he slipped on the edge of a waterfall. In his memory, Crawford Gates called his tune MARSDEN. Thus both text and music of this hymn honor the memory of a beloved friend.

We Are Sowing 216

*Text: Anonymous (*Pure Diamonds, *Cleveland, 1872)*
Music: Henry A. Tuckett (1852–1918; LDS)
Tune name: WESTWOOD

One of the truths we endeavor to teach our children is that our words, thoughts, and actions have consequences. Our responsibilities to ourselves, to others, and to our Heavenly Father require us to consider these consequences before we act. "We Are Sowing" reminds adults, too, of the ongoing importance of pondering the outcome of each seed we sow.

The word *sowing* in the hymn's title might lead some to assume that it is based on the parable of the sower, found in Matthew, chapter 13. But when we read Jesus' interpretation of this parable, and compare his message with that of "We Are Sowing," we see that the parable and the hymn teach different truths, though both use the analogy of seeds and sowing.

Jesus explained that the seeds in his parable, as they are cast upon different soils, represent varying degrees of receptiveness to the words of truth. Some seeds flourish and take root; others are choked out by "the care of this world, and the deceitfulness of riches." (Matthew 13:22.)

In the hymn, on the other hand, the seeds represent our words, thoughts, and deeds, and the harvest—or lack of it—symbolizes the consequences of those words, thoughts, and deeds. It expands upon the teaching found in Galatians 6:7: "Whatsoever a man soweth, that shall he also reap."

In his book *The Law of the Harvest,* Elder Sterling W. Sill presented a similar message: "One of the greatest of life's privileges is that we may prepare our own seed beds. We may sow our own seeds and reap our own harvests.

"There are some people who get their greatest pleasures from creating strains of beautiful music. Others paint inspiring pictures. Some gather the seeds of great literature and transplant them into the rich soil of their own lives. . . . Suppose that we take the seeds of great ideals, ambitions, spirituality and Godliness, and by proper planting produce in abundance the golden fruit of eternal life." ([Salt Lake City, Utah: Bookcraft, 1963], p. 293).

The unusual hymn tune gives the melody to the altos in the third line. The tune name, WESTWOOD, honors the composer's mother. The hymn entered Mormon hymnody in the *Deseret Sunday School Union Music Book* in 1884. In the 1985 hymnal, the phrase "our words and looks and actions" in line four of verse three became "our words and thoughts and actions," strengthening the hymn's message.

Come, Let Us Anew 217

Text: Charles Wesley (1707–1788)
Music: Attributed to James Lucas (b. 1726)
Tune name: LUCAS

Synergism (SIN-er-jiz-em) occurs when separate parts cooperate in such a way that the total effect is greater than the sum of the parts could have been if the parts had worked independently. A wonderful synergism can happen in Church meetings when the Saints gather to worship together and to encourage one another. The heartening sentiments of "Come, Let Us Anew" are an opportunity for just such synergism to happen.

When we gather together to sing, pray, worship, and offer mutual encouragement, we reinforce one another in our righteous efforts and desires. We share our energies and resolve. Alone, we may feel discouraged and disheartened; but together, we can feel our morale soar.

Charles Wesley's message of encouragement is that we should renew our energies "and never stand still" in our good works. He uses many comparisons to underlie one of the main points of his text: that time passes quickly, almost without our realizing it. Life is as fleeting as a dream that vanishes the instant we awaken; it flows past us as quickly as a drop of water in a rushing stream; it flies like an arrow; the "fugitive moment" (literally, the moment that flies) is gone almost before it is here. Time does not wait, no matter how many good works remain undone.

The moments, days, and years are hastening toward one final event: the second coming of the Messiah, Jesus Christ. That moment will come before most people are prepared for it. This is the link between the hymn's two main ideas: first, that time hastens, and we must fulfill our duties without delay; and second, that the Messiah's return, the day for which we must diligently and daily prepare, will soon be upon us.

The third verse expresses Charles Wesley's hope for all of us, the goal we prayerfully seek as individuals and that we wish for one another.

It is that we may one day say, like Paul, "I am now ready to be offered, and the time of my departure is at hand.

"I have fought a good fight, I have finished my course, I have kept the faith." (2 Timothy 4:6–7.)

Charles Wesley's 1750 text was first published with the James Lucas tune in 1833 in a hymn collection edited by Lowell Mason.

Two changes in the 1985 hymnal make this hymn easier to sing. First, tenor and bass parts have been added for the last two measures in line four. Second, the words *for* and *and* have been added in verse two, line three, making the meter of that verse more consistent with the other verses: "For the arrow is flown and the moments are gone."

We Give Thee But Thine Own 218

Text: William Walsham How (1823–1897)
Music: Anonymous; arranged by Lowell Mason (1792–1872) and George J. Webb (1803–1887)
Tune name: SCHUMANN

This hymn expresses a beautiful sentiment: our offerings to the Lord are not a grudging fulfillment of the law's letter. They are a privilege, returned to the Lord in a spirit of love and gratitude. We consecrate our goods to the Lord as a small token of the immense debt we owe to him.

"We Give Thee But Thine Own" was originally written as an offertory hymn—that is, a hymn to be sung as the congregation is invited to drop money into a basket or pouch that is circulated through the congregation. It is not the Latter-day Saint custom to take collection during the course of meetings, but this hymn perfectly reflects the feelings we would wish to have in our hearts as we pay our tithes or make other financial contributions. One author said: "The hymn does not confine itself to our duty to give, but it opens up to our imagination the great needs of the world which our gifts are meant to fill—heartache, poverty, waywardness, woe, loneliness, captivity to sin; or more positively, the need of Christ's gospel. . . . This is a different approach from that of the usual offertory hymn in which giving is represented as a duty we owe to God or as an investment on which God will repay us a thousand-fold." (Albert Edward Bailey, *The Gospel in Hymns* [New York: Charles Scribner's Sons, 1950], p. 422.)

The opening words of this hymn, "we give thee but thine own," are somewhat old-fashioned in their phrasing, but an understanding of these words is important in sensing the hymn's message. In saying "we give thee but thine own," we mean that the "gifts" we give to the Lord—our tithes and offerings—are really just a means of returning to him what is already his: "we give thee only what already belongs to thee." *All* we have, all the possessions we are in the habit of thinking of as ours, we in fact hold in stewardship for the Lord. An editing change for the 1985 hymnal reinforces this idea while improving the word accents: in verse one, "All that we have" has been changed to "For all we have."

William Walsham How wrote this hymn in about 1858. J. Spencer Cornwall quoted him as saying, "A good hymn should be like a good prayer—simple, real, earnest, and reverent." (*Stories of Our Mormon Hymns*, p. 198.)

Lowell Mason gave the name SCHUMANN to this hymn tune. It was thought that the German composer Robert Schumann had written this melody; however, it does not appear among his known compositions, and his widow once stated that she did not believe her husband had written it.

Because I Have Been Given Much 219

Text: Grace Noll Crowell (1877–1969); altered
Music: Phillip Landgrave (b. 1935)
Tune name: SEMINARY

The world's wealth increases, yet "ye have the poor always with you." (Matthew 26:11.) In this hymn, new to the 1985 hymnbook, we joyfully promise to share both our material wealth and our loving compassion with those who have less. Such a sharing is "thanks indeed," the most meaningful way we can show the Lord that we are gratefully aware of our blessings.

Verse one mentions "bounty" and "gifts" in general terms. Verse two tells more specifically what these gifts are: shelter, warmth, food. Verse three is crucial to the sense of this hymn: the sharing of love and emotional support is just as important as the sharing of temporal things, though usually more difficult.

In his poem titled "Holy Thursday" from *Songs of Experience*, English poet William Blake cries out against a society that thinks its hungry children are adequately cared for when they are "fed with a cold and usurous hand." The hunger may be removed, but when the hand that offers the food is "cold and usurous" (*usurious*—profit-motivated or self-interested), the sharing does not bless the giver.

The author noted in 1940: "I wrote the poem [originally titled 'The Shared Loaf'] after a long and serious illness. I was convalescing, and in a sudden, glad up-rush of gratitude for my release from pain, recalling the many mercies and blessings that had been mine those long hard days, and through all my past life, remembering the love that had been around and about me ever, I wrote the words of this hymn. Surely I have been given much; surely love has been showered upon me. God grant I may never forget to 'divide my gifts with every brother that I see who has the need of help from me,' and I trust I shall not hoard the love that has been so abundantly showered upon me." (John Barnes Pratt, *Present Day Hymns and How They Were Written* [New York: A. S. Barnes and Co., 1940], p. 27.)

The original third verse is as follows:

Because Love has been lavished so
Upon me, Lord,
A wealth I know that was not meant
For me to hoard—
I shall give love to those in need,
The cold and hungry clothe and feed,
Thus shall I show my thanks indeed.

If the congregation were to sing a revised version of the first verse, substituting plural pronouns *we* and *us* for *I* and *me*, they would find that the hymn is not nearly as strong. When we sing it as it is written, we are making a personal and an individual commitment.

Note that the hymn is written to be sung in unison. The keyboard left hand (bass clef) is written as an accompaniment and is not suitable for singing in parts.

The tune name, SEMINARY, honors the Southern Baptist Theological Seminary in North Carolina, where the composer was both a student and a teacher.

Lord, I Would Follow Thee 220

Text: Susan Evans McCloud (b. 1945; LDS)
Music: K. Newell Dayley (b. 1939; LDS)
Tune name: I WOULD FOLLOW THEE

"Lord, I Would Follow Thee" is the prayer of someone who seeks to love and emulate Jesus Christ. To help another in misfortune, to refrain from judging unrighteously, to heal and comfort—as we sing this hymn we ask the Lord to bless us with the opportunity and the willingness to fulfill these Christlike roles.

The text of this hymn, new to the 1985 hymnal, is an expansion of its first line: "Savior, may I learn to love thee, / Walk the path that thou hast shown." If we truly learn to love the Savior, we will want to be like him. What are the characteristics of the path he has shown? How can we be like the Savior? The hymn specifies some important ways: by pausing "to help and lift another," by resisting the temptation to judge hastily, by showing a "gentle heart" to the "wounded and the weary," and by following the example of the Savior in the love we show to others.

Author Susan Evans McCloud stated that she felt a need for "a song on brotherly love and compassion, on the need to be Christlike in our treatment of others." She described her feelings when writing this hymn: "I tried to think back to the occasions most precious to me when I obtained my own testimony of the Savior's sacrifice for us and of my Heavenly Father's personal love. I wanted the song to have both tenderness and conviction. I thought of how I felt when my little sister lost her three-month-old baby and asked me to go with her the following day to find a dress for the funeral and a locket for the baby. I was so acutely aware of the need for tenderness in our dealings with others; I yearned for it in all the people we met on our way, wishing they could somehow know of the need and pain which did not show." These feelings became the spirit of the hymn, correlating closely with the words "In the quiet heart is hidden / Sorrow that the eye can't see."

Composer K. Newell Dayley noted that the hymn tune is simple and easily remembered. Musically, measures one and two are the reverse of measures nine and ten, lending variety and emphasis to the opening line of each verse of the text as it is repeated near the conclusion of the verse. This repetition helps us to focus on the main message of each verse before we repeat with the prayer that is at the center of this hymn: "Lord, I would follow thee."

Dear to the Heart of the Shepherd 221

Text: Mary B. Wingate (b. 1899)
Music: William J. Kirkpatrick (1838–1921)
Tune name: SHEPHERD

This hymn praises the watchfulness and compassion of the Savior. It pictures him as the Good Shepherd, basing the comparison on the parable of the lost sheep, one of the best-known and most evocative passages in all the New Testament.

Jesus was addressing not a group of disciples or followers but a group of "publicans and sinners" when he spoke this parable, given in Luke 15:4-7:

"What man of you, having an hundred sheep, if he lose one of them, doth not leave the ninety and nine in the wilderness, and go after that which is lost, until he find it?

"And when he hath found it, he layeth it on his shoulders, rejoicing.

"And when he cometh home, he calleth together his friends and neighbours, saying unto them, Rejoice with me; for I have found my sheep which was lost.

"I say unto you, that likewise joy shall be in heaven over one sinner that repenteth, more than over ninety and nine just persons, which need no repentance."

After verse three of the hymn text asks, " 'Will you not seek for my lost ones . . . ?' " verse four answers in the affirmative. We who are singing the hymn become involved in the parable and its message. We are among the disciples, ready to enlist as "undershepherds" to seek the lost sheep. Though it might be assumed that the hymn would conclude with a call to all straying sheep to return to the fold, it is instead a call to the followers of Jesus to seek out those who are lost.

It is interesting that even though Mary B. Wingate was not a Latter-day Saint, the chorus of her text correlates closely with the Joseph Smith translation of Luke 15:4, which adds the detail that the lost sheep has wandered into the wilderness. The King James Version states only that the ninety and nine are *left* in the wilderness as the shepherd goes to find the lost sheep.

Hear Thou Our Hymn, O Lord 222

Text and music: Frank W. Asper (1892–1973; LDS)
Tune name: REBECCA

Calling upon his long experience as a musician and a Latter-day Saint, Frank W. Asper wrote both words and music to this simple and effective hymn of prayer. It is suitable as a closing hymn but is not limited to that purpose.

The requests included in our prayer are simple ones, yet they imply a large-scale commitment within their compass. In this prayer we are asking to be changed in our innermost being; the word *hearts,* in fact, occurs in both verses. If our prayer is granted, we will be living on a high spiritual plane. We will walk the narrow path of obedience, we will remember the words of the Lord, and we will have his Spirit as our companion. As we sing the prayer of this hymn text, we aspire to lofty spiritual goals.

This text involves no complex theology, no self-congratulation, no exhortation. It is just a prayer for guidance, relevant to any occasion and to any member of the Church. The first line is made up of one-syllable words—"Hear thou our hymn, O Lord"—and the remaining lines are almost as simple. The tune is equally straightforward and dignified, with a simple melodic line and a rhythm made up entirely of quarter notes and dotted half notes.

The tune name, REBECCA, honors the mother of Frank W. Asper.

Have I Done Any Good? 223

Text and music: Will L. Thompson (1847–1909); altered
Tune name: EAST LIVERPOOL

President David O. McKay proclaimed, "The willingness to serve others is ready for expression in the hearts of millions, if only nations or groups in nations will but point the way." (*Gospel Ideals* [Salt Lake City, Utah: Improvement Era, 1953], p. 208.) This hymn, "Have I Done Any Good?" provides us just such an opportunity—to point the way toward service and good works, to "wake up" to the importance of helping others.

Latter-day Saints would be the last to belittle the importance of prayer, meditation, and study. But we also take pride in having a gospel of action. On November 30, 1856, Brigham Young was conducting a Church service in the Salt Lake Tabernacle when word came of the arrival of an immigrant party in the Salt Lake Valley. This ill-fated handcart company had faced cold and starvation, and they were in need of every kind of comfort and assistance. President Young announced, "The afternoon meeting will be omitted, for I wish the sisters to go home and prepare to give those who have just arrived a mouthful of something to eat, and to wash them and nurse them up. . . . Were I in the situation of those persons who have just come in, . . . I would give more for a dish of pudding and milk or a baked potato and salt, . . . than I would for all your prayers, though you were to stay there all afternoon and pray. Prayer is good, but when baked potatoes and milk are needed, prayer will not supply their place." (Quoted in Leonard J. Arrington, *Great Basin Kingdom* [Cambridge, Mass.: Harvard University Press, 1958], p. 159.)

An alteration in the second verse was made for the 1985 hymnal. The original lines were, "Only he who does something is worthy to live, / The world has no use for the drone." Many Latter-day Saints found these words problematic, because they seemed to imply that a person who is ill or disabled has somehow forfeited the right to a place on this earth. Human life is sacred and needs no justification, though no able person has the right to be idle.

The changed words read, "Only he who does something helps others to live. / To God each good work will be known."

In addition to these textual changes, musical editing smoothed out several measures that previously had more intricate rhythms. Two other reasons the music looks easier and more inviting in the 1985 hymnal: the measures aren't as crowded on the page; the hymn now fills two pages rather than one and one-half. And eighth and sixteenth notes that were previously written with flags on each note—which may be visually confusing—have been "beamed" together within the beat.

The author-composer's home town, East Liverpool, Ohio, is the source of the tune name. The hymn was first published in 1904.

I Have Work Enough to Do 224

Text: Josephine Pollard (1834–1892)
Music: William J. Kirkpatrick (1838–1921)
Tune name: DUNCANNON

As each of us sings this hymn, we are singing a reminder to ourselves. No one lacks for work to do. Yet, inexorably, the night comes—at the end of the day and, symbolically, at the end of our lives—and the time is past to do the work we should have done during the day.

The message of this hymn, that the demands of our work are urgent because the daylight will soon pass, is one that Jesus spoke of with reference to his own earthly mission: "I must work the works of him that sent me, while it is day: the night cometh, when no man can work." (John 9:4.)

This hymn has undergone some revisions as it has appeared in Latter-day Saint hymn collections. In *Deseret Sunday School Songs,* published in 1909, it included a refrain or chorus, in typical gospel-song style. The words were these:

Ere the sun goes down,
Ere the sun goes down;
I must do my daily duty,
Ere the sun goes down.

In the 1950 hymnal, the men's voices echoed "ere the sun, ere the sun goes down" in a distinctive rhythm at the ends of the first two phrases. The present musical arrangement is more dignified and hymnlike.

The tune name, DUNCANNON, refers to the town in Pennsylvania where the composer was born.

We Are Marching On to Glory 225

Text and music: John M. Chamberlain (1844–1928; LDS)
Tune name: LEICESTER

This vigorous hymn invites us to imagine ourselves as members of a great host of righteous Saints, part of a grand procession toward a heavenly goal. It has been popular among Latter-day Saints since it was first published in 1879 in the *Juvenile Instructor.*

In J. Spencer Cornwall's volume, *Stories of Our Mormon Hymns,* is a charming personal reminiscence about John M. Chamberlain:

"Your compiler well remembers John M. Chamberlain. As a small boy, I went into his music store in Salt Lake City, with my father. As soon as Brother Chamberlain found out that I was interested in music and attempting to learn to play, he sat down at the piano and played some of his piano compositions for me. They were filled with elaborate arpeggios and other flourishes. As a youngster I was intrigued. His tall stature and grey hair were very becoming to his gentle words. As we left he gave me a printed copy of one of his compositions and told me to take it home and learn to play it." (P. 204.)

What we would not give today for a videotape of this little scene that so impressed the young J. Spencer Cornwall!

The birthplace of John M. Chamberlain, Leicester, England, accounts for the tune name.

Improve the Shining Moments 226

Text and music: Robert B. Baird (1855–1916; LDS)
Tune name: GWENTHLYN

J. Spencer Cornwall observed: " 'Improve the Shining Moments' contains a most valuable exhortation on making the most of 'time.' It is not a hymn but is a song that is not out of place in a hymn collection because of its subject matter." (*Stories of Our Mormon Hymns,* p. 89.)

It is certainly true that an admonition to use time wisely is in keeping with Latter-day Saint doctrine and tradition. From the earliest days of the Church, our leaders have spoken out on this subject. In 1903, President Joseph F. Smith stated in a conference address: "I desire to say to this congregation at this time that I have felt very strongly of late a desire, a responsibility, I may say, resting upon me, to admonish the Latter-day Saints everywhere to cease loitering away their precious time, to cease from all idleness. It is said in the revelations that the idler in Zion shall not eat the bread of the laborer, and there is . . . far too much precious time wasted by the youth of Zion, and perhaps by some that are older and more experienced and who ought to know better." (*Gospel Doctrine,* 5th ed. [Salt Lake City, Utah: Deseret Book Co., 1939], p. 235.)

And Elder Bruce R. McConkie expressed a similar thought: "Without work there would be neither existence, creation, redemption, salvation, or temporal necessities for mortal man. . . . Work is a blessing that brings salvation, idleness a curse that assures damnation." (*Mormon Doctrine,* 2d ed. [Salt Lake City, Utah: Bookcraft, 1966], p. 847.)

The tune name, GWENTHLYN, honors Robert B. Baird's wife, Anne Gwenthlyn Davis. The hymn was first published in 1879 in the *Juvenile Instructor.*

There Is Sunshine in My Soul Today 227

Text: Eliza E. Hewitt (1851–1920)
Music: John R. Sweney (1837–1899)
Tune name: SUNSHINE

J. Spencer Cornwall's comment about this song was that "this number is a gospel song with its characteristic verse and chorus. It is popular because of its 'catchy' melody and joyful text." (*Stories of Our Mormon Hymns,* p. 192.)

This hymn is simply an expression of the happiness that comes to a person who accepts and follows the teachings of Jesus Christ. Such expressions benefit us all; when we rejoice in the happiness that righteousness brings, we lift our own morale and encourage one another's good efforts. As we learn from the wisdom of Proverbs, "A merry heart doeth good like a medicine: but a broken spirit drieth the bones." (Proverbs 17:22.)

Since the joy of discipleship is difficult to express in words, the author of the text sought to make this joy more vivid through comparisons. She likened it to things that naturally suggest pleasure and contentment: sunshine, "glorious and bright"; music, "a carol to my King"; and springtime, with birds and flowers.

This hymn was first printed in 1890 in a collection of gospel songs titled *The Finest of the Wheat,* and it entered Latter-day Saint hymnody in *Songs of Zion* (1908). The 1985 hymnal changed the first word of each line – "There's" – to a more singable "There is." And the larger type face used in the 1985 book dictated the omission of the tenors' and basses' echoing phrases in the chorus; in order to keep this hymn to a single page in length, those antiphonal phrases had to be dropped.

You Can Make the Pathway Bright 228

Text: Helen Silcott Dungan (ca. 1899)
Music: James M. Dungan (1851–1925)
Tune name: BRIGHT

If we feel downcast, we tend to focus inward: our own problems and our own small world consume our energy and attention. But if we have a cheerful disposition, we are more apt to forget ourselves and give encouragement and help to others. "Sunshine in your heart" leads to unselfishness. That is the message of this hymn.

As is true of several of the gospel-song hymns in our hymnal, "You Can Make the Pathway Bright" is worthy of inclusion more for the sake of its message than for the quality of its poetry or music. But no one can deny the truth of what it teaches: kindness and cheer will bless all around us and ultimately ourselves as well.

Although this hymn is not Latter-day Saint in origin, members of our Church certainly subscribe to its message. The gospel cannot protect us from trials, but its ultimate design is to make us happier. Brigham Young once made this statement: " 'Mormonism' has done everything for me that ever has been done for me on the earth; it has made me happy; . . . it has filled me with good feelings, with joy and rejoicing. Whereas, before I possessed the spirit of the Gospel I was troubled with that which I hear others complain of, that is, with, at times, feeling cast down, gloomy, and despondent; with everything wearing to me, at times, a dreary aspect. . . . But since I have embraced the Gospel not for one-half minute, to the best of my recollection, has anything worn to me a gloomy aspect; under all circumstances I have felt pleasant and cheerful." (*Discourses of Brigham Young,* sel. John A. Widtsoe [Salt Lake City, Utah: Deseret Book Co., 1978], pp. 452–53.)

The hymn was first published in *The Gospel Hymnal* (1899) and entered Latter-day Saint hymnnody in the privately printed *Songs of Zion* (1908).

Today, While the Sun Shines 229

Text: L. Clark (ca. 1880); altered
Music: Evan Stephens (1854–1930; LDS)
Tune name: CONSTANT

J. Spencer Cornwall stated, "The text of the hymn 'Today While the Sun Shines' amplifies in a most forceful manner, the old saying 'yesterday is gone, tomorrow may never come, but today is here.' " (*Stories of Our*

Hymns, p. 226.) This hymn strengthens our determination to make use of the present moment.

Several of our hymns admonish us to use our time to good advantage. "Today, While the Sun Shines" is particularly emphatic. By the time we have sung the three verses with the refrain that follows, we have sung the word *today* no fewer than twenty-eight times! No one can miss the message of this hymn.

In the 1950 hymnal this hymn ended with the words "There is no tomorrow, but only today." This sentiment was intended to have the meaning referred to by J. Spencer Cornwall: we cannot depend upon a tomorrow in which to accomplish the things we have procrastinated today.

But through the years, members of the Church called or wrote the General Music Committee's office to express concern over the phrase. Latter-day Saints certainly do believe in an eternal tomorrow. Furthermore, the line almost had the ring of "Eat, drink, and be merry, for tomorrow we die." Thus the line was altered to appear as it does in the 1985 hymnal: "Prepare for tomorrow by working today." It was felt that this conclusion more accurately reflects the message of the hymn.

Another word change acknowledges that our choices in life are sometimes between two good options: "choose the good part" was changed to "choose the better part" in verse two.

Both the words and the music of this hymn appeared in the *Juvenile Instructor* in September 1877.

Scatter Sunshine 230

Text: Lanta Wilson Smith
Music: Edwin O. Excell (1851–1921)
Tune name: UNIONTOWN

In this hymn we encourage others as we encourage ourselves. It is a reminder to us that an attitude of cheerfulness best becomes the followers of the Savior. The more at peace with ourselves we feel, the more peace we can radiate. Cheerfulness helps us toward important goals: the removal of suffering, loneliness, and strife.

In the entry under "Cheerfulness" in *Mormon Doctrine,* Elder Bruce R. McConkie noted that "one of the frequent bits of counsel, comfort, and solace coming from God to his people is, 'Be of good cheer.' " (2d ed. [Salt Lake City, Utah: Bookcraft, 1966], p. 124.) To prove the point, Elder McConkie then listed no fewer than nine citations from scriptures both ancient and modern. Though the message of this hymn is not complex or poetically profound, it reiterates an important truth: the Lord truly wishes his people to be cheerful.

"Scatter Sunshine" is the original title of this hymn, known recently by its somewhat misleading first line: "In a world where sorrow." It is a typical gospel song or revival song. Standard features of the gospel song are the dotted rhythms (in the case of this hymn, written as triple rhythms), the energetic and admonitory text, and the verse-chorus structure, with the words of the chorus repeated as a refrain after each verse.

The name of the composer's home town, Uniontown, Pennsylvania, is the source of the tune name. This hymn was first published in 1892 in E. O. Excell's *Triumphant Songs, No. 3.*

Father, Cheer Our Souls Tonight 231

Text: Ellis Reynolds Shipp (1847–1939; LDS)
Music: Orlando Gibbons (1583–1625); altered
Tune name: SONG 13 or SIMPLICITY

This hymn, a beautiful prayer for comfort, acknowledges that life may inflict "burdens" or "dark waves." But in a trusting and simple way, we turn to our Father, asking first for personal comfort and then for a blessing upon distant loved ones. Though not grouped with the other closing hymns in our hymnal, this hymn—new to the 1985 hymnbook—serves this purpose very well.

Almost three centuries separate the music of this hymn from the words. Orlando Gibbons, a famous English musician born in the sixteenth century, wrote the tune for a collection of hymns gathered by the English Puritan poet, George Wither. It was the thirteenth tune in the hymnal; thus the tune name, SONG 13. It has an alternative title, SIMPLICITY.

The tune's elegant simplicity makes it a beautiful setting for the words written by one of the most remarkable women in the early history of the LDS Church. Ellis Shipp, mother, physician, and poet, blessed the lives of all around her with her many gifts. One of her daughters commented: "She had absolutely conquered herself. Her thought was for humanity—for you. What would you like? What do you need?" (Quoted in Susan Evans McCloud, *Not in Vain* [Salt Lake City, Utah: Bookcraft, 1984], p. 186.) Her unselfish nature is reflected in an excerpt from her poem "Love Divine":

Oh, help me love humanity,
And all its virtues see,
For those who love most tenderly
Are surely most like Thee.

At the end of sixty years of medical practice, thousands of dollars were owing to Dr. Shipp. She canceled all the debts and told her wondering children: "When people have sickness they are having trouble enough; they should not be burdened with a single thought of debt. I want these books burned." (Quoted in *Not in Vain,* p. 183.)

Ellis Shipp's life was the embodiment of love and solicitude. Her life's work was to ease the burden of others. What could be more natural for her than to sense that our Father would wish to show his love for us in the same way? His love will lift us and cheer us.

Let Us Oft Speak Kind Words 232

Text: Joseph L. Townsend (1849–1942; LDS)
Music: Ebenezer Beesley (1840–1906; LDS)
Tune name: BICESTER

The song of birds, the light of the morning sunbeam, the murmur of fountains – the most pleasant and universally loved beauties of nature – are metaphors for this hymn's central message, the beauty and comfort of kind words. And here also is a perfectly matched tune, "sweet tones" of music to reflect the "sweet tones of the heart."

Joseph L. Townsend was still living when George D. Pyper was writing *Stories of Latter-day Saint Hymns* in 1939. George D. Pyper wrote, "Brother Townsend is one of those who seek retirement in home life rather than publicity but at the solicitation of the writer, he very kindly furnished the information concerning the origin of a few of his songs." Here is George D. Pyper's summary of the information Joseph Townsend provided at that time about "Let Us Oft Speak Kind Words," which had first been published in the *Juvenile Instructor* in 1879:

" 'Kind Words are Sweet Tones of the Heart' ['Let Us Oft Speak Kind Words'], one of the most popular and appealing of Brother Townsend's songs, was composed while he was laboring in the superintendency of a very large Sunday School. He heard a number of fault-finding remarks among the people. It occurred to him how much finer it would be if he could hear kind words spoken oftener. With this thought in mind he wrote the song which has been translated into many languages. Some have called it his best sermon. It is said that it stopped the gossiping tongues of the people and produced a kindlier feeling in the town where he lived." (Pp. 111–12.)

This hymn is unusual in that the accompaniment of the verse section does not include the usual four parts sung by the congregation. Since the bass cleff (lower) staff is for the accompanist only, the men of the congregation should sing either the melody or harmony line given in the upper staff. (The verse is marked *Duet* for this reason. In the 1950 hymnbook, the verse was written in a unison arrangement.) The chorus, marked *Harmony,* is written as usual with four parts. The effect of this contrast, when the congregation is alert to it, can be very striking: the verse is a sweet, lyrical reminder; the chorus is a more vigorous admonition, with fuller harmony and dotted rhythms.

Nay, Speak No Ill 233

Text and music: Anonymous (ca. 1853)
Tune name: KINDLY WORD

"Gossip bespeaks either a vacant mind or one that entertains jealousy or envy," counseled President David O. McKay. (*Improvement Era,* Dec. 1954, p. 931.) "Nay, Speak No Ill" is a reminder that fault-finding and criticism usually bring waste and unhappiness in their wake. As J. Spencer Cornwall said of this hymn, "The ever timely admonition of its message . . . will make it a permanent favorite in the Latter-Day Saint hymnal." (*Stories of Our Mormon Hymns,* p. 123.)

Although the title of this hymn is cautionary, it is a hymn that tells us what we *should* do as well as what we should *not* do. We must replace negative words with words of kindness and encouragement: "Let's speak of all the best we can."

At some future time a scholar may succeed in establishing the origins of this hymn beyond any doubt, but for the present time we do not know the name of author or composer for certain. In his "Source Book for *Hymns* (1950)," Bruce David Maxwell reported on research that has led to some tentative attributions: "Mary Musser Barnes writes the following on page 17 of her unpublished Master's thesis, 'An Historical Survey of the Salt Lake Tabernacle Choir of the Church of Jesus Christ of Latter-Day Saints' (State University of Iowa, June 1936): 'Elizabeth Foster Lindsay Thomas was a concert singer in Scotland before she came to Utah. Besides being a soloist in the [Salt Lake Tabernacle] Choir, she was the first president of the Mutual Improvement Association. She was both composer and author of the song, "Nay, Speak No Ill." ' . . . Unfortunately, Miss Barnes gives no references to back up her statements. . . . The attribution of authorship is another matter. Although most of the early sources publish the text without the name of the author, *The Mountaineer* published it in 1860 as the work of Eliza Cook." (Eliza Cook was an English poet well known in the nineteenth century for her didactic verse.) Bruce David Maxwell noted further that the poem had appeared anonymously in the *Deseret News* in 1853. (P. 42.)

Jesus, Mighty King in Zion 234

Text: John Fellows (d. 1785)
Music: Tracy Y. Cannon (1879–1961; LDS)
Tune name: VIOLA

This hymn reaffirms the baptismal covenants we have made as followers of Jesus Christ. Just as Jesus rose to a new life as a resurrected being, so after our baptism we may rise to a life of renewed commitment. We first imitate Jesus by being baptized in similitude of his death and burial; the ensuing responsibility is to imitate him in our lives.

Though previously printed in Latter-day Saint hymnals as a hymn of unknown authorship, these lines are now known to be by an English hymn writer, John Fellows, whose collection of poetry was published in 1773. The hymn's original title was "Believers buried with Christ in Baptism."

But even though the writer was not a Latter-day Saint, the relevance of this hymn to Latter-day Saint thought is so great, especially in the reference to baptism by immersion, that the lines caught the attention of Emma Smith as she was compiling the 1835 hymnal, and she included it in the section of the hymnal headed "On Baptism." (Author John Fellows was a Baptist, and thus baptism by immersion would have been a central tenet of his beliefs.)

Latter-day Saints have sung this hymn ever since Emma Smith deemed it worthy of inclusion in the 1835 hymnal. The present musical setting was written by Tracy Y. Cannon especially for the 1948 hymnal. The tune name, VIOLA, honors his sister-in-law.

Should You Feel Inclined to Censure 235

Text: Anonymous (ca. 1863)
Music: Philip Paul Bliss (1838–1876)
Tune name: LOWER LIGHTS or CENSURE

"Should You Feel Inclined to Censure," a hymn in the gospel-song tradition, serves to caution us against one of the most frequent failings of human nature: the tendency to find fault. Impatient or critical words often exact a high price in human relationships; in this hymn we admonish one another to exercise discretion and tolerance.

No one would pretend that the poetry or music of "Should You Feel Inclined to Censure" represents a first-rate contribution to Christian hymnody, but neither would anyone deny the relevance of the hymn's message. Since both ancient and latter-day scriptures are full of admonitions that parallel the message of this hymn, Latter-day Saints should lead the way in refusing to repeat or hear gossip, ascribe selfish motives, or see anything but the best in others. Doctrine and Covenants 20:54 warns us, "And see that there is no iniquity in the church, neither hardness with each other, neither lying, backbiting, nor evil speaking."

Harsh judgments not only can destroy good feelings among family members, neighbors, and Church associates but also can undermine the work and calling of Church authorities. President David O. McKay once gave this useful counsel: " 'Speak not against the authorities.' What does it mean? Be not a murmurer; that is what it means. It is one of the most poisonous things that can be introduced into the home of a Latter-day Saint—this murmuring against presidents of stakes, high councilors. . . . Better stop murmuring and build. . . . Backbiting and evil speaking throw us into the class of malefactors rather than the class of benefactors." (*Gospel Ideals* [Salt Lake City, Utah: Improvement Era, 1953], p. 143.)

The tune for this hymn is LOWER LIGHTS (the same as for no. 335), first published in 1871.

Lord, Accept into Thy Kingdom 236

Text: Mabel Jones Gabbott (b. 1910; LDS)
Music: Alexander Schreiner (1901–1987; LDS)
Tune name: WORSHIP

"Lord, Accept into Thy Kingdom" was written especially for baptismal services, and it refers to the latter-day doctrine of baptism for the dead. It also serves beautifully as a general hymn of prayer and worship and as a reminder of the meaning of the ordinances of baptism and confirmation.

As with so many of our hymns, this hymn came about because a talented individual responded to an assignment from the General Music Committee of the Church. Mabel Jones Gabbott recalled the circumstances: "We were living [in the 1940s] in Salt Lake City, where my husband was bishop. We had two small children. As a poet, I was invited to a meeting at Church headquarters. There Alexander Schreiner, George D. Pyper, and others instructed us in the making of a hymn—line length, meters, regularity of accents, and quality of tone. A list of suggested subjects was given to each of us. I submitted some texts." Three, including this hymn, were accepted and published in the 1950 hymnal.

She commented further: "The line 'Know ye not that he was holy' is reminiscent of many such phrases in the Book of Mormon. [See, for example, 2 Nephi 31:7.] I think it is a beautiful phrase, and I borrowed it."

Do What Is Right 237

*Text: Anonymous (*The Psalms of Life, *Boston, 1857)*
Music: George Kaillmark (1781–1835)
Tune name: OAKEN BUCKET

The opening words of this hymn have become a personal motto for many a Latter-day Saint. The twelve repetitions of "Do what is right" have engraved this phrase upon the conscience of young and old, and the continuing relevance of this important message has ensured this hymn's popularity through several generations of Latter-day Saint hymn-singers.

George D. Pyper commented as follows in *Stories of Latter-day Saint Hymns:* "[It] is one of those soulful poems adopted by the Church – a waif in the realm of song. How it came to be included in our hymn book is told by Assistant Church Historian, A. William Lund. He says that in a conversation with the late Duncan M. McAllister, which occurred just before Brother McAllister's death, the latter said that while George Q. Cannon was presiding over the British Mission, on one occasion he attended a conference in Scotland and there heard sung for the first time, the hymn 'Do What Is Right.' He was so impressed with it that when the twelfth edition of the Latter-day Saints' hymn book was published in 1863 under George Q. Cannon's direction, this hymn was included in the collection, but no one had any knowledge of who wrote it.

" 'Do What Is Right' cannot be classified as a sacred hymn, and it is doubtful if the author ever considered it as such. . . . But if it is not a message of divine truth there never was one written. It is a simple sermon and contains admonitions that appeal to the Mormon heart. George Q. Cannon recognized its value when he heard it in that Scottish conference. He saw in it a message of hope; a song of promise; an urge to be 'faithful and fearless,' and one that fitted in with Mormon philosophy. . . . It is a beloved, adopted child in Mormon hymnody." (Pp. 85–86.)

The elusive composer was an Englishman named George Kaillmark, 1781–1835. His melody, "Araby's Daughter," originally was a setting for an excerpt from *Lalla Rookh: An Oriental Romance,* by Thomas Moore (author of no. 115). The first stanza is as follows:

Farewell—farewell to thee, Araby's daughter!
(Thus warbled a Peri beneath the dark sea,)
No pearl ever lay, under Oman's green water,
More pure in its shell than thy Spirit in thee.

In the United States, some new words by Samuel Woodworth, "The Old Oaken Bucket," gave great popularity to the tune; hence the tune name. In spite of J. Spencer Cornwall's lament that "it is regrettable that such a forthright, positive challenge as is found in this hymn could not have been traditionally associated with more worthy music and a less ignoble connotation" (*Stories of Our Mormon Hymns,* p. 37), the popularity of this tune persists.

Behold Thy Sons and Daughters, Lord 238

Text: Parley P. Pratt (1807–1857; LDS)
Music: Alexander Schreiner (1901–1987; LDS)
Tune name: PARLEY

The sacred ordinance of confirmation is the subject of this hymn text. As J. Spencer Cornwall noted, "The hymn is completely one of our own, in authorship, and more important, in doctrine." (*Stories of Our Mormon Hymns,* p. 32.)

The choir or congregation that sings this hymn is singing a prayer, asking a beautiful blessing upon the head of a person or a group of people who have just been baptized members of The Church of Jesus Christ of Latter-day Saints. A new member on whose behalf this hymn is sung is fortunate indeed. What more significant blessings could be asked? Within the hymn's four verses, the new member is blessed with peace, joy, love, purity, fellowship ("And may they find, from this good hour, / They are adopted in"), faith, hope, and spiritual guidance.

Elder Parley P. Pratt's text, first published in 1840, was undoubtedly one of the first poetic expressions in the history of the Church having to do with the laying on of hands for the gift of the Holy Ghost. Though written a century later, the musical setting is a perfect match for the straightforward words. Alexander Schreiner's simple hymn tune beautifully reflects the sacredness of this moment.

Elder Bruce R. McConkie expressed the significance of the ordinance of confirmation: "Following baptism in water, the bestowal of the Holy Ghost takes place by the laying on of hands of the elders. . . . Those who receive this conferral, in a very real sense, have the hand of the Lord laid upon them." (*Mormon Doctrine,* 2d ed. [Salt Lake City, Utah: Bookcraft, 1966], p. 438.)

Choose the Right 239

Text: Joseph L. Townsend (1849–1942; LDS)
Music: Henry A. Tuckett (1852–1918; LDS)
Tune name: AGNES

By the time we have finished this hymn, we have sung the phrase "choose the right" fourteen times! Each time we sing it, we "program our conscience" over and over again with this useful admonition.

The hymn has been a favorite with Latter-day Saints since it was first printed in *Deseret Sunday School Songs* in 1909. It is in typical gospel-song style, with a verse and a chorus, vigorous rhythms, and a message of cheerful admonition. It was dropped from the 1948 hymnal but then was included in the 1950 hymnal.

The second verse warns, "Let no spirit of digression / Overcome you. . . . This expression simply means, "Don't let any impulse cause you to deviate (or *digress*) from the path of right." It is a phrase somewhat difficult to understand, and sometimes the members of a congregation mispronounce *digression* as *discretion.* This error gives the line an exactly opposite meaning!

J. Spencer Cornwall recalled a delightful memory of this hymn's composer: "Henry A. Tuckett was a candy maker in Salt Lake City who made music a hobby. Your writer remembers, when he was a small boy, attending a children's music class taught by Henry A. Tuckett. The class culminated with a concert, featuring Brother Tuckett's own compositions." (*Stories of Our Mormon Hymns,* p. 119.)

Henry A. Tuckett's wife, Agnes, is honored in the tune name.

Know This, That Every Soul Is Free 240

Text: Anonymous (ca. 1805, Boston, Massachusetts)
Music: Roger L Miller (b. 1937; LDS)
Tune name: BRAMWELL

"Man's greatest endowment in mortal life is the power of choice—the divine gift of free agency," stated President David O. McKay. "No true character was ever developed without a sense of soul freedom." (*Gospel Ideals* [Salt Lake City, Utah: Improvement Era, 1953], p. 299.) Every prophet of the Church has voiced a similar sentiment.

Latter-day Saints believe that next to life itself, agency is the greatest of our Heavenly Father's gifts. Though other hymns in our hymnal admonish us to make right choices (see the five other hymns listed under "Agency" in the index of topics in the hymnal), "Know This, That Every Soul Is Free" is the only one that focuses upon agency as a principle. It was the first hymn in Emma Smith's 1835 hymnal. Clearly, this text fills an important and unique role for Latter-day Saints.

The hymn as it appeared in the 1927 hymnal was not often sung, however. And neither was the new tune that appeared in the 1950 hymnal. The 1985 Hymnbook Committee felt that yet another musical setting might bring renewed interest.

Composer Roger Miller felt that the text, with its powerful opening line and its confident assertion of the importance of human agency, deserved a "strong, stately setting. I imagined the reverberations of a great organ in an old English church or cathedral, with the congregation singing at full voice." He admired the tune ELLACOMBE (no. 41), and he wanted something equally dignified. In addition, the vigorous opening rhythms of the tune SINE NOMINE (no. 82) were the direct inspiration for the first four notes of his new tune.

Roger Miller named the tune BRAMWELL in honor of his great-great-grandfather, George Walter Bramwell, an English convert and musician. According to family tradition, George Bramwell brought one of the first pianos to the Salt Lake Valley, transporting it by wagon from the east.

The composer suggested: "The hymn works in unison, in two parts (soprano and bass), or in four parts. The tempo should be deliberate and the organ registration full, using strong diapasons and perhaps reeds." He noted that he did not realize that his tune also works as a round until he heard it performed as a canon (round) by the Tabernacle Choir at general conference.

In the 1927 hymnal, this text was attributed to William C. Gregg; in the 1950 hymnbook, William C. Clegg was listed as author. More recent scholarship indicates, however, that the text was first published in a non–Latter-day Saint publication in approximately 1805.

Count Your Blessings 241

Text: Johnson Oatman, Jr. (1856–1922)
Music: Edwin O. Excell (1851–1921)
Tune name: BLESSINGS

Many a Latter-day Saint has found it useful to recall or think of this popular hymn in moments of discouragement. The hymn's repeated reminder, "count your blessings," is a motto that can change our outlook from self-pity and discouragement to one of gratitude.

Gratitude is essential for our spiritual well-being. President Joseph

F. Smith wrote many years ago in the *Juvenile Instructor:* "The spirit of gratitude is always pleasant and satisfying because it carries with it a sense of helpfulness to others; it begets love and friendship, and engenders divine influence. Gratitude is said to be the memory of the heart.

"And where there is an absence of gratitude, either to God or man, there is the presence of vanity and the spirit of self-sufficiency." (Quoted in *Gospel Doctrine,* 5th ed. [Salt Lake City, Utah: Deseret Book Co., 1939], p. 262.)

We are commanded throughout the scriptures to "thank the Lord thy God in all things" (D&C 59:7), to "let thy heart be full of thanks unto God" (Alma 37:37), and to be "always returning thanks unto God for whatsoever things ye do receive" (Alma 7:23). Our gratitude opens the way for the Lord to pour out additional blessings: "And he who receiveth all things with thankfulness shall be made glorious; and the things of this earth shall be added unto him, even an hundred fold, yea, more." (D&C 78:19.)

Some people look at life with no other purpose than to find out what is missing. This hymn exhorts us to move beyond such a narrow outlook, to rise above the corrosive effects of envy, and to realize that followers of Jesus Christ are heirs to the greatest of all blessings. J. Spencer Cornwall stated, " 'When upon Life's Billows' is a hymn for the moralist. Its value cannot be gainsaid, because many a worshipper on hearing or singing it is induced to contemplation on the blessings with which he is surrounded." (*Stories of Our Mormon Hymns,* p. 215.)

This hymn was first published in E. O. Excell's *Songs for Young People* in 1897. In the 1985 hymnal, the original title was restored, the key was lowered, some intricate rhythms were simplified in the chorus, and one note of the melody was changed: the last melody note in line 4 was raised to A instead of staying on G, reflecting the way the line is generally sung.

Praise God, from Whom All Blessings Flow 242

Text: Thomas Ken (1637–1711)
Music: Louis Bourgeois (ca. 1510–1561)
Tune name: OLD HUNDREDTH

For more than three hundred years, Christians the world over have worshiped Heavenly Father by means of this dignified and concise hymn of praise. In four short lines, praise echoes from heaven and earth to glorify God, "from whom all blessings flow."

George D. Pyper pointed out that although Emma Smith did not include "Praise God, from Whom All Blessings Flow" in her 1835 hymnal, she did select two other hymns by Thomas Ken for that collection: "Awake

My Soul and with the Sun" and "Glory to Thee, My God, This Night." "Praise God, from Whom All Blessings Flow" is actually the refrain that occurs in three of his longer hymns: "A Morning Hymn," "An Evening Hymn," and "A Midnight Hymn." (See *Stories of Latter-day Saint Hymns,* pp. 189–90.)

These four lines are sometimes called "the Doxology." In addition to referring to this specific stanza, the term *Doxology* can be applied more widely to hymns of praise.

The precise origin of the tune has been the subject of much discussion. It may have originated as a French *chanson;* Louis Bourgeois, if not its composer, at least deserves credit for first harmonizing the hymn and including it in an important hymn collection. In any case, it was first matched with a metrical version of Psalm 100. Thus the tune acquired its familiar name, OLD HUNDREDTH. Here, in modern spelling, is the hymn version of Psalm 100 as it was printed in 1640 in the *Bay Psalm Book,* the first book to be printed in the American colonies:

Shout to Jehovah, all the earth;
Serve ye Jehovah with gladness;
Before Him come with singing mirth;
Know that Jehovah, he God is.

Let Us All Press On 243

Text and music: Evan Stephens (1854–1930; LDS)
Tune name: COURAGE

The enthusiasm and determination conveyed in this song have made it a popular choice among Latter-day Saints, young and old, for many years. It is a hymn of the gospel-song type, with vigorous rhythms that correlate well with the vitality of its message.

The hymn refers to fighting, to wielding a sword, to vanquishing the enemy. But as in all our hymns that employ military imagery, these references are figurative. Paul often used military figures of speech, but he made it clear that he was not trying to stir up actual fighting. His purpose was symbolic:

"Put on the whole armour of God, that ye may be able to stand against the wiles of the devil.

"For we wrestle not against flesh and blood, but against principalities, against powers, against the rulers of the darkness of this world, against spiritual wickedness in high places." (Ephesians 6:11–12.)

Evan Stephens, who wrote many of our most popular Latter-day Saint hymns, did not hesitate to use metaphors of armed battle. He usually sought to write hymns that would be especially appealing to the youth. And he knew that the vision of a mighty army, with its connotations of courage, loyalty, bravery, and glory, would serve his purposes in this hymn. The sword referred to here is "the mighty sword of truth."

This hymn first appeared in a hymn collection in 1888, when the Deseret Sunday School Union published *Hymns and Sacred Songs.* In the 1985 hymnal, a slight change was made in the melody on the word *wicked* in the chorus: the melody originally stayed on the A; now, reflecting popular usage, it goes from the A to a G#.

Come Along, Come Along 244

Text: William Willes (1814–1890; LDS)
Music: A. C. Smyth (1840–1909; LDS)
Tune name: SPENCER

"Come Along, Come Along" is a cheerful reminder of a serious truth: leadership flows from the power of example and good-natured guidance, rather than from the power of force. The second verse reinforces the importance of teaching by example: the Savior invites us but does not drive us.

This hymn text by William Willes reflects the author's philosophy as a devoted Sunday School worker in the early Church. J. Spencer Cornwall said that William Willes and a companion, George Goddard, became known as " 'the Sunday School Twins.' Their stories, songs, and long beards were familiar to Sunday School children from one end of the Territory of Utah to the other. In the words of George D. Pyper: 'It was a gala day when these two men visited a Sunday School.' " (*Stories of Latter-day Saint Hymns,* p. 26.)

Brigham Young's advice to parents on guiding their children applies equally well to anyone in any leadership position: "How often we see parents demand obedience, good behavior, kind words, pleasant looks, a sweet voice and a bright eye from a child or children when they themselves are full of bitterness and scolding! How inconsistent and unreasonable this is! . . .

"Parents should never drive their children, but lead them along, giving them knowledge as their minds are prepared to receive it. Chastening may be necessary betimes, but parents should govern their children by faith rather than by the rod, leading them kindly by good example into all truth and holiness." (*Discourses of Brigham Young,* sel. John A. Widtsoe [Salt Lake City, Utah: Deseret Book Co., 1978], p. 208.)

The spirit behind this advice is that suggested by Doctrine and Covenants 121:41–42:

"No power or influence can or ought to be maintained by virtue of the priesthood, only by persuasion, by long-suffering, by gentleness and meekness, and by love unfeigned;

"By kindness, and pure knowledge, which shall greatly enlarge the soul without hypocrisy, and without guile."

The hymn first appeared in July 1878 in the *Juvenile Instructor*.

This House We Dedicate to Thee 245

Text: Henry W. Naisbitt (1826–1908; LDS)
Music: Frank W. Asper (1892–1973; LDS)
Tune name: LAUREL

"This House We Dedicate to Thee" is a hymn suitable for the dedication of a Church building. As they sing this hymn, the worshipers consecrate the building to sacred purposes, asking the Lord to bless all that takes place within its walls.

Although written for a building dedication, the hymn may appropriately be used at other times. Through their faithfulness, Latter-day Saints constantly seek to dedicate and rededicate their meetinghouses to holy purposes, to renew the prayers and feelings that have taken place as part of the formal dedication service. As the building fills its function—as devoted members of the Church pray, serve, sing, and teach one another within its walls—these activities are a continuing consecration.

The hymn is specific in its petitions. In a series of questions, it asks the Lord to bless our efforts, to bless those who speak within the building, and to bless those who seek the Lord. The hymn text reaches out from the present generation to the years past—"our fathers' God"—and to the years to come—"Here may our sons and daughters come."

The hymn as printed in the 1950 hymnal was a five-verse hymn. The three-verse hymn printed in the 1985 hymnal is actually more useful and more inclusive, since the two omitted verses (made up of one sentence) refer specifically to temples. Thus they limited the more general subject of the hymn, since the "house of the Lord" can be a ward or stake building as well as a temple. The omitted verses are as follows:

And may pollution ne'er have place
Within this shrine we give;
And in it through the years to come,
Awake the dead to live;

Live to thy kingdom; live to thee
While life shall pass away;

Then greet again with praise and song,
In heaven's eternal day.

The hymn text was first published in 1871. The tune was named LAUREL after the street where the composer lived in Salt Lake City. This tune was first printed with this text in *Hymns* (1948).

Onward, Christian Soldiers 246

Text: Sabine Baring-Gould (1834–1924)
Music: Arthur S. Sullivan (1842–1900)
Tune name: ST. GERTRUDE

Though Latter-day Saints do not glory in the thought of violence, the "war against evil" is a metaphor that has meaning for us in its spiritual sense. In this hymn, we march "*as* to war," Christian soldiers who do not seek actual warfare but who are enlisted forever as soldiers in another kind of battle.

Is it the stirring text or the vigorous, appealing tune that makes this hymn so popular among so many Christian denominations? J. Spencer Cornwall observed that in the case of this hymn it is impossible to know whether Sabine Baring-Gould or Arthur S. Sullivan made the more important contribution. (See *Stories of Our Mormon Hymns,* p. 133.)

Sabine Baring-Gould commented many years later on the hymn text he had written in 1864: "Whitmonday [the eighth Monday after Easter] is a great day for school festivals in Yorkshire. One Whitmonday . . . it was arranged that our school should join forces with a neighboring village. I wanted the children to sing when marching from one village to another, but couldn't think of anything quite suitable; so I sat up at night, resolved that I would write something myself. 'Onward, Christian soldiers' was the result. It was written in great haste, and I am afraid some of the rhymes are faulty. Certainly nothing has surprised me more than its popularity." (Quoted in Charles S. Nutter and Wilbur F. Tillett, *The Hymns and Hymn Writers of the Church* [New York: Methodist Book Concern, 1911], p. 205.)

The original hymn was six stanzas long. A stanza omitted from our hymnal is this:

Crowns and thrones may perish,
Kingdoms rise and wane.
But the Church of Jesus
Constant will remain.
Gates of hell can never
'Gainst the church prevail;

We have Christ's own promise,
And that cannot fail.

Another stanza, beginning "What the saints established, / That I hold for true," is consistently omitted from hymnals today because it is Sabine Baring-Gould's personal statement of his allegiance to English High Church principles.

Arthur Sullivan wrote his fine tune, ST. GERTRUDE, specifically for these words seven years later. The tune name honors Mrs. Gertrude Clay-Ker-Seymour, in whose home he was a guest at the time.

We Love Thy House, O God 247

Text: William Bullock (1797–1874)
Music: Leroy J. Robertson (1896–1971; LDS)
Tune name: FOUNTAIN GREEN

After a temple or a ward meetinghouse has been consecrated to the Lord, his Spirit dwells within to aid the Saints who gather to be taught and strengthened. In this hymn, the opening line could refer to either the "house" where ward or branch members meet weekly or to one of the temples.

"We Love Thy House, O God" is a hymn addressed to Deity, an expression of gratitude for these sacred places of worship and their importance in our lives. It is not merely as buildings that they are important; the hymn says nothing about the beauty of the physical structure. They have value and importance because "thou, O Lord, art there."

The first line of this hymn could well echo through the thoughts of a busy Latter-day Saint man or woman who, with all the distractions and discouragements of the world left behind, steps within the walls of a chapel or a temple. The joys of discipleship and fellowship help to restore tranquility, priorities, and contentment. In simple, moving phrases, the hymn lists these joys: prayer, the meeting with fellow Saints, the feeling of the Lord's presence, and the hearing of "the word of life."

The text, written in 1854, was inspired by Psalm 26:8: "Lord, I have loved the habitation of thy house, and the place where thine honour dwelleth." The footnote in the 1979 Latter-day Saint edition of the King James Bible tells us that the Hebrew word for *honor* can also be translated as "glory" or "presence."

The title of Leroy J. Robertson's dignified and singable hymn tune honors his birthplace, Fountain Green, Utah.

Up, Awake, Ye Defenders of Zion 248

Text: Charles W. Penrose (1832–1925; LDS); altered
Music: Attributed to Thomas E. Williams (d. 1854)
Tune name: COLUMBIA

At the time of this hymn's writing, the possibility of armed combat was real and immediate for the Latter-day Saints. Though hostile armies do not threaten us today, we can still feel a thrill of response to the call to be "defenders of Zion." Loyalty, strength, and sacrifice are still needed.

As was the case with "O Ye Mountains High" and other hymns, the original text included very warlike phrases. As we read phrases like "God-hating foe" and "plundering wretches" in the original version of this text, first published in 1857, it is instructive to contemplate, from a historical point of view, how threatened the early Saints must have felt. A small band of Saints faced a hostile world, and in their settlements and migrations they had learned some tragic lessons about the devastation that an angry mob or army can inflict. They had lost family members; they had lost the Prophet Joseph and other beloved Church leaders.

Today, when Latter-day Saints have taken their place in many communities and nations throughout the world, less vengeful language is appropriate. We do not need to view ourselves as defenders of a fortress who must constantly be on guard against attack. Threats and dangers surround us, of course, but they do not usually take the form of armed mobs. So, in our modern hymnal, "God-hating foe" has become "enemy host"; "plundering wretches" has become "plundering foemen"; reference to "the blood of our prophets" is deleted. Other appropriate word changes were also made.

Did this tune originate in England, under the name "Brittania, the Pride of the Ocean," or in America, under the name "Columbia, the Gem of the Ocean"? After it was first published in Philadelphia in 1843, an Englishman named Stephen Meany claimed that he had written the words a year earlier and his friend Thomas Williams the tune. But the American edition credited David T. Shaw with both words and music. To complicate matters further, another American, Thomas A. Becket, claimed to have helped Shaw with the writing. Those arguing for English origin point out that "Columbia" seems to be a makeshift reference, hardly a common term to refer to America. On the other side, defenders of American origin point to the 1843 American copyright, as opposed to an 1852 date when the English version was first deposited in the British Museum archives. The riddle of the tune's origin may never be solved.

Called to Serve 249

Text: Grace Gordon; altered
Music: Walter G. Tyler
Tune name: CALLED TO SERVE

Even the most sophisticated of Latter-day Saints respond to the vigorous challenge of this children's marching song. As we sing it, we speak with pride and energy of our dedication to the "heavenly King of Glory" and his cause.

This hymn was not at first scheduled for inclusion in the hymnal. But in April 1985 a meeting to which every mission president in the Church had come was held in the Assembly Hall on Temple Square in Salt Lake City. In an event that had a powerful effect on all the Area Presidents, Regional Representatives, and mission presidents, including those who were about to depart for their new assignments, missionaries from the Missionary Training Center marched into the Assembly Hall singing "Called to Serve." The effect was electrifying. An editorial in the *Church News* stated, "The impact of this experience was so moving that tears were flowing and deep emotions were stirred. It was an unforgettable spiritual moment." (11 Aug. 1985, p. 16.)

The shared feeling following that meeting was, "But *of course* 'Called to Serve' is going to be in the new hymnal!" It was in fact the very last to be added to the list of hymns approved for the 1985 hymnbook. Even though this song was originally written for children, it was decided to place it among such rallying songs as "Behold! A Royal Army" and "We Are All Enlisted," rather than with the other children's songs.

This hymn, long a favorite with Primary children, has undergone some editorial changes. The 1951 Primary songbook, *The Children Sing,* included a verse omitted from the subsequent Primary songbook as well as from our present hymnal:

Called to serve his path of service loyal,
Called to lead to his eternal light;
Rich reward awaits in mansions royal.
Forward then in heavenly might.

The line that now reads "Sons and daughters, children of a King" was originally "Sons of God, and children of a King." It was altered to make the language more inclusive. The word *homage,* somewhat difficult for children, was changed to *praises.* In the chorus, the phrase "God our strength will be" originally read "Joy our strength shall be."

We Are All Enlisted 250

*Text: Anonymous (*The New Golden Chain, *New York, 1866)*
Music: William B. Bradbury (1816–1868)
Tune name: MONTCLAIR

This vigorous hymn conveys the enthusiasm and dedication of an army of righteous followers of Christ and asks, "Who'll volunteer?"

Like several other hymns in our hymnal (for example, "Hope of Israel," no. 259), this hymn uses the metaphor of a fighting army to parallel the loyalty and zeal of followers of Jesus Christ. The military terminology does not refer to an actual earthly battle; it is an army that has accepted Paul's exhortation to "put on the whole armour of God, that ye may be able to stand against the wiles of the devil." (Ephesians 6:11.)

The hymn stresses not only the dedication of those soldiers but also their happiness in the task to which they have committed themselves. The soldiers in this army serve with a joyful heart: "Happy are we! Glad to join the army, we will sing as we go." Elder Neal A. Maxwell wrote on the importance of this attitude: "To think of enduring to the end as 'hanging in there,' doing one's duty relentlessly, is not inaccurate. Yet enduring to the end is more than outlasting and surviving, though it includes those qualities. We are called upon, as was the Prophet Joseph, to 'endure it well,' gracefully, not grudgingly." (*Wherefore, Ye Must Press Forward* [Salt Lake City, Utah: Deseret Book Co., 1977], p. 109.)

The composer, William B. Bradbury, was a resident of Montclair, New Jersey, at the time of his death. The tune name, MONTCLAIR, reflects this fact.

Behold! A Royal Army 251

Text: Fanny J. Crosby (1820–1915)
Music: Adam Geibel (1885–1933)
Tune name: ROYAL ARMY

In the words of J. Spencer Cornwall, "Many hymns of exhortation have in them a militant connotation to establish an atmosphere of conquering determination in worshipers. Such an one is 'Behold the Royal Army' with its 'Victory, Victory,' chorus." (*Stories of Our Mormon Hymns,* p. 10.)

This hymn, first published in 1894, is unique in that it represents the collaboration of a blind author and a blind musician. The author, Fanny Crosby, lost her eyesight when she was only six weeks old. She went on to become perhaps the most popular writer of Sunday School song texts that the United States has ever produced. Her favorite saying was, "I think that life is not too long and therefore I determine that many people read a song who will not read a sermon."

J. Spencer Cornwall quoted the famous poem Fanny Crosby wrote on her blindness when she was only nine years old:

O what a happy soul am I!
Although I cannot see;
I am resolved that in this world
Contented I will be.
How many blessings I enjoy,
That other people don't;
To weep and sigh because I'm blind,
I cannot and I won't.

Among the popular compositions of blind composer Adam Giebel are "Stand Up for Jesus" and "Kentucky Babe."

Put Your Shoulder to the Wheel 252

Text and music: Will L. Thompson (1847–1909)
Tune name: WILLING

For many Latter-day Saints who have been members of the Church since childhood days, this song brings back vivid memories. Young Latter-day Saints love the energetic rhythms and catchy tune of "Put Your Shoulder to the Wheel." As we sang this song at the tops of our voices, we were being schooled in an important principle: the value of good work.

"Put Your Shoulder to the Wheel" has all the characteristics of the type of hymn known as the gospel song. Its words are an exhortation to good deeds; it has the distinctive dotted rhythms of the gospel song; and it is divided into verse and chorus. Also typical of the gospel song is the way in which the men's voices, in the chorus, answer the melody by repeating the words "push along" and "full of song."

This hymn is not Latter-day Saint in origin, but it achieved immediate popularity among members of the Church. It was included in *Deseret Sunday School Songs* in 1909, only five years after it was first published in a gospel-song hymnal in 1904. In the 1950 hymnal, it carried the title "The World Has Need of Willing Men."

This hymn's message will never be out of date. Every willing worker is needed for the cause of righteousness. The scriptures abound in exhortations to join in the cause of right with full energy, to be "anxiously engaged in a good cause." (D&C 58:27.) President David O. McKay said, "Let us teach [our children] to work and to realize that the *privilege* to work is a gift, that *power* to work is a blessing, that *love* to work is success." (*True to the Faith* [Salt Lake City, Utah: Bookcraft, 1966], p. 287.)

Like Ten Thousand Legions Marching 253

Text: Jean L. Kaberry (b. 1918; LDS)
Music: Robert P. Manookin (b. 1918; LDS)
Tune name: ROBERT II

This hymn honors the hosts of young missionaries who travel by assignment to distant parts of the world to spread the gospel message. It links them with glorious company: Abraham, Jacob, and Joseph. The final verse invites all nations to accept what has been referred to in the hymn as a "glorious song"—the message of the restored gospel.

Composer Robert P. Manookin stated: "My wife and I had become acquainted, during our mission in New Zealand, with a wonderful Australian sister, Jean L. Kaberry, who has a great literary ability, along with a fine testimony of the gospel. Knowing that the new [1985] hymnbook was under consideration and that hymns of various subjects were sought, I challenged Jean to write a missionary hymn. This poem was the result, and my intent was to set it to music with a kind of martial strength or implication, denoting the marching bands of youth all over the world." The tune name, ROBERT II, honors the composer's oldest son.

Jean L. Kaberry worked for several years as a secretary and typist in the New Zealand Temple. Young missionaries would often come to the temple, and she was impressed with their enthusiasm. When Robert Manookin asked her to write a missionary hymn text, it was natural for her to think of these young people. "I visualized the Roman legions going forth to conquer the world, and applied the vision to our missionaries," she said.

Both words and music invite energetic singing, and congregations will enjoy this march-like hymn. To bring the hymn to a more emphatic close, Robert Manookin lengthened the rhythm of the next to last measure, giving half-notes in the melody where we might expect quarter notes.

True to the Faith 254

Text and music: Evan Stephens (1854–1930; LDS)
Tune name: ANN

Generations of Latter-day Saint youth have had their hearts and spirits lifted through this energetic song of resolve and dedication. As they sing this song, the youth of the Church, as a united body, pledge their faith. Against all odds, they will be "faithful and true" to "God's command" and to the faith their "parents have cherished."

In an article titled "Songs and Music of the Latter-day Saints," composer Evan Stephens expressed his views on the hymnody of the Church:

"The songs and music of the Latter-day Saints are in perfect accord with the spirit of the newly revealed gospel of Jesus Christ, as restored in modern times through the medium of the Prophet, Joseph Smith.

"In contrast to that generally used by the churches of the day in which this Church was set up anew upon the earth, they are as light to darkness, or brightness to gloom. Expressions of fear and sorrow, the terrible confessions of and lamentations over sin, the constant dwelling upon the sufferings of our crucified Savior, and the eternal tortures in store for sinners, give place in the songs of the Latter-day Saints to expressions of hope, joy and the sense of sins forgiven. More emphasis is placed upon the love and the glorious conquest of our Redeemer than upon his earthly sufferings; more, on the final redemption of all erring humanity than upon a never-ending torment of souls. When the heartstrings and the fount of tears are to be touched at all, it is with tenderness, sympathy and joy, rather than with terror and sorrow. . . .

"[The 'Mormonistic' in music is] that which breathes optimism and not pessimism; music in which the sombre must not predominate, but be used only as a means of contrast to heighten the effects of the bright." (*Improvement Era,* June 1914, p. 760.)

George D. Pyper reported that Evan Stephens composed "True to the Faith" in response to a sermon by President Joseph F. Smith on "The Third and Fourth Generations." He was so inspired by the vision of the youth of Zion that he composed this hymn to be sung by the Sunday School at their conferences in 1905. He wrote a dedication on the copy: "Lovingly dedicated to my 20,000 pupils of Zion."

In George D. Pyper's opinion, this song "contains more of the composer's emotional enthusiasm than any other of his writings. Professor Stephens loved the youth of Zion. . . . This song was his spiritual advice to them." (*Stories of Latter-day Saint Hymns,* pp. 118–19.)

Carry On 255

Text: Ruth May Fox (1853–1958; LDS)
Music: Alfred M. Durham (1872–1957; LDS)
Tune name: PAROWAN

"Onward with Mormon Ideals." This was the theme of the Mutual Improvement Association conference of June 1930, held during the Church's centennial year. These two influences—the thought of a hundred years of heritage and the admonition "onward"—combined to suggest the idea that became "Carry On."

J. Spencer Cornwall obtained the following information from Leonard Grant Fox, son of Ruth May Fox: "An invitation had been sent throughout the Church for a song—words and music—which would be appropriate for the M-Men and Gleaners to sing at the conference. . . . A number of songs were submitted, but none was quite what had been hoped for. At a meeting of the executive officers of the M. I. A. the subject was discussed with some concern as the time was getting short. The meeting closed about noon, and Sister Fox was heard to say, 'I guess I'll have to see what I can do.' Sister Van Noy recalls, 'That same afternoon she came and said, "Elsie, will you type this up?" It was the lyrics to "Carry On." Next morning she brought the song, having changed only one word, and asked me to make several copies.' "

J. Spencer Cornwall continued the story: "But the music was needed. Brother Alfred M. Durham was invited by Sister Fox to write the music for 'Carry On.' A few days later he called on Sister Fox. They found a piano where Brother Durham played his composition. For some time they went over the song together. After this interview Sister Fox remarked, 'The music is lovely, just what I had in mind, something lively and catchy, a tune everyone can sing easily.' "

When someone commented to Alfred M. Durham that "the music does much for the song," he modestly deflected the compliment and turned it toward Ruth May Fox: "The music was inspired by the words[;] they are the body of the song, the music is the adornment." (*Stories of Our Mormon Hymns,* pp. 48–49.)

Alfred M. Durham's birthplace, Parowan, Utah, is the source of the tune name.

As Zion's Youth in Latter Days 256

Text: Susan Evans McCloud (b. 1945; LDS)
Music: Irish melody
Tune name: CLONMEL

An Irish melody of unknown origin matches the firm determination of the words of "As Zion's Youth in Latter Days." This song truly embodies the "strength to dare," the resolve to "love, and learn, and overcome."

Susan Evans McCloud accepted a request from the 1985 Hymnbook Committee to write a song for youth, one that would reflect the viewpoint of youth rather than the viewpoint of adults admonishing the youth. She passed along to them the entry from her journal, April 1, 1984, when she sat down to write the hymn:

"Cold, gray skies, then snow, increasing, thick & heavy. Late when I decided to try lyrics. I prayed, very fervently and sincerely, cried over many of my inner anguishes. Arose—went to my desk—and the song came. A song for youth. Four verses with barely a stop. Took it downstairs & Heather played while James & I sang it. Could hardly keep the tears away. Late up. Everyone else asleep. I prayed again. A closeness, a gratitude."

As a teenager, the author herself went through what she described as "a difficult, trying situation." She had to leave her Salt Lake home for what seemed to her like "exile in the mission field." She said, "I felt a loneliness for home that tore at my heart." But at this difficult time, she recalled: "I received great sustenance, courage, and joy from the songs for youth. I wanted this song to do that for some suffering or confused or vacillating youth."

On May 18, 1986, after an Aaronic Priesthood fireside held in the Salt Lake Tabernacle, she had an opportunity to speak to a chorus of young people who had just performed her song. She reported: "I expressed my desire that the song might mean to some of them what the songs of the youth had meant to me when I was struggling through my own teenage years in Illinois. It was a moment of pure joy and spirit-to-spirit communication. I felt my Heavenly Father's love, and my heart sang with gratitude for the opportunity he had afforded me to serve in his kingdom in this way."

Rejoice! A Glorious Sound Is Heard 257

Text: W. O. Robinson (1876–1979; LDS)
Music: Frank W. Asper (1892–1973; LDS)
Tune name: ELINORE

Exultation and exhortation are both important in this joyful hymn. For two verses, we declare the joy we feel as we hear the "glorious sound" of voices raised in praise to Jehovah. These voices are our own, and the triumphant shout, or song, is to continue "down the ages, on and on." The third verse admonishes us to remain a faithful part of that "joyous strain": "Arise and sing, ye sons of men."

The first line of this hymn as it appeared in the 1950 hymnal was "Oh hark! a glorious sound is heard." The 1985 Hymnbook Committee felt that it would be more in keeping with the hymn's purpose to begin with the word *Rejoice!* An additional word change was made in verse two, where the phrase "manhood, grace, and power" was changed to "honor, grace, and power," because many women serve as part of our missionary force.

A hymn such as "Rejoice! A Glorious Sound Is Heard" gives us an opportunity to follow the scriptural admonition to praise the Lord. Offering praise is something we Latter-day Saints perhaps do not do often enough, even though we are frequently told to do so in both ancient scripture and modern revelation. Praise of the Lord is a constant theme of the psalms: "I will bless the Lord at all times: his praise shall continually be in my mouth." (Psalm 34:1.)

In Romans 15:11, Paul instructed, "Praise the Lord, all ye Gentiles; and laud him, all ye people." In Alma 26:8, Ammon said to his brethren, "Blessed be the name of our God; let us sing to his praise, yea, let us give thanks to his holy name, for he doth work righteousness forever."

The tune name, ELINORE, is the middle name of the composer's first wife.

O Thou Rock of Our Salvation 258

Text: Joseph L. Townsend (1849–1942; LDS)
Music: William Clayson (1840–1887; LDS)
Tune name: IRCHESTER

As a symbol of fortitude and eternal stability, the metaphor of the rock has inspired many writers, both in our scriptures and in our hymns. This hymn is a call to battle, in which the leader of the army is a "rock," unconquerable and firm.

Under the entry "Rock of Heaven" in *Mormon Doctrine* (2d ed. [Salt Lake City, Utah: Bookcraft, 1966], p. 657), Elder Bruce R. McConkie stated:

"Christ is the Rock (Deut. 32:3–4, 18, 30–31; 1 Cor. 10:1–4), or the *Rock of Heaven*. (Moses 7:53.) Such name-titles carry a connotation of strength and stability (1 Sam. 2:2), as for instance when David exulted: 'The Lord is my rock, and my fortress, and my deliverer; The God of my rock, in him will I trust: he is my shield, and the horn of my salvation, my high tower, and my refuge, my saviour.' (2 Sam. 22:1-4; 23:3; Psa. 18:1–3, 31.)"

The author and composer of this hymn were associated as officers of the Sunday School in Payson, Utah. Their Sunday School callings inspired many hymn collaborations. This hymn follows many characteristics of the gospel-song tradition: the dotted-note rhythms, the energetic message of exhortation, and the refrain. It is somewhat unusual, however, in having a different set of words for the final chorus. This final chorus is in fact a rephrasing of verse one; it helps to give a feeling of unity to the hymn text as the conclusion of the hymn recalls the prayer of the opening.

Before his emigration to America in 1861, William Clayson presided over the Irchester Branch in England for two years. This fact is reflected in the tune name. The hymn was first published in the *Juvenile Instructor* in 1877.

Hope of Israel 259

Text: Joseph L. Townsend (1849–1942; LDS)
Music: William Clayson (1840–1887; LDS)
Tune name: WILBY

In the words of J. Spencer Cornwall, "One could sermonize at length on the apt title of the song 'Hope of Israel.' The perpetuation and growth of the church membership is in large measure dependent on the continuing faith of the youth. 'Onward, Onward, Youth of Zion' is a militant command to the 'Children of the Promised Day' to rise in might 'With the Sword of Truth and Right.' " (*Stories of Our Mormon Hymns,* pp. 72–73.)

The image of Church members as a military body fighting a fierce war serves some useful purposes. It is natural to think of the metaphor of a battling army when we are concerned with such characteristics as loyalty, courage, and determination. Throughout scripture, battle imagery has represented the war against evil.

Paul even described the armor that a Christian should wear in preparation for battle: "Stand therefore, having your loins girt about with truth, and having on the breastplate of righteousness;

"And your feet shod with the preparation of the gospel of peace;

"Above all, taking the shield of faith, wherewith ye shall be able to quench all the fiery darts of the wicked.

"And take the helmet of salvation, and the sword of the Spirit, which is the word of God." (Ephesians 6:14–17.)

Clearly the armor Paul was describing, "the whole armour of God" (Ephesians 6:13), is a figurative armor, meant to be symbolic, not a literal suit of armor for an actual battle. Though some denominations have decided to omit from their hymnals all references to battle and warfare, several such hymns were retained in our 1985 hymnal on the assumption that we, like Paul, are able to picture a symbolic battle. When "Hope of Israel" mentions "the sword of truth and right," clearly this is a "sword" meant to convert and enlighten, not one meant to maim and kill.

As was the case with the preceding hymn, "O Thou Rock of Our Salvation," this hymn was a result of the collaborative efforts of Joseph

L. Townsend and William Clayson during the time they served in the Sunday School organization in Payson, Utah. It was first published in the *Juvenile Instructor* in 1880.

William Clayson's birthplace, Wilby, Northamptonshire, England, is the source of the tune name.

Who's on the Lord's Side? 260

Text: Hannah Last Cornaby (1822–1905; LDS)
Music: Henry H. Russell (1812–1900); altered
Tune name: OCEAN WAVE

"I know thy works, that thou art neither cold nor hot: I would thou wert cold or hot.

"So then because thou art lukewarm, and neither cold nor hot, I will spue thee out of my mouth." (Revelation 3:15–16.)

The time is here when we must declare ourselves and answer the question posed by this song: "Who's on the Lord's side?"

This song is an example of the adaptation of a popular tune to gospel-song use. Many will already know this melody by its original title: "A Life on the Ocean Wave." This tune was first published in 1839.

J. Spencer Cornwall wrote: "The hymn 'Who's on the Lord's Side, Who?' was a great rally hymn in the early days of the Latter-day Saint Church. When Elder George Goddard sang it he would call for all those who were 'on the Lord's side' to rise and sing the refrain." (*Stories of Our Mormon Hymns,* p. 193.)

Hannah Last Cornaby's text, first published in the *Millennial Star* in 1884, included two additional verses. The final reference to the "olive branch" shows an effort to temper the military imagery somewhat. These are the omitted verses:

The Lord has armies great
Which at his bidding go,
His chariots are strong;
Who's on the Lord's side? Who?
When He made bare His arm
To lay the wicked low,
Then is the time to ask,
Who's on the Lord's side? Who?

Then rally to the flag;
Our God will help us through;
The victory is ours:
Who's on the Lord's side? Who?

Stainless our flag must wave,
And to the nations show
The olive branch of peace;
Who's on the Lord's side? Who?

Thy Servants Are Prepared 261; 329

Text: Marilyn McMeen Brown (b. 1938; LDS)
Music: Willy Reske (b. 1897; LDS)
Tune name: JULIUS

In strong, confident language, we pledge our service to the Lord as we sing this hymn, new to the 1985 hymnal. We are not only *willing* to serve as his missionaries but we are also *prepared.* With great dedication, the Lord's servants will spread the light of truth throughout the world.

Verse one compares the gathering of converts to the gathering of sheep into a fold; it ends by addressing the Savior with a title appropriate to this comparison: "O Lamb of God." Verses two and three draw upon the metaphor of light versus darkness. Author Marilyn McMeen Brown envisioned the missionary force as lighting the "world's dark lamps" with the light of the gospel message, until the darkness draws away. As the truth is spread, "love shall conquer night."

The hymn text uses simple, self-assured language. The first verse commits us to the missionary call, the second prays for missionary success, and the third looks confidently to the future and foresees the dark world transformed by the "revealing light" of the gospel. If the congregation is sincere in the words as they sing them, they have made a serious collective commitment.

Because of the stepwise movement of the melody (measures five and six move upward along the tones of a major scale), congregations will have no trouble learning it.

Go, Ye Messengers of Glory 262

Text: John Taylor (1808–1887; LDS)
Music: Leroy J. Robertson (1896–1971; LDS)
Tune name: THE BIG EAST

The zeal of the great missionary years of 1839 through 1842 are reflected in this hymn text by John Taylor. At the time he wrote this hymn, his heart was on fire with missionary fervor as he preached throughout

Britain. Some forty years later, he would be sustained as President of The Church of Jesus Christ of Latter-day Saints.

In the summer of 1839, members of the Quorum of the Twelve Apostles, with other missionaries as well, departed for the British Isles. They had been called by revelation to preach the gospel overseas. Within two years, because of the persuasive powers of such great missionaries as Wilford Woodruff and John Taylor and because the Lord chose to pour out his Spirit upon whole congregations of the honest in heart, almost six thousand converts were added to The Church of Jesus Christ of Latter-day Saints.

John Taylor's missionary efforts did not cease after his return to Nauvoo, Illinois. In 1846, he departed for a second mission to the British Isles, and in 1850, he filled a mission to France and Germany.

John Taylor wrote "Go, Ye Messengers of Glory" for an 1840 hymnal of which he was one of the editors. The text conveys the enthusiasm and confidence of the missionary work being carried on in the British Isles at that time, when such large numbers of people were so anxious to embrace the gospel message.

The phrase "legates of the skies" is unusual but perfectly in keeping with the spirit and message of the text. A *legate* is an ambassador or representative; thus "legates of the skies" are bearers of a heavenly message.

THE BIG EAST refers to the mountains in eastern Sanpete County, Utah, where the composer, Leroy J. Robertson, herded sheep as a youth.

Go Forth with Faith 263

Text: Ruth M. Gardner (b. 1927; LDS)
Music: Lyall J. Gardner (b. 1926; LDS)
Tune name: PAUL

Our hymnbook is richer for the addition of this fine missionary hymn. Sung at a missionary farewell or as a reminder to all Saints of the responsibility and rewards of preaching the gospel, it sets forth the qualities of a good missionary and outlines the missionary's basic message.

When Paul Gardner, son of Ruth M. and Lyall J. Gardner, received his mission call to Japan, he asked his parents to speak as part of the farewell sacrament meeting. But he made two requests: first, they were not to give advice, and second, they were not to give praise!

"These were hard restrictions but we tried to abide by his wishes," stated Lyall Gardner. Instead of offering advice through their talks, Lyall and Ruth Gardner decided, as a surprise for their son, to write a new hymn to be performed by the ward choir at the meeting.

The hymn's original title was "Go Forth, My Son." Lyall Gardner noted: "It was written for only one performance; however, friends and relatives asked for copies, and it found its way to Argentina, Australia, the Philippines, South Africa, and many wards and stakes in the United States. The hymn was not written for fame or glory or money. It was written simply out of love for one of our children." The tune name, PAUL, honors that missionary son.

"If this hymn is successful and is accepted by the people of the Church," said Lyall Gardner, "it will be for three reasons. First, the message is true. Ruth has an unusual gift of being able to phrase profound gospel principles in simple, effective, and poetic language. There is an air of dignity and fervency to the ageless truths that are proclaimed. Second, the music is simple and relates to common people. Third, the message is what most parents would express to their young missionaries going out to serve the Lord on a mission."

Hark, All Ye Nations! 264

Text: From a German text by Louis F. Mönch (1847–1916; LDS)
Music: George F. Root (1820–1895)
Tune name: COME TO THE SAVIOR

In "Hark, All Ye Nations!" a hymn of strong rhythms and fervent declaration, the vitality of a devoted convert and missionary finds its expression. Those who have the gospel long to share it with "every land and people," and in this hymn we call on the world to listen to our message.

This hymn has a distinctive history. Like many, it is a hybrid of Latter-day Saint and non–Latter-day Saint creativity. Louis F. Mönch, a German immigrant whose spiritual history is no less dramatic than his educational achievements (see Biographies), resigned as principal of Ogden City Schools in Utah to return to Europe as a Latter-day Saint missionary. While in Switzerland, he translated many songs and talks for the benefit of the German-speaking Saints.

He also wrote some original works in his native German, one of them *"Sehet, Ihr Volker"* ("Behold, Ye People"), a missionary-centered text for a popular gospel tune, "Come to the Savior," that he had evidently learned while he was in the United States. Both words and music for "Come to the Savior" were by George F. Root, also the composer of "Tramp, Tramp, Tramp" (the tune of "In Our Lovely Deseret," no. 307) and "The Battle Cry of Freedom." The original first verse of George F. Root's hymn was as follows:

Come to the Savior, make no delay;
Here in His word He's shown us the way;

Here in our midst He's standing today,
Tenderly saying, "Come!"
Joyful, joyful will the meeting be,
When from sin our hearts are pure and free;
Here in our midst He's standing today,
Tenderly saying, "Come!"

Louis F. Mönch's missionary text to George F. Root's tune became so popular among Latter-day Saint members and missionaries in German-speaking countries that some today consider it the most beloved and most often sung hymn among the Saints of Germany, Austria, and German-speaking Switzerland. The author of this book became aware of this fact in a dramatic way: the first time I went with my husband to a reunion of returned Swiss-Austrian missionaries, I didn't know the hymn at all, but all those who had any link with German-speaking Mormonism considered it their "theme-song" hymn, and its singing was the emotional high point of the evening.

Elder Thomas S. Monson referred to this hymn, new to the 1985 hymnal, in a meeting in the Assembly Hall on Temple Square in September 1985; his remarks underline the hymn's international appeal: "I heard 'Hark, All Ye Nations' first sung in Italy. I was impressed with its missionary spirit. When I went to Germany, I told the Saints that the Italians have a good missionary hymn. They said, 'Oh, yes, the Italians stole it from us!' The same hymn is also sung by the Maoris of New Zealand in a slower tempo."

Thus we have a native American gospel-song hymn given a new text and a new meaning a century ago by a German-speaking Latter-day Saint and today returned to English-speaking Saints in a new English version with a message appropriate to its history: the worldwide relevance of gospel truth.

Arise, O God, and Shine — 265

Text: William Hurn (1754–1829)
Music: John Darwall (1731–1789)
Tune name: DARWALL

We often pray on behalf of missionary work, asking the Lord to lead the missionaries to the doors of the honest in heart and to bless the people of the world that they may hear and know his word. This powerful hymn is just such a prayer. We are entreating our Father in Heaven to "bring distant nations near."

It is wonderful to think that a hymn text and a hymn tune more than two hundred years old could provide such a fine addition to the 1985 hymnal, and one so relevant to the desires of Latter-day Saints. For many years, the choice of hymns for missionary farewell services or for missionary-theme sacrament meetings has been fairly limited. But the 1985 hymnal increased to thirty-five the number of hymns listed under the topical heading "Missionary Work." No new missionary hymn is more exciting or effective than "Arise, O God, and Shine."

The original first line of the text was "Rise, gracious God, and shine." An editor changed it to its present form in 1857. The text recalls Isaiah 60:1–3, a scriptural passage set to music by Handel in his oratorio *Messiah.* It is Isaiah's triumphant prophecy concerning the spread of the Lord's truth:

"Arise, shine; for thy light is come, and the glory of the Lord is risen upon thee.

"For, behold, the darkness shall cover the earth, and gross darkness the people: but the Lord shall arise upon thee, and his glory shall be seen upon thee.

"And the Gentiles shall come to thy light, and kings to the brightness of thy rising."

The tune is sometimes called DARWALL'S 148TH because when it was first published in 1770 it was the setting for a version of the 148th Psalm, beginning "Ye boundless realms of joy." Many denominations use this tune for the words to "Rejoice, the Lord Is King!" (no. 66). It also works well with the text "An Angel from on High" (no. 13), if the repeat is omitted in the refrain.

Although the language of the text may seem quite abstract to some members of the congregation, it is basically a prayer to our Father in Heaven to hasten the spread of his gospel throughout every land. This fine hymn tune has a remarkable characteristic that makes it especially suitable for this optimistic, forward-looking text: the movement of almost every musical phrase is upward.

The Time Is Far Spent 266

Text: Eliza R. Snow (1804–1887; LDS)
Music: German folk song
Tune name: KRAMBAMBULI

The lively tune and the powerful admonition of this hymn perfectly convey the sense of urgency that is part of its message. A great responsibility rests upon the Saints if they are to prepare the people of the world for the Savior's coming, for "the time is far spent; there is little remaining."

An observation by J. Spencer Cornwall concerning this hymn is a useful warning against assuming a hymn's content based on title alone. He wrote: " 'The Time Is Far Spent' is a missionary hymn of exhortation. Frequently it is mistaken to be a closing hymn [when] . . . the first line is . . . read out of its context. Such is far from its real import—that of 'publishing glad tidings by sea and by land.' "

He continued: "The tune which in some way became associated with 'The Time Is Far Spent' is a German drinking song called 'Krambambule.' . . . It had been used previously in at least two other hymn collections with religious texts. These collections were evidently known to the early Mormon hymn-writers." (*Stories of Our Mormon Hymns,* p. 200.)

In the opening line of verse three, "What, tho, if the favor of Ahman possessing," the word *Ahman* will be unfamiliar to some people. Elder Bruce R. McConkie explained: "In the pure language spoken by Adam—and which will be spoken again during the millennial era (Zeph. 3:9)—the name of God the Father is *Ahman,* or possibly *Ah Man,* a name-title having a meaning identical with or at least very closely akin to *Man of Holiness.*" (*Mormon Doctrine,* 2d ed. [Salt Lake City, Utah: Bookcraft, 1966], p. 29.) Orson Pratt discussed the revelation that was the source of this information. (In *Journal of Discourses* [London: Latter-day Saints' Book Depot, 1855], 2:342.)

One word change in the 1985 hymnal expanded the use of this hymn to include sisters: in verse three, the phrase "Go, brethren" was changed to "Go forward."

How Wondrous and Great 267

Text: Henry U. Onderdonk (1789–1858)
Music: Attributed to Johann Michael Haydn (1737–1806)
Tune name: LYONS

When we rejoice in our knowledge of God's goodness, our instinctive wish is to share this knowledge and the happiness it brings with the entire world. The hymn "How Wondrous and Great" follows just such a train of thought. In verse one, we worship and praise the Lord in joyful exclamations. In verse two, we look forward to the time when all nations will awaken to the light of truth.

The hymn text is a poetic rendering of Revelation 15:3–4, known as "Moses' Song of the Lamb":

"And they sing the song of Moses the servant of God, and the song of the Lamb, saying, Great and marvellous are thy works, Lord God Almighty; just and true are thy ways, thou King of saints.

"Who shall not fear thee, O Lord, and glorify thy name? for thou only art holy: for all nations shall come and worship before thee; for thy judgments are made manifest."

The hymn's message is simple: since our God is a God of such power, it is inevitable that his name and worship should spread to all nations. As a missionary-oriented people, we should be filled with great hope and satisfaction for the opportunity to sing such a hymn and ponder such a prophecy.

This popular hymn tune is sung in most denominations to a text by Robert Grant. The first verse is as follows:

O worship the King, all glorious above!
O gratefully sing his power and his love!
Our Shield and Defender, the Ancient of Days,
Pavilioned with splendor, and girded with praise.

Come, All Whose Souls Are Lighted 268

Text: Reginald Heber (1783–1826)
Music: Lowell Mason (1792–1872)
Tune name: MISSIONARY HYMN

From the beginning of the nineteenth century, when the Protestant world was just beginning to awaken to the missionary possibilities among the non-Christian nations of the world, comes this best known of all Christian missionary hymns. Latter-day Saints have sung this hymn since the days of Emma Smith's first hymnal in 1835.

In the year 1829, Reginald Heber's father-in-law, Dean Shipley, was planning a special church service in which the subject of the sermon would be "The Society for the Propagation of the Gospel in Foreign Parts." He asked Reginald Heber to write a special hymn for the meeting. Within only a few short minutes he had written the entire hymn, originally titled "Missionary Hymn," which was sung the next day and soon became popular with Christians the world over.

Previous hymnals, including Emma Smith's, included a verse omitted from the 1985 hymnal:

What though the spicy breezes
Blow soft o'er Ceylon's isle;
Though every prospect pleases,
And only man is vile?
In vain with lavish kindness
The gifts of God are strewn;
The heathen in his blindness
Bows down to wood and stone.

The Reverend Reginald Heber, at that point in his life, had not ventured out into the world as a missionary. The catalogue of scenes from every corner of the globe are those that would have occurred naturally to the romantic imagination of an eager young Church of England clergyman—a sort of idealized missionary travelogue. (As one writer pointed out, "India has no coral strands [beaches] except in this poem.") But his later life validated the hymn's sentiments in the strongest way. He was called as bishop of Calcutta and died in India in missionary service.

The hymn's title in the 1950 hymnbook was "From Greenland's Icy Mountains." Our present version uses the original third verse as the first, and alters "Shall we, whose souls are lighted" to "Come, all whose souls are lighted." Michael Moody, chairman of the Church's General Music Committee, commented: "While this hymn is widely used among other denominations, it has not really been discovered by Latter-day Saints. The verses were rearranged in the hope that the new title would give a better idea of the hymn's message."

About seven years after the hymn was written, a woman in Savannah, Georgia, obtained a copy of the text and wished to have it set to music. She remembered a young man working as a clerk in a local bank who was said to have musical talent, and at her request, he wrote the present tune. He was Lowell Mason, later to become perhaps the most important name in American church music.

Early Latter-day Saints used this hymn tune for the text "O God, the Eternal Father" (no. 175) before the Felix Mendelssohn tune replaced it.

Jehovah, Lord of Heaven and Earth 269

Text: Anonymous
Music: Oliver Holden (1765–1844)
Tune name: CORONATION

As we sing this hymn, we petition the Lord to hasten the day when "every tongue" will join in his praise. The blessing of the gospel's going forth to others is also a blessing to us: "we long to see thy Church increase."

Prophecies such as Habakkuk 2:14 make it clear that one day the gospel will spread throughout the world: "For the earth shall be filled with the knowledge of the glory of the Lord, as the waters cover the sea."

In the meantime, it is human nature that the Lord's followers should feel impatient. The Saints wish the Lord to pour out his Spirit so that these events may come to pass without delay: "Roll on thy work in all its power!"

The tune name, CORONATION, relates to the hymn text by Edward

Perronet that is paired with this melody in many Protestant hymnals. Verse one reads:

All hail the power of Jesus' name!
Let angels prostrate fall;
Bring forth the royal diadem,
And crown him Lord of all.

The anonymous text was published in the *Millennial Star* in 1860.

I'll Go Where You Want Me to Go 270

Text: Mary Brown (1856–1918)
Music: Carrie E. Rounsefell (1861–1930)
Tune name: CONSECRATION

A traditional hymn for Latter-day Saint missionary farewells, this song embodies the faith of a true servant of the Lord—willing to alter plans, give up worldly goods, and travel to the far corners of the earth to do the Lord's bidding. And if the call should be less dramatic, less visible—not to the mountain or the battle but to a "lowly place"—the sustaining faith is still as great.

"I'll Go Where You Want Me to Go" has been a popular Christian gospel song since its publication in 1899. Editor Homer Rodeheaver wrote in the 1920s: "Mrs. Rounsefell is a tiny woman who lives in Boston. She used to do evangelistic work, and accompanied her singing with an old-fashioned zither. One day a friend handed her the words of this hymn and immediately a tune came to her and she struck a chord on her zither and sang the song." (Quoted in Phil Kerr, *Music in Evangelism* [Glendale, Calif.: Gospel Music Publishers, 1939], p. 142.)

In his book *That All May Be Edified,* Elder Boyd K. Packer made a point that relates closely to the message of this hymn: "The faith of the members of the Church in earlier days was tested many, many times. In a conference report for 1856, we find the following. Heber C. Kimball, a counselor in the First Presidency, is speaking:

" 'I will present to this congregation the names of those whom we have selected to go on missions. Some are appointed to go to Europe, Australia, and the East Indies. And several will be sent to Las Vegas, to the north, and to Fort Supply, to strengthen the settlements there.'

"Such announcements often came as a complete surprise to members of the Church sitting in the audience. Because of their faith, I suppose the only question they had on their minds in response to such a call was 'When?' 'When shall we go?' I am not so sure but that a similar call made today would call forth the response from many among us, not 'When?'

but 'Why?' 'Why should *I* go?' . . . Never say no to an opportunity to serve in the Church. If you are called to an assignment by one who has authority, there is but one answer." ([Salt Lake City, Utah: Bookcraft, 1982], pp. 241–43.)

Oh, Holy Words of Truth and Love 271

Text: Joseph L. Townsend (1849–1942; LDS)
Music: Edwin F. Parry (1850–1935; LDS)
Tune name: SMITH

One of the distinctive beliefs of The Church of Jesus Christ of Latter-day Saints is the principle of ongoing revelation. We have the words of the scriptures, but in addition, we have the words referred to in this hymn—"holy words of truth and love"—from modern-day apostles and prophets, the leaders of the Church. The Saints of today, more than ever before, have access to the words of the Lord and of the presiding Brethren. Church publications, radio, television, personal visits to stakes and missions around the world—all bring the counsel of our General Authorities to each member. This hymn expresses gratitude for that counsel.

Why do Latter-day Saints place such importance upon the words of their leaders? A scripture such as Doctrine and Covenants 1:38–39 helps to answer this question:

"What I the Lord have spoken, I have spoken, and I excuse not myself; and though the heavens and the earth pass away, my word shall not pass away, but shall all be fulfilled, whether by mine own voice or by the voice of my servants, it is the same.

"For behold, and lo, the Lord is God, and the Spirit beareth record, and the record is true, and the truth abideth forever and ever."

The first hymn collection in which this hymn appeared was the 1892 *Deseret Sunday School Song Book*. The tune name is for the composer's wife, Margaret Smith.

Oh Say, What Is Truth? 272; 331

Text: John Jaques (1827–1900; LDS)
Music: Ellen Knowles Melling (1820–1905; LDS)
Tune name: JAQUES

In lofty language, this hymn asserts the priority and eternal nature of truth. All else may disappear; earthly power and riches count for nothing;

but "truth, the sum of existence, will weather the worst / Eternal, unchanged, evermore."

The hymn was written by an early Latter-day Saint missionary. It is likely that John Jaques was weighed down many times by the hardships of his calling, but he took comfort in recalling the all-consuming and overriding value of the truth whose messenger he was. These words might well serve as a morale-building reminder to a discouraged missionary. If truth is really "the brightest prize / To which mortals or Gods can aspire," then it is worth any sacrifice.

George D. Pyper commented on this hymn in *Stories of Latter-day Saint Hymns:* "Among the hymns written by John Jaques is one which has taken its place as a classic among the writings of Mormon hymnists." George D. Pyper's account of the circumstances of this hymn's origin is highly speculative but interesting nevertheless:

"Elder Jaques was called upon to return to England as a missionary from 1869 to 1871. His appointments frequently took him to Stratford-upon-Avon. On one occasion he sat there in an attractive nook, lost in reverie, perhaps feeling the influence of the great Shakespeare himself, pondering the words of Pilate, when he asked the Master, 'What is Truth?'

"That question, he thought, has come down through the ages. Truth is a tiny word. Yet within it is encompassed the very foundation of the universe. In a figurative sense, those five letters stand as the supporting pillars of the bridge of experience, across which only mankind may enter into the fullness of earthly existence and reach the portals of that higher intelligence which leads, in our belief, to eternal life and happiness. Truth, the key to knowledge, its quest the noblest desire of man, underlies all our progress—our civilization. In a religious sense, it is the everlasting way to everlasting life. It offers an explanation to the deep riddle of our being—the past, the present, and the hereafter. And thus meditating upon the faith he had espoused, his surroundings brought to mind the lines of Shakespeare, 'It is all as true as it is strange, nay, it is ten times ten times true, for truth is truth to the end of reckoning.' [*Measure for Measure,* Act V.] It was no doubt such thoughts as these that inspired him to write 'O Say, What Is Truth?' which has a high place in Latter-day Saint hymnody." (Pp. 121–22.)

The hymn text was first published in the *Millennial Star* in 1850. It was printed with the present tune, JAQUES, in the 1887 *Improvement Association Song Book.*

Truth Reflects upon Our Senses 273

Text: Eliza R. Snow (1804–1887; LDS);
chorus by M. E. Abbey
Music: Charles Davis Tillman (1861–1943)
Tune name: RAILWAY TO HEAVEN

In singing these words of Eliza R. Snow, each of us pledges to obey the admonition spoken by Jesus in Matthew 7:1: "Judge not, that ye be not judged." The comparison of the mote and the beam from this same scriptural passage drives home this important precept—"judge not"—and reminds us that if we disobey it, we displease our Lord and pay a great personal price in the form of remorse.

Latter-day Saints have an added understanding of Matthew 7:1 because of a significant word added in the Joseph Smith Translation of the King James Version of the Bible: "Judge not *unrighteously,* that ye be not judged."

President Nathan Eldon Tanner, in his book *Seek Ye First the Kingdom of God,* offered some important counsel that correlates closely with the message of this hymn: "Let us remember . . . that the further out of line or out of tune we ourselves are, the more we are inclined to look for error or weaknesses in others and to try to rationalize and justify our own faults rather than to try to improve ourselves." ([Salt Lake City, Utah: Deseret Book Co., 1973], p. 57.)

In 1909, when the editors of *Deseret Sunday School Songs* included this text, they used a familiar tune that Charles Tillman had written for a text by M. E. Abbey called "Life's Railway to Heaven." But this hymn tune continued on with a chorus; Eliza R. Snow's words do not. The editors needed two more lines of verse to go with the chorus of this tune, and their solution was just to use M. E. Abbey's original words for the chorus. As a grafted-on addition, they do not correlate particularly well with the meaning of Eliza R. Snow's poem.

Here are the words to the first verse of "Life's Railway to Heaven":

Life is like a mountain railroad, with an engineer that's brave;
We must make the run successful, from the cradle to the grave;
Watch the curves, the fills, the tunnels; never falter, never quail;
Keep your hand upon the throttle, and your eye upon the rail.

The Iron Rod 274

Text: Joseph L. Townsend (1849–1942; LDS)
Music: William Clayson (1840–1887; LDS)
Tune name: PAYSON

For all Latter-day Saints, the iron rod is a symbol of security, obedience, and righteous progression. This hymn exhorts us toward our destiny; it also reminds us of the dangers that threaten us if we choose to release our hold on the one sure guide.

The text of this favorite hymn can be understood only with reference to its scriptural source. In the Book of Mormon, Nephi recounted a vision that had come to his father, Lehi. The details of this important scriptural passage can only be sketched here:

Beckoned to do so by a man dressed in a white robe, Lehi entered a "dark and dreary waste," and after wandering many hours he prayed to the Lord for deliverance. He then beheld a "large and spacious field," a tree growing in the field, and a river running near the tree. After eating of the fruit of this tree, his soul was filled with "exceedingly great joy." His immediate concern was for his family. How could he bring them to the tree so that they, too, could eat of this fruit? His wife and two of his sons succeeded in finding their way to the tree, but two other sons failed.

Lehi said, "And I beheld a rod of iron, and it extended along the bank of the river, and led to the tree by which I stood." "Numberless concourses of people" attempted to follow the path to the tree, but the only ones who succeeded were those who "did press forward through the mist of darkness, clinging to the rod of iron, even until they did come forth and partake of the fruit of the tree." (See 1 Nephi 8:5–24.)

In a later passage, Nephi interpreted his father's vision. (See 1 Nephi 12:17–18.) The meaning of the iron rod is explained most fully in 1 Nephi 15:23–24:

"And they said unto me [Nephi]: What meaneth the rod of iron which our father saw, that led to the tree?

"And I said unto them that it was the word of God; and whoso would hearken unto the word of God, and would hold fast unto it, they would never perish; neither could the temptations and the fiery darts of the adversary overpower them unto blindness, to lead them away to destruction."

That great promise inspired this hymn. Originally written for the Payson Sunday School (thus the tune name) while the author and composer were officers in that organization, this hymn has made "hold to the rod" a watchword for many Latter-day Saints. The hymn was first published as a Sunday School music card in 1878 and then was included in the 1892 *Deseret Sunday School Song Book*. The restoration of its original title, "The Iron Rod" in the 1985 hymnal may encourage more frequent use of this strong Book of Mormon text.

Men Are That They Might Have Joy 275

Text: J. Marinus Jensen (1868–1945; LDS)
Music: J. J. Keeler (b. 1913; LDS)
Tune name: JENSEN

Perhaps no words from the Book of Mormon are more beloved or more often quoted than those of 2 Nephi 2:25: "Adam fell that men might be; and men are, that they might have joy." This hymn on the coming forth of the Book of Mormon emphasizes the happy message of this scripture.

In 1942, J. Marinus Jensen wrote the hymn text of "Men Are That They Might Have Joy" and asked his grandson, J. J. Keeler, who was an organist and a Brigham Young University faculty member, to set it to music. J. J. Keeler named the hymn tune JENSEN in his grandfather's honor.

The hymn's first line, "A voice hath spoken from the dust," refers to Nephi's prophecy about the destiny of his people. He foretold the destruction of his seed and the seed of his brethren; yet, he said, "the prayers of the faithful shall be heard, and all those who have dwindled in unbelief shall not be forgotten.

"For those who shall be destroyed shall speak unto them [unto their destroyers, the Gentiles] out of the ground, and their speech shall be low out of the dust." (2 Nephi 26:15–16.)

The expression "without alloy" may be unfamiliar to some. A pure metal that is mixed with a base metal is said to be, or to contain, an *alloy*. The message of the Book of Mormon, the "voice from the dust," is pure in its truthfulness.

This hymn was part of the choir section of the 1950 hymnal. It has now been transposed to a lower key for easier congregational singing, and the last phrase of the hymn melody has been simplified. The name of the hymn, originally "A Voice Hath Spoken from the Dust," has been changed to "Men Are That They Might Have Joy." It is a more inviting title and a more accurate indication of the spirit and message of the hymn.

Come Away to the Sunday School 276

Text and music: Robert B. Baird (1855–1916; LDS)
Tune name: GLASGOW

Weather statistics would probably not corroborate the claim that "nature breathes her sweetest fragrance / On the holy Sabbath day." Some Sunday mornings are cloudy, not at all infused with a "rosy light." But for all who look forward to meeting with fellow Saints and sharing gospel truths, Sunday mornings do have the unique, invigorating quality described in this hymn.

Robert B. Baird, who wrote both the words and the music of "Come Away to the Sunday School," used a typical gospel-song format, with dotted rhythms and a repeated chorus or refrain. His goal in this song was more than just to urge all the Saints to gather together on a given Sunday; he looked toward nothing less than "salvation / Through the Lord's appointed way." Each class that is held, each truth that is taught, is one more step toward this goal. He pictured the Sunday School congregation as a group of seekers for truth, "each one striving for salvation," devoting their energies toward spiritual growth and good works. In a beautiful line he reminded us that "God will not withhold his blessings / From the eager, seeking mind."

The birthplace of Robert B. Baird was Glasgow, Scotland, and the tune name honors this city. This hymn was first published in the *Juvenile Instructor* in February 1882 and then was included in the *Deseret Sunday School Union Music Book* in 1884.

As I Search the Holy Scriptures 277

Text and music: C. Marianne Johnson Fisher (b. 1932; LDS)
Tune name: ABIDING PEACE

"As I Search the Holy Scriptures" is a moving, personal prayer for the Spirit of the Lord to accompany scripture study. It is a beautiful reminder that rich blessings of peace and knowledge are in store for those who will enhance their scripture study through prayer, meditation, and careful thought.

Each of the four verses cites a different blessing that comes from searching the scriptures. Verse one asks for wisdom and knowledge; verse two asks, "May life's mysteries be unfolded"; verse three asks for comfort—the healing of wounds and the soothing of a troubled spirit; and verse four asks the Lord's help in following the path to life eternal.

It was a conscious decision on the part of author-composer Marianne

Fisher to use the word *search* instead of *read.* To her, searching involves being able to "read and reread, ponder, pause in meditation, search for other related passages, underline."

Marianne Fisher's method of underlining is to recopy a particularly meaningful passage in braille, since she has no way of marking passages in her braille scriptures, which total thirty-two large volumes. Blind since birth, she commented: "How fortunate for those who read the ink-print edition to have their scriptures always at hand. Those of us who are blind cannot always have our scriptures literally 'at our fingertips.' "

When the announcement appeared in Church publications that new hymns were being sought for a forthcoming hymnbook (1985), Marianne Fisher chose a topic that, in her words, was "dear to our hearts but had not been the subject of any hymn in our hymnbook." Her goal was to write a "meaningful, singable text, one that would be easy to remember."

She wished to share credit for this hymn: "I must acknowledge two special people in my life, who did much in the preparation of this hymn. One was my former husband, James Wallace Fisher. As a noble man and dedicated servant of our Heavenly Father, he provided the necessary transportation for me to get to the home of my dear friend, Emma Furness. There I would dictate my previously brailled text as well as each musical voice part. Emma, in her extraordinarily beautiful penmanship, transcribed my dictation into manuscript to be submitted to the Church Music Committee." She continued, "How in error I would be if I did not also express my gratitude to my Father in Heaven, who I know, beyond all question, caused me to have clarity of mind, recalling my musical skills and poetic talents."

First printings of the hymnbook gave a tempo range of 76–92, but in subsequent printings this range was changed to 66–88 to correspond more closely with Marianne Fisher's suggestion that it be sung prayerfully.

Thanks for the Sabbath School 278

Text: William Willes (1814–1890; LDS)
Music: James R. Murray (1841–1905)
Tune name: ANDOVER

The mission of the Sunday School is nothing less than that of perfecting the Saints. "Thanks for the Sabbath School" grows out of a jubilant vision of this task. Sunday School training is not an end in itself; each class is a step toward the day when "evil and error are fleeing away."

This enthusiastic testimony of the purpose and value of Sunday School grew out of years of dedicated service to the Sunday School organization. Called in 1885 as a Sabbath School missionary, author William

Willes and his companion George Goddard were known as " 'the Sunday School Twins.' Their stories, songs, and long beards were familiar to Sunday School children from one end of the Territory of Utah to the other. In the words of George D. Pyper: 'It was a gala day when these two men visited a Sunday School. They sang "Who's On the Lord's Side, Who?" and "A Mormon Boy." These two men, I venture to say, by their songs and stories, had a greater influence in indoctrinating the boys and girls in the Word of Wisdom than any other medium.' " (J. Spencer Cornwall, *Stories of Our Mormon Hymns,* pp. 26–27.)

Composer James R. Murray also wrote the most familiar of the many musical settings for "Away in a Manger." (It does not happen to be the setting newly added to our hymnal.) He was a native of Andover, Massachusetts; his birthplace is the source of the name of the hymn tune.

Thy Holy Word 279

Text: Marvin K. Gardner (b. 1952; LDS)
Music: Robert Cundick (b. 1926; LDS)
Tune name: GENTLE WAY

"The Lord has said that when we hear or read his words—given by his Spirit unto us—we can testify that we have heard his voice and know his words," said Marvin K. Gardner. (See D&C 18:34–36.) "Many times while hearing a stirring testimony or while reading the scriptures, I have felt a spirit of rejoicing and a great desire to thank the Lord for giving us his word. This hymn text is an expression of that gratitude."

Verse one (hearing the word) was prompted by "that spirit of thanksgiving and rededication we feel at the conclusion of general conference," he said. Verse two (reading the word) was inspired by a scripture the Gardner family memorized in home evening about Nephi's love for the scriptures: "My soul delighteth in the scriptures, and my heart pondereth them." (2 Nephi 4:15.) Verse three (sharing the word) refers to the many opportunities Church members have to share the gospel through teaching classes, giving talks, bearing testimony, and serving missions. Verse four expresses the desire to *learn* and then to *live* the Lord's word. "I hope this hymn articulates the feelings of gratitude other Latter-day Saints may have as they hear, read, or teach the word of the Lord," said Marvin K. Gardner.

GENTLE WAY, the name of Robert Cundick's hymn tune, is the title of a text that Edward L. Hart wrote in honor of President David O. McKay. Robert Cundick's setting was originally composed for that text, and the tribute, "The Gentle Way," was performed by the Tabernacle Choir. For the 1985 hymnal, this appealing hymn tune was matched with "Thy Holy Word," and it complements these words equally well.

Welcome, Welcome, Sabbath Morning 280

Text: Robert B. Baird (1855–1916; LDS)
Music: Ebenezer Beesley (1840–1906; LDS)
Tune name: WELCOME

J. Spencer Cornwall called "Welcome, Welcome, Sabbath Morning" "undoubtedly the most popular Sunday School song in the Latter-day Saint hymnal." (*Stories of Our Mormon Hymns,* p. 203.) The vigorous rhythms and the cheerful text embody the sense of joy and purpose that underlie an ideal Sunday School experience.

The four verses take us through the events of a Sabbath morning, with the focus on Sunday School (always a Sunday morning meeting at the time this hymn was written). First comes the dawning of the new day, when we can look forward to resting not only from physical labors but also from "every care" that may beset us during the week. The hymn then pays tribute to the Sunday School teachers who "labor hard to teach us."

We may not literally hear bells or children's voices bidding us to the meetinghouse, but verse two conveys a pressing, joyful invitation: "Hasten, hasten, come away." Whoever chooses to do something else will miss spiritual enlightenment and happy fellowship.

Verse three lists the components of the Sunday School meeting: prayer, song, and learning. And verse four acknowledges frankly that while the principal mission of the Sunday School is to teach the gospel, socialization is also one of the great benefits of gathering together in worship on the Sabbath. Our Sabbath meetings renew our resolution to live righteously, and verse four concludes with an avowal that "we will brave the tempest longer," no matter what adversity may stand in our way.

The happy, energetic tune with its repeated chorus correlates well with the joyful encouragement of the text. This appealing song calls up many pleasant connotations, especially for those Church members who learned and loved "Welcome, Welcome, Sabbath Morning" as children.

Help Me Teach with Inspiration 281

Text and music: Lorin F. Wheelwright (1909–1987; LDS)
Tune name: VALBORG

All of us are teachers. As we emulate the Master Teacher, Jesus Christ, we constantly seek to lift and enlighten our family members, friends, and fellow Saints, whether we have a formal teaching assignment or not. What are the qualities of a dedicated teacher? This hymn outlines those qualities in a beautiful, inspiring way.

In 1957, Lorin F. Wheelwright, then a member of the Sunday School General Board, first introduced this hymn to a group of Sunday School workers in Wells Stake in Salt Lake City. He recorded the remarks with which he introduced the hymn:

"I often wonder when I look at empty benches in a Sunday School class, as you do, and I look at the roll and I see a name. That name is not a mere statistic. That empty bench is not just wood. That empty bench represents somebody who is wandering; that name is a soul who should be close to Christ. . . . Upon us rests the mantle of the teacher. I have thought a great deal about it. . . . How do we *feel* about being teachers? How do we express ourselves about our responsibilities and our opportunities? I searched the entire hymnbook to find the hymn that said it. I could not find a hymn that said it just the way I felt it, so I did what I hope any of you would do. I sat down and wrote a hymn. . . . This is a prayer for teachers."

Small changes for the 1985 hymnbook, such as substituting the word *friend* for *child* in verse two, now make the hymn applicable to "all who aspire to gospel learning," in the words of its writer. Two additional verses that were part of the hymn as published in the January 1958 *Instructor* (p. 23) are as follows:

Mold my will to do Thy bidding,
Open, Thou, mine eyes to see;
Free my soul with truth eternal,
Leave Thy Comforter with me.

Let my vision of tomorrow,
See the man this child will be;
Living by a good example,
Living nearer, Lord, to Thee.

The author suggested that each singer think about each verb in this hymn: "This word tells me what it means to teach." The verbs are at the center of the hymn: "*Fill* my mind with understanding; *Tune* my voice to echo thine. *Touch* my hand with gentle friendship; *Warm* my heart with love divine." (Italics added.)

He commented that the melody—named VALBORG in honor of his mother, Valborg Rasmussen Wheelwright—was "composed to induce contemplation. The phrases form a prayer ascending and a blessing descending."

We Meet Again in Sabbath School 282

Text: George Manwaring (1854–1889; LDS)
Music: Ebenezer Beesley (1840–1906; LDS)
Tune name: SABBATH BELL

The habit of Sunday School attendance, as this hymn conveys so well, brings many rewards. We love the pleasant fellowship, we love the songs of praise, and we love the gospel teachings. Our response at the conclusion of each Sunday School meeting is reflected in the line that concludes this hymn: "Oh, let us meet again."

George Manwaring's description of Sunday School as a place "where joyful gladness is the rule" corresponds well with the aspirations for the Sunday School expressed by President David O. McKay in 1945, when he was a member of the First Presidency:

"I commend the General Sunday School Union Board for emphasizing joy in the life of Sunday School officers, teachers, and children. Joy is sweeter than pleasure. . . . Joy is pleasure not to be repented of. Children are entitled to joy." (*Instructor*, Dec. 1945, pp. 560–61.)

"We Meet Again in Sabbath School" first appeared in the *Juvenile Instructor* in 1877.

The Glorious Gospel Light Has Shone 283

Text: Joel H. Johnson (1802–1882; LDS)
Music: Gottfried W. Fink (1783–1846)
Tune name: BETHLEHEM

Latter-day Saints treasure their unique beliefs concerning the salvation of the dead and the responsible role all worthy members of the Church are to assume in making this salvation come to pass. In this hymn, we give voice to our gratitude for these doctrines and then exhort one another to "act for those we love."

Such a complex topic is difficult to express in the form of a hymn text, and thus Joel H. Johnson's words, first printed in *Times and Seasons* in 1841, fill an important role in the hymnal. They were not chosen often for congregational use from the 1950 hymnbook, however, even though

Leroy J. Robertson had provided a dignified musical setting in keeping with the solemnity of the words.

The 1985 Hymnbook Committee decided that another hymn tune might increase the use of the text. The choice was an old tune, BETHLEHEM, so called because it was once used as a setting for "While Shepherds Watched Their Flocks" (no. 211). It is a tune with immediate appeal, one that gives great power to the words.

In the 1950 hymnal, this eight-verse hymn had the last four "extra" verses printed at the bottom of the page. An advantage of the present tune is that it is exactly twice the length of the previous one. Thus Joel H. Johnson's original eight short verses can be combined into four long ones, and the entire hymn text can now be accommodated between the lines of the music. The hymn is far more meaningful when the entire text is sung. Whereas most congregations singing from the 1950 hymnal would have ended with the old verse four, singing words that do not really conclude the hymn satisfactorily ("So many Saints have gone to teach / The gospel to the dead"), we now finish with a ringing call to action:

Then let us rise without restraint
And act for those we love,
For they are giving their consent
And wait for us to move.

If You Could Hie to Kolob 284

Text: William W. Phelps (1792–1872; LDS)
Music: English melody; arranged by Ralph Vaughan Williams (1872–1958)
Tune name: KINGSFOLD

" 'If You Could Hie to Kolob' challenges the finite mind to understand the infinite," commented J. Spencer Cornwall. "What is the meaning of 'Everlasting?' Nothing is final. Everything is intermediary between two other things. The beginning is as illusive as the end. There is no end—only eternity." (*Stories of Our Mormon Hymns,* p. 258.)

Under the entry "Kolob" in *Mormon Doctrine* (2d ed. [Salt Lake City, Utah: Bookcraft, 1966], p. 428), Elder Bruce R. McConkie explained that "*Kolob* means 'the first creation.' It is the name of the planet 'nearest to the celestial, or the residence of God.' It is 'first in government, the last pertaining to the measurement of time. . . . One day in Kolob is equal to a thousand years according to the measurement of this earth.' (Book of Abraham, pp. 34–35; Abra. 3:3–9.)"

Elsewhere in *Mormon Doctrine* Elder McConkie noted: "*Eternity* refers to the eternal worlds, to the spheres of existence outside the realm of time, those outside the temporal limitations circumscribing mortal life on this earth. Spirit beings and immortal persons live in *eternity;* mortal man lives in *time.* Eternity goes on forever and is of infinite duration. . . . As men view things from their mortal perspective, there was a *past eternity* and there will be a *future eternity.*" (Pp. 239–40.)

It is to stretch our thinking on such matters that William W. Phelps wrote this remarkable text, first published in the *Deseret News* in 1856. The effective repetition set up in verse three, "There is no end . . . ," mirrors poetically the ongoing nature of eternity.

The verb *hie* is an archaic word meaning "hasten."

This hymn, included in the choir section of the 1950 hymnal, was too difficult for congregational use and was not often chosen by choirs. Thus the 1985 Hymnbook Committee decided to print the hymn text with a new musical setting. From the first moment the committee tried KINGSFOLD, they felt that this tune captured the ethereal contemplation, the sense of wonder, and the almost mysterious wistfulness of the hymn text. The tune name, KINGSFOLD, is the name of the town in Surrey, England, where Ralph Vaughan Williams noted a version of this lovely folk melody.

God Moves in a Mysterious Way 285

Text: William Cowper (1731–1800)
Music: William B. Bradbury (1816–1868)
Tune name: HARVEY'S CHANT or COWPER

One hymn scholar, Albert Edward Bailey, commented: "The word majestic best describes this hymn. It reveals at work in the world a God who preserves the grandeur of the ancient Jehovah and the personal concern of the Christian's Father." (*The Gospel in Hymns* [New York: Charles Scribner's Sons, 1950], p. 133.)

William Cowper originally gave this hymn the title "Conflict: Light shining out of Darkness" (1774). It is the finest expression in Christian hymnody of an important and comforting truth: that the darkest events and circumstances may in fact turn out to be a blessing, even though God's purposes, at the time, are difficult to discern.

Albert Edward Bailey continued: "We do not know under what circumstances Cowper wrote this hymn. It is somehow connected with his mental breakdown in 1773 when he made an attempt upon his life; probably written about six months afterward in 1774 when the cloud had lifted somewhat. . . . The main thesis of the hymn had already been documented more than once in the poet's own life. His first fit of insanity had landed him in St. Alban's Asylum; yet that misfortune was what led to his brother's visits and his own 'conversion.' That was 'light shining out of darkness.' Again, happily established in the Unwin home [the Unwins were the family who had taken him in after his release from the asylum], he was crushed by another disaster—the death of Mr. Unwin and the threatened break-up of that providential haven. But this calamity brought Mr. Newton [with whom he later wrote a book of hymns] upon the scene, and the new home, happiness and creativity at Olney. . . . Still other incidents in his life justify his conclusion that faith and confidence are better than despair." (Pp. 133–34.)

The 1950 hymnal included two verses omitted from the 1985 hymnal:

Deep in unfathomable mines
Of never failing skill,
He treasures up his bright designs
And works his sovereign will.

Judge not the Lord by feeble sense,
But trust him for his grace;
Behind a frowning providence
He hides a smiling face.

Oh, What Songs of the Heart 286

Text: Joseph L. Townsend (1849–1942; LDS)
Music: William Clayson (1840–1887; LDS)
Tune name: SUSAN

This hymn focuses on a single ecstatic vision: the reunion with loved ones in the life after this. No matter what our suffering has been, no matter how many loved ones have preceded us in death or how many remain behind, all will be restored one day in a joyful reunion, not only with loved ones we knew on earth but also with our "heavenly parents."

As they so often did when they were colleagues in the Payson, Utah, Sunday School, Joseph L. Townsend and William Clayson collaborated on this hymn for a specific purpose. When J. Spencer Cornwall solicited some information concerning the origin of this hymn, Joseph L. Townsend replied that the hymn was "an inspiration intended to throw a brighter light on some of our doleful funerals." (*Stories of Our Mormon Hymns*, p. 75.)

The joyful words of this hymn express a profound faith in life after death. Not only does life continue but our individual identity is eternal as well, as are our relationships with the loved ones we have known on earth. And these loving relationships can be even more serene and joyful than they were on earth, because this time we have met "ne'er to part." The dangers and vicissitudes of earth life no longer will threaten.

These thoughts would indeed be a comfort to a grieving family or individual who must endure, for the time being, separation from a loved one.

The hymn first appeared in the *Juvenile Instructor* in 1879 and then was included in the *Deseret Sunday School Song Book* in 1892. The tune name, SUSAN, honors William Clayson's wife Susan Moulton.

Rise, Ye Saints, and Temples Enter 287

Text: Jean L. Kaberry (b. 1918; LDS)
Music: Robert P. Manookin (b. 1918; LDS)
Tune name: MARIE

In the six words of its opening line, this hymn, new to the 1985 hymnbook, states its message: "Rise, ye Saints, and temples enter." The remaining lines of verses one and two support this vital admonition by citing blessings to be obtained through temple attendance: we seal our loved ones, we learn the plan of exaltation, and we enter into sacred covenants. Verse three asks the Father's blessing on those who follow the hymn's admonition.

The New Zealand Temple was the "temple home" of the author and composer of this hymn at the time it was written. Robert Manookin said: "While my wife and I were serving a mission in the New Zealand Temple, the temple president, William Roberts, organized a special sacrament meeting program among the temple missionaries to try to spur understanding and interest in temple work among the members of the Church. He asked that I write music for the occasion. I then approached Sister Jean L. Kaberry, a typist and secretary in the temple, to write a poem that could be set to music. 'Rise, Ye Saints, and Temples Enter' was the result. The temple missionaries were then organized into a small choir that sang the hymn for the sacrament meeting program."

Two items in the text might bear comment. The first is the expression "quick and dead." This phrase is often misapplied, but Jean Kaberry uses it here in its correct and original meaning: the *living* and the dead. Second, the word *Elohim* does not occur often in our hymn texts, and some Latter-day Saints may wish to have a clearer understanding of its meaning. In *Mormon Doctrine,* Elder Bruce R. McConkie noted that "*Elohim* is the plural of the Caananite *El* or the Hebrew *Eloah;* consequently, its literal meaning is *Gods. . . . Elohim,* plural word though it is, is also used as the exalted name-title of God the Eternal Father, a usage that connotes his supremacy and omnipotence, he being God above all Gods." (2d ed. [Salt Lake City, Utah: Bookcraft, 1966], p. 224.)

Robert P. Manookin wrote a straightforward and singable hymn tune that congregations will be able to learn and enjoy without difficulty. The tune name, MARIE, honors the composer's daughter.

How Beautiful Thy Temples, Lord 288

Text: Frank I. Kooyman (1880–1963; LDS)
Music: Tracy Y. Cannon (1879–1961; LDS)
Tune name: JUDITH

One of the most beautiful and comforting doctrines of the restored gospel of Jesus Christ is that of the redemption of the dead. Those who die without the privilege of hearing the gospel message in this life will be able to receive it in the hereafter. This hymn gives thanks for temples and temple work, through which we may make these blessings available to those who have departed.

J. Spencer Cornwall quoted Frank I. Kooyman's account of his writing of this hymn:

"When in 1945 the Church Music Committee sent out a call to song-writers for additional sacred songs to be included in a contemplated new hymnbook, this hymn was one of the several written in response to that appeal. From the laboratory of his old-world experience the author could bring forth nothing pertaining to the work for the dead. It was a brand-new principle to him, appealing strongly to the devotional side of his nature. A spiritual experience of his paternal grandfather which he heard from his mother's lips after he embraced the restored gospel also impressed him deeply. The grandfather, at one time, in vision—as father Lehi calls an inspired dream-experience (1 Nephi 8:2)—found himself in the spirit-world in front of what seemed to be the gates of heaven. Many were entering, and [my] sincere grandfather (who had conscientiously lived according to the light granted him) was about to enter also when somebody held him back, placing a hand on his shoulder: 'No, Kooyman, you cannot go in yet; something has to be done first.' Greatly surprised, he woke up and for the balance of his earthly life wondered what it was that 'had to be done first.' The Rev. Polman, his dominie [pastor], too, was puzzled. 'Why, my good friend, you are one of the best sheep of my flock,' he exclaimed. 'If you cannot go to the green pastures of heaven, what will become of the rest of us!' " (In *Stories of Our Mormon Hymns,* p. 77.)

Temple work is the "something that must be done." Grandfather Kooyman and other righteous men and women who have gone before will receive a full measure of blessings because of men and women upon the earth who perform temple ordinances in their behalf.

The tune name, JUDITH, honors the daughter of composer Tracy Y. Cannon.

Holy Temples on Mount Zion 289

Text: Archibald F. Bennett (1896–1965; LDS)
Music: Alexander Schreiner (1901–1987; LDS)
Tune name: CLIFFORD

"Temples are the Holy of Holies to Latter-day Saints," wrote J. Spencer Cornwall in commenting on the message of this hymn. "Only the faithful attend there, seeking blessings and divine inspiration. The idea of a temple which is more than a mere church meeting place is unique to the Church of Jesus Christ of Latter-day Saints." (*Stories of Our Mormon Hymns,* p. 71.)

Verse one of this hymn focuses on the beauty of the buildings themselves, "symbols of a love divine." Verse two asks a divine blessing on those who enter the temple to do work on behalf of their kindred. Verse three is a shout of praise for the redemption and joy that come through temple work. The "prisoners" referred to in the hymn's final line are the dead who have waited patiently in the next world for temple work to be completed in their behalf.

Archibald F. Bennett supplied this information to J. Spencer Cornwall: "When the 1950 edition of the Latter-day Saint Hymnal was being planned, I received a request from Alexander Schreiner of the Church Music Committee, to prepare the words of a hymn on temple work with the object of its being included in the new hymnbook then in the course of preparation. He stated that the committee had informed Elder Mark E. Petersen that they needed some more hymns on temple work and that Brother Petersen had suggested that I write these words." (P. 71.)

J. Spencer Cornwall wrote further about the suitability of Alexander Schreiner's musical setting for this text: "The melody has a character of exultation, of joyful, vital energy." The melody begins in a rising pattern, "suitable to the ideas of high temple spires, of the upward reach. The third and contrasting line expresses the quieter sentiment of serenity and prayer and is followed by the upward motive of sacred service." (P. 71.)

Rejoice, Ye Saints of Latter Days 290

Text: Mabel Jones Gabbott (b. 1910; LDS)
Music: R. Paul Thompson (b. 1926; LDS)
Tune name: SING PRAISE TO GOD

In our day, new temples are being built throughout the world. The greater availability of temple blessings for worthy Saints is truly a cause for rejoicing. Verse one expresses this joy, and then verses two, three, and four outline the blessings more specifically: the privilege of personal covenant and commitment, the redeeming of the dead, and the perfecting of the Lord's earthly kingdom in preparation for his coming.

"Rejoice, Ye Saints of Latter Days" has been updated through rewriting. In 1940 Mabel Jones Gabbott wrote the text, "Rejoice, Ye Saints of Latter Days," that became part of the 1950 hymnal. When the time came for it to be considered for the 1985 hymnal, however, it was clear that its usefulness was limited for two reasons.

In the first place, as the author herself expressed it, "The words seemed slanted to temples in America." With the lines "Another temple to our God / Now stands upon this chosen sod," the text seemed to ignore temples in countries other than the United States. In addition, because this text grew out of a poem written for the dedication of the Idaho Falls Temple, the earlier version of the hymn related specifically to the dedication of a temple, and thus could be used only rarely. It included such lines as "Again is reared from earth's deep sod / A temple to the Most High God. . . . / Oh, workmen, rear it tenderly." In other words, it was a hymn for temple dedications rather than a hymn about temples and temple work.

In 1984, at the invitation of the Hymnbook Committee, Mabel Jones Gabbott accepted the challenge of rewriting the text she had written four decades earlier. The new version encompasses all the temples that have now been built worldwide, and it refers in a dignified way to the blessings of the temple as they relate to the living and the dead.

R. Paul Thompson provided the new musical setting. He stated that his goal was to "capture the special meanings of the text. The melodic line came through the inspiration provided by the text."

Turn Your Hearts 291

Text: Paul L. Anderson (b. 1946; LDS)
Music: Gaylen Hatton (b. 1928; LDS)
Tune name: MARYANNE

This hymn is about genealogy—not just the mechanical process of gathering names and dates but also the reasons this research is vital and the blessings that result from it. It is also about temple work, the source of blessings for generations that have gone before and those yet to be.

Verse one refers to Malachi's prophecy that Elijah will return in the latter days and "turn the heart of the fathers to the children, and the heart of the children to their fathers." (Malachi 4:6.) Verse two points out that we are bound "to all men throughout all time"; verse three then emphasizes our link with those gone before; verse four, our link with those yet to come.

Paul L. Anderson reported that a friend and fellow ward member, Lynn R. Carson, made the initial suggestion that resulted in this hymn. Lynn Carson was employed by the Church Family History Department as a researcher, with the specific responsibility of collecting records from third-world countries. He suggested to Paul Anderson that it should be possible to write a hymn about genealogy that would have a broad scope, referring not only to responsibility for immediate ancestors but also to responsibility to the patriarchs and prophets of old who were promised their seed would be blessed and to the generations yet to come who will be blessed through righteous ancestors who are alive today. Paul Anderson said that to him, "turning your heart" means creating an emotional bond with someone you may not even know through an act of love and service.

The original hymn text included two additional verses:

Turn your hearts to Eve and Adam,
Abraham, who heard God's call,
Isaac, Jacob, Sarah, Ruth,
Who lived God's law and loved His truth
And called down blessings on us all.

Turn to Joseph and to Emma
Who, through persecution, pain,
Shared the keys of our salvation,
Binding ev'ry generation
In a grand eternal chain.

Gaylen Hatton composed the hymn tune specifically for Paul Anderson's words at the request of the 1985 Hymnbook Committee. The author felt that his words received "a dignified, appropriate tune that reflects the spirit of temple service."

O My Father 292

Text: Eliza R. Snow (1804–1887; LDS)
Music: James McGranahan (1840–1907)
Tune name: MY REDEEMER

"Implicit in the Christian verity that all men are the spirit children of an *Eternal Father* is the usually unspoken truth that they are also the offspring of an *Eternal Mother,*" wrote Elder Bruce R. McConkie. "This glorious truth of celestial parentage, including specifically both a Father and a Mother, is heralded forth by song in one of the greatest of Latter-day Saint hymns, *O My Father* by Eliza R. Snow." (*Mormon Doctrine,* 2d ed. [Salt Lake City, Utah: Bookcraft, 1966], pp. 516–17.)

Latter-day Saints love the beauty of this hymn's poetry and the importance of its unique doctrine. George D. Pyper pointed out that Eliza R. Snow was wife of the Prophet Joseph Smith at the time she wrote this hymn and thus had many opportunities to discuss matters of doctrine. He continued:

"It was during this period that Zina D. Huntington (afterwards Zina D. Young) was grieved over an unusual circumstance. Her mother, who had died some time before, had been buried in a temporary grave and it became necessary to remove the body to a permanent resting place. When the remains were exhumed it was discovered that they were partially petrified. It seemed to Zina as if the very foundation of the doctrine of the resurrection crumbled. To the question 'Shall I know my mother when I meet her in the world beyond?' the Prophet responded emphatically, 'Yes, you will know your mother there.' A firm believer in Joseph's divine mission, Zina D. Huntington was comforted by the promise. From the discussions on the resurrection and the relationship of man to Deity no doubt came the inspiration to Eliza R. Snow for the writing of 'O My Father.' The poem was written in the home of Stephen Markham, and was penned on a wooden chest, the only table available in her meagerly furnished room.

"The hymn is in four stanzas and is an epitome of the great drama of eternal life as revealed by the restored Gospel of Jesus Christ.

"The Prologue: The first stanza proclaims the literal Fatherhood of God; that we were nurtured by His side in our ante-mortal existence, connoting the truth that we were instructed in the great plan, obedience to which would enable us to regain His presence 'and again behold His face.'

"The Play: Stanza II shifts the scene to earth-life, where we are placed in a school to see whether we will do the things required of us and prove our right to the promised restoration to God's presence. Our recollection of ante-mortal life is withheld in order that we may walk by faith; yet, not to be left wholly in the dark, a 'secret something,' a key that opens the door to knowledge, is given us, and through it (Stanza III) is revealed the new and glorious doctrine that we are children of a Mother in heaven.

"The Epilogue: Back again into the Eternal Presence our thoughts are projected. Through obedience, and through having completed all we have been commanded to do, with the 'mutual approbation' of our heavenly Parents, we claim the promise made in our ante-mortal state.

"Truly 'O My Father' is the drama of eternal life: not merely a hymn, but a prophecy and a revelation." (*Stories of Latter-day Saint Hymns,* pp. 4–6).

Eliza R. Snow's poem was first published in *Times and Seasons* in 1845. It has been sung to many different tunes; Stephen Foster's GENTLE ANNIE was one of the first. In *Deseret Sunday School Songs* (1909), it was printed with the tune AUSTRIA, the tune to "Glorious Things of Thee Are Spoken" (no. 46). Also, many Latter-day Saint composers have written musical settings for Eliza R. Snow's text. But it was a non–Latter-day Saint, James McGranahan, whose tune has emerged as the most popular. James McGranahan's melody (with the second two lines in 4/4 time rather than in 3/4, by the way) was published in 1877 as a setting for words by Philip Paul Bliss, three of whose hymns are in the 1985 hymnal (nos. 131; 235; 335). The first stanza of that hymn is as follows:

I will sing of my Redeemer
And His wond'rous love to me;
On the cruel cross He suffered
From the curse to set me free.
Sing, oh, sing of my Redeemer,
With His blood He purchased me.
On the cross He sealed my pardon,
Paid the debt, and made me free.

Each Life That Touches Ours for Good 293

Text: Karen Lynn Davidson (b. 1943; LDS)
Music: A. Laurence Lyon (b. 1934; LDS)
Tune name: HERMANA

Most of the richest blessings of life come to us through other people. President Spencer W. Kimball made this interesting comment: "God does notice us, and he watches over us. But it is usually through another person that he meets our needs." (*Ensign,* Oct. 1985, p. 3.)

The author of this hymn text is also the compiler of this book. When the 1985 Hymnbook Committee expressed a wish for a hymn that could be used at funerals, I realized that such a hymn could also be an opportunity to express thanks for the blessing of human relationships. It is a sentiment I feel strongly. At various times during my life, my work and schooling have taken me into many different places and circumstances. I was a single woman for many years, living in dormitories, apartments, and finally a home of my own, moving quite often to a new city and a new ward or branch. Now, I am married, and my residence and associations have changed once again.

One truth has emerged from all these experiences: *any* geographical location, marital status, professional activity, and Church assignment can be a component of a happy life, as long as one blessing remains constant—the blessing of close, supportive personal relationships, whether friends or family, in whose lives the Savior's love is manifest. This hymn is a prayer of thanks for those relationships.

This hymn is appropriate for any occasion honoring friends or friendships; it doesn't need to be limited to funerals or farewells. "If verse three sounds too funereal, it can be omitted," said the composer. "But a careful reading of the text does not necessarily indicate that the departed one is dead."

A. Laurence Lyon originally wrote this hymn tune for a text by his great-grandfather, Latter-day Saint poet John Lyon, titled "O Lord, Responsive to Thy Call." That text appeared in previous Latter-day Saint hymnals. The composer stated: "The hymn-tune title, HERMANA, is my mother's first name. I dedicated this piece to her memory."

Love at Home 294; 318

Text and music: John Hugh McNaughton (1829–1891)
Tune name: CALEDONIA

One of the most prized of all earthly blessings is that of a happy, loving home. "Love at Home" is a hymn in praise of this blessing. It is not a prayer, an exhortation, or a scriptural paraphrase; it is simply a description of the beautiful influences that emanate from a happy home.

President David O. McKay taught: "The home is the first and most effective place for children to learn the lessons of life: truth, honor, virtue, self-control; the value of education, honest work, and the purpose and privilege of life. Nothing can take the place of home in rearing and teaching children, and no other success can compensate for failure in the home." (*Family Home Evening Manual,* 1968–69, p. iii.)

The message of "Love at Home" expresses the reverse side of this coin. President McKay's point was that if the home *fails,* no other success can compensate; "Love at Home" reminds us that if the home *succeeds,* everything else is more beautiful and satisfying. For those who are fortunate enough to dwell in a happy home, the outside world is transformed as well: roses appear, the brook sings a more beautiful song, and the sky is brighter. Most important, our Heavenly Father is pleased: "Oh, there's One who smiles on high / When there's love at home."

This hymn was first published in *The American Sunday School Hymn-Book,* new edition, in 1860. An early verse that is not part of the version in our hymnbook was published in *The New Golden Chain* in 1866:

Jesus, show thy mercy mine,
Then there's love at home;
Sweetly whisper, I am thine,
Then there's love at home.
Source of love, thy cheering light
Far exceeds the sun so bright—
Can dispel the gloom of night;
Then there's love at home.

The tune name, CALEDONIA, honors the city in New York that was the birthplace of John Hugh McNaughton.

O Love That Glorifies the Son 295

Text and music: Lorin F. Wheelwright (1909–1987; LDS)
Tune name: ILA

Originally written to be used in family home evenings, this serene hymn, new to our hymnal, is a plea for the pure love of Christ to fill our souls. If we are granted this blessing, what is the result? A host of additional blessings will follow: greater unity, spirituality, harmony, courage, and optimism.

In the *Instructor* of August 1967 (p. 319), Lorin F. Wheelwright wrote: "When invited . . . to compose a hymn that would 'renew a right spirit within me' (Psalm 51:10)—and thus enrich a family activity—I thought of Christ's great statement of the law of love: first is love of God, and second is love of man. 'On these two commandments hang all the law and the prophets.' (Matthew 22:40.) I also thought of Paul's epistle, in which he told us that love 'rejoiceth in the truth; beareth all things, believeth all things, hopeth all things, endureth all things.' (1 Corinthians 13:6–7.) It is Paul's sense of priority, interpreting the teachings of Jesus, which prompts me to emphasize love as the greatest hunger and deepest need of the human soul. In another context I have stated it this way:

When in conflict with personal gain, love comes first.
When in conflict with our cultural pursuits, love comes first.
When in conflict with our sense of scholarship and accuracy,
love comes first. . . .
It is this fundamental thinking that we must share if we would
be Christlike ourselves. . . .
It completely identifies us with the Savior,
And with God,
And fills our hearts with Their Holiness and Their Glory.

"To invite this refining influence into our lives is the purpose of the hymn."

Concerning the music, Lorin F. Wheelwright noted: "The choir or congregation should relish each dissonance in search of a final consonance. The inner tensions of the music are purposefully designed to push the singers toward a strong desire to 'Come, fill my soul today.' As each stanza is completed, the final phrase will induce a quiet contemplation which softens the volume without losing its intensity."

The hymn tune name honors Ila Spilsbury, Lorin F. Wheelwright's wife of more than five decades.

Our Father, by Whose Name 296

Text: F. Bland Tucker (1895–1984); altered
Music: John David Edwards (1806–1885)
Tune name: RHOSYMEDRE

This hymn, new to the 1985 hymnbook, is a prayer to our Father in Heaven in his role as a father—a parent who understands and values the bonds within a family and who will bless earthly parents as they strive to fulfill their responsibilities. As he taught and blessed his Only Begotten Son, so we ask him to bless our children and our homes.

This hymn is a welcome addition to Latter-day Saint hymnody. Although the sanctity of the family is central to our beliefs, we had few hymns in our book addressing this topic. "Our Father, by Whose Name," with specific reference to fatherhood as well as general reference to home and family, should find much use in our home and church worship services.

The original text of this hymn is a three-part prayer. The original verse one is just as we have it in our hymnbook. The original verse two is a prayer to Jesus Christ, beginning—

O Christ, thyself a child
Within an earthly home,

With heart still undefiled,
Thou didst to manhood come . . . .

And verse three is a prayer to the Holy Spirit, beginning—

O Spirit, who dost bind
Our hearts in unity,
Who teachest us to find
The love from self set free. . . .

The 1985 Hymnbook Committee felt that if the text were revised so that all three verses were a prayer to our Father in Heaven, the hymn would be more consistent with Latter-day Saint doctrine on prayer. In particular, it is not Latter-day Saint practice to address prayers directly to the Savior or the Holy Spirit.

Representatives of the estate of author F. Bland Tucker granted the right to reprint the text in altered form and made a few perceptive suggestions of their own.

The tune name, RHOSYMEDRE, is the name of the village in North Wales where composer John David Edwards served as vicar for many years. This melody has achieved some fame in a hymn prelude arrangement by Ralph Vaughan Williams.

From Homes of Saints Glad Songs Arise 297

Text: Vernald W. Johns (b. 1902; LDS)
Music: G. William Richards (b. 1918; LDS)
Tune name: DYRENG

The scene of individuals and families singing praises to the Lord in their homes is central to this hymn. "Then sing, O saints," the hymn exhorts, and the invitation is difficult to resist. To raise "glad songs" to our Father in Heaven is a natural response to the many blessings enumerated in the hymn: faith, peace, scriptures, prophetic guidance. And singing symbolizes the faith that invites protection when "error's ways allure."

The two distinctive words in the hymn's title are *homes* and *songs.* According to the hymn, the home is the source, or at least a principal source, of many of the blessings for which we praise the Lord in song.

Author Vernald W. Johns reported that "the thought of the joy the gospel brings to those who live its principles, as felt in our own and other families, provided the title line that had to be expanded. Because I am a music director in the Church, it was natural for me to think of joyfulness in terms of song."

Composer G. William Richards, who served as a member of the 1985

Hymnbook Executive Committee, reported that in the work of that committee "many texts were passed around each week which had been submitted without tunes. This one was circulated for a month or so and appeared to be an orphan, so I took it home with me one night." He studied the text and soon had written out the complete hymn tune and harmonization. He submitted the music anonymously, and it was later chosen as the setting for this text.

It is a simple and dignified hymn tune that lies within a one-octave compass (plus one half-step). G. William Richards named the tune DYRENG because his wife's home in Manti, Utah, the Dyreng home, "had many glad songs arise in it."

Home Can Be a Heaven on Earth 298

Text: Carolyn Hamilton Klopfer (b. 1936; LDS)
Music: W. Herbert Klopfer (b. 1936; LDS)
Tune name: ALISA

This forthright statement of the blessings of a loving home can enrich any meeting or lesson that deals with home and family. The text, newly created for the 1985 hymnbook, echoes the teachings of our prophets—that prayer, kindness, family home evening, service, scripture study, and other spiritual building blocks are essential to a happy family life.

The composer and author of this hymn, who are husband and wife, found that a few people were skeptical of the hymn's optimism; they "criticized us for having the nerve to state a condition that is impossible in mortality," said Herbert Klopfer.

"But," Carolyn Klopfer stated, "I have come to realize that the words were given to me as a testimony that even under trying circumstances, I must never lose faith or give up hope in those who are part of my home. Not all of my children may choose to remain faithful; yet I must continue to teach and show the way, providing loving moments when we work, play, and pray together. I shall cherish *these* moments, though sometimes brief, when heaven is in my home.

"I shall feel the peace that comes from knowing that one sweet daughter, Alisa, who left our earthly home at the tender age of five years, has safely reached her heavenly home, leading the way where my family and I want to be worthy to stay."

Commenting on his hymn tune, Herbert Klopfer suggested: "Each voice part ought to be taught independent of the others and then put together in a smoothly fitting four-part harmony. If musical harmony is not achieved, the message of having harmony in our homes is not taught as effectively as it could be."

Children of Our Heavenly Father 299

Text: Caroline V. Sandell-Berg (1832–1903);
translated by Ernst W. Olson (1870–1958)
Music: Traditional Swedish melody
Tune name: SWEDISH

"Who shall separate us from the love of Christ?" asked Paul the Apostle. "Shall tribulation, or distress, or persecution, or famine, or nakedness, or peril, or sword? . . .

"Nay, in all these things we are more than conquerors through him that loved us.

"For I am persuaded that neither death, nor life, . . . nor any other creature, shall be able to separate us from the love of God, which is in Christ Jesus our Lord." (Romans 8:35, 37–39.)

This hymn, with its simple expression of faith, echoes the testimony of Paul and of other prophets who have borne witness of God's care for all things—from the greatest to the least.

Its song-like quality is simple enough even for children to learn easily; indeed, it is often considered a hymn for children. Latter-day Saints of all ages will find that this hymn, new to the 1985 hymnal, has the sort of abiding, simple song-message that remains with them always. This brief hymn could be a valuable item in a mental index of thoughts to call upon in times of stress or doubt. Its message also makes it suitable as a funeral hymn.

The words and melody of this beautiful hymn work together so effectively to convey a spirit of sweet comfort that it is difficult to know which plays the more important role. In simple but convincing tones, the hymn bears witness of the constant, unfailing watchfulness of the Father.

So many tunes related to this one have been found in Europe and Scandinavia that it is impossible to say with certainty what its origins are. Most agree that the Swedish song which was the hymn tune's immediate source probably had its origins in Germany near the beginning of the nineteenth century. Possibly it is even older.

This translation of the text, by Ernst W. Olson, was first published in a Lutheran hymnal in 1925.

Our hymnal omitted one verse. Like the other verses, it asserts a message of ultimate, unquestioning trust in our Father's goodness. It is as follows:

God his own doth tend and nourish;
In his holy courts they flourish.
From all evil things he spares them;
In his mighty arms he bears them.

Families Can Be Together Forever 300

Text: Ruth M. Gardner (b. 1927; LDS)
Music: Vanja Y. Watkins (b. 1938; LDS)
Tune name: NORMA

The title of this song, "Families Can Be Together Forever," summarizes its all-important message, one that is engraved more boldly on the hearts of Latter-day Saint children each time they sing this song. In the simplest possible terms, these words highlight the role of the temple in creating an eternal family unit.

In 1979, when representatives from the Primary and Sunday School general boards were discussing the message and format of a forthcoming children's sacrament meeting presentation about temples, they decided that the single most important thing to teach children about temples was that by participating in the temple ordinances, families could be together forever. Author Ruth M. Gardner, then a member of the Primary General Board, said that "after much prayer, I decided to try to write a song to express this idea. As I worked on the song, the words and a musical setting came at the same time. I wanted the children to express their desires to be with their families through all eternity, just as I want to be with my family.

"As we wrote the presentation," she continued, "each member of the committee voiced concerns about the many children whose parents had not yet been to the temple. So the second verse was written to let the children know that, even though their parents might not have had a temple marriage, they could prepare themselves to be married in God's temple.

"As I refined the song, it was apparent that while the words had a good message, the music did nothing to enhance that message. So I took the words to Vanja Watkins and asked her to set them to music."

Vanja Watkins, who was serving on the General Music Committee of the Church at the time, continued the story: "I was pleased to be asked and began work immediately in order to meet the request. The right tune did not come immediately, however, and there are several vain attempts the world will never hear! When this melody began to flow into my mind, I had a good feeling it was the right setting and I felt the blessing of the Lord as I wrote it and harmonized it." This song and several other children's songs were added to the hymnal in 1985.

The importance of the last line of the chorus is highlighted by the repetition of the words, "the Lord has shown me how I can." "The melody for these words is different the second time," said Vanja Watkins, "but the importance of the word *Lord* is highlighted once by the highest note in the song and again by the longest note in the phrases."

When asked for a tune name, the composer said that she "without hesitation selected the name NORMA, for that is the name of my mother, whom I love and appreciate for all she has given and done for me."

I Am a Child of God 301

Text: Naomi W. Randall (b. 1908; LDS)
Music: Mildred T. Pettit (1895–1977; LDS)
Tune name: CHILD OF GOD

Few songs in the history of The Church of Jesus Christ of Latter-day Saints have touched more hearts than "I Am a Child of God." Sister Camilla Kimball once commented, "It is the whole gospel plan in a few simple words." Originally written for a Primary presentation, it has become a favorite of children and adults alike.

In 1957 the Primary General Board was planning a Primary general conference program to be held in the Salt Lake Tabernacle in April of that year. The program was to center on the need of children to be taught the gospel. The board asked Naomi W. Randall to write a new song and suggested that she enlist the help of composer Mildred T. Pettit, then a resident of Pasadena, California. Although the two women were not acquainted, they discussed the project by telephone.

Naomi Randall reported: "That evening, I got down on my knees and prayed aloud, pleading that our Heavenly Father would let me know the right words. Around 2:00 A.M. I awakened and began to think again about the song. Words came to my mind. . . . I immediately got up and began to write the words down as they had come to me. Three verses and a chorus were soon formed. I gratefully surveyed the work, drank of the message of the words, and returned to my bedroom where I knelt before my Father in Heaven to say 'Thank you!' "

The general board approved the words the next morning, and Naomi Randall sent them to Mildred Pettit, who returned the tune by special delivery mail in less than a week. "I Am a Child of God" was sung at the April meeting and was first published Churchwide in the June 1957 *Children's Friend.*

The words of the chorus originally read, "Teach me all that I must *know* / To live with him some day." (Italics added.) A few years after the song was published, Spencer W. Kimball, then a member of the Quorum of the Twelve Apostles, attended a conference in Elko, Nevada, where a Primary children's chorus sang the song. Naomi Randall said: "On the trip home he talked with a Primary General Board member who had attended that same conference. He expressed his love for the song, then stated that there was one word in the chorus that concerned him. He wondered if Sister Randall would consider changing the line that says 'Teach me all that I must *know*' to 'Teach me all that I must *do*.' Of course I gladly accepted his suggestion.

"I wondered why I didn't include that thought at the time the lyrics were first written. But as time went on I came to feel very sincerely that this was the way the Lord wanted the song to evolve, because it became a teaching moment for members all over the Church and impressed upon their minds that knowing the gospel is not all that is required; it is the day-by-day *doing* the Lord's will and keeping the commandments that help us reach our eternal goal."

From the time of that incident, said the author, President Kimball was fond of saying, "Naomi Randall wrote most of the words, but I wrote one!"

An additional verse was not included in our hymnal:

I am a child of God
His promises are sure
Celestial glory shall be mine
If I can but endure.

I Know My Father Lives 302

Text and music: Reid N. Nibley (b. 1923; LDS)
Tune name: MAGGIE

Both the words and music of this song further Reid Nibley's stated purpose: "to express a testimony as a child would." The simple statement of faith in the most elementary gospel truths is movingly paired with an equally simple tune.

The motivation for this song was a letter from Tabernacle organist Robert Cundick requesting a song for a new children's song book. "He suggested several categories," Reid Nibley said, "and I was immediately drawn to 'Testimony.' The words 'I know my Father lives' came to my mind, and the music came almost simultaneously. The remainder of the piece came very quickly, but I thought it was too simple, so I began working on it. It became more and more complicated and less and less spontaneous. After two weeks of struggling with it, I began to erase all the excess notes, and soon it emerged in its original form."

He concluded, "I have been deeply touched when I have heard children sing this little song. I have the feeling that it no longer belongs to me, but it is the most worthwhile thing I have ever done."

The musical simplicity of this song requires that the music director and organist heed the two editorial suggestions included with this hymn:

first, that it be sung in unison, whether the singers are children or adults; and second, that manuals only be used – no pedals – if the accompanying instrument is an organ.

Keep the Commandments 303

Text and music: Barbara A. McConochie (b. 1940; LDS)
Tune name: PEACE

Peace and safety come from only one source – the keeping of divine commandments, as counseled by the prophets of the Lord. Though originally written with children in mind, the simple message of this beautiful song is important to every Latter-day Saint.

Barbara McConochie, writer of both the words and the music, wished credit for the words also to be given to President Harold B. Lee. It was a quotation from President Lee – "words of a prophet," as stated in the song – that she drew upon. "Keep the Commandments" was first performed in a Primary sacrament meeting presentation in her home ward in Palo Alto, California. The children liked the song so much that she sent it to the general Primary office. It has since been sung by Latter-day Saint children all over the world.

What more simple, important idea can we instill in children or in ourselves than the importance of keeping the commandments? Repetition is the key to the effectiveness of this song. "Note the use of repetition to emphasize key phrases and truths," said Barbara McConochie. "The hymn states the counsel in the first half and in the second half states the promise or reward, followed by a repetition of the plea to 'keep the commandments.' This phrase is the highest point musically, the climax of the song. The final phrase reminds us once again of the peace that will follow obedience."

Teach Me to Walk in the Light 304

Text and music: Clara W. McMaster (b. 1904; LDS)
Tune name: AUTUMN

This unusual and effective song conveys its message through a dialogue. The first verse, a child's simple request for guidance, calls forth the response of teacher or parent in verse two. Verse three is a combined prayer of gratitude.

While serving on the music committee of the Primary General Board, Clara McMaster was given the assignment to write a song to be presented by the Primary at the April 1958 general conference. In her words, "The scriptures are filled with this great important message—'walk in the light'—and I have often gone to the scriptures for guidance and direction in my assignments." For the first performance, a chorus of Primary children sang the first verse, teachers and parents in the audience sang the second, and all joined together for verse three.

The author-composer of this hymn named the hymn tune after her favorite time of year.

The Light Divine 305

Text: Matilda Watts Cahoon (1881–1973; LDS)
Music: Mildred T. Pettit (1895–1977; LDS)
Tune name: LIGHT DIVINE

Originally written for a chorus of Primary children, "The Light Divine" is a poetic description of the beauty of the light of faith. Just as the heavenly light permeates every creation of nature, so it will abide within the hearts of those who seek it.

Verses one and two tell of the warmth and growth that accompany the light of faith. Faith brings hope and radiance, and it will grow within the heart of a child, just as a bud will blossom into a flower. The third verse and the chorus are a prayer asking our Heavenly Father to continue to touch us with his light. Matilda Watts Cahoon's purpose was to offer to the Primary children the same reminder that Paul sent to the Corinthians: "For God, who commanded the light to shine out of darkness, hath shined in our hearts." (2 Corinthians 4:6.)

On September 3, 1985, a meeting was held in the Assembly Hall on Temple Square in Salt Lake City to celebrate the completion of the new hymnal. One of the speakers on this occasion, President Gordon B. Hinckley, paid tribute to Matilda Watts Cahoon:

"She was my music teacher in junior high school. The only claim I have to musical fame is that I was a part of the boys' chorus in junior high which won two district championships of the Salt Lake and Granite school districts. Since then I've forgotten how to read music and all about it, but I do hold up my hand to Matilda Watts Cahoon who somehow coaxed a tune out of me as a part of the boys' chorus of that junior high school. She was a great and delightful and lovely teacher."

Dr. William A. Pettit, son of composer Mildred T. Pettit, recalled his mother's concern over the last line of the tune, "which she at first thought should go up rather than down." But the firm downward motion of the last five notes of the tune seems to correlate well with the assertion that truth is "our guiding star."

"The Light Divine" was first printed in *The Primary Song Book* in 1939.

God's Daily Care 306

Text: Marie C. Turk
Music: Willy Reske (b. 1897; LDS)
Tune name: LOUISE

Several hymns in our book, such as "Now the Day Is Over" (no. 159), speak with great feeling of the close of day. "God's Daily Care" is a delightful response to the *dawn* of day. In the simple words of a child, the singer offers gratitude for the Father's care. The sight of a beautiful sunrise has brought thoughts of the Father's all-encompassing watchfulness.

Willy Reske's hymn tune has a simple, folklike quality that gives it great appeal. Most of Willy Reske's compositions are large-scale works for organ or choir, and by comparison, this eight-measure melody may seem almost inconsequential. But it suits perfectly the simplicity and directness of the words. Any group, children or adults, will be able to sing this hymn easily. The second half of the tune is simply a descending major scale, with one small variation.

Willy Reske himself remarked, "It is just a 'little ditty,' but if people love it and sing it, that is all that matters."

The tune name, LOUISE, honors Martha Louise Wiemer, the wife of the composer.

In Our Lovely Deseret 307

Text: Eliza R. Snow (1804–1887; LDS)
Music: George F. Root (1820–1895)
Tune name: SHEFFIELD

George F. Root wrote both words and music to a popular Civil War song, a sentimental favorite called "Tramp! Tramp! Tramp!" The words to the original first verse, supposedly giving forth the thoughts of a captured Union soldier, are as follows:

In the prison cell I sit,
Thinking, Mother dear, of you,
And our bright and happy home so far away;
And the tears they fill my eyes
Spite of all that I can do,

Though I try to cheer my comrades and be gay.
Tramp, tramp, tramp, the boys are marching;
Cheer up, comrades, they will come,
And beneath the starry flag
We shall breathe the air again
Of the freeland in our own beloved home.

Eliza R. Snow knew that children would respond to the catchy tune of this popular song, and she took advantage of an opportunity to write some new words to it that would teach a whole range of valuable lessons, from prayer to politeness.

Generations of Latter-day Saint Primary children have loved "In Our Lovely Deseret." President Spencer W. Kimball once shared this delightful reminiscence of this song's influence on him:

"I remember the song 'In Our Lovely Deseret.' . . . I can remember how lustily we sang:

Hark! Hark! Hark! 'tis children's music,
Children's voices, O, how sweet. . . .

" . . . I remember we sang:

That the children may live long,
And be beautiful and strong.

"I wanted to live a long time and I wanted to be beautiful and strong—but never reached it.

Tea and coffee and tobacco they despise.

"And I learned to despise them. . . . The song goes on:

Drink no liquor, and they eat
But a very little meat.

I still don't eat very much meat.

They are seeking to be great and good and wise.

"And then we'd 'Hark! Hark! Hark!' again." (*Ensign,* May 1978, p. 47.)

Love One Another 308

Text and music: Luacine Clark Fox (b. 1914; LDS)
Tune name: LOVE ONE ANOTHER

Only if we know and exemplify the Savior's teachings can we claim to be his followers. Some of the last words Jesus spoke to his disciples emphasized the most important mark of that discipleship and reminded them what they must do to be recognized as his true followers: they would be known as disciples of Jesus because of their "love one to another." (See John 13:34–35.)

Luacine Clark Fox, who wrote both words and music for "Love One Another," always approached her creative work with a serious sense of spiritual dedication. She stated: "I have purposely, with very few exceptions, focused my writings, compositions, and artistic endeavors on the Church, feeling that there can be no greater fulfillment in the exercise of a God-given talent than to use it in connection with the work of the Lord. I have a strong testimony of the truthfulness of the gospel of Jesus Christ."

She told this story of the writing of "Love One Another":

"It is always my habit to pray before doing any writing or composing. This I did while in the process of working on *Psalm of Easter*, from which 'Love One Another' is taken. In searching the scriptures, I came to the words of the Savior at the Last Supper wherein he gave his new commandment to love one another. I knew that I had found the theme I wanted. As I jotted down the words in my notebook, taken from John 13:34–35, the melody to accompany them came into my mind, and I wrote it down as well. The final result of words and music was exactly the same as had come to me initially, with no variation whatsoever. It is my witness that whatever is of worth in the song came from the Lord."

As Sisters in Zion 309

Text: Emily H. Woodmansee (1836–1906; LDS)
Music: Janice Kapp Perry (b. 1938; LDS)
Tune name: SAUNDERS

In this energetic song, new to the 1985 hymnal, the vision of Relief Society and its high-minded purposes reaches from the nineteenth century into this one. "The errand of angels" is surely nothing less than to do the direct and immediate bidding of our Father in Heaven, and "this is a gift that, as sisters, we claim."

The text, titled "Song of the Sisters of the Relief Society," was first published in 1874 in the *Woman's Exponent* (vol. 3, p. 98), a periodical that was the forerunner of the *Relief Society Magazine*. The author, Emily H. Woodmansee, was one of the many gifted and intellectual women of early Utah who were dedicated to bringing culture, idealism, and education to their community. Her poem, originally ten verses long (with the tenth verse a repetition of the first), shows how determined these early sisters were to carry out a vast number of responsibilities in the name of the Relief Society. The omitted verses are as follows:

We'll turn from our follies, our pride and our weakness,
The vain, foolish fashions of Babel despise;
We'll seek for the garments of truth and of meekness,
And learn to be useful and happy and wise.

We'll wear what is sensible, neat and becoming
The daughters of Zion—the angels of light;
We'll work with a will, while the angels are scanning
Our aims and our actions from morning till night.

We'll bring up our children to be self-sustaining;
To love and to do what is noble and right;
When we rest from our labors, these dear ones remaining,
Will bear off the kingdom and "fight the good fight."

Nor shall our attention be wholly restricted
To training our children or shaping our dress;
The aged, the feeble, the poor and afflicted,
Our labors shall comfort, our efforts shall bless.

The Lord hath established the cities of Zion,
The poor of His people are trusting in Him,
He makes us a source for His poor to rely on;
Oh! shall we not brighten the eyes that are dim.

Oh! shall we not hasten to soothe the condition
Of the humble, the needy, the honest and pure?
Oh! let us remember, whate'er our ambition—
'Tis our duty, our mission, to comfort the poor.

The next two verses are those printed as verses two and three in our hymnbook. Note that the word *tuition,* in verse three, is used in its older meaning of "instruction." Our word *tutoring* is a related word with a similar meaning.

The skills of composer Janice Kapp Perry provided a strong and engaging melody for these words. She wrote the music in response to a request from the 1985 Hymnbook Committee. At a later time, when she was touring with the cast of *It's a Miracle,* a musical for which she wrote the music, she received word that a three-part women's arrangement of this hymn was needed at once for a women's conference satellite broadcast from Salt Lake City. She reported: "My only opportunity to write the arrangement came one afternoon when our tour bus was broken down in a poor section of Philadelphia, Pennsylvania. All cast members were stranded in a vacant lot for hours while the bus was repaired. I sat against a telephone pole in the weeds, with my electronic keyboard on my lap, and wrote the arrangement—a real exercise in being '*in* the world but not *of* the world.' "

A Key Was Turned in Latter Days 310

Text: Jan Underwood Pinborough (b. 1954; LDS)
Music: Charlene A. Newell (b. 1938; LDS)
Tune name: KEY

The Nauvoo Relief Society minutes record that on April 28, 1842, the Prophet Joseph Smith stood to address this new women's organization. The words he spoke have served from that day forward as a summation of the spirit and mission of the Relief Society. In the singing of "A Key Was Turned in Latter Days," Relief Society sisters can recall and enjoy this message.

Author Jan Underwood Pinborough said: "I became aware that the 1950 hymnbook had no hymns specifically about or for women. I felt that the women of the Church would enjoy singing about the gifts and missions that are distinctly theirs." This hymn was written specifically for the 1985 hymnbook.

The text is based directly on Joseph Smith's promises to the Relief Society. As we refer to the Prophet's statements, we can understand more clearly the meaning of the word *key* in the title of this hymn:

"This Society is to get instruction through the order which God has established—thro' the medium of those appointed to lead—and I now turn the key to you in the name of God and this Society shall rejoice and knowledge and intelligence shall flow down from this time." (*Words of Joseph Smith,* ed. Andrew F. Ehat and Lyndon W. Cook [Provo, Utah: Brigham Young University Religious Studies Center, 1980], p. 118.)

Jan Underwood Pinborough stated that the promises contained in Joseph Smith's address to the Relief Society have always had great meaning for her, because they "link our ability to receive knowledge with our responsibility to serve. In other words," she pointed out, "as we turn our attention to those who need our care, we receive the knowledge and blessings we need so much. This teaching in itself is a great liberating key for women, particularly in a time when the world encourages us to focus on our own rights and needs."

Her hymn text, with its reminder that "light and knowledge will attend / Our service in his name," beautifully reflects this link between compassionate service and the resultant blessings of knowledge and intelligence. The entire hymn is in harmony with Joseph Smith's assurance to the Relief Society sisters that if they will act according to their feelings of charity, "the angels cannot be restrain'd from being [their] associates." (*Words of Joseph Smith,* p. 117).

Jan Underwood Pinborough pointed out that "the idea of *turning* is central to this text. The Prophet turned a key to the women of the Church in organizing the Relief Society. As a result, we turn our hearts to each other, looking to the Savior, who shows us how to serve those in need. Together, we turn toward God to seek to know him. He then turns his face toward us, sending us light, knowledge, and assurance. In this chain of turning, the whole earth is blessed."

Composer Charlene Newell indicated that the harmonic changes of the second line might be difficult to hear at first, but the sisters would soon be able to sing the hymn comfortably, especially if they are invited to sing in unison at first.

We Meet Again As Sisters 311

Text: Paul L. Anderson (b. 1946; LDS)
Music: Bonnie Lauper Goodliffe (b. 1943; LDS)
Tune name: SISTERHOOD

Worship, compassionate service, increased knowledge, the seeking of righteous paths—all of these familiar aims of the Relief Society are honored and highlighted in "We Meet Again As Sisters." If a Relief Society meeting opens with this hymn, new to the 1985 hymnbook, no sister can have any doubt about the possibilities and importance of that meeting.

As author Paul Anderson was contemplating what the exact nature of this hymn's text would be, his wife, Lavina Fielding Anderson, suggested that he read Joseph Smith's first address to the Relief Society. The hymn text reflects the spirit and vision of that address, in which the Prophet Joseph Smith promised the sisters of the Relief Society that their good works would cause the blessings of "knowledge and intelligence [to] roll down from this time." He told them, "If you live up to your privilege the angels cannot be restrain'd from being your associates." (*The Words of Joseph Smith,* ed. Andrew F. Ehat and Lyndon W. Cook [Provo, Utah: Brigham Young University Religious Studies Center, 1980], pp. 118, 117.) The hymn text, with such phrases as "May God be our companion / And angels be our friends," brings these admonitions and promises forward to our day.

To the obvious question of whether (or why) a man should write a Relief Society hymn, Paul Anderson's answer was: "I wrote it out of a sincere belief. As women respect and honor the priesthood, so men can appreciate and honor the dignity of women." Thus he wrote a hymn to emphasize that what women do is important and noble, a hymn that includes a reference to our "heavenly parents" and a statement that women are heirs "to every gospel blessing"—to serve as a companion hymn to those that honor the calling of the priesthood.

Paul Anderson pointed out that the text also works well with the tune ST. THEODULPH (no. 69). The sisters might try ST. THEODULPH as well as SISTERHOOD, since it is interesting to contrast the different mood each tune imparts to the text. ST. THEODULPH is more determined, SISTERHOOD more devotional.

Bonnie Lauper Goodliffe, associate Tabernacle organist, stated that SISTERHOOD was intended to "highlight the text and be easily learned and easily sung. I used a narrow vocal range, simple rhythms, and relatively easy key. Because I am an alto, I also wanted the hymn to have an interesting alto part." Thus, in line three, the melody switches to the altos.

She noted further that the left-hand part is strictly accompaniment, not intended to be sung.

We Ever Pray for Thee 312

See the discussion of hymn 23.

God Is Love 313

See the discussion of hymn 87.

How Gentle God's Commands 314

See the discussion of hymn 125.

Jesus, the Very Thought of Thee 315

See the discussion of hymn 141.

The Lord Is My Shepherd 316

See the discussion of hymn 108.

Sweet Is the Work 317

See the discussion of hymn 147.

Love at Home 318

See the discussion of hymn 294.

Ye Elders of Israel 319

Text: Cyrus H. Wheelock (1813–1894; LDS)
Music: Thomas H. Bayly (1797–1839); altered
Tune name: BABYLON

The text of this simple, sincere missionary hymn renews for us the dedication that burned in the hearts of those who preached the gospel in the early days of the Church. No matter what the odds, no matter what the difficulties, the hope and idealism of Zion shone above all.

How well these words reflect those early days. The laborers were indeed few, but their spirit of cheerfulness and service was undaunted. When Cyrus H. Wheelock, author of the text, departed for missionary service in England, one of his traveling companions was Elder Parley P. Pratt. Truly he was at the center of the Church's early missionary work, and he knew its trials as well as its rewards. Later he served as a missionary in the United States and eventually presided over the Northern States Mission.

An early convert to the Church not only made a spiritual commitment but often made a geographical commitment as well. Being baptized a Latter-day Saint usually meant that the next step was to emigrate to "Zion"—the home of the Saints in Utah Territory. Thousands of converts from the British Isles, Scandinavia, and elsewhere found their way across ocean and plain to join their fellow Latter-day Saints. And the problems of hunger and poverty, addressed in the third verse of this hymn, were not just idle phrases, although the standard of living was often somewhat higher once the converts arrived in Utah.

This hymn, first published in 1851, reflects that spirit of gathering. After the children of Israel had suffered amidst the wickedness of the Egyptians in a spiritual Babylon, the Lord led them to the promised land; in the same way, the missionaries in the early days of the Church sought out the righteous to "bring them to Zion" in the "mountains of Ephraim."

Today, our missionaries lead their converts to Zion in a spiritual, figurative sense—*Zion* represents the truths of the gospel.

The tune, which has been slightly altered to fit the words in our hymnal, is familiar to many as the melody of Thomas H. Bayly's *Long, Long Ago.* He is also the author of the original words. The first verse is as follows:

Tell me the tales that to me were so dear,
Long, long ago,
Long, long ago.
Sing me the songs I delighted to hear,
Long, long ago, long ago.

The Priesthood of Our Lord 320

Text and music: John Craven (b. 1929; LDS)
Tune name: DAWN

Not "by rank or wealth or sword" does the power come; these are the sources of fleeting earthly influence. The power that is stronger than any other is the priesthood, given by God to be used worthily and faithfully.

This hymn, new to the 1985 hymnal, speaks of bearing the priesthood worthily, of listening to "the Spirit's whispered word," and of being part of a great host of "deacons, teachers, priests, and elders, / Seeking virtue side by side."

Author-composer John Craven wrote the melody of this hymn in the early 1960s, when he was head of the music department at the Dudley College of Education, West Midlands, England. It was performed by the Dudley Teacher Training Choir to another text, "All the Scenes of Nature," in a popular devotional program broadcast over BBC. John Craven later wrote the text "The Priesthood of Our Lord" for one of the first stake conferences in the United Kingdom.

He noted that the immediate source of inspiration for these words was Ephesians 6:11: "Put on the whole armour of God, that ye may be able to stand against the wiles of the devil." As originally written, the second verse began, "It is ours, the total armour, by Apostle Paul inferred."

The author-composer stated, "A competent leader, a forewarned accompanist, and the resident music-readers in almost any priesthood assembly, should bring about immediate unison rendition of this hymn." The note below the hymn advises that it "may be sung without accompaniment as a round in unison by beginning every two measures." But in John Craven's opinion, "canonic [round] treatment is best reserved for campfire or published choral arrangement."

The tune name, DAWN, honors John Craven's wife, Dawn Ansell, who passed away in 1985.

Ye Who Are Called to Labor 321

Text: Mary Judd Page (1818–1907; LDS)
Music: Daniel B. Towner (1850–1919)
Tune name: LONGWOOD

"Ye Who Are Called to Labor" is a hymn of admonition to all who have received the call to missionary service. It holds up a high standard of courage and character for those who accept the responsibility to "minister for God." First published in 1841, this hymn text represents a heritage of Latter-day Saint missionary commitment that is ours to the present day.

The hymn is based closely on the spirit and some of the wording of Doctrine and Covenants 75:2–5: "Hearken, O ye who have given your names to go forth to proclaim my gospel. . . .

"Labor with all your might–

"Lifting up your voices as with the sound of a trump, proclaiming the truth according to the revelations and commandments which I have given you.

"And thus, if ye are faithful ye shall be laden with many sheaves, and crowned with honor, and glory, and immortality, and eternal life."

The 1841 text by Mary Judd Page was paired later with a gospel-song tune by Daniel B. Towner. J. Spencer Cornwall informed us that he himself arranged the hymn for men's voices, "with the thought that missionaries would have more opportunity to use it than mixed voice groups." (*Stories of Our Mormon Hymns,* p. 292.)

Verse four in the 1950 hymnal was not included in the 1985 hymnal, and the original fifth verse became the fourth. The Hymnbook Committee felt that most groups are more likely to sing four verses than five. Here is the omitted verse:

And while you roam as pilgrims and strangers on this earth,
O do not be discouraged; with songs of joy go forth;
Rejoice in tribulation, for your reward is sure.
Remember that your Savior like sorrows did endure.

Come, All Ye Sons of God 322

Text: Thomas Davenport (1815–1888; LDS)
Music: Orson Pratt Huish (1851–1932; LDS)
Tune name: DAVENPORT

The first verse of "Come, All Ye Sons of God" rallies priesthood holders to the cause of missionary work; theirs is the assignment to "gather scattered Israel" into the fold. Verses two, three, and four address the lost sheep themselves, admonishing them to listen to the voice of the Shepherd and be led back into Zion's fold. "Heavenly bliss" in the presence of God is the promised reward.

Thomas Davenport, the author of this text, estimated that during the years 1847 through 1849 he walked almost two thousand miles through England in the cause of missionary work. When he and other dedicated Latter-day Saint missionaries preached the gospel to men and women of other nations in the early years of the Church, the converts usually undertook to gather to Zion in a literal sense; part of becoming a Latter-day Saint was the duty and privilege of assisting fellow Saints in establishing Mormon settlements in the United States. For Thomas Davenport, the phrase "bring you home to Zion" had an immediate, literal meaning.

We sing these same words today but with a different meaning. When converts hear and accept the gospel, they come "home to Zion" by recognizing eternal truths and becoming part of the Lord's chosen kingdom, wherever they might live.

Those who wish to understand the significance of this hymn's message can be well served by reading the Doctrine and Covenants passages cited at the bottom of the page in the hymnal.

Rise Up, O Men of God 323; 324

Text: William Pierson Merrill (1867–1954)
Music (KENILWORTH): Frank W. Asper (1892–1973; LDS)
Music (FESTAL SONG): William H. Walter (1825–1893)
Tune names: KENILWORTH and FESTAL SONG

"A clarion call to all religious men"—these are the words J. Spencer Cornwall used to describe this stirring text. (*Stories of Our Mormon Hymns,* p. 289.) In their hearts, most followers of Christ wish to devote their time and energies "to serve the King of Kings," but the distractions of daily life—some of them petty—sidetrack and fragment this devotion. The exhortation of this hymn is powerful and unequivocal: "Have done with lesser things."

The 1985 hymnbook included two musical settings for these words. One, by Frank W. Asper, appeared first in the 1948 hymnal. It is an anthem-like setting, suitable for men's choir. The other setting, FESTAL SONG by William H. Walter, is an easier setting, suitable for a congregation of men's voices. FESTAL SONG appeared for the first time in a Latter-day Saint hymnbook in the 1985 edition.

William Pierson Merrill left this account of the writing of "Rise Up, O Men of God": "I wish there were interesting and inspiring details connected with the composition of this hymn. The real story is most prosaic. I was asked to write a 'Brotherhood Hymn,' adapted to use in religious meetings for men. I had just been reading a stirring article by Gerald Stanley Lee, entitled 'The Church of the Strong Men,' and this hymn came to me entirely without effort or forethought, as I was crossing Lake Michigan on a steamer one day." (Quoted in John Barnes Pratt, *Present Day Hymns and How They Were Written* [New York: A. S. Barnes and Co., 1940], p. 69.)

Some hymnals include these additional words:

Rise up, O men of God!
His kingdom tarries long;
Bring in the day of brotherhood
And end the night of wrong.

Rise up, O men of God!
The Church for you doth wait,
Her strength unequal to her task;
Rise up, and make her great!

Kenilworth, after which the Frank W. Asper tune is named, is the home of the composer's daughter, near Price, Utah.

Rise Up, O Men of God — 324

See the discussion of hymn 323.

See the Mighty Priesthood Gathered 325

Text: Jean L. Kaberry (b. 1918; LDS)
Music: Robert P. Manookin (b. 1918; LDS)
Tune name: RICHARD

This stirring hymn for men's voices causes to happen the very scene it describes: "the mighty priesthood [is] gathered," and "proud their voices blend together, / Raising hymns to Father's praise." The power of the priesthood will usher in the time when "all darkness flees away."

An important part of this hymn's message is that priesthood authority and tradition are a family heritage, passed down from father to son. Verse one mentions "Son and father jointly serving." Verse two mentions the precepts taught by Adam to his son Seth. And verse three is an admonition to younger priesthood holders to cherish and maintain these traditions: "Come, ye sons, and walk uprightly, / As your noble fathers trod." This latter phrase also implies that sons without priesthood-bearing fathers follow in the footsteps of their spiritual fathers – faithful priesthood holders of past years and of earlier dispensations.

Robert P. Manookin shared this background of the hymn: "While we were in New Zealand as temple missionaries, my wife and I received correspondence from our friends Jerry Ottley [director of the Tabernacle Choir] and his wife JoAnn. In that correspondence Jerry asked for an anthem for male chorus that could be used in a priesthood session of general conference. I asked our dear friend, Jean L. Kaberry, to write a priesthood poem, and this was the result. The men of the Tabernacle Choir and Mormon Youth Chorus subsequently sang the anthem version in general conference. Later, during the preparation of the 1985 hymnbook, Brother Michael Moody approached me to ask if I would make a hymn setting of the anthem that could be used in the hymnbook."

The tune name, RICHARD, honors the son of the composer.

Verse one includes an unusual word, *serried.* From a French word meaning "to press," it means "pressed together, as in ranks." Jean Kaberry noted: "I have always thrilled to the sight of a large gathering of priesthood. I used the word *serried,* hoping to create an impression of row upon row of fathers and sons."

When the singers are learning this hymn, it would be helpful to mention in advance that they should be prepared to skip to the third ending as they finish the final verse. Some may not be familiar with this convention of music-printing, and the congregation will need to be ready to skip from the word *Loudly* to the word *sound.*

Come, Come, Ye Saints 326

See the discussion of hymn 30.

Go, Ye Messengers of Heaven 327

Text: John Taylor (1808–1887; LDS)
Music: F. Christensen; arranged
Tune name: TRANSPORT

When a missionary has served faithfully as a preacher of the gospel, many prayers of gratitude will be offered on his behalf, and many a thankful new convert will call down the blessings of heaven upon him. This hymn sings of the glory that will come to both missionary and new member as the result of missionary service.

John Taylor, one of the great missionaries in the early days of the Church, wrote this hymn to reflect the missionary fervor he shared with his companions in the British Isles. Because of the labors of such legendary missionaries as Wilford Woodruff and John Taylor, thousands of British men and women were baptized members of the Church; the reference in the third verse to "when your thousands all are gathered" is not at all an exaggeration of the missionary success of that time.

This hymn was included in the 1927 hymnal and then was omitted from the 1950 hymnal. It is included once again in the 1985 hymnal, this time in an arrangement for men's choir. The only change in the text is that the word *nations* in verse four was originally *heathen.*

This hymn is similar in message and language to "Go, Ye Messengers of Glory" (no. 262), which also was written by John Taylor. See the discussion of that hymn for additional information about his missionary activities.

An Angel from on High 328

See the discussion of hymn 13.

Thy Servants Are Prepared 329

See the discussion of hymn 261.

See, the Mighty Angel Flying 330

Text: Robert B. Thompson (1811–1841; LDS)
Music: Evan Stephens (1854–1930; LDS)
Tune name: CARMARTHEN

With strong rhythms and a forceful melody, "See, the Mighty Angel Flying" sends forth the news of the restoration of the gospel. Its words embody the simple but profound truths that are our message to the world: the gospel has been restored; its message is the word of life; it prepares mankind for the last days; the righteous who obey its precepts will be rewarded.

The "angel" of the hymn's title is the heavenly messenger mentioned in Revelation 14:6: "And I saw another angel fly in the midst of heaven, having the everlasting gospel to preach unto them that dwell on the earth, and to every nation, and kindred, and tongue, and people."

This hymn enjoins all people first to *see* the angel; then, in verse two, to *hear* his message, the truth of the everlasting gospel. In verse three, the imperative (command) verb comparable to *see* in verse one and *hear* in verse two is *make*: "Make the Lord of Hosts your friend!" These three steps represent the logical progression for someone hearing the gospel for the first time and accepting its truths: recognizing the fact that the gospel has been restored, then hearing its message, and then seeking the Lord and becoming his follower. The final verse promises the blessings that will come to all who follow this path: salvation with "all the Saints of Zion."

Because author Robert B. Thompson died in 1841, the same year in which this text was published, he witnessed the struggles of the Church in its beginnings but did not live to see the Saints prosper in the West. How he must have longed for the "dangers . . . around you" to come to an end! The thought of the final reward of the just, as expressed in verse four, sustained many an early Saint during difficult times.

Oh Say, What Is Truth? 331

See the discussion of hymn 272.

Come, O Thou King of Kings 332

See the discussion of hymn 59.

High on the Mountain Top 333

See the discussion of hymn 5.

I Need Thee Every Hour 334

See the discussion of hymn 98.

Brightly Beams Our Father's Mercy 335

Text and music: Philip Paul Bliss (1838–1876)
Tune name: LOWER LIGHTS

Though not written by a Latter-day Saint, the message of this hymn relates directly to Latter-day Saint priesthood responsibility: because our Heavenly Father is not physically present to carry out his ordinances in person or to minister in person to each needy soul, he depends for these tasks upon his agents, the dedicated members of his Church.

The underlying metaphor of the hymn is drawn from sea-going experience. The hymn's lesson is somewhat difficult to understand, however, without knowing the meaning of "lower lights" and their relationship to the "lighthouse." The message is much more clear once we are acquainted with an anecdote told by Dwight L. Moody, a famous and dynamic revival preacher. This story was the immediate inspiration for the hymn by Philip Paul Bliss:

"On a dark, stormy night . . . a boat, rocking and plunging, neared the Cleveland harbor. 'Are you sure this is Cleveland?' asked the captain, seeing only one light from the light-house. 'Quite sure,' replied the pilot. 'Where are the lower lights?' 'Gone out, sir.' 'Can you make the harbor?' 'We must, or perish, sir!'

"With a strong hand and a brave heart the old pilot turned the wheel. But alas, in the darkness he missed the channel, and with a crash upon the rocks the boat was shivered, and many a life lost in the watery grave. Brethren, the Master will take care of the great light-house; let *us* keep the lower lights burning." (Quoted in Phil Kerr, *Music in Evangelism* [Glendale, Calif.: Gospel Music Publishers, 1939], p. 163.)

The beam of light from the lighthouse, "our Father's mercy," never goes out. But some struggling people—metaphorically, the sailors lost on the dark sea—need more immediate aid than the distant beam of the lighthouse. Those who seek to carry out the will of the Father will keep the lower lights burning, so that anyone who wishes to find the safety of the harbor can turn at once in the right direction.

The tune, LOWER LIGHTS, is the same as the tune to "Should You Feel Inclined to Censure" (no. 235). "Brightly Beams Our Father's Mercy" was first published in 1871 in a collection titled *The Charm.*

School Thy Feelings 336

Text: Charles W. Penrose (1832–1925; LDS)
Music: George F. Root (1820–1895)
Tune name: ABBOTT

The scriptures are full of warnings against the destructive effects of anger and resentment; the costs of these negative emotions are greatest for the person who harbors them. "School Thy Feelings" expresses a great message of self-control. Whoever chooses to commit this hymn to memory will be able to draw upon its wise words whenever an angry impulse threatens to rise to the surface.

George D. Pyper quoted Charles W. Penrose's memorable story about the circumstances that motivated him to write "School Thy Feelings":

"This hymn was not intended for singing; it was written for myself, about 1860, when I was in Birmingham, England, before I immigrated. I had been insidiously accused, not openly, but certain things had been said about me and my presidency of the Birmingham Conference [District], and particularly in relation to my family affairs and possessions. . . . When I went to Birmingham . . . I had taken there a good deal of furniture and stuff belonging to my family that did not belong to the conference. It was intimated by one of the Elders from Zion that I was endeavoring [when reclaiming the furniture prior to moving] to lay claim to the property that belonged to the Birmingham Conference, and it touched me to the quick. I had labored then over ten years in the ministry, most of the time as traveling elder, literally without purse or scrip. I started that way and had continued, suffering a great many hardships and difficulties and trials that I need not refer to now, and this touched me right to the heart. I did not know how to bear it. Weltering under these feelings I sat down and wrote that little poem, right from my soul, and intended it for myself. . . . President Brigham Young . . . later told me that he had it read to him several times when he had a deputy marshal guarding him in his house." (*Stories of Latter-day Saint Hymns,* pp. 158–59.)

In an article in the October 1924 *Improvement Era,* Elder Orson F. Whitney, then a member of the Quorum of the Twelve Apostles, expressed his admiration for the hymn and the man behind it:

"Here was one who knew himself to be 'falsely, basely slandered,' pleading, not with his accuser, but with himself, against the passing of condemnation 'on friend or foe.' . . . Except for the infamy of his act, I could almost thank 'the accuser of the brethren' for that 'quiet slander,' which wounded the poet's sensitive soul and gave us as the indirect and unintended result this beautiful hymn." (Quoted in Pyper, *Stories of Latter-day Saint Hymns*, p. 159.)

The author of this hymn text, Charles W. Penrose, later became an Apostle and a Counselor in the First Presidency to Joseph F. Smith and Heber J. Grant.

Two figures of speech in the hymn text might pose some difficulty. An *acrid vial* (in verse three) is a bottle of harsh or bitter liquid, a symbol of affliction. Verse four includes these lines:

Noblest minds have finest feelings;
Quiv'ring strings a breath can move;
And the gospel's sweet revealings
Tune them with the key of love.

The "quivering strings" moved by a breath refer to a figure of speech common among poets of the nineteenth century: the image of the aeolian harp. This was a box strung with harmoniously tuned strings, designed to be placed in an open window so that the breeze would cause the strings to vibrate and produce a sweet sound. A *key* can refer to a small wrench for tuning any harplike instrument. Thus the gospel's "key of love" prepares the "noblest mind" to respond sweetly and gently, like the strings of a well-tuned aeolian harp.

George F. Root, popular writer of gospel and Civil War songs, wrote the tunes of two other hymns in our book: "Hark, All Ye Nations!" (no. 264) and "In Our Lovely Deseret" (no. 307). This hymn, like the other two, preserves a tune that he originally wrote for other words. "The Vacant Chair," sung to this tune, was a text by H. S. Washburn about a fallen soldier. The first verse is as follows:

We shall meet, but we shall miss him;
There will be one vacant chair;
We shall linger to caress him,
When we breathe our evening prayer.
When a year ago we gathered,
Joy was in his mild blue eye,
But a golden cord is severed,
And our hopes in ruins lie.

O Home Beloved 337

Text: Evan Stephens (1854–1930; LDS)
Music: Joseph Parry (1841–1903)
Tune name: SWANSEA

"O Home Beloved" is known and loved by many Latter-day Saints. It is frequently performed by the men of the Tabernacle Choir, and its rich harmonies have given pleasure to listeners over the years.

For many decades, the men's choirs of Wales have been known as among the finest in the world, and Welshmen continue this tradition with great enthusiasm today. Competitions and festivals enhance the pride that the Welsh feel in their local singing groups.

Evan Stephens and Joseph Parry, the author and composer respectively of "O Home Beloved," were both born in Wales; it is not surprising that both took a strong interest in the rich possibilities available when a group of men with trained voices sing together.

The music was originally written in about 1875 for the words of a love song. Evan Stephens, who usually composed the music for his own texts, chose in this case to borrow the tune of Joseph Parry instead. The tune name, SWANSEA, is the name of the Welsh city where Joseph Parry conducted a music school for several years.

Although its text is moving and thought-provoking, "O Home Beloved" is not, strictly speaking, a hymn. It is an expression of nostalgia rather than a hymn of worship or exhortation. J. Spencer Cornwall referred to it as a "missionary hymn" (*Stories of Our Mormon Hymns,* p. 290), and it is not difficult to imagine a Latter-day Saint missionary longing for his home as he preaches the gospel abroad. Missionary sentiments are not explicit in the hymn, however. We enjoy it because it suits so well the pleasing sound of men's voices and because an appreciation of home is a praiseworthy message in its own right.

America the Beautiful 338

Text: Katharine Lee Bates (1859–1929)
Music: Samuel A. Ward (1847–1903)
Tune name: MATERNA

Behind the inspiration for this patriotic hymn are the scenic wonders of America—the skies, the fields, the mountains, and the cities. But equally important, it is a tribute to the people of America's past who "more than self their country loved."

"America the Beautiful" is a remarkable combination of national feeling and religious feeling. In each verse, the first two lines allude to some of the numberless blessings Americans enjoy—the heritage of heroes, patriots, and pilgrims, as well as the "amber waves of grain" and "purple mountain majesties." The author's gratitude bursts forth in a panoramic series of allusions to American landscape and American history. Following these exclamations, lines three and four of each verse are a prayer, almost in the form of a warning: Americans must not take these blessings for granted but must continually pray for the grace and guidance of God.

Katharine Lee Bates was a professor of English at Wellesley College in Massachusetts. During the summer of 1893, she had been invited to lecture at Colorado College in Colorado Springs. She wrote that on one summer day in Colorado she stood at the summit of Pike's Peak and "gazed in wordless rapture over the far expanse of mountain ranges and sealike sweep of plain." Earlier, as she had journeyed west, she had attended the Columbian Exhibition at the Chicago World's Fair, "whose White City," she stated, "made such strong appeal to patriotic feeling that it was in no small degree responsible for at least the last stanza of 'America the Beautiful.' It was with this quickened and deepened sense of America that we went on, my New England eyes delighting in the wind-waved gold of the vast wheat-fields." (Quoted in John Barnes Pratt, *Present Day Hymns and How They Were Written* [New York: A. S. Barnes and Co., 1940], p. 6.)

By the 1920s her text had become permanently associated with MATERNA, a tune which Samuel A. Ward had written in 1882. The tune name derives from the fact that the anonymous text for which it was originally written began with the words "O mother dear, Jerusalem."

My Country, 'Tis of Thee 339

Text: Samuel Francis Smith (1808–1895)
*Music: Anonymous (*Thesaurus Musicus, *London, 1744)*
Tune name: AMERICA

Within the images of this memorable text, the majesty of America's scenic beauty comes to symbolize America's heritage of freedom. In four short verses, the word *liberty* occurs twice, the words *free* or *freedom* four times.

In 1829 a man named William C. Woodbridge returned to America from his European travels with a number of German music books. He passed these books on to the noted hymn writer and musician Lowell Mason. But Mason could not read German either, so he gave them to Samuel F. Smith, at that time a student of theology at Andover, and asked him to translate them. As Samuel F. Smith leafed through the books, he came across a tune that caught his attention immediately. He recalled later: "I think I instantly felt the impulse to write a patriotic hymn of my own adapted to the tune. Picking up a scrap of waste paper which lay near me, I wrote at once, probably within half an hour, the hymn 'America' as it is now known everywhere." (Quoted in Marilyn Kay Stulken, *Hymnal Companion to the Lutheran Book of Worship* [Philadelphia, Pa.: Fortress Press, 1981], pp. 568–69.)

The first performance of the hymn was at an Independence Day celebration in a Boston, Massachusetts, church in 1831. A year later, it was included in a collection of church music published by Lowell Mason.

The melody that had so attracted Samuel F. Smith was matched with a patriotic German text in the book he was perusing. He was probably unaware that the tune had also served for patriotic hymns in Danish, Dutch, French, Swiss, Russian, and Austrian versions. In the 1740s it had also been matched to an English text that was to become the national hymn of Great Britain.

J. Spencer Cornwall noted that "the imagery of the hymn is not that of America as a whole, but only that part east of the Alleghenies northward where the author lived. Woods and templed hills, for example, certainly does not portray the plains of the middle states or the mountains of the west. But the universal passion for 'sweet freedom, sweet land of liberty,' and God's mighty protection forever with which the hymn is imbued, makes it a vital, living essence of patriotism." (*Stories of Our Mormon Hymns*, p. 122.)

Oliver Wendell Holmes, a Harvard classmate and close friend of Samuel Smith, made this comment: "He wrote 'My Country, 'Tis of Thee.' If he had said 'our,' the hymn would not have been immortal, but that 'my' was a master stroke. Everyone who sings the song at once feels a personal ownership in his native land. The hymn will last as long as the country." (Quoted in C. A. Browne, *The Story of Our National Ballads* [New York: Thomas Y. Crowell Co., 1919], p. 75.)

The Star-Spangled Banner 340

Text: Francis Scott Key (1779–1843)
Music: John Stafford Smith (1750–1836)
Tune name: NATIONAL ANTHEM (USA)

The pen of the poet transformed one suspenseful night into words that symbolize for all Americans not only the sacrifices that have been made for freedom but also the vigilance with which this blessing must be guarded.

During America's war with England in 1812, Francis Scott Key, poet and zealous patriot, had gone to a British flagship in Baltimore harbor under a flag of truce. His mission was to procure the release of his friend, Dr. William Beanes, who had been captured by the British. He expected to be able to return to shore without much delay, but because the British fleet was preparing to bombard Fort McHenry, he and Dr. Beanes were detained. They had to remain on board for the night and witness the attack against their own flag.

In the darkness of night, the two men had no way of knowing whether the enemy attack had been successful. But at the first light of dawn, they could see the American flag still waving from Fort McHenry. Their relief and gratitude were overwhelming, and Francis Scott Key immediately began to write "The Star-Spangled Banner."

In his mind as he wrote these words was the tune of "Anacreon in Heaven," an English drinking song; he had previously written other words to this melody. The tune had been composed by English musician John Stafford Smith to be sung by members of a London club called the Anacreontic Society. (*Anacreontic* means "joyful" or "convivial," like the verse of Anacreon, poet of ancient Greece.) The original words, written by Ralph Tomlinson, were as follows:

To Anacreon in Heaven, where he sat in full glee,
A few sons of harmony sent a petition
That he their inspirer and patron would be,
When their answer arrived from the jolly old Grecian:
Voice, fiddle, and flute no longer be mute;
I'll lend ye my name, and inspire ye to boot.
And besides, I'll instruct you, like me, to entwine
The myrtle of Venus with Bacchus's vine.

How different the connotations of a melody, depending on the words and experiences with which it is linked! What began as a drinking song has become a stirring and dignified patriotic anthem.

Consistent with most contemporary printings of the United States national anthem, the 1985 hymnal does not include the original third verse of Francis Scott Key's text:

And where is that band, that so vauntingly swore,
That the havoc of war and the battle's confusion,
A home and a country shall leave us no more?
Their blood has washed out their foul footsteps' pollution.
No refuge could save the hireling and slave,
From the terror of flight, or the gloom of the grave;
And the star-spangled banner in triumph doth wave
O'er the land of the free and the home of the brave!

God Save the King 341

Text: Anonymous (18th century)
*Music: Anonymous (*Thesaurus Musicus, *London, 1744)*
Tune name: NATIONAL ANTHEM (United Kingdom)

Written almost two and a half centuries ago, "God Save the King" serves the British people today as an expression of loyalty to monarch and country. This national anthem is a prayer for blessings to be poured out on the monarch.

Obscurity veils the origins of "God Save the King." Henry Carey is sometimes named as author of both words and music, but this attribution rests on uncertain evidence. Various melodies written by John Bull, Henry Purcell, and other early British composers bear some resemblance to the tune, but it is not possible to credit any one person with the music. Many other countries use, or have used, this melody as a national hymn, including the United States, Russia, Denmark, and Germany.

Nor do we know the name of the author of the text. The words first appeared in *Harmonia Anglicana* (soon reprinted as *Thesaurus Musicus,* the source named in our hymnal), published in 1743 or 1744, with a different second verse from the one we know today. The earlier second verse was as follows:

O Lord our God, arise,
Scatter his enemies
And make them fall!
Confound their politics,
Frustrate their knavish tricks,
On him our hopes are fixed,
O save us all!

In 1745, a periodical called *Gentleman's Magazine* printed "God Save the King," adding a third verse. Again, no author was given. The rather negative and combative second verse given above fell into disuse, and the third verse from *Gentleman's Magazine* became the second verse that is sung today.

Advance Australia Fair 342 (Australia)

Text and music: Peter Dodds McCormick (1834–1916)

National hymns can sometimes seem a bit repetitious; after all, how many ways are there of expressing feelings of patriotism and loyalty? But the words of "Advance Australia Fair" are distinctively Australian. With their pride in the immense size of their country and its natural resources, with their generous willingness to share these riches with "those who've come across the sea," Australians can sing these words with honest conviction.

For a century and a half, various composers and poets of Australia attempted to write a distinctive national song that would capture national interest. "Advance Australia Fair" was first performed in Sydney in 1878. Not until 1973 did the New South Wales Council of the Returned Services League endorse "Advance Australia Fair" as an unofficial anthem, stipulating that "God Save the Queen" should be used instead for any occasion on which a member of the Royal Family was present.

The reference to the "radiant Southern Cross" in verse two is to the southern constellation *Crux*.

Three verses of McCormick's original text have not been included in our book. The omitted verses—originally verses two, four, and five—refer to the landing of the British explorer Captain James Cook on the coast of Australia in 1770 (*Albion* is an ancient literary name for Britain) and to the determination of Australians past and present to safeguard their country:

When gallant Cook from Albion sail'd,
To trace wide oceans o'er,
True British courage bore him on
Till he landed on our shore.
Then here he raised old England's flag,
The standard of the brave;
With all her faults we love her still—
"Britannia rules the wave."
In joyful strains then let us sing,
"Advance Australia Fair."

While other nations of the globe
Behold us from afar,
We'll rise to high renown and shine
Like our glorious southern star.
From England, Scotia, Erin's Isle,
Who come our lot to share,
Let all combine with heart and hand
To advance Australia fair.
In joyful strains then let us sing,
"Advance Australia Fair."

Should foreign foe e'er sight our coast
Or dare a foot to land,
We'll rouse to arms like sires of yore
To guard our native strand.

Britannia then shall surely know,
Beyond wide oceans' roll,
Her sons in fair Australia's land
Still keep a British soul.
In joyful strains then let us sing,
"Advance Australia Fair."

"Advance Australia Fair" is available to Latter-day Saints living in Australia so that they may include it in their hymnbooks. Because it is not printed as part of the hymnbook itself, the text is given here:

1. *Australians all let us rejoice,*
For we are young and free;
We've golden soil and wealth for toil,
Our home is girt by sea.
Our land abounds in nature's gifts
Of beauty rich and rare;
In history's page, let every stage
Advance Australia fair.
In joyful strains then let us sing,
"Advance Australia fair."

2. *Beneath our radiant Southern Cross*
We'll toil with hearts and hands,
To make this Commonwealth of ours
Renowned of all the lands.
For those who've come across the seas
We've boundless plains to share,
With courage let us all combine
To advance Australia fair.
In joyful strains then let us sing,
"Advance Australia fair."

God Defend New Zealand 342 (New Zealand)

Text: Thomas Bracken (1843–1898)
Music: John Joseph Woods (1849–1934)

Stressing moral responsibility rather than material wealth, the vigorous national hymn "God Defend New Zealand" truly is a hymn. It is a prayer for protection and guidance, asking the Father not only to "defend New Zealand" but also to make New Zealand an exemplar among nations, "preaching love and truth to man."

Thomas Bracken, the author of the text, was born in Ireland. Left an orphan at age nine, he was sent to join an uncle in Australia. He later made his way to New Zealand, where he eventually established a career in letters and politics. He founded a successful weekly newspaper called the *Saturday Advertiser.*

It was in this newspaper, in 1875, that he first published "God Defend New Zealand." He offered a prize of ten guineas to the composer who could provide the best musical setting. Out of twelve composers who entered the competition, the winner was John Joseph Woods, a music teacher and instrumental performer who had been born and educated in Tasmania and who had later settled in Lawrence, New Zealand.

Two additional verses by Bracken not included in our hymnbook version are these:

Peace not war shall be our boast,
But should foes assail our coast,
Make us then a mighty host,
God defend our free land.
Lord of battles in thy might,
Put our enemies to flight,
Let our cause be just and right,
God defend New Zealand.

Let our love for thee increase,
May thy blessings never cease,
Give us plenty, give us peace,
God defend our free land.
From dishonour and from shame,
Guard our country's spotless name,
Crown her with immortal fame,
God defend New Zealand.

In 1940, following a request by the New Zealand Centennial Council, "God Defend New Zealand" was officially designated the national hymn of New Zealand. In 1977, it was announced that with the consent of Her Majesty Queen Elizabeth II, "God Defend New Zealand" and the traditional anthem "God Save the Queen" would both have equal status as national anthems. A letter (April 22, 1986) from the New Zealand Department of Internal Affairs to the LDS General Church Music Office noted that " 'God Save the Queen' would be especially appropriate at any occasion where Her Majesty the Queen, or a member of the Royal Family or the Governor-General as Her Majesty's personal representative, when within New Zealand, is officially present, . . . while 'God Defend New Zealand' would be specifically appropriate whenever the national identity of New Zealand is to be stressed, even in association with a toast to Her Majesty as Queen of New Zealand."

"God Defend New Zealand" is available to Latter-day Saints living in New Zealand so that they may include it in their hymnbooks. Because it is not printed as part of the hymnbook itself, the text is given here. The first verse is printed in both English and Maori.

1. *God of Nations! At Thy feet*
In the bonds of love we meet;
Hear our voices we entreat,
God defend our free land.
Guard Pacific's triple star
From the shafts of strife and war,
Make her praises heard afar,
God defend New Zealand.

E Ihowa, Atua.
O nga Iwi! Matou ra,
Ata whakarongona,
Me Aroha noa.
Kia hua ko te pai,
Kia tau To ata' whai,
Manaakitia mai
Aotearoa.

2. *Men of ev'ry creed and race,*
Gather here before thy face,
Asking thee to bless this place,
God defend our free land.
From dissension, envy, hate,
And corruption guard our State,
Make our country good and great,
God defend New Zealand.

3. *May our mountains ever be*
Freedom's ramparts on the sea;
Make us faithful unto Thee,
God defend our free land.
Guide her in the nations' van,
Preaching love and truth to man,
Working out thy glorious plan
God defend New Zealand.

O Canada 342 (Canada)

English text: Robert Stanley Weir (1856–1926)
French text: Adolphe B. Routhier (1839–1920)
Music: Calixa Lavallée (1842–1891)

"O Canada" pays tribute to a country rich in natural beauty and national pride—a land of freedom, of "pines and maples," "shining skies," and "glorious rivers." Canada can depend on her sons and daughters to value and protect these blessings. Verse four concludes the anthem with a prayer to the Lord to "hold our Dominion in thy loving care."

Adolphe B. Routhier's French text, of which our version for the English-language hymnal prints only one verse, was the original text of "O Canada." It was these words that were set to music by Calixa Lavallée, a pianist, teacher, and composer from the province of Quebec. Calixa Lavallée moved to the United States as a young man, fighting on the side of the Union Army during the Civil War. He established a teaching career in Boston, Massachusetts. In 1874 he became director of the Grand Opera House in New York, the predecessor of the Metropolitan Opera House. He wrote the prayerlike musical setting for "O Canada" in 1880 at the request of a group of patriotic French-Canadians.

The English words of Robert Stanley Weir are in the spirit of the French original but they are not in fact a direct translation. Robert Stanley Weir commented in 1908 that he wrote the English words "because Mr. Lavallée's splendid melody (one worthy to rank with the finest national airs of any of the older lands) has hitherto lacked an English setting in the song style." (Quoted in Paul Nettl, *National Anthems* [New York: Frederick Ungar Publishing Co., 1967], p. 217.)

"O Canada" is available to Latter-day Saints living in Canada so that they may include it in their hymnbooks. Because it is not printed as part of the hymnbook itself, the text is given here. The first verse is printed in both English and French.

1. *O Canada! Our home and native land!*
True patriot love in all thy sons command.
With glowing hearts we see thee rise
The True North, strong and free
From far and wide, O Canada,
We stand on guard for thee.

O Canada! Terre de nos aïeux,
Ton front est ceint de fleurons glorieux!
Car ton bras sait porter l'epée,
Il sait porter la croix!

Ton histoire est une épopée
Des plus brillants exploits.

Chorus:
God keep our land
Glorious and free!
O Canada we stand on guard for thee,
O Canada! We stand on guard for thee.

Et ta valeur,
De foi trempée,
Protégera nos foyers et nos droits,
Protégera nos foyers et nos droits.

2. *O Canada! Where pines and maples grow.*
Great prairies spread and lordly rivers flow.
How dear to us thy broad domain,
From East to Western sea!
Thou land of hope for all who toil!
Thou True North strong and free.

3. *O Canada! Beneath thy shining skies*
May stalwart sons and gentle maidens rise
To keep thee steadfast through the years
From East to Western sea,
Our own beloved native land,
Our True North strong and free!

4. *Ruler supreme Who hearest humble pray'r,*
Hold our Dominion in thy loving care.
Help us to find, O God; in thee
A lasting rich reward,
As waiting for the better day,
We ever stand on guard.

BRIEF BIOGRAPHIES OF THE AUTHORS AND COMPOSERS

This section gives biographical information about the authors, composers, translators, adapters, and arrangers whose work was included in the 1985 hymnal. Sources of hymns are given here if information about the authors or composers was not available. (See, for example, *Bohemian Brethren's Songbook.*)

Abbey, M. E.

The only information available concerning M. E. Abbey is that he was "an old Baptist preacher" in Atlanta, Georgia, in the 1890s. (See Phil Kerr, *Music in Evangelism* [Glendale, Calif.: Gospel Music Publishers, 1939], p. 163.)

Truth Reflects upon Our Senses, 273 (Text of the refrain)

Adams, Sarah Flower

English, 1805–1848, born in Essex. Her father was the editor of a radical newspaper, and her pastor was a reform-minded Unitarian. So it is not surprising that she became a contributor to *The Repository,* a newspaper of advanced ideas published by her pastor. Her husband-to-be, William B. Adams, was also a contributor. She was friend to many prominent literary figures of her day, including Leigh Hunt and Robert Browning.

Nearer, My God, to Thee, 100 (Text)

Addison, Joseph

English, 1672–1719, born in Wiltshire. Oxford-educated and a fine classical scholar, he became a friend of such notable literary figures of his time as Sir Richard Steele and Jonathan Swift. He contributed to Sir Richard Steele's newspaper, *The Tatler,* and joined with him to publish *The Spectator.* The famous literary critic Samuel Johnson praised Addison's literary style as "familiar but not coarse, elegant but not ostentatious." (Quoted in *British Literature,* ed. Hazelton Spencer et al. [Lexington, Mass.: D. C. Heath and Co., 1974], 1:891.)

The Lord My Pasture Will Prepare, 109 (Text)

Alexander, Cecil Frances

Irish, 1818–1895, born in County Wicklow. She married the Reverend William Alexander, who eventually became archbishop of Ireland for the Church of England. Before her marriage, she had helped establish a school for the deaf, and she was known for her charitable work. She was devoted to religious education. Her *Hymns for Little Children* went through at least seventy editions, and the proceeds from its publication went to an Irish school for the handicapped. She wrote the popular children's hymn "All Things Bright and Beautiful."

There Is a Green Hill Far Away, 194 (Text)
He Is Risen! 199 (Text)
Once in Royal David's City, 205 (Text)

Alford, Henry

English, 1810–1871, born in London. The son of a rector, he graduated with honors from Trinity College, Cambridge. He was then ordained a clergyman of the Church of England and eventually became dean of Canterbury Cathedral. He was widely known as a Greek scholar and spent twenty years preparing a four-volume commentary on the Greek New Testament.

Come, Ye Thankful People, 94 (Text)

LDS. Mexican-born American, 1892–1943. A native of Colonia Juarez, a Latter-day Saint settlement in Mexico, she moved to Douglas, Arizona, in 1912. Her husband, Leo Alldredge, worked as a merchant in Douglas and later in Mesa, Arizona.

They, the Builders of the Nation, 36 (Text)

Alldridge, Richard

LDS. English-born American, 1815–1896. He was born in Northampton, but following his marriage he moved with his wife, Ann Blunt, to Birmingham, where he heard the Latter-day Saint missionaries and was baptized in 1847. He and his wife emigrated to America in 1861 to join with other Latter-day Saints. He made his living in Utah as a shoemaker. Five of his hymn texts were included in the first English edition of *Latter-day Saint Hymns,* and two of these remain in our present hymnal. He was a resident of Cedar City, Utah, at the time of his death.

Lord, Accept Our True Devotion, 107 (Text)
We'll Sing All Hail to Jesus' Name, 182 (Text)

Allen, James

English, 1734–1804. Born in Yorkshire, he was educated for the ministry but was not satisfied with the established church. He joined the Sandemanians (or Glassites), a group that did not have a paid clergy. He built a chapel on his own estate and ministered to the congregation there until his death.

Glory to God on High, 67 (Text)

Allen, Penelope Moody

LDS. American, born 1939 in Castro Valley, California. She moved with her family to San Jose, California, when she was eight years old, after the death of her father. She graduated with highest honors from San Jose State College and then obtained her master of arts degree from Brigham Young University. In 1963 she married Gary L. Allen, and they have four children. She has published stories, poems, and articles in the *Ensign* and other periodicals, and she also writes historical novels. She presently lives in Bountiful, Utah, and is an avid gardener.

With Songs of Praise, 71 (Text)
Let the Holy Spirit Guide, 143 (Text)

Anderson, Paul Lawrence

LDS. American, born 1946 in Pasadena, California. He received a bachelor of arts degree in architecture from Stanford University and a master's degree in the same field from Princeton University. After a mission to Japan, he worked as an architect in California before moving to Salt Lake City to work with Church historic sites. He helped restore the Peter Whitmer Log Home in Fayette, New York; the Whitney Store in Kirtland, Ohio; the Hiram and Sarah Kimball home in Nauvoo, Illinois; and the Manti Temple interior. He also helped plan the Museum of Church History and Art and is now manager of exhibits for that museum. He has published many articles on Mormon architectural history and historic sites. He and his wife, Lavina Fielding, have one son.

In Fasting We Approach Thee, 139 (Text)
Sabbath Day, 148 (Text)
Turn Your Hearts, 291 (Text)
We Meet Again As Sisters, 311 (Text)

Arndt, Ernst Moritz

German, 1796–1860. Born in Schoritz, he studied theology but became a university lecturer rather than a clergyman. His fiery patriotic writings, calling upon Germans to challenge the tyranny of Napoleon, attracted so much attention that he had to flee to Sweden, where he remained for four years. Eventually he returned to Germany and became professor of history at the University of Bonn. He was later honored with the title of rector of that university.

God Speed the Right, 106 (Music)

Asper, Frank W.

LDS. American, 1892–1973, born in Utah. After music study with Annie Maeser (daughter of Karl G. Maeser) and Ebenezer Beesley, he performed his first organ solo in the Assembly Hall on Temple Square at age twelve. He studied in Europe and Boston, and after graduating from the New England Conservatory of Music, he became an instructor there. In 1924 he was appointed Tabernacle organist, and through recordings and broadcasts his playing became known to millions. He directed the McCune School

Symphony Orchestra, which filled a cultural need in Utah before the establishment of the Utah Symphony. He held music posts with Methodist and Jewish congregations in Salt Lake City. He gave numerous concerts throughout the world and was organizer of the Utah chapter of the American Guild of Organists.

God Is in His Holy Temple, 132 (Music)
'Tis Sweet to Sing the Matchless Love, 176 (Music)
O Thou, Before the World Began, 189 (Music)
Hear Thou Our Hymn, O Lord, 222 (Text and music)
This House We Dedicate to Thee, 245 (Music)
Rejoice! A Glorious Sound Is Heard, 257 (Music)
Rise Up, O Men of God, 323 (Music)

Bach, Johann Sebastian

German, 1685–1750, born in Eisenach. The most gifted member of a remarkable family of musicians that flourished in Germany from the sixteenth through the eighteenth centuries, Bach acquired most of his musical knowledge from family members or through independent study. He was the father of seven children by his first wife and of thirteen more by his second. A skilled performer on both organ and violin, he wrote some three hundred church cantatas and many volumes of instrumental music. Though Bach was largely unrecognized as a composer during his life, he is now established as one of the musical giants of all time. The depth and feeling of his religious music have never been surpassed.

O Savior, Thou Who Wearest a Crown, 197 (Musical adaptation)

Baird, Robert Bell

LDS. Scottish-born American, 1855–1916. A native of Glasgow, he emigrated to Utah as a child, and was baptized a Latter-day Saint in 1876. He was closely associated with Evan Stephens and directed the ward choir in Willard, Utah. He taught music in the public schools of Willard and the surrounding communities; he also served as a city councilman in the town of Willard.

Improve the Shining Moments, 226 (Text and music)
Come Away to the Sunday School, 276 (Text and music)
Welcome, Welcome, Sabbath Morning, 280 (Text)

Baker, Mary Ann

American, 1831–? She was orphaned at an early age when her parents died of tuberculosis, and she later lost a brother to the same disease. At the invitation of her Baptist minister, the Reverend H. R. Palmer of Chicago, she wrote "Master, the Tempest Is Raging." In later years she became an enthusiastic worker for the Women's Christian Temperance Union.

Master, the Tempest Is Raging, 105 (Text)

Baker, Theodore

American, 1851–1934. He was trained for a business career but decided instead upon a career in music. He traveled to Europe for study, and his doctoral thesis was the first serious musicological treatment of American Indian music. He worked for the publishing house of G. Schirmer as an editor and translator. Among his important contributions to American music are dictionaries of musical terms and a biographical dictionary of musicians, as well as English translations of many songs. He spent the last six years of his life in Germany.

Prayer of Thanksgiving, 93 (Translation)

Baring-Gould, Sabine

English, 1834–1924, born on his family estate in Exeter. The child of wealthy parents, he spent much of his early life in France and Germany. He became a clergyman of the Church of England, eventually serving as rector of the estate that had been in his family for three hundred years. He was noted for his democratic and generous personality; his marriage to a penniless young woman of fine character was a happy one, and they had fifteen children. Most of his writings were religious in nature—his *Lives of the Saints* fills fifteen volumes—though he also wrote novels.

Now the Day Is Over, 159 (Text)
Onward, Christian Soldiers, 246 (Text)

Barnby, Joseph

English, 1838–1896, born in York. By age twelve he was organist and choirmaster; he later studied at the Royal College of Music. He was widely known as a conductor and conducted the first English performance of Wagner's *Parsifal* and Bach's *St. John Passion.* Always devoted to the cause of music education, he became principal of the Guildhall School of Music. He was a fellow of the Royal Academy of Music and received a knighthood from Queen Victoria. He composed the popular lullaby "Sweet and Low."

Now the Day Is Over, 159 (Music)

Bates, Katharine Lee

American, 1859–1929. A graduate of Wellesley College, she taught at Dana Hall, a preparatory school for Wellesley, and then joined the Wellesley faculty, where she remained for thirty-four years and became chairman of the English department. She received honorary degrees from Oberlin, Middlebury, and Wellesley. She wrote children's works and scholarly books as well as poetry.

America the Beautiful, 338 (Text)

Bayly, Thomas Haynes

English, 1797–1839. Educated at Winchester and at Oxford University, he was a songwriter, novelist, and dramatist. He wrote many sentimental ballads and dramatic pieces. He was primarily known as an author rather than a composer, yet it is two songs for which he wrote music as well as words, "Gaily the Troubador" and "Long, Long Ago," that are best known today.

Ye Elders of Israel, 319 (Music)

Beesley, Ebenezer

LDS. English-born American, 1840–1906, a native of Oxfordshire. After their baptism as Latter-day Saints, the Beesley family emigrated to Utah in 1859. Ebenezer Beesley settled in Salt Lake City. J. Spencer Cornwall listed his activities: "Leading the singing in the Sunday School, revising and preparing music for the *Juvenile Instructor,* directing the ward choir, studying the violin under Professors C. J. Thomas and George Careless, composing Sunday School music, compiling songbooks for Sunday Schools and Mutual Improvement Associations, later directing the production of the *Latter-day Saints' Psalmody.*" (*Stories of Our Mormon Hymns,* p. 107.) In 1880 he was appointed director of the Tabernacle Choir; he held this position for nine years.

High on the Mountain Top, 5; 333 (Music)
What Glorious Scenes Mine Eyes Behold, 16 (Music)
The Happy Day at Last Has Come, 32 (Music)
God of Our Fathers, We Come unto Thee, 76 (Music)
Great Is the Lord, 77 (Music)
Sing We Now at Parting, 156 (Music)
'Tis Sweet to Sing the Matchless Love, 177 (Music)
Reverently and Meekly Now, 185 (Music)
Let Us Oft Speak Kind Words, 232 (Music)
Welcome, Welcome, Sabbath Morning, 280 (Music)
We Meet Again in Sabbath School, 282 (Music)

Beirly, Alfred

No information is available concerning Alfred Beirly.

In Hymns of Praise, 75 (Music)

Bennett, Archibald Flower

LDS. American, 1896–1965, born in Bear Lake County, Idaho. His family moved to Canada when Archibald Bennett was three years old. He graduated from Calgary Normal School in 1915 and as a member of the Canadian Mounted Rifles served in France during World War I. He became a schoolteacher in Canada but moved to Salt Lake City after his marriage in

1921 to Ann Ella Milner. He received his bachelor of arts and master of arts degrees from the University of Utah. His Church service included membership on the Sunday School General Board. He achieved wide recognition as an authority on genealogy, publishing numerous genealogy textbooks and serving as secretary of the Genealogical Society of Utah.

Holy Temples on Mount Zion, 289 (Text)

Bennett, Wallace F.

LDS. American, born 1898 in Salt Lake City, Utah. His lifelong interest in the music of The Church of Jesus Christ of Latter-day Saints has shown itself in his work as a choir director, a member of the General Church Music committee, and a member of the Sunday School General Board. He married Frances Grant, daughter of President Heber J. Grant. He interrupted a business career to serve for twenty-four years as United States Senator from Utah, from 1950 through 1974. He is the author of three books, including *Why I Am a Mormon,* first published in 1956 and then reissued by Deseret Book in 1964.

God of Power, God of Right, 20 (Text)

Bennett, William Sterndale

English, 1816–1875, born in Sheffield. In *The New Grove Dictionary of Music and Musicians,* he is called "the most distinguished English composer of the Romantic school." ([London: Macmillan, 1980], 2:499.) Left an orphan at an early age, he received musical training from his grandfather and was admitted at age nine to the Royal Academy of Music, where he studied violin, piano, and composition. Mendelssohn became his friend after hearing his first piano concerto, and both Mendelssohn and Schumann encouraged him to continue to compose. But his duties as teacher, conductor, editor, and administrator kept him from fulfilling his early promise as a composer. He collaborated with Otto Goldschmidt on *The Chorale Book for England*. He was knighted by Queen Victoria in 1871.

Praise to the Lord, the Almighty, 72 (Musical arrangement)

Bernard of Clairvaux

French, 1091?–1153. Born near the city of Dijon into a noble family, Bernard became a monk in the Cistercian order and in 1115 founded a branch of the order at Clairvaux (pronounced approximately *clair VOE*). In spite of the wish of the Catholic Church to promote him, he remained an abbot at Clairvaux until his death. His reputation and influence spread widely, however, because of the eloquence of his sermons and poems and his reputation for a holy life. He undertook many journeys to promote peace and had a reputation for protecting the poor and weak against the more powerful. In 1174 he was canonized a saint of the Catholic Church.

Jesus, the Very Thought of Thee, 141; 315 (Text)

Blenkhorn, Ada

No information is available concerning Ada Blenkhorn.

In Hymns of Praise, 75 (Text)

Bliss, Philip Paul

American, 1838–1876. Born in poor circumstances in Pennsylvania, he left home at age eleven to do farm and timber work, gaining what education he could. At age twelve he joined the Baptist church, later affiliating with both the Methodists and the Congregationalists. For many years he worked as an itinerant musician, traveling by horse with his melodeon to teach singing. He traveled as a singing evangelist with the famous preacher Dwight L. Moody, and he published at least ten hymn collections, some of which became very popular.

More Holiness Give Me, 131 (Text and music)
Should You Feel Inclined to Censure, 235 (Music)
Brightly Beams Our Father's Mercy, 335 (Text and music)

Bohemian Brethren's Songbook

The tune MIT FREUDEN ZART was first printed in the 1566 *Kirchengesang* (*"Church Hymns"*) of the Bohemian Brethren. This volume, edited by Petrus Herbert, Johannes Geletzky, and Michael Tham, was the third edition of a hymnal originally published by Johann Horn, who was born in Bohemia about 1490.

Sing Praise to Him, 70 (Music)

Borthwick, Jane

Scottish, 1813–1897, born in Edinburgh. A dedicated member of the Free Church of Scotland, she was widely known as a writer and translator of hymns. With her sister Sarah, she published a four-volume work called *Hymns from the Land of Luther*. These translations of German hymns—104 in all—have found their way into many Christian hymnals. She lived in Edinburgh all her life, devoting herself to social work and to the support of missionary labors.

Be Still, My Soul, 124 (Translation)

Bortniansky, Dmitri Stepanovich

Russian, 1751–1825, born in Gluchov, Ukraine. After traveling to Italy to study with the Italian master Baldassare Galuppi, he returned to Russia in 1796, when the Empress Catherine the Great asked him to become conductor of the Imperial Chapel Choir. He set a new standard and style for Russian church music, combining Russian and Italian influences. His numerous sacred compositions, which were edited by Tchaikovsky, filled ten volumes.

The Lord My Pasture Will Prepare, 109 (Music)

Bourgeois, Louis

French, 1510?–1561? Born in Paris, he went to Geneva, Switzerland, as a follower of the Protestant reformer John Calvin and there became a choirmaster. Calvin assigned him the responsibility for the musical editorship of the Genevan Psalter, one of the most important collections in the history of Christian hymnody. He prepared psalm collections and textbooks and was highly regarded in Geneva as an innovative and devoted teacher of music. He harmonized many unison hymn tunes, a practice so controversial that he was jailed for a short time because of it. He is credited with the invention of the hymn board, which posted the hymn numbers in front of the church so that worshipers could find them more easily.

Praise God, from Whom All Blessings Flow, 242 (Music)

Bradbury, William Batchelder

American, 1816–1868. He left his native state of Maine to study at the Boston Academy of Music, where one of his teachers was Lowell Mason. He gave lessons in voice and piano and later obtained a position as organist at the Baptist Temple in New York, where he gave free singing classes for children. During the last decade of his life, he manufactured and sold pianos.

Come, All Ye Saints Who Dwell on Earth, 65 (Music)
Sweet Hour of Prayer, 142 (Music)
We Are All Enlisted, 250 (Music)
God Moves in a Mysterious Way, 285 (Music)

Bradshaw, Merrill

LDS. American, born 1929 in Lyman, Wyoming. He received his bachelor of arts and master of arts degrees from Brigham Young University and his doctorate from the University of Illinois. He has written more than two hundred musical compositions during his twenty-nine years as teacher and composer at BYU. Additional activities include extensive writing and speaking on musical and general academic subjects. In 1981 he was named BYU Distinguished Faculty Lecturer, and presently he is the John R. Halliday Professor of Music and composer-in-residence at BYU. He was a member of the General Music Committee of the Church and was chairman of the Hymnbook Committee responsible for the initial work on the 1985 hymnal. He has served on the board of directors of the Barlow Endowment for Music Composition. He and his wife are the parents of seven children, and his many Church callings have included that of bishop.

We Will Sing of Zion, 47 (Text and music)

Brooks, Phillips

American, 1835–1893, born in Boston, Massachusetts. He received his bachelor of arts degree from Harvard University and also studied at the Virginia Theological Seminary. As Episcopalian minister of Trinity Church, Boston, he was one of the most influential churchmen of his day. His reputation as a great preacher was widespread, and many of his sermons were published.

O Little Town of Bethlehem, 208 (Text)

Brown, Marilyn McMeen

LDS. American, born 1938 in Denver, Colorado. When she arrived at Brigham Young University as a freshman, she had already begun working toward her goal: to write fiction, poetry, and essays that would find recognition both within the LDS Church and outside it. To date she has published six books, twenty-five articles and short stories, and more than forty poems. Her novels *The Earthkeepers* and *Goodbye, Hello* have received favorable reviews. Presently she is working on a book about her childhood experiences in Colorado. She and her husband, Bill Brown, are parents of six children.

Thy Servants Are Prepared, 261; 329 (Text)

Brown, Mary

American, 1856–1918. No other information is available concerning Mary Brown.

I'll Go Where You Want Me to Go, 270 (Text)

Brown, Newel Kay

LDS. American, born 1932 in Salt Lake City, Utah. He began the study of composition with Leroy J. Robertson at the University of Utah, and he continued these studies at the University of California at Berkeley. As a missionary, he conducted a missionary chorus that performed throughout West Germany. He earned his doctorate at the Eastman School of Music, studying under Howard Hanson, Bernard Rogers, and Wayne Barlow. He has taught in New Jersey and Arkansas and presently teaches composition and theory at North Texas State University. Church callings have included those of choir director, bishop, and branch president. He is married to Myrna Weeks, and they are the parents of five children.

With Songs of Praise, 71 (Music)

Bruce, Michael

Scottish, 1746–1767, born in Kinross. His father was a weaver. In order to raise funds for his studies at the University of Edinburgh, Bruce taught school during the university holidays. Before his death at the age of twenty-one, he had written several hymns for a singing class. After Bruce's death, an acquaintance by the name of John Logan apparently was credited with authorship of some of his writings, but modern scholarship gives credit to Bruce.

Behold, the Mountain of the Lord, 54 (Text)

Bullock, William

English, 1797–1874. He served in the British Navy, became a medical doctor, and labored thirty-two years as a missionary. He received his doctor of divinity degree from Cambridge and was made dean of Halifax, Nova Scotia.

We Love Thy House, O God, 247 (Text)

Cahoon, Matilda Rozelle Watts

LDS. American, 1881–1973, born in Murray, Utah. While still in her teens, she began a teaching career that took her to other parts of Utah and to Nevada. At age nineteen, she went to Chicago for further music study. After the death of her husband, she obtained her bachelor's degree from the University of Utah. In a meeting in the Assembly Hall on Temple Square on September 3, 1985, Gordon B. Hinckley of the First Presidency paid tribute to Matilda Watts Cahoon who, he stated, "somehow coaxed a tune out of me as a part of the boys chorus in junior high school. She was a great and delightful and lovely teacher."

The Light Divine, 305 (Text)

Calkin, John Baptiste

English, 1827–1905. He received most of his musical training from his father. After serving as organist and choirmaster in various churches in London, he became a professor of music at Guildhall School of Music and Croydon Conservatory. He was also organist and choirmaster at St. Columba's College in Ireland.

I Heard the Bells on Christmas Day, 214 (Music)

Cannon, Tracy Y.

LDS. American, 1879–1961, born in Salt Lake City, Utah. The adopted son of George Q. Cannon, at age fifteen he joined the Tabernacle Choir and sang under Evan Stephens. He studied music with John J. McClellan and traveled to Europe, New York, and Chicago for additional training. In 1909 he began twenty years of service as a Tabernacle organist, playing for many network broadcasts. He was appointed to the General Music Committee of the Church when it was organized in 1920, becoming chairman in 1939. For twenty-five years he was director of the McCune School of Music and Art. He established a far-reaching educational program for church organists and choristers.

Come, Rejoice, 9 (Text and music)
God of Power, God of Right, 20 (Music)
Praise the Lord with Heart and Voice, 73 (Text and music)
The Lord Be with Us, 161 (Music)
Come, Let Us Sing an Evening Hymn, 167 (Music)
Jesus, Mighty King in Zion, 234 (Music)
How Beautiful Thy Temples, Lord, 288 (Music)

Careless, George Edward Percy

LDS. English-born American, 1839–1932. Born in London, he studied music at the Royal Academy in London. After his conversion to The Church of Jesus Christ of Latter-day Saints he directed LDS choirs in London, then emigrated to Salt Lake City, Utah in 1864. In 1875 he conducted the first performance of Handel's *Messiah* in the Rocky Mountains. Under his direction, the Salt Lake Theater Orchestra became a professional group.

Because of his initiative, Salt Lake City residents were among the first people in the world to see and hear full-scale productions of some of the new operettas of Gilbert and Sullivan. He eventually became director of the Tabernacle Choir. Some seventy hymn tunes by this gifted composer have appeared in LDS hymn collections.

The Morning Breaks, 1 (Music)
Arise, O Glorious Zion, 40 (Music)
Though Deepening Trials, 122 (Music)
Prayer Is the Soul's Sincere Desire, 145 (Music)
O Thou Kind and Gracious Father, 150 (Music)
O Lord of Hosts, 178 (Music)
Again We Meet Around the Board, 186 (Music)
Behold the Great Redeemer Die, 191 (Music)
He Died! The Great Redeemer Died, 192 (Music)

Carr, Benjamin

English-born American, 1768–1831, born in London. His father was a music publisher in London, and the family continued this work after their arrival in Philadelphia, Pennsylvania. The Carr family became especially well known as publishers of patriotic music. Through the *Musical Journal,* a weekly publication which he founded, Benjamin Carr was responsible for bringing much European music to the attention of the American public. He was one of the most important composers of the Federalist era. Church music was also a strong interest; he served for thirty years as director of music at St. Peter's Roman Catholic Church in Philadelphia.

Come, Ye Children of the Lord, 58 (Musical arrangement)

Carson, Lynn R.

LDS. American, born 1942 in Salt Lake City, Utah. After he served a mission in Austria, he married Pamela L. Gillie; they have four children. He lives in Salt Lake City and works for the Family History Department of the Church as manager of the microfilming and oral genealogy programs in Africa, India, and the Middle East. He has been a ward or stake organist since the age of fourteen and since age sixteen has written hymns for his own enjoyment as a sort of musical journal. Other musical interests include the study of early Latter-day Saint hymnody.

Sabbath Day, 148 (Music)

Carter, Daniel Lyman

LDS. American, born 1955 in Caldwell, Idaho. He attended Brigham Young University and was graduated with a degree in composition in 1985. From his father, an accomplished tenor, he learned to love classical music, and from his mother he came to appreciate country and western music as well. He has published poetry in the *New Era* and has had several songs, choral pieces, and keyboard pieces published by Jackman Music Corporation and Sonos Music Resources. He has served as a specialist for the General Music Committee of the Church.

As Now We Take the Sacrament, 169 (Music)

Caswall, Edward

English, 1814–1878, born in Yately. The son of a clergyman, he obtained both a bachelor of arts and a master of arts degree from Oxford, graduating with honors. In 1839, he was ordained a priest of the Church of England. He became increasingly interested in the Oxford, or Tractarian, cause (also known as the High Church movement), a group founded by members of the Church of England who wished to restore the older rituals and tenets. After the death of his wife, he followed the pattern of John Henry Newman and was reordained a member of the Catholic clergy. He divided the remainder of his life between writing and charitable works; virtually all of his hymn texts were written and published after he became a Catholic. He was especially well known for his translations from Latin.

Jesus, the Very Thought of Thee, 141 (Translation)

Chamberlain, John Marvin

LDS. English-born American, 1844–1928. A native of Leicestershire, he emigrated with his family to Salt Lake City, Utah, after they were baptized members of The Church of Jesus Christ of Latter-day Saints. It is said that the Chamberlain family received the first organ to arrive in the Salt Lake Valley. He and his wife, Louise M. E. Rawlings, were members of the

Tabernacle Choir for many years. He left numerous hymns as well as piano and organ selections.

We Are Marching On to Glory, 225 (Text and music)

Christensen, F.

No information is available concerning F. Christensen.

Go, Ye Messengers of Heaven, 327 (Music)

Christiansen, Clay

LDS. American, born 1949 in Price, Utah. Of pioneer Utah and Idaho stock, he began piano lessons at age eight and then at age thirteen began organ study under J. J. Keeler. He received his bachelor of arts degree in organ performance from Brigham Young University in 1971 and a master of music degree from the University of Utah as the last of Alexander Schreiner's master's candidates. He also studied organ under Dr. Robert Noehren. He is presently working toward a doctorate in composition at the University of Utah. He has published original compositions and arrangements for organ and for voice. In 1982 he was appointed Tabernacle organist. He is married to Diane Francom, and they are parents of twelve children.

In Fasting We Approach Thee, 139 (Music)

Clark, L.

Born 1880? No other information is available concerning L. Clark.

Today, While the Sun Shines, 229 (Text)

Clayson, William

LDS. English-born American, 1840–1887. A native of Northamptonshire, he was left lame for life by an injury he received while doing farm work at only ten years of age. He was largely self-taught as a musician, and his principal instrument was the flute. He joined The Church of Jesus Christ of Latter-day Saints and emigrated to Utah in 1861, settling in Payson. He became associated with J. L. Townsend through their work in the Payson

Sunday School, and they collaborated as composer and author on many hymns. All hymns by William Clayson in our present hymnal have texts by J. L. Townsend.

The Day Dawn Is Breaking, 52 (Music)
Nearer, Dear Savior, to Thee, 99 (Music)
O Thou Rock of Our Salvation, 258 (Music)
Hope of Israel, 259 (Music)
The Iron Rod, 274 (Music)
Oh, What Songs of the Heart, 286 (Music)

Clayton, William

LDS. English-born American, 1814–1879. His birthplace was Lancashire. An ardent convert and a devoted missionary, he labored in England for the cause of The Church of Jesus Christ of Latter-day Saints until his emigration in 1840. The Prophet Joseph Smith recognized his abilities and chose him as his secretary. He also became clerk and recorder in the Nauvoo Temple and was elected treasurer of the city of Nauvoo, Illinois. Under the leadership of Brigham Young, he was one of the original pioneers to make the trek westward in 1847.

Come, Come, Ye Saints, 30; 326 (Text)

Clegg, William

LDS. English-born American, 1823–1903. He was born in Hull, Yorkshire, to a musical family who were among the first Latter-day Saint converts in England. At age fourteen he was apprenticed to a file cutter. In 1850, after his marriage to Sarah Elizabeth Oates, he was baptized a Latter-day Saint. The family sailed to America in 1863 and settled in Springville, Utah, after an arduous journey. Clegg was a scholar of the scriptures and the author of several literary works. He was a friend of the noted LDS artist John Hafen, who painted his portrait.

Let Earth's Inhabitants Rejoice, 53 (Text)

Coles, George

English-born American, 1792–1858. For several years he served as editor of the *Christian Advocate* in New York.

A Poor Wayfaring Man of Grief, 29 (Music)

Converse, Charles Crozat

American, 1832–1918. Born in Warren, Massachusetts, he traveled to Leipzig, where he studied law, philosophy, and music theory. He there made the acquaintance of such famous figures in the world of music as Franz Liszt and Louis Spohr. He returned to the United States to establish himself as a lawyer, and he also supervised an organ manufacturing company. He wrote many larger works as well as hymn tunes. He received an honorary doctor of laws degree from Rutherford College.

Israel, Israel, God Is Calling, 7 (Music)

Cornaby, Hannah Last

LDS. English-born American, 1822–1905. Born in Suffolk County to Anglican parents, she married Samuel Cornaby and together they accepted the Latter-day Saint religion, with which they had become acquainted through anti-Mormon literature. They suffered much persecution after their baptism, and they sailed for America in 1853, settling in Spanish Fork, Utah. During a long illness, she was visited by Bishop Thurber of Spanish Fork and Elder Orson Pratt, who, in the course of administering to her for the restoration of her health, blessed her with the gift to write. In her words, "I realize that if I have received but one talent, I am accountable to the Giver for the proper use of the same." (Quoted in J. Spencer Cornwall, *Stories of Our Mormon Hymns,* p. 194.)

Who's on the Lord's Side? 260 (Text)

Cornwall, J. Spencer

LDS. American, 1888–1983. He was born in Salt Lake City, Utah. After studies at the University of Utah, Northwestern University, and the Chicago Conservatory of Music, he served as music supervisor in San Luis County, Colorado; the Granite School District, Utah; and the Salt Lake City Schools. In 1935 he was called to be conductor of the Tabernacle Choir. Under his twenty-seven-year leadership, the choir's renown grew in America as well as abroad. He served on the YMMIA General Board and on the General Music Committee of the Church. He was a beloved teacher and conductor and was busy lecturing and conducting in choral festivals throughout the United States until he was in his nineties. He and his wife, Mary Alice Haigh, were the parents of seven children. He was the author of *Stories of Our Mormon Hymns* (Salt Lake City, Utah: Deseret Book, 1963).

Softly Beams the Sacred Dawning, 56 (Music)

Coslett, Joseph

LDS. Welsh-born American, 1850–1910. Born in Cardiff, South Wales, to a musical family, he grew up in a household where vocal and instrumental music were a part of everyday life. He emigrated to the United States as a teenager, and with his brother he made his living as a mason. They moved to Cedar City, Utah, in 1870, where Joseph Coslett married Emmaline Haight and became well known as a musician and choir director. In 1880 he received a license to act as music instructor in any school run by The Church of Jesus Christ of Latter-day Saints. He also ran a music store for many years. A photograph that includes the sign over this store shows that he sometimes spelled his name "Cosslett."

We'll Sing All Hail to Jesus' Name, 182 (Music)

Cowper, William

English, 1731–1800. His birthplace was Hertfordshire. He was admitted to the bar but did not pursue law because of poor physical and emotional health; his entire life was a struggle against despair and mental illness. The humane and pleasant tone of much of his poetry, particularly his famous long poem *The Task,* stands as a remarkable contrast to the hardships of his personal life. His interest in hymn writing was stimulated by his friendship with the evangelical clergyman John Newton.

God Moves in a Mysterious Way, 285 (Text)

Cox, Frances Elizabeth

English, 1812–1897, born in Oxford. She published *Sacred Hymns from the German* in 1841, and she revised and enlarged this volume for a second edition in 1864. Known as a skilled translator of German hymn texts, she published fifty-six translations in all, together with biographical notes on the authors of these texts.

Sing Praise to Him, 70 (Translation)

Craven, John

LDS. English, born 1929 in Doncaster. The only child of Baptist parents, both teachers, he attended boarding school in Yorkshire and later received his bachelor of music degree from the University of Glasgow. He was introduced to The Church of Jesus Christ of Latter-day Saints by Dawn R. Ansell, whom he later married. He and his wife served in many ward and stake positions. He was head of the music department at Dudley College of Education for twenty-four years and was active in many music groups as baroque violinist and continuo accompanist. He is now retired and living in Canada, and his interests include student opera direction, historical keyboard tuning systems, and the composition of organ preludes.

The Priesthood of Our Lord, 320 (Text and music)

Crawford, Jane Vilate Romney

LDS. American, 1883–1956, born in Salt Lake City, Utah. She attended the University of Utah and also pursued private instruction in music, art, and kindergarten work. A lifetime of Church service included a mission to the Northern States, a later mission to England in the company of her husband, and membership on the Primary General Board and the General Music Committee of the Church. She was a skilled organist.

Father in Heaven, We Do Believe, 180 (Music)

Croft, William

English, 1678–1727. His birthplace was Warwickshire. A pupil of the famous John Blow at Chapel Royal, he became organist there in 1704 and also served as tutor to the royal children. After holding various positions as organist, he became organist at Westminster Abbey, serving from 1708 to 1727. In 1713 he received a doctor of music degree from Oxford University, and he was one of the founders of the Academy of Vocal Musick. Although he wrote a considerable amount of secular music, including music for theater, he is best remembered for his sacred choral works.

O God, Our Help in Ages Past, 31 (Music)

Crosby, Fanny Jane

American, 1820–1915. A native of Putnam County, New York, she was completely blind almost from birth. She triumphed over this handicap to become one of America's best-loved writers of gospel songs. Her poetic talents at first took a different direction—she wrote the words for the popular song "There's Music in the Air"—but at age forty-four she began writing religious verse. It is estimated that she wrote more than eight thousand religious poems. She married Alexander Van Alstyne, a blind musician.

Behold! A Royal Army, 251 (Text)

Crowell, Grace Noll

American, 1877–1969. A native of Iowa and a devoted member of the Methodist church, she wrote more than twenty books of uplifting verse in addition to publishing some thirty-five hundred poems in various periodicals. She was the mother of three sons, and in 1938 she received the distinction of being named American Mother of the Year. She was awarded an honorary degree from Baylor University.

Because I Have Been Given Much, 219 (Text)

Crüger, Johann

Prussian, 1598–1662. After a considerable period of travel and study throughout Europe, he became tutor to the children of a prominent family. In 1662 he entered Wittenberg University to study theology, but after two years he accepted a position as cantor in a Berlin church. In 1644 he published a collection of hymns that is now recognized as the most important of the seventeenth century.

Now Thank We All Our God, 95 (Music)

Cundick, Robert

LDS. American, born 1926 in Salt Lake City, Utah. He found his musical interests kindled when the Sandy Utah Second Ward installed a new Hammond organ, and he went on to serious study of organ and composition. Among his teachers were Alexander Schreiner, Leroy J. Robertson, and Maurice Abravanel. In 1955 he received his doctorate in composition from the University of Utah. He taught at Brigham Young University until 1962, when he was called to England to serve as organist at London's Hyde Park Chapel until 1964. In 1965 he was appointed Tabernacle organist. He holds associate and fellowship certificates from the American Guild of Organists. He and his wife, Charlotte Clark, have five children.

That Easter Morn, 198 (Music)
Thy Holy Word, 279 (Music)

Curtis, Theodore Edward

LDS. American, 1872–1957, born in Salt Lake City, Utah. He earned his living as an employee of ZCMI. He was proficient on both mandolin and guitar, performing frequently throughout the Salt Lake Valley. The author of several books of poetry, he is well known among Latter-day Saints for "The Trail Builders' Hymn," which he wrote at the request of the Primary General Presidency. He published poetry in all the Latter-day Saint magazines, and a booklet of his poetry, *Mother, Heart of Gold,* was for many years distributed in LDS wards on Mother's Day. He filled three local missions in the Granite Stake. A lifetime of Church service included his ordination as patriarch in 1946.

Awake and Arise, 8 (Text)
Come unto Him, 114 (Text)
Lean on My Ample Arm, 120 (Text)
Again, Our Dear Redeeming Lord, 179 (Text)

Dalrymple, Andrew

LDS. American, born 1817. He crossed the plains with Captain Daniel Robinson's handcart company in 1860 and was ordained a member of the seventieth quorum of seventies in Davis County, Utah, in 1865. He made his home in Centerville, Utah. He and his wife, Caroline Holland, were the parents of several children.

O Lord of Hosts, 178 (Text)

Darwall, John

English, 1731–1789, born in Staffordshire. A graduate of Oxford, he was ordained a clergyman of the Church of England in 1761. He combined his religious duties with a lifelong devotion to music of many kinds. He composed two volumes of piano sonatas and wrote musical settings for all the psalms.

Arise, O God, and Shine, 265 (Music)

Davenport, Thomas

LDS. English-born American, 1815–1888. Born in Derbyshire, he was baptized a Latter-day Saint in 1847 and for two years served as a missionary in England, walking, by his own estimate, more than eighteen hundred miles during his missionary labors. He settled in Parowan, Utah.

Come, All Ye Sons of God, 322 (Text)

Davidson, Karen Lynn

LDS. American, born 1943 in Glendale, California. She attended Brigham Young University as an English major, receiving bachelor of arts and master of arts degrees. Education also included a doctorate in medieval English literature from the University of Southern California; a USC dean's exchange fellowship to Cambridge University in Cambridge, England; and one year at the University of Chicago on a National Endowment for the Humanities fellowship. As a member of the BYU English faculty, she was Honors Program professor of the year and director of the Honors Program. Her work has appeared in the *Ensign*, *New Era*, and other publications. She has been a member of the General Music Committee of the Church and the 1985 Hymnbook Executive Committee. She and her husband, David A. Davidson, live in southern California, where she has a private music studio in her home.

O Savior, Thou Who Wearest a Crown, 197 (Text)
Each Life That Touches Ours for Good, 293 (Text)

Davies, Henry Walford

English, 1869–1941, born in Shropshire. After showing early talent as a singer and organist, he became a teacher at the Royal College of Music, conductor of the London Bach Choir, and professor of music at the University of Wales. He received a knighthood and was appointed master of the king's music. An honorary doctorate was bestowed upon him in 1935 by Oxford University.

'Twas Witnessed in the Morning Sky, 12 (Music)

Davis, John S.

LDS. Welsh-born American, 1813–1882. A printer and publisher, he joined The Church of Jesus Christ of Latter-day Saints in his native Wales in 1846. He became a devoted missionary among the Welsh, serving as counselor to the president of the Welsh Mission. At his own expense he translated and published the Book of Mormon and the Doctrine and Covenants in Welsh, and in 1852 he helped edit and publish the only Welsh-language Latter-day Saint hymnbook. He was the first Latter-day Saint to be ordained a high priest in Wales. In 1854 he emigrated to Salt Lake City, Utah, where he played a prominent role among the Welsh-speaking people of Utah.

What Was Witnessed in the Heavens? 11 (Text)

Dayley, K. Newell

LDS. American, born 1939 in Twin Falls, Idaho. He is well known as a composer of Church music and of musical theater productions, including the soundtrack of the show at the Polynesian Cultural Center. He was the founding director of Synthesis, the award-winning jazz ensemble at Brigham Young University. He served at BYU as director of bands and director of the entertainment division. For eight years he was a member of the General Music Committee of the Church, and other Church callings have included that of bishop. He has been chairman of the Brigham Young University music department. He and his wife, Diane, live in Provo and are parents of eight children.

Lord, I Would Follow Thee, 220 (Music)

Daynes, Joseph J.

LDS. English-born American, 1851–1920, born in Norwich. When he was eleven years old, he and a brother emigrated to America with their parents, who had been converted to The Church of Jesus Christ of Latter-day Saints. At age sixteen he was appointed to play the organ that had been brought from Australia in 1867 and installed in the old Salt Lake Tabernacle. He continued as organist in the new Tabernacle under Charles J. Thomas, George Careless, Ebenezer Beesley, and Evan Stephens. He organized the first Tabernacle organ recitals, and he composed marches for the funerals of Brigham Young and Wilford Woodruff.

Come, Listen to a Prophet's Voice, 21 (Music)
Now We'll Sing with One Accord, 25 (Music)
Great God, Attend While Zion Sings, 88 (Music)
Lord, Accept Our True Devotion, 107 (Music)
As the Dew from Heaven Distilling, 149 (Music)

de Jong, Gerrit, Jr.

LDS. Dutch-born American, 1892–1978. A native of Amsterdam, Gerrit de Jong (pronounced *dee YONG*) received a rigorous Dutch education in music, art, languages, and other subjects. In 1906 he and his parents settled in Salt Lake City, Utah. He moved to Provo, Utah, in 1925 to become the founding dean of the college of fine arts at Brigham Young University. He received his doctorate in the field of Germanic literature from Stanford University in 1933. For thirty-four years he was a member of the Sunday School General Board, giving conferences and workshops in the various native languages of the Saints throughout the Western hemisphere. He was also a member of the General Music Committee of the Church for twenty years. He wrote and lectured in six languages, achieved renown as an organist and a composer, and received many honors and recognitions. The de Jong Concert Hall at BYU was named in his honor.

Come, Sing to the Lord, 10 (Text and music)

Dean, Harry A.

LDS. American, 1892–1987. He was born in Salt Lake City, Utah. After serving a mission in Samoa and receiving bachelor's and master's degrees from Brigham Young University, he taught music on the college level at three different institutions: Gila College in Arizona for three years, Ricks College in Idaho for eight years, and Snow College in Ephraim, Utah, until his retirement. During his lifetime he directed fifty-nine performances of Handel's *Messiah* for school and community groups. Seven children were born to him and his wife, Gladys Cutler.

God Bless Our Prophet Dear, 24 (Music)
Savior, Redeemer of My Soul, 112 (Music)
Lord, We Come Before Thee Now, 162 (Music)

Dean, Joseph H.

LDS. English-born American, 1855–1947. He and his parents emigrated from England to America in 1859 and eventually settled in Morgan, Utah. In 1870 he moved to Salt Lake City. He worked for seven years as a stonecutter for the Salt Lake Temple, and in 1893, at the time of the temple's dedication, he was appointed chief caretaker. He was a member of the Tabernacle Choir. He wrote articles for Church publications, missionary tracts, and instructions for Samoan missionaries. He filled two missions for the Church in Hawaii and one in Samoa, later assisting in translating hymns into both languages. In 1940 he was ordained patriarch of the Shelley Idaho Stake.

Before Thee, Lord, I Bow My Head, 158 (Text and music)

Denney, Charles, Jr.

LDS. English-born American, 1849–1937, a native of Middlesex. He emigrated to America in 1866 and worked as a typesetter and proofreader at the *Deseret News.* He and his wife both sang in the Tabernacle Choir, and he also served as ward choir director and Sunday School superintendent. He served two foreign missions, one in Germany and one in England. He was a prolific poet.

O Thou Kind and Gracious Father, 150 (Text)

Dibble, Philo

LDS. American, 1806–1895. Born in Massachusetts, he heard the Latter-day Saint missionaries in Kirtland, Ohio, and was baptized by Parley P. Pratt in 1830. Known as a staunch friend of the Prophet Joseph Smith, he raised money to pay the debt on the Kirtland farm where Joseph Smith was living. He served as a lieutenant colonel in the Mormon militia. His journal accounts of mob actions, tribulations, and other historical events in the early days of the Church make him an important eyewitness to the unfolding of Mormonism. He was a resident of Springville, Utah, at the time of his death.

The Happy Day at Last Has Come, 32 (Text)

Doane, George Washington

American, 1799–1859, born in Trenton, New Jersey. After practicing law for two years, he decided to enter the Episcopalian ministry. He taught at Trinity College in Hartford, Connecticut, and became rector of Trinity Church in Boston and then bishop of New Jersey. He was known as the "missionary bishop" because of his intense devotion to missionary work. He is remembered as the founder of Burlington College.

Softly Now the Light of Day, 160 (Text)

Doddridge, Philip

English, 1702–1751, born in London. His duties as a Congregationalist minister included not only serving his parish but also managing a theological academy in which he prepared some two hundred young men for the ministry. In spite of a constant battle against tuberculosis, he was a tireless worker who had a reputation for making use of every minute of time, even to the extent of having a student read to him while he shaved in the mornings. He left behind some four hundred hymns. He was a friend and admirer of Isaac Watts.

How Gentle God's Commands, 125; 314 (Text)

Dougall, Hugh W.

LDS. American, 1872–1963, born in Salt Lake City, Utah. A grandson of Brigham Young, he served a mission to the southern states and then traveled to Europe and New York for musical training in preparation for his career as a professional singer. He became a successful singing teacher in Salt Lake City, where he guided students for almost fifty years.

Come unto Him, 114 (Music)
Jesus of Nazareth, Savior and King, 181 (Text and music)

Draper, William H.

English, 1855–1933, born in Warwickshire. He received both bachelor of arts and master of arts degrees from Oxford. As a clergyman in the Church of England, he held many prestigious positions. He wrote more than sixty hymns; many of the finest were translations from Latin and Greek.

All Creatures of Our God and King, 62 (Translation)

Dungan, Helen Silcott

No information is available concerning Helen Silcott Dungan.

You Can Make the Pathway Bright, 228 (Text)

Dungan, James M.

1851–1925. No other information is available concerning James M. Dungan.

You Can Make the Pathway Bright, 228 (Music)

Dunn, Loren C.

LDS. American, born 1930 in Tooele, Utah. He was educated in journalism and economics at Brigham Young University and received his master of science degree in communications at Boston University. Throughout his life he has written poetry for personal enjoyment. While living in Boston in 1968, he was called to be a General Authority. He is a member of the First Quorum of the Seventy. His Church assignments have taken him throughout the world: he and his family have lived in Australia, New Zealand, and Brazil. He is married to Sharon Longdon, and they are the parents of five children.

Testimony, 137 (Text)

Durham, Alfred M.

LDS. American, 1872–1957. Born in Parowan, Utah, he taught music in Utah schools for forty-two years after studying at the Juilliard Conservatory under Frank Damrosch. He also served in the Utah State legislature for ten years. He was active in Kiwanis and was a charter member of the Logan Kiwanis. He took pride in his many years of service as a guide on Temple Square.

Sweet Is the Peace the Gospel Brings, 14 (Music)
They, the Builders of the Nation, 36 (Music)
Again, Our Dear Redeeming Lord, 179 (Music)
Carry On, 255 (Music)

Durham, George Homer

LDS. American, 1911–1985, born in Parowan, Utah. He received his bachelor of arts degree from the University of Utah and his doctorate from the University of California at Los Angeles. He was director of the institute of government at the University of Utah and head of the political science department, then vice-president of the university. He became president of Arizona State University in 1960, serving for nine years. After seven years as Utah commissioner of higher education, he became director of the historical department of The Church of Jesus Christ of Latter-day Saints. In addition to holding numerous advisory and volunteer positions, he became a member of the First Quorum of the Seventy in 1977.

My Redeemer Lives, 135 (Music)

Durham, Lowell M.

LDS. American, born 1917 in Boston, Massachusetts. After graduation from the University of Utah and a mission in Great Britain, he received his master of arts and doctoral degrees from the University of Iowa. He has written program notes for the Utah Symphony and served as music director for radio station KSL in Salt Lake City, Utah. He is presently professor of music at the University of Utah, where he also has been dean of the college of fine arts. Conductors who have directed performances and recordings of his compositions and arrangements include Maurice Abravanel, Eugene Ormandy, and Leonard Bernstein. He was a member of the Sunday School General Board from 1947 to 1956. He and his wife, Betty Rivers, have three children.

With All the Power of Heart and Tongue, 79 (Music)
As the Shadows Fall, 168 (Music)

Durham, Lowell M., Jr.

LDS. American, born 1943 in Iowa City, Iowa. He grew up in Salt Lake City where he attended the University of Utah. Later schooling included the University of Washington in Seattle, Washington. He has published extensively in the magazines of the Church, and has received awards for his poetry. He served as associate editor of the *New Era* and was president of Deseret Book Company from 1981 to 1983. He was a board member for the Utah Endowment for the Humanities from 1980 to 1984. He is president and chief executive officer of ZCMI and has served in the presidency of the Salt Lake Olympus Stake. He is married and the father of seven children.

As the Shadows Fall, 168 (Text)

Durham, Thomas L.

LDS. American, born 1950 in Salt Lake City, Utah. He is descended from a long line of Latter-day Saint musicians, beginning with his great-grandfather, Thomas Durham, a member of the ill-fated Martin Handcart Company of 1856. He received bachelor's and master's degrees in music at the University of Utah and then attended the University of Iowa where he earned a doctorate in music composition. He is associate professor of music at Brigham Young University. He is married to Rebecca Christensen, and they are the parents of three children. His principal musical interest is church music, and he has published several compositions and arrangements.

With Humble Heart, 171 (Music)

Dykes, John Bacchus

English, 1823–1876, born in Kensington-upon-Hull. At ten he became organist in his grandfather's church and later received his bachelor of arts degree from Cambridge. It is said that his decision to devote his talents to church music came when he heard the famous soprano Jenny Lind perform in Mendelssohn's oratorio *Elijah.* He was vicar of St. Oswald's Church, Durham, and composed more than three hundred hymn tunes.

Lead, Kindly Light, 97 (Music)
Jesus, the Very Thought of Thee, 141; 315 (Music)

Edwards, John David

English, 1806–1885. He received a bachelor of arts degree from Oxford and was ordained a priest three years later. His pastoral assignments were mainly in Wales.

Our Father, by Whose Name, 296 (Music)

Edwards, Lewis D.

LDS. Welsh-born American, 1858–1921. Born in Aberdare, South Wales, he emigrated to Pennsylvania, where, like many of his native countrymen, he enjoyed singing in choirs. He journeyed west and became a Latter-day Saint in 1878 and thereafter became a music student of Evan Stephens. He conducted singing classes, taught music in the public schools, and founded and conducted many choirs and glee clubs. His vigorous songs won several prizes.

I Know That My Redeemer Lives, 136 (Music)

Ellerton, John

English, 1826–1893. He received his bachelor of arts and master of arts degrees from Cambridge and was then ordained a clergyman of the Church of England. He served in many ecclesiastical positions and maintained a lifelong interest in the writing, translating, and study of hymns, including hymns for children. John Julian made this comment on John Ellerton's texts: "Ordinary facts in sacred history and in daily life are lifted above the commonplace rhymes with which they are usually associated, thereby rendering the hymns bearable to the cultured, and instructive to the devout." (*A Dictionary of Hymnology,* 2 vols. [1907; reprint, New York: Dover Publications, 1957], 1:327.)

The Lord Be with Us, 161 (Text)

Ellis, J.

Ca. 1889. No other information is available concerning J. Ellis.

How Firm a Foundation, 85 (Musical attribution)

Elser, Rosalee

American, born 1925 in Independence, Missouri. A serious music student from the age of six, she received her bachelor of arts degree in music from the Kansas City Conservatory of Music (University of Missouri) and also studied at Graceland College in Lamoni, Iowa, and Willamette University in Salem, Oregon. She is a member of the American Guild of Organists and the Hymn Society of America and serves as staff organist at the Stone Church in Independence. As a member of the hymnal committee for the Reorganized Church of Jesus Christ of Latter Day Saints, she carried out the major responsibility for hymn harmonizations in their current hymnal, *Hymns of the Saints.* She is the granddaughter of Joseph Smith III and the great-granddaughter of the Prophet Joseph Smith.

Away in a Manger, 206 (Musical harmonization)

Elvey, George Job

English, 1816–1893. Born in Canterbury, he studied music, specifically organ, with private instructors and at the Royal Academy of Music in London. He received his bachelor of music and doctor of music degrees from Oxford University. For forty-seven years he held the position of organist at St. George's Chapel, Windsor. During this time he was music teacher to several members of the British royal family. He was honored by Queen Victoria with a knighthood in 1871.

Come, Ye Thankful People, 94 (Music)

Excell, Edwin Othello

American, 1851–1921, born in Uniontown, Pennsylvania. His father was a minister of the German Reformed Church; from him he inherited musical interest and a fine singing voice. He went about the country organizing singing schools and soon became involved in revival work. For the rest of his life he pursued musical evangelism, published many songs, and was recognized as one of the great song-leaders of the day. He wrote a song popular among Latter-day Saint Primary children, "Jesus Wants Me for a Sunbeam."

Scatter Sunshine, 230 (Music)
Count Your Blessings, 241 (Music)

Faber, Frederick William

English, 1814–1863. Born in Yorkshire, he was educated at Oxford, where he came under the influence of John Henry Newman, one of the leaders of the Oxford Movement, a group that sought to bring back to the Church of England certain doctrines and practices of the Roman Catholic Church. He entered the ministry of the Church of England, but eventually Faber, like Newman, became a Roman Catholic. All of his 150 hymns were published after his conversion to Catholicism.

Faith of Our Fathers, 84 (Text)

Fawcett, John

English, 1740–1817, born in Yorkshire. Apprenticed to a tailor as an orphan boy of twelve, he taught himself to read and decided to become a preacher. He was ordained a Baptist minister, and he and his family were much loved by the congregation whom they served. He stayed with this congregation even after he received offers for far more lucrative posts. King George III also offered financial support, but John Fawcett declined, preferring a simple life of religious service and devotion. He is the author of the text "Blest Be the Tie That Binds," sung in many Christian denominations to the tune DENNIS (the tune to no. 125 in our hymnal, "How Gentle God's Commands").

Lord, Dismiss Us with Thy Blessing, 163 (Text)

Fellows, John

English, ?–1785. He left many volumes of writings, including tracts, long religious poems, catechisms, a verse history of the Bible, and theological works as well as hymns. Few facts are known about his life. He is said to have been an indigent shoemaker. A Baptist, he wrote some fifty-five hymns having to do with baptism. The fact that most of his books were printed in Birmingham suggests that he lived in that area.

Jesus, Mighty King in Zion, 234 (Text)

Fink, Gottfried Wilhelm

German, 1783–1846. Born in Sulza, Thuringia, he was known as an excellent minister and teacher, and his professional activities centered more on the written word than on musical composition. He wrote music criticism, worked as a newspaper editor, and published many theoretical and historical works having to do with music.

The Glorious Gospel Light Has Shone, 283 (Music)

Fisher, Cleta Marianne Johnson

LDS. American, born 1932 in Las Vegas, Nevada. Totally blind since birth, she attended the School for the Blind in Ogden, Utah, and won a scholarship to the Perkins School for the Blind in Massachusetts. She then obtained a bachelor's degree from Brigham Young University in sociology and two master's degrees from the University of Utah, one in music and the other in speech pathology/audiology. She runs her own medical secretarial service and has taught in Salt Lake City schools. She has assisted the Church in developing curriculum for the handicapped and is a member of the Tabernacle Choir.

As I Search the Holy Scriptures, 277 (Text and music)

Flemming, Friedrich Ferdinand

German, 1778–1813, born in Neuhausen, Saxony. A physician, he studied medicine in France, Germany, and Austria, and then entered medical practice in Berlin. He was active in the musical life of Berlin and was affiliated with a men's choral society, for which he did a great deal of composing.

Father in Heaven, 133 (Music)

Fones, Joseph G.

LDS. English-born American, 1828–1906. He was a self-taught musician, by trade a coal miner. After suffering a serious mining accident, he was administered to by elders of The Church of Jesus Christ of Latter-day Saints. His miraculous healing led him to join the Church. After his emigration to America, he organized choirs and bands in several towns in southern Utah.

Beautiful Zion, Built Above, 44 (Music)

Fowler, William

LDS. Australian-born American, 1830–1865. Of English and Irish parentage, William Fowler was born in Australia, where his father's regiment was serving. Further military duty took the family to the East Indies and eventually back to England. Left an orphan at fifteen, he searched seriously for a religion that would satisfy him and was baptized a Latter-day Saint in 1849. He labored extensively as a missionary in England and wrote several poems published in the *Millennial Star.* He and his family emigrated to America in 1863 and settled in Manti, Utah, where he worked as a schoolteacher.

We Thank Thee, O God, for a Prophet, 19 (Text)

Fox, Luacine Clark

LDS. American, born 1914 in Washington, D.C. The daughter of President J. Reuben Clark, Jr. and Luacine Annetta Savage, she lived in Washington, D.C.; Salt Lake City, Utah; and Mexico City. She attended the University of Utah; her piano teachers included Florence Bennion, José Velasquez, and Mabel Borg Jenkins, and she studied harmony and composition with Tracy Y. Cannon. She wrote and produced a radio program, "Story Telling Time," for KSL for many years; other creative work includes award-winning media productions, Book of Mormon dramas, general conference productions, and two cantatas. She was a member of the YWMIA General Board, and she and her husband, Orval C. Fox, served as missionaries in Nauvoo, Illinois. They have three children.

Love One Another, 308 (Text and music)

Fox, Ruth May

LDS. English-born American, 1853–1958, a native of Wiltshire. After her mother died when Ruth May was only sixteen months old, her father emigrated to America, leaving her in the care of a widow. A short time later he sent for his daughter, the widow, and the widow's young daughter, and he and the widow were married after her arrival in America. They lived in Philadelphia for two years and then set out for Salt Lake City. Ruth May Fox's adulthood was marked by decades of Church service, most notably forty years on the YWMIA General Board, eight of those as president. She was also active in Travelers' Aid and the Red Cross. She was the mother of twelve children and lived to be 104 years old.

Carry On, 255 (Text)

Francis of Assisi

Italian, 1182–1226. He is one of the most beloved of all Catholic saints. The son of a wealthy merchant, he went against the wishes of his father and declared that he would devote himself to a life of poverty and good works. His preaching drew many people to him, and he established a rule of holy life, known as the Franciscan Order, which was to spread throughout the Catholic world. Because he was known for his love of nature, pictures and statues of St. Francis usually portray him as surrounded by birds and animals.

All Creatures of Our God and King, 62 (Text)

Gabbott, Mabel Jones

LDS. American, born 1910 in Malad, Idaho. One of nine children, she received her education at the University of Idaho and the University of Utah. After serving a mission in the Northwestern States under President Preston Nibley, who encouraged her aspirations as a writer, she returned to Salt Lake City to work as secretary to Elder LeGrand Richards. She married John Donald Gabbott, and they are parents of five children. She has served on the staffs of the *Friend, Improvement Era,* and *Ensign*. She was also a member of the YWMIA General Board and the General Music Committee of the Church, serving as chairman of the Hymnbook Text Committee and contributing much to the initial work on the 1985 hymnal.

We Have Partaken of Thy Love, 155 (Text)
In Humility, Our Savior, 172 (Text)
Lord, Accept into Thy Kingdom, 236 (Text)
Rejoice, Ye Saints of Latter Days, 290 (Text)

Gabriel, Charles H.

American, 1856–1932. He was born in humble circumstances in Iowa, but early followed his family's interest in music. He saw his first piano at age fourteen, and by the time he was twenty he was becoming well known as a composer. He settled in Chicago, became known to important music publishers in that area, and soon found that his songs were in wide demand. He edited more than a hundred volumes of religious music.

I Stand All Amazed, 193 (Text and music)

Gardner, Lyall J.

LDS. American, born 1926 in Salt Lake City, Utah. He grew up in Oregon and received his bachelor of arts degree from the University of Oregon. He then obtained a master's degree in musicology and organ from the Eastman School of Music in Rochester, New York, with additional graduate work at Brigham Young University, the University of Utah, and the University of Michigan. He worked for a manufacturing company and oil refinery until 1962, when he returned to Salt Lake City to join the Church's Advanced Planning Department. Presently he is manager of the Church Consultation Center and also president of Gardner Micro-Systems, Inc., a software development company. For several years he was a member of the General Music Committee of the Church. He is married to Ruth Muir, and they are the parents of four children.

Go Forth with Faith, 263 (Music)

Gardner, Marvin Kent

LDS. American, born 1952. He lived in Duncan, Arizona, until age fifteen, when his family moved to Provo, Utah. After serving a mission in Colombia, he taught Spanish and supervised teachers at the Missionary Training Center in Provo. He received his bachelor and master of arts degrees in English from Brigham Young University, where he also studied music and taught English composition. Since 1978 he has been an editor and writer for the *Ensign,* where he is assistant managing editor. Church callings have included those of high councilor, elders quorum president, choir director, and organist. He has been a member of the General Music

Committee of the Church and of the Hymnbook Executive Committee, and he was responsible for much of the text editing in the 1985 hymnal. He is married to Mary Catherine Hoyt; they live in Bountiful, Utah, with their five children.

Press Forward, Saints, 81 (Text)
Thy Holy Word, 279 (Text)

Gardner, Ruth Muir

LDS. American, born 1927 in Salt Lake City, Utah. A graduate of the University of Utah, she served as a member of the Primary General Board for fourteen years. During that time she worked extensively as a specialist in children's music. She has also served as a member of the General Music Committee of the Church. Over the years, many of her stories, poems, songs, and programs have been published by the Primary Association, and she has written many roadshows and other special programs. She is married to Lyall J. Gardner, and they are the parents of four children.

Go Forth with Faith, 263 (Text)
Families Can Be Together Forever, 300 (Text)

Gates, Brigham Cecil

LDS. American, 1887–1941. Born in Hawaii, the son of Jacob F. and Susa Young Gates, he began music study at an early age and attended conservatories in Boston and Berlin. In 1919 he organized the McCune School of Music and Art in Salt Lake City and five years later became head of the music department at Utah State University at Logan. He was director of the Lucy Gates opera company and the Salt Lake Oratorio Society and served as a member of the General Music Committee of the Church. His settings of "The Lord's Prayer" and "My Redeemer Lives" are known to many.

How Long, O Lord Most Holy and True, 126 (Music)

Gates, Crawford

LDS. American, born 1921. A native of San Francisco, California, he obtained a bachelor of arts degree from San Jose State, a master of arts degree from Brigham Young University, and a doctorate from the Eastman School of Music. After a mission to the eastern states, he served with the United States Navy in the Pacific theatre from 1942 to 1946. He composed *Promised Valley* for the Utah Centennial Celebration. From 1950 to 1966 he was a member of the BYU music faculty. He has served on the MIA General Board and the General Music Committee of the Church. Composer of over 650 works, including music for the Hill Cumorah Pageant, he has received twenty awards from ASCAP (American Society of Composers, Authors, and Publishers). He conducted the Rockford Symphony for sixteen years and has served as music department chairman at Beloit College, Wisconsin. He and his wife, Georgia Lauper, are the parents of four children.

Our Savior's Love, 113 (Music)
Ring Out, Wild Bells, 215 (Music)

Gauntlett, Henry John

English, 1805–1876, born in Shropshire. Educated in both law and music, he spent thirteen years as a lawyer because of his father's insistence. Finally turning to music, he was a prolific composer, leaving some ten thousand hymn tunes at the end of his career. He was also known as an expert in the field of organ design and building, and he maintained a lifelong interest in improving the level of congregational singing. He received an honorary doctor of music degree from the archbishop of Canterbury, and Felix Mendelssohn referred to him as "one of the most remarkable professors of the age." (Quoted in *New Grove Dictionary of Music and Musicians*, ed. Stanley Sadie [London: Macmillan, 1980], 7:190.)

Once in Royal David's City, 205 (Music)

Geibel, Adam

American, 1885–1933. A native of Germany, he came to the United States as a child but suffered the misfortune of going blind at age eight. He became known as an organist, conductor, and composer, and he formed his own publishing company. "Kentucky Babe" was one of his most popular songs, and "Sleep, Sleep, Sleep" became well known as the theme song for many years of the Fred Waring radio program.

Behold! A Royal Army, 251 (Music)

Giardini, Felice de

Italian, 1716–1796, born in Turin. He was a brilliant violinist; his European concert tours established him as a performer, conductor, and teacher. He moved to London to undertake opera management, but financial losses forced him to leave England for Italy. He returned to England six years later to begin a comic opera troupe. He died in Moscow while this troupe was touring Russia.

Glory to God on High, 67 (Music)

Gibbons, Orlando

English, 1583–1625, born in Oxford. After some years as a boy chorister at King's College, Cambridge, he became organist of the Chapel Royal and retained this position for the rest of his life. In 1606 he received his bachelor of music degree from Cambridge and in 1622 an honorary doctor of music degree from Oxford. The outstanding organist of his time, he left a legacy of sacred compositions, particularly anthems, that ensure his position in the history of English music. In 1623 he was named organist of Westminster Abbey.

Father, Cheer Our Souls Tonight, 231 (Music)

Gill, George

1820–1880. No other information is available concerning George Gill.

Beautiful Zion, Built Above, 44 (Text)

Goldschmidt, Otto Moritz David

German, 1829–1907, born in Hamburg. Widely known as a pianist, composer, and conductor, he studied with Felix Mendelssohn at the Leipzig Conservatory and served as accompanist to the famous Swedish soprano Jenny Lind, whom he later married. He collaborated with William Sterndale Bennett on *The Chorale Book for England* (1863), a book of German chorales adapted to English texts. He taught piano at the Royal Academy of Music. The first performance in England of Bach's B Minor Mass was given by the London Bach Choir, a group he founded.

Praise to the Lord, the Almighty, 72 (Musical arrangement)

Goode, William

English, 1762–1816, born in Buckinghamshire. Attracted by the religious life, he abandoned the business career for which his family intended him and enrolled at Oxford University, where he received both bachelor and master of arts degrees. He was ordained by the Church of England in 1786, and as a clergyman he held several different posts during his lifetime. Noted for his interest in foreign missionary work, he helped to found the Church Missionary Society.

Lo, the Mighty God Appearing! 55 (Text)

Goodliffe, Bonnie Lauper

LDS. American, born 1943 in San Francisco, California. She studied piano at the San Francisco Conservatory of Music and received her bachelor and master of arts degrees in music theory from Brigham Young University. She studied organ with J. J. Keeler at BYU and with Oskar Peter at the Mozarteum in Salzburg, Austria. From 1974 to 1976 she sang with the Cleveland Orchestra Chorus. An associate of the American Guild of Organists, she was guest organist at the Salt Lake Tabernacle in 1979, was named associate Tabernacle organist in 1984, and has performed as organist for the Sunday morning Tabernacle Choir broadcast. She served as a member of the General Music Committee of the Church and of the 1985 Hymnbook Executive Committee. She and her husband, Glade P. Goodliffe, have seven children.

We Meet Again As Sisters, 311 (Music)

Gordon, Grace

No information is available concerning Grace Gordon.

Called to Serve, 249 (Text)

Gottschalk, Louis Moreau

American, 1829–1869. Born in New Orleans of French parentage, he was a pianist who toured throughout Europe and the Americas. He also became widely known as a composer and conductor, often making use of Creole and Caribbean folk melodies in his compositions. Chopin and other notable musical figures of the day praised his playing. He was well known in his time for melodic piano pieces such as "The Dying Poet."

God, Our Father, Hear Us Pray, 170 (Music)

Gould, John Edgar

American, 1822–1875. Born in Maine, he established a business in New York as a dealer in pianos and musical merchandise. He later engaged in the same business in Philadelphia. He was a noted choral conductor, tune composer, and hymnal publisher. In 1871 he was advised to travel for the sake of his health; he died in Africa, without having returned to the United States.

Jesus, Savior, Pilot Me, 104 (Music)

Gower, John Henry

English-born American, 1855–1922. Born in Warwickshire, he first served as assistant organist at Windsor Castle at age twelve. He later received his bachelor of music and doctor of music degrees from Oxford University and became organist and music master at Trent College, Nottingham. Emigrating to America to pursue a mining career, he settled in Denver, Colorado. There he continued his activities as a church musician and choirmaster.

There Is a Green Hill Far Away, 194 (Music)

Greatorex, Henry Wellington

English-born American, 1813–1858. A native of Derbyshire, he was born into a family with a strong church-music tradition. He emigrated to the United States in 1836 and served as organist of various churches. In 1851 he published the *Collection of Sacred Music*, a volume that included thirty-seven of his own hymn tunes and several by his father, Thomas Greatorex, and his grandfather Anthony Greatorex.

Softly Now the Light of Day, 160 (Musical arrangement)

Green, Carolee Curtis

LDS. American, born 1940 in Salt Lake City, Utah. She attended the University of Utah. Her compositions have been awarded prizes in *Ensign* contests. Other interests include playing piano and organ, oil painting, mathematics, and family activities. She has held many teaching and music positions in the Church. She is married to Jack L. Green, and they are the parents of seven children.

Awake and Arise, 8 (Music)

Griggs, Thomas Cott

LDS. English-born American, 1845–1903. Born in Dover, he emigrated to America with his mother in 1857, after their conversion to Mormonism. For four years they lived in Boston, where he became interested in music and learned to play brass instruments. He sang for many years with the Tabernacle Choir and was named to the conducting staff in 1880, functioning as assistant to Ebenezer Beesley. He was a member of the Sunday School General Board for fourteen years and helped to compile the first *Deseret Sunday School Song Book.*

God Is Love, 87; 313 (Music)
Gently Raise the Sacred Strain, 146 (Music)

Gruber, Franz Xaver

Austrian, 1787–1863, born in Hochburg. He studied music against the preference of his father, a linen weaver, who wished him to choose a different profession. After studying both violin and organ, he obtained school positions that also allowed him to serve as church organist. For thirty years he was headmaster of a school at Berndorf and organist at Hallein.

Silent Night, 204 (Music)

Hammond, William

English, 1719–1783, born in Sussex. He was educated at St. John's College, Cambridge. He joined the Calvinistic Methodists in 1743 and then in 1745 became a member of the Moravian Brethren. (This sect had arisen in Bohemia three centuries earlier among some of the followers of the martyr John Huss and had spread to many parts of the world. The Moravians were, and are, noted for the quality and enthusiasm of their music.) He was a scholar of Latin and Greek, choosing even to write his autobiography in Greek, and he translated many hymns into English in addition to writing hymns in English.

Lord, We Come Before Thee Now, 162 (Text)

Handel, George Frideric

German-born, 1685–1759; born in Halle but took up permanent residence in England in 1712. The son of a barber-surgeon, he studied organ, composition, and law before being employed by George I of England as composer and conductor. His immense number of compositions included forty-six operas, thirty-two oratorios, and many instrumental works. His most celebrated work is his oratorio *Messiah*. His anthem "Zadok, the Priest," performed in 1727 at the coronation of George II, has been performed at every subsequent English coronation. He is buried in Westminster Abbey.

Joy to the World, 201 (Music)

Hanks, Marion Duff

LDS. American, born 1921 in Salt Lake City, Utah. He received a juris doctor degree from the University of Utah. His activities have included extensive writing, editing, and teaching. He served in the Northern States mission and saw active duty in the Pacific during World War II. He and his family have lived in London and Hong Kong on Church assignment, and he has served several United States presidents in advisory capacities, most recently on the President's Physical Fitness Council. He is a civic leader and a national leader with the Boy Scouts of America. He has been a General Authority since 1953 and serves in the presidency of the First

Quorum of the Seventy. He and his wife, Maxine Christensen, are the parents of five children.

That Easter Morn, 198 (Text)

Harrison, Elias L. T.

LDS. American, 1830–1900. He was a gifted writer who eventually lost his standing in the Church of Jesus Christ of Latter-day Saints because of his support of William Godbe. Godbe founded an apostate group known as the Church of Zion (usually referred to as Godbeites); his original association with Harrison was as cofounder of *The Utah Magazine,* ancestor of today's *Salt Lake Tribune.* During the time Elias Harrison was a Latter-day Saint, he made many contributions through his skills as a writer and editor. He also served as secretary of the Swedish Mission.

Sons of Michael, He Approaches, 51 (Text)

Hart, Edward L.

LDS. American, born 1916 in Bloomington, Idaho. One of eleven children reared on a farm, he went on to distinguish himself as a track runner and a scholar at the University of Utah, where he was chosen as a Rhodes scholar and a member of Phi Beta Kappa. He received a master of arts degree from the University of Michigan and a doctorate from Oxford University. He has taught English for thirty years at Brigham Young University and held a Fulbright Fellowship for study in Pakistan. He has written poetry since high school and has published in various journals. For eight years he served on the board of the Utah Arts Council. He and his wife, Eleanor Coleman, are the parents of four children, and he has served as bishop of a BYU student ward.

Our Savior's Love, 113 (Text)

Hassler, Hans Leo

German, 1564–1612, born in Nuremberg. The son of an organist, he traveled to Venice for organ study and became court organist to Emperor Rudolph II in Prague. Later he accepted a position as court organist to Christian II, Elector of Saxony, at Dresden. He wrote many choral works, both sacred and secular, as well as works for organ. The beauty of the melody PASSION CHORALE (see no. 197) so impressed Bach that he used it five times in his "St. Matthew Passion" and several other times in choral and organ works.

O Savior, Thou Who Wearest a Crown, 197 (Music)

Hastings, Thomas

American, 1784–1872. A native of Connecticut, he lived in New York state from the age of twelve. In 1823 he began a nine-year editorship of a weekly religious newspaper called *The Western Recorder.* At the invitation of a group of churches in New York City, he went there to become their choir director. For many years he directed the choir at Bleeker Street Presbyterian Church. The University of New York City awarded him an honorary doctor of music degree. He wrote a total of six hundred hymns and one thousand hymn tunes.

Hail to the Brightness of Zion's Glad Morning! 42 (Text)
Rock of Ages, 111 (Music)
Come, Ye Disconsolate, 115 (Verse three of text)

Hatton, Gaylen

LDS. American, born 1928 in Red Mountain, California. He moved to Salt Lake City, Utah, at age fifteen and has also lived in Sacramento, California, and in Provo, Utah. He received his bachelor and master of arts degrees from Brigham Young University and his doctorate from the University of Utah, where he studied under Leroy Robertson. His compositions have been played by the Utah Symphony, the Charlotte Symphony, the Sacramento Symphony, the Bedford Festival Orchestra, and the Sun Valley Festival Orchestra. In 1958 he received the Rosenblatt Award. His many commissions include those from the National Endowment for the Arts, the Sacramento Civic Ballet, and the Intermountain Concert Society. He is a member of the BYU faculty and has served as a specialist for the General Music Committee of the Church.

Turn Your Hearts, 291 (Music)

Hatton, John

English, ?–1793. Almost nothing is known about John Hatton except that he resided in St. Helen's, England, on Duke Street, after which his famous tune is named.

From All That Dwell below the Skies, 90 (Music)

Hawkes, Annie S.

American, 1835–1918. Born in New York, she lived most of her life in Brooklyn. She wrote many verses for the hymn collections of Robert Lowry, who was the pastor of the Baptist congregation of which she was a member.

I Need Thee Every Hour, 98; 334 (Text)

Haydn, Franz Joseph

Austrian, 1732–1809, born in Rohrau. He was one of the great masters of the classical period, the composer of works of lively melody and immense appeal. After struggling for years as a music teacher and accompanist, he attracted the attention of the Esterhazy princes, the patrons who were to support him financially in most of his prodigious output: over one hundred symphonies, eighty string quartets, fifty piano sonatas, numerous songs, operas, and chamber works. He was a friend of Mozart and a teacher of Beethoven, and his compositions influenced the course of western musical history.

Glorious Things of Thee Are Spoken, 46 (Music)

Haydn, Johann Michael

Austrian, 1737–1806, born in Rohrau. The younger brother of Franz Joseph Haydn, he played both organ and violin. He served most of his life as musical director to Archbishop Sigismund of Salzburg, retaining this position for forty-four years. He devoted his life to Catholic church music.

How Wondrous and Great, 267 (Music)

Heber, Reginald

English, 1783–1826. Born in Cheshire with advantages of wealth and culture, he was a precocious child, able to translate Latin verse at age seven. As a young clergyman of the Church of England, he sought to improve hymn-singing and foster interest in new hymns. He compiled a forward-looking collection of hymns written by himself and others. He was appointed bishop of Calcutta, but after three years he succumbed to the climate and died in India. Edward VII of England later established a monument in his honor. Among Protestants he is best known for the hymn "Holy, Holy, Holy."

Come, All Whose Souls Are Lighted, 268 (Text)

Hemans, Felicia Dorothea Browne

English, 1793–1835, born in Liverpool. During her lifetime, she was immensely popular in both England and America for her sentimental and lofty verse. Today she is remembered principally for "Casabianca" ("The boy stood on the burning deck . . . ") and "The Landing of the Pilgrim Fathers."

For the Strength of the Hills, 35 (Text)

Hemy, Henri Frederick

English, 1818–1888, born at Newcastle-on-Tyne. The son of German parents, he became organist at St. Andrew's Roman Catholic Church in Newcastle and later professor of music at St. Cuthbert's College in Durham. He published a method book for piano instruction that went through several reprintings, but his main interest was church music.

Faith of Our Fathers, 84 (Music)

Hewitt, Eliza E.

American, 1851–1920. A native of Philadelphia, she was a devoted Sunday School teacher in the Presbyterian church but suffered from a spinal malady that made it impossible for her to carry out vigorous teaching activity.

There Is Sunshine in My Soul Today, 227 (Text)

Hibbard, Angus S.

No information is available concerning Angus S. Hibbard.

Father in Heaven, 133 (Text)

Hickson, William Edward

English, 1803–1870. A boot manufacturer who maintained a lifelong interest in hymnody, he compiled a volume called *The Singing Master,* published in 1836. He was also noted for his work in the field of education and social reform.

God Speed the Right, 106 (Text)

Hinckley, Gordon B.

LDS. American, born 1910 in Salt Lake City, Utah. He graduated from the University of Utah and served a mission to Great Britain. After serving as executive secretary to the General Music Committee beginning in 1951, he was called as Assistant to the Council of the Twelve in 1958 and as a member of the Quorum of the Twelve Apostles in 1961. After his call as Counselor in the First Presidency in 1981, he was called as Second Counselor to President Spencer W. Kimball in 1982 and as First Counselor to President Ezra Taft Benson in 1985. He is the General Authority adviser to the Salt Lake Mormon Tabernacle Choir and has been a great champion of music in the Church. He is married to Marjorie Pay, and they have five children.

My Redeemer Lives, 135 (Text)

Hine, Stuart Wesley Keene

English, born in London in 1899. He served in France during World War I. Thereafter he and his wife lived in various parts of the world, including Poland and Czechoslovakia, as Protestant missionaries. Their missionary work gave them knowledge of several languages. Recently they have worked among displaced foreign persons in England.

How Great Thou Art, 86 (Text; musical arrangement)

Hofford, Lowrie M.

No information is available concerning Lowrie M. Hofford.

Abide with Me; 'Tis Eventide, 165 (Text)

Holbrook, Joseph P.

American, 1822–1888. A native of Boston, he compiled several collections of hymns, including a major Methodist hymnal in 1878.

Jesus, Lover of My Soul, 102 (Music)

Holden, Oliver

American, 1765–1844, born in Shirley, Massachusetts. His skills as a carpenter helped him to rebuild Charlestown, Massachusetts, after it had been burned by the British during the Battle of Bunker Hill. He acquired considerable property and served as preacher of a Puritan church that he built himself in Charlestown. He served for fifteen years on behalf of Charlestown in the Massachusetts house of representatives. He edited or helped to edit several collections of hymns.

Jehovah, Lord of Heaven and Earth, 269 (Music)

Hopper, Edward

American, 1818–1888. Born in New York City, he attended New York University and graduated from Union Theological Seminary. Ordained a Presbyterian minister, he served in several New York churches, including Mariner's Church at New York Harbor, where many in his congregation were sailors.

Jesus, Savior, Pilot Me, 104 (Text)

How, William Walsham

English, 1823–1897, born in Shrewsbury. Educated at Oxford, he was the Church of England bishop of Wakefield and of Bedford. He had spiritual charge of large numbers of Londoners from the poor sections of the city and was known as "the poor man's bishop." He was the author or editor of a great number of pastoral and theological publications. Honorary doctorates were bestowed upon him by the archbishop of Canterbury and by Oxford.

For All the Saints, 82 (Text)
We Give Thee But Thine Own, 218 (Text)

Howe, Julia Ward

American, 1819–1910, born in New York. She was a poet, social worker, and public speaker, best known for her work on behalf of woman suffrage and the abolition of slavery. A Unitarian, she was a persuasive and popular speaker in church meetings. She joined her husband, Dr. Samuel G. Howe, in editing the *Boston Commonwealth*, an antislavery paper.

Battle Hymn of the Republic, 60 (Text)

Hughes, John

Welsh, 1873–1932. Born in Dowlais, he earned his living as an official of the Great Western Colliery Company, where he worked his way up from door-boy. He followed family tradition by participating devotedly as a member of the Baptist church.

Guide Us, O Thou Great Jehovah, 83 (Music)

Huish, Orson Pratt

LDS. English-born American, 1851–1932. When he was nine years old his family emigrated to America, and he spent his early life in farming and cattle raising. Later he became a proprieter of general stores and a pharmacy. After settling in Payson, Utah, he and six of his brothers and sisters formed the Huish Band, which traveled and entertained throughout the southern part of Utah.

Guide Me to Thee, 101 (Text and music)
Come unto Jesus, 117 (Text and music)
Come, All Ye Sons of God, 322 (Music)

Hunter, Nan Greene

LDS. American, born 1938 in Salt Lake City. She graduated from Brigham Young University in 1961. She has directed many musical and dramatic productions for children and was recently recognized by the Republican party of California for her work with children. She is the founder and director of the Country School of Almaden, a private elementary school with prekindergarten through eighth grade and a student body of four hundred. She is married to Richard A. Hunter, and they are the parents of eight children. They have lived in San Jose, California, for the past twenty years.

Father, This Hour Has Been One of Joy, 154 (Text)

Hurn, William

English, 1754–1829. Born in Norfolk, he was well educated and worked as a teacher of classical languages. He was ordained a clergyman of the Church of England in 1781 after a brief career in the army.

Arise, O God, and Shine, 265 (Text)

Hymns of the Spirit

Edited by Samuel Longfellow and Samuel Johnson, this Unitarian hymnal was published in 1864. The collection shows the influence of Transcendentalist philosophy, which was an important liberalizing force in nineteenth century American religious thought.

God Is in His Holy Temple, 132

Jaques, John

LDS. English-born American, 1827–1900, born in Leicestershire. After his baptism into The Church of Jesus Christ of Latter-day Saints in 1845, he carried out missionary work in England, finally emigrating to America in 1856. He was a member of the ill-fated Martin Handcart Company, and his eldest daughter was among those who died before they were rescued from the snowstorms. He served again in England as a missionary from 1869 to 1871, and after his return he worked for the *Deseret News*. For seventeen years he served as assistant Church historian.

Softly Beams the Sacred Dawning, 56 (Text)
Oh Say, What Is Truth? 272; 331 (Text)

Jensen, J. Marinus

LDS. American, 1868–1945. A native of Provo, Utah, he received his master's degree from the University of Chicago. A journalist and teacher by profession, he wrote for the early newspapers of Provo and was also active in drama. He became a professor of English and journalism at Brigham Young University.

Men Are That They Might Have Joy, 275 (Text)

Johns, Vernald W.

LDS. American, born 1902 in Pleasant View, Utah. He attended Weber College, where his interest in writing was awakened. He edited the Weber College yearbook and later was associate editor of the Utah State University yearbook. He was editor and publisher of the Garland, Utah, newspaper, for fifteen years, and he was also postmaster of Garland. He and his wife Franke served a mission together in Colombia, South America. Varied ward and stake assignments have included a calling as member of the Bear River stake presidency.

We Meet, Dear Lord, 151 (Text)
From Homes of Saints Glad Songs Arise, 297 (Text)

Johnson, Joel Hills

LDS. American, 1802–1882. Born in Grafton, Massachusetts, he was baptized a Latter-day Saint in 1831 after hearing the missionaries speak in Ohio. He did missionary work throughout New York and Ohio, and, as the owner of a sawmill, furnished lumber for the Kirtland Temple. He arrived in Salt Lake City in 1848 and was soon called to fill a mission in Iowa and Nebraska, then to settle in southern Utah. He was a witness to many important events in Church history, including the ordination of the first twelve Apostles and the dedication of the Kirtland Temple. His journal contains about one thousand original songs and hymns.

High on the Mountain Top, 5; 333 (Text)
The Glorious Gospel Light Has Shone, 283 (Text)

Jones, Stephen M.

LDS. American, born 1960 in Murray, Utah. He began his musical studies at age nine and began composing at age sixteen. He graduated magna cum laude in music composition from Brigham Young University in 1983. He is enrolled at the College-Conservatory of Music in Cincinnati, Ohio, where he received his master's degree in 1986 and anticipates receiving his doctorate in 1988. He has taught at both BYU and the College-Conservatory of Music. He has published many compositions for various combinations of voice, instruments, and electronics, and his awards include a Barlow endowment grant, first place in the National Federation of Music Clubs Young Composers' Contest, and other commissions and fellowships.

When Faith Endures, 128 (Music)

Kaberry, Jean L.

LDS. Australian, born 1918 in Melbourne. She joined the Church in 1952 in Perth, Western Australia, and has done office work most of her life while maintaining an interest in creative writing. Her specialty is the writing of song lyrics and hymn texts, and she has collaborated with Robert Manookin on a number of works. She is the mother of four sons.

Like Ten Thousand Legions Marching, 253 (Text)
Rise, Ye Saints, and Temples Enter, 287 (Text)
See the Mighty Priesthood Gathered, 325 (Text)

Keeler, J. J.

LDS. American, born 1913 in Provo, Utah. He received bachelor's and master's degrees in music from Brigham Young University. He studied privately with Charles Shepherd and Alexander Schreiner and at the McCune School of Music under Frank W. Asper. He received additional

musical training at Leipzig Conservatory, the Royal College of Music in London, the Chicago Musical College, and the Aspen Institute in Aspen, Colorado. He was a faculty member at Brigham Young University for forty-three years, where he was associate professor of music, university organist, and coordinator of the organ department. His publications include works in the field of organ pedagogy as well as hymn arrangements.

Men Are That They Might Have Joy, 275 (Music)

Keen, Robert

English, later eighteenth century. Little is known of this hymn writer except that he was a leader of music in the Baptist church in London. Pastor of the church was Dr. John Rippon, who published an anthology in 1787 that was the first appearance of "How Firm a Foundation." One of Dr. Rippon's collections was apparently a source of hymns borrowed for Emma Smith's 1835 hymnbook. Robert Keen's name is occasionally spelled "Keene."

How Firm a Foundation, 85 (Text)

Kelly, Thomas

Irish, 1769–1854, born in County Queens. A graduate of Trinity College, Dublin, he studied law but turned instead to a career as an Anglican clergyman. Because of conflict with his ecclesiastical superiors, he was stopped from preaching, but he built several chapels at his own expense and continued work as an independent preacher. He and his wife were known for their generosity to the people of Ireland, especially during the famine of the 1840s.

Zion Stands with Hills Surrounded, 43 (Text)
As the Dew from Heaven Distilling, 149 (Text)

Ken, Thomas

English, 1637–1711, born in Hertfordshire. The family of his brother-in-law, the famous writer Izaak Walton, provided a home for him after he was left an orphan at age eleven. He obtained bachelor and master of arts degrees from Oxford and became a clergyman of the Church of England, serving as a preacher and chaplain to royalty. He was made bishop of Bath and Wells, but he lost this position because he refused to take an oath of allegiance to William of Orange. He was known as a brilliant preacher and a man of integrity. John Dryden wrote of him, "David left him, when he went to rest, / His lyre; and after him he sang the best."

Praise God, from Whom All Blessings Flow, 242 (Text)

Key, Francis Scott

American, 1779–1843. He graduated from St. John's College, Annapolis, Maryland. At one time he considered taking holy orders, and throughout his life he remained a devoted and supportive member of the Episcopal church. Though a serious poet, he was by profession an attorney and served as United States attorney for the District of Columbia from 1833 to 1841.

The Star-Spangled Banner, 340 (Text)

Kaillmark, George

English (German-born), 1781–1835. Early printings of the hymnal wrongly give the first initial as "E." He was a violinist, teacher, and composer of popular music.

Do What Is Right, 237 (Music)

Kidder, Mary A. Pepper

American, 1820–1905. A Methodist, she was born in Boston but lived most of her life in New York.

Did You Think to Pray? 140 (Text)

Kimball, Edward P.

LDS. American, 1882–1937. He attended the Latter-Day Saints College in Salt Lake City, Utah, and Brigham Young University. After a mission and further study in Germany, he returned to Salt Lake City and served on the Sunday School General Board and the General Music Committee of the Church. In 1905 he was appointed Tabernacle organist and served in that capacity for twenty-five years. He also served as president of the

German-Austrian Mission. His activities included extensive public speaking and civic work.

The Wintry Day, Descending to Its Close, 37 (Music)
Great God, to Thee My Evening Song, 164 (Music)
God Loved Us, So He Sent His Son, 187 (Text)

Kipling, Rudyard

English, 1865–1936, born in Bombay, India. The first Englishman to win the Nobel Prize for literature, he was an articulate spokesman for the cause of British imperialism in the last decades of the nineteenth century. He alienated some of his countrymen because of his support of militarism and colonialism, but his vigorous preaching of a life of action, duty, and cheerfulness won many admirers in his day. Today he is perhaps best known for *The Jungle Book* and for his poems, including the popular "If."

God of Our Fathers, Known of Old, 80 (Text)

Kirkpatrick, William James

American, 1838–1921. A lifelong resident of Pennsylvania, he received his early musical training from his father. By age twenty-one he had published a collection of camp-meeting songs, and the publication of gospel hymns was the consuming interest of his life. By the time of his death he had participated in the publication of about a hundred collections of gospel songs. Many were published by his own company, Praise Publishing Company of Philadelphia.

Away in a Manger, 206 (Music)
Dear to the Heart of the Shepherd, 221 (Music)
I Have Work Enough to Do, 224 (Music)

Klopfer, Carolyn Hamilton

LDS. American, born 1936 in Murray, Utah. She met her husband-to-be when both were employees at the Church Genealogical Society. She has served in Church callings as organist, administrator, and is presently ward music chairman of the Eighteenth North Ward in the Salt Lake Eagle Gate Stake. Her other interests include hiking and calligraphy. She and her husband, W. Herbert Klopfer, are the parents of four children.

Home Can Be a Heaven on Earth, 298 (Text)

Klopfer, W. Herbert

LDS. German-born American, born in Berlin in 1936. He lived in East Germany until the age of fourteen, then emigrated to the United States. He served a mission in Switzerland and Austria and has filled numerous Church positions in music and administration. For many years he has been a professional organist and music teacher. He has served as a member of the General Music Committee of the Church and as president of the Salt Lake Eagle Gate Stake. He and his wife, Carolyn Hamilton, have four children.

Home Can Be a Heaven on Earth, 298 (Music)

Kocher, Conrad

German, 1786–1872, born in Württemberg. His admiration for the music of Haydn and Mozart caused him to leave his position as a tutor and take up music as a full-time vocation. A publishing house recognized his talent as a composer and sent him to Rome for further study. There he came to admire the music of the great Italian composer Palestrina. Upon his return to Germany he embarked upon a reform of German church music. He especially encouraged the tradition of four-part singing.

For the Beauty of the Earth, 92 (Music)

Kooyman, Frank Iemke

LDS. Dutch-born American, 1880–1963. A native of Terschelling, he became a Latter-day Saint at age nineteen and served as a missionary in his native Holland for three years. He then emigrated to Utah and worked as a bookkeeper while maintaining vigorous Church activity. He served a second mission in the Netherlands and was eventually called to preside over that mission. He translated many hymns and important Church volumes into Dutch and assisted with the editing of the 1948 LDS hymnbook. (The first syllable of Kooyman rhymes approximately with *boy*.)

Thy Spirit, Lord, Has Stirred Our Souls, 157 (Text)
Thy Will, O Lord, Be Done, 188 (Text)
In Memory of the Crucified, 190 (Text)
How Beautiful Thy Temples, Lord, 288 (Text)

Koschat, Thomas

Austrian, 1845–1914. A professional singer, he became a member and then director of the Court Opera chorus in Vienna. He wrote three operas and many compositions for male quartets.

The Lord Is My Shepherd, 108; 316 (Music)

Kremser, Edward

Austrian, 1838–1914. Born in Vienna, he became director of the Vienna Men's Chorus in 1868. His compositions include operettas as well as solo instrumental and vocal works. He maintained a strong interest in the popular and folk music of the Austrian people.

Prayer of Thanksgiving, 93 (Musical arrangement)

Landgrave, Phillip

American, born 1935. He was educated at Emory University, Eastern Kentucky State University, and the Southern Baptist Theological Seminary, where he received a doctor of musical arts degree in 1966. He also undertook postdoctoral study at the University of Southern California. He became professor of church music at the Southern Baptist Theological Seminary. His choral compositions for children and adults are well known.

Because I Have Been Given Much, 219 (Music)

Laudis Corona

This hymnbook was published in Boston, Massachusetts, in 1885; it is the earliest known non–Latter-day Saint source for "With Wondering Awe." Bruce David Maxwell pointed out ("Source Book for Hymns [1950]," p. 74) that this Christmas hymn in fact appeared one year earlier in a Latter-day Saint hymnbook, the *Deseret Sunday School Union Music Book* (second edition). But we would not be justified in concluding that it is a hymn of Latter-day Saint origin. In all likelihood an earlier non–Latter-day Saint source for "With Wondering Awe" has yet to be discovered.

With Wondering Awe, 210 (Text and music)

Leavitt, Marylou Cunningham

LDS. American, born 1928 in the state of Washington. Reared in a Catholic family, she attended convent school for four years. At age nine, she began to take her interest in writing seriously. She pursued this interest as a student at the University of Washington. At age twenty-one, she was baptized a Latter-day Saint. After rearing a family of ten children and two stepchildren, she joined the Ricks College administrative staff as a writer/editor. She served as a text specialist for the 1985 hymnal. She has published many song lyrics and poems and presently continues her writing career in Salt Lake City, Utah.

We Listen to a Prophet's Voice, 22 (Text)

Lewis, Freeman

American, 1780–1859. He was a composer of hymn tunes who was a surveyor by profession. He lived most of his life in Uniontown, Pennsylvania. His tune book, *The Beauties of Harmony,* was published in 1813 and went through two editions.

Reedemer of Israel, 6 (Music)

Longfellow, Henry Wadsworth

American, 1807–1882. Born in Portland, Maine, he created or popularized a whole group of romantic American legends in such well-known narrative poems as *The Song of Hiawatha, The Courtship of Miles Standish, Evangeline,* and "Paul Revere's Ride." Educated at Bowdoin College, he traveled extensively as a student of European languages and literature. He taught at Harvard for eighteen years, where he was an associate of such figures as Oliver Wendell Holmes and James Russell Lowell. His translation of Dante's *Divine Comedy* was motivated by the accidental death of his beloved second wife. He was the first American to be honored with a memorial bust in Poets' Corner, Westminster Abbey.

I Heard the Bells on Christmas Day, 214 (Text)

Longhurst, John

LDS. American, born 1940 in Sacramento, California. His bachelor of music and master of music degrees were from the University of Utah, where he studied organ with Alexander Schreiner, and his doctorate was from the Eastman School of Music. In 1969 he joined the music faculty at Brigham Young University, where he taught organ and music theory. Since his appointment as Tabernacle organist in 1977, he has toured extensively with the Tabernacle Choir and performs regularly on the Choir's weekly broadcasts. He is a fellow of the American Guild of Organists and has recorded for the Philips and CBS Masterworks labels. Church service has included membership on the Sunday School General Board. He is married to Nancy Meldrim, and they have four children.

We're Not Ashamed to Own Our Lord, 57 (Music)
I Believe in Christ, 134 (Music)

Lowry, Robert

American, 1826–1899. Born in Philadelphia, Pennsylvania, he graduated from Bucknell University, became a Baptist minister, and preached throughout Pennsylvania and New York. He did not begin the study of music until the age of forty. He loved children and was a tireless Sunday School worker. His Sunday School hymnals went through several printings, and his sentimental ballad "Where Is My Wandering Boy Tonight?" was extremely popular.

I Need Thee Every Hour, 98; 334 (Music)

Lucas, James

Born 1726. No other information is available concerning James Lucas.

Come, Let Us Anew, 217 (Music)

Luther, Martin

German, 1483–1546, born in Eisleben. After he was ordained a Catholic priest, his study of scripture caused him to question certain practices of the Catholic church. The sale of indulgences (an indulgence is the remission of a certain amount of punishment after death) was especially abhorrent to him. At the time he wrote his ninety-five theses, he still saw himself as a Catholic reforming the church from within; however, his increasing outspokenness led inevitably to excommunication. His ideas commanded a great following, and the establishment of Protestantism was the first major break in the unity of the Catholic church. His writings, including a translation of the Bible, helped fix the standard for modern German.

A Mighty Fortress Is Our God, 68 (Text and music)

Lyon, A. Laurence

LDS. American, born 1934 in Rotterdam, Holland, where his parents were presiding over the Dutch mission. He grew up in Salt Lake City, Utah, and received his bachelor of science and master of arts degrees from the University of Utah, where he studied under Leroy J. Robertson. In 1965 he obtained a doctorate in composition from the Eastman School of Music. He has more than one hundred compositions in print, and his works have been performed by the Eastman-Rochester Symphony, the Utah Symphony, the Oregon Symphony, and the Tabernacle Choir. He has received many prizes and commissions. He served on the Sunday School General Board and has been a member of the General Music Committee of the Church. He and his wife, Donna, have four children.

Saints, Behold How Great Jehovah, 28 (Music)
Each Life That Touches Ours for Good, 293 (Music)

Lyra Davidica

This collection of hymns was published in London in 1708 by the English music printer John Walsh. The complete title was *Lyra Davidica; or, A Collection of Divine Songs and Hymns, partly new composed, partly translated from German and Latin Hymns: and set to easy and pleasant tunes.*

Christ the Lord Is Risen Today, 200 (Text)

Lyte, Henry F.

Scottish, 1793–1847, born in Kelso. While still a child he was left an orphan. He was educated as a charity student and graduated from Trinity College, Dublin. He decided against a medical career and instead entered the Church of England ministry at age twenty-one. He served for twenty-four years as a clergyman in an English fishing village. He published three volumes of poetry during his lifetime and is also remembered for his work as editor of the poetry of Henry Vaughan (1622–1695); Lyte's efforts brought Vaughan to notice as one of the great metaphysical poets. A memorial tablet in Henry Lyte's honor was placed in Poets' Corner, Westminster Abbey.

Abide with Me! 166 (Text)

McBurney, Samuel

Scottish, born 1847 in Glasgow. He was a student at Glasgow University. In 1879 he traveled for his health to Australia. By 1890 he had returned to Ireland where he received a doctor of music degree from the University of Dublin. He later became inspector of music for the Melbourne Educational Department.

Come, Follow Me, 116 (Music)
While of These Emblems We Partake, 173 (Music)

McClellan, John J.

LDS. American, 1874–1925. A native of Utah, his musical talents led him to study in the Midwest and in Europe. Returning to Salt Lake City, he became Tabernacle organist and director of the Salt Lake Opera Company. J. Spencer Cornwall wrote of him in *Stories of Our Mormon Hymns:* "His artistic bow seemed to be always bent to the limit. It was seldom unstrung. . . . He was able to put such soul into the grand old Tabernacle organ of ours and through its instrumentality preach the gospel to the world." (P. 186.)

Sweet Is the Work, 147; 317 (Music)

McCloud, Susan Evans

LDS. American, born 1945 in Ogden, Utah. As a child she lived in Utah and Illinois, and her subsequent education was at Brigham Young University. Through her numerous publications she has been able to satisfy a lifelong ambition to be a writer. Her list of works in print includes fiction, biography, children's books, poetry, and journalism credits. She has also written successfully for film and stage. She married James W. McCloud, and they and their six children are enthusiastically involved in Scottish activities, including Scottish music and dancing.

Lord, I Would Follow Thee, 220 (Text)
As Zion's Youth in Latter Days, 256 (Text)

McConkie, Bruce R.

LDS. American, 1915–1985. A graduate of the University of Utah, he earned the degrees of bachelor of arts and juris doctor. He became a General Authority in 1946 and an Apostle in 1972. He also served as president of the Southern Australian Mission and as servicemen's coordinator. His many scholarly volumes have been widely read and praised: they include *Mormon Doctrine*; the three-volume *Doctrinal New Testament Commentary*; a six-volume series on the life and mission of Jesus Christ; and *A New Witness for the Articles of Faith.* He served on the Church Board of Education and the Board of Trustees of Brigham Young University. Nine children were born to him and his wife, Amelia Smith.

Come, Listen to a Prophet's Voice, 21 (Verse four of text)
I Believe in Christ, 134 (Text)

McConochie, Barbara A.

LDS. American, born 1940 in Ogden, Utah. She began piano studies at the McCune School of Music and Art at age five. At age thirteen she was called as ward organist and began teaching her first piano students. She graduated from the University of Utah and taught high school English for two years. After moving to California, she taught piano privately and directed the Oakland Temple Pageant *And It Came to Pass* for its premiere run of twelve performances. She enjoys choral directing and has written several compositions for chorus. She and her husband, Douglas A. McConochie, are the parents of nine children.

Keep the Commandments, 303 (Text and music)

Macfarlane, John Menzies

LDS. Scottish-born American, 1833–1892. A native of Sterling and the son of a coachman, he emigrated to America while in his teens and settled in Cedar City, Utah, where his abilities as a choir director were widely recognized. After he moved to St. George, he brought much pleasure into the difficult pioneer life of southern Utah through his continued musical activity. He was a valuable citizen in other ways, serving as a district judge, a surveyor, and a builder. In *Stories of Latter-day Saint Hymns,* George D. Pyper related: "When the late Bishop Scanlan of the Catholic Church visited Silver Reef, a flourishing mining camp in those days, he expressed a desire to hold mass in St. George. The Latter-day Saint authorities, with a liberality for which they are noted, consented and Brother Macfarlane trained his choir for six weeks learning the Latin mass." (P. 83.)

Dearest Children, God Is Near You, 96 (Music)
Far, Far Away, 212 (Text and music)

McGranahan, James

American, 1840–1907. The son of a Pennsylvania farmer who did not approve of his musical interests, he nevertheless managed to obtain music study in New York and Chicago. He decided to devote himself to sacred music rather than to an operatic career, and under the influence of Philip Paul Bliss, he followed a career in evangelism. He was coeditor of fifteen volumes of gospel songs.

O My Father, 292 (Music)

McIntyre, Thomas

LDS. Scottish-born American, 1833–1914, a native of Edinburgh. Upon his baptism as a Latter-day Saint in 1854, he became director of the Latter-day Saint choir in Edinburgh. He emigrated to Utah in 1859, traveling by handcart to the Salt Lake Valley. He did many kinds of work, including printing for the *Deseret News*, and played French horn in the theater orchestra. He formed a band that played in many Utah cities, and for many years he sang in the Tabernacle Choir.

How Great the Wisdom and the Love, 195 (Music)

McMaster, Clara Elizabeth Watkins

LDS. American, born 1904 at Beaver Dam, Box Elder County, Utah. The eleventh child born into a musical family, she has maintained a lifelong interest in children's music, and her songs are well known to all Latter-day Saint children. She served as a member of the Primary General Board for fourteen years and sang with the Tabernacle Choir for twenty-three years. She and her husband, J. Stuart McMaster, are the parents of four children. From 1970 to 1973 the McMasters lived in Independence, Missouri, where he served as president of the Kansas-Missouri Mission. In 1978 the McMasters received the Franklin S. Harris Fine Arts Award from Brigham Young University in recognition of their musical service.

Teach Me to Walk in the Light, 304 (Text and music)

McNaughton, John Hugh

American, 1829–1891, born in Caledonia, New York. He wrote many popular songs, including "The Blue and the Gray" and "Faded Coat of Blue."

Love at Home, 294; 318 (Text and music)

Malin, Annie Pinnock

LDS. English-born American, 1863–1935, a native of London. When she was six years old, she came to America with her parents, converts to The Church of Jesus Christ of Latter-day Saints. She found time for a great deal of writing while rearing the five children born to her and her husband, Millard Fillmore Malin. Many of her stories and poems were published in Latter-day Saint magazines.

God, Our Father, Hear Us Pray, 170 (Text)

Manookin, Robert P.

LDS. American, born 1918 in Salt Lake City. He began piano study at the age of eight, then went on to study organ with Frank W. Asper and Alexander Schreiner, choral conducting with J. Spencer Cornwall, and composition with B. Cecil Gates, Leon Dallin, and Carl Fuerstner. He received his bachelor of arts degree from Brigham Young University, his master of music degree from the University of Illinois, and his doctoral degree in composition from the University of Utah. He served as a member of the BYU music faculty for many years. He and his wife have served as temple missionaries in New Zealand and the Philippines, and he has written music for the New Zealand temple pageant. His works are frequently performed by the Tabernacle Choir.

O Saints of Zion, 39 (Music)
We Have Partaken of Thy Love, 155 (Music)
Thy Will, O Lord, Be Done, 188 (Music)
Like Ten Thousand Legions Marching, 253 (Music)
Rise, Ye Saints, and Temples Enter, 287 (Music)
See the Mighty Priesthood Gathered, 325 (Music)

Manwaring, George

LDS. English-born American, 1854–1889, a native of Cheshire. His family joined The Church of Jesus Christ of Latter-day Saints and emigrated to America in 1871, eventually settling in Springville, Utah. He learned the draper's trade in England, and he was employed by ZCMI and other retail establishments in Utah. Largely self-taught, he became an accomplished organist and singer, and for a while studied art with John Hafen. He died of pneumonia when only thirty-five years of age.

Joseph Smith's First Prayer, 26 (Text)
Lord, We Ask Thee Ere We Part, 153 (Text)
Sing We Now at Parting, 156 (Text)
'Tis Sweet to Sing the Matchless Love, 176; 177 (Text)
We Meet Again in Sabbath School, 282 (Text)

Mason, Lowell

American, 1792–1872. Born in Medford, Massachusetts, he was a charter member of the First Presbyterian Church of Savannah, Georgia. His musical gifts showed themselves early, and he pursued the study of composition while working as a bank clerk. He helped compile a hymn collection which sold so widely after its publication in 1822 that he was thereafter able to turn his full-time attention to music. For fourteen years he served as music director of Bowdoin Street Church in Boston, where Lyman Beecher was pastor. He worked enthusiastically on behalf of music instruction in the Boston public schools, and he is sometimes called the father of American music education. His travels in Europe enabled him to bring back to America much English, French, and German music.

Nearer, My God, to Thee, 100 (Music)
How Gentle God's Commands, 125 (Musical arrangement)
Joy to the World, 201 (Musical arrangement)
We Give Thee But Thine Own, 218 (Musical arrangement)
Come, All Whose Souls Are Lighted, 268 (Music)

Medley, Samuel

English, 1738–1799, born in Hertfordshire. A leg wound he received during service in the navy forced him to spend some time in recuperation. To while away the time, his grandfather read to him from the sermons by Isaac Watts, and Samuel Medley was profoundly moved. He joined the Baptist church and became a pastor. Because of his experiences at sea, he could relate particularly well to his Liverpool congregation, many of whom were seafaring men and their families.

I Know That My Redeemer Lives, 136 (Text)

Melling, Ellen Knowles

LDS. English-born American, 1820–1905, born in Lancashire. The daughter of a family who were among the first in England to join The Church of Jesus Christ of Latter-day Saints, she was baptized by Heber C. Kimball and confirmed by Orson Hyde. She sailed to America in 1855 with her family, and after a difficult trek across the continent, during which she gave birth to a daughter, they arrived in Salt Lake City. They settled in Ogden, where her husband, John Melling, became conductor of the Ogden Tabernacle choir and made a living for the family as a tailor and music teacher.

Oh Say, What Is Truth? 272; 331 (Music)

Mendelssohn, Felix

German, 1809–1847, born in Hamburg. His grandfather was the famous Jewish philosopher Moses Mendelssohn; however, his father converted to Christianity, and Felix Mendelssohn himself was a devoted Christian. Since he was surrounded from birth by every cultural advantage, his precocious gifts bloomed early, and at age seventeen he wrote his first mature composition, the overture to *A Midsummer Night's Dream.* He was known as a conductor throughout Europe, and he helped to stimulate interest in the then little-known Johann Sebastian Bach. Felix Mendelssohn's two famous oratorios are *Elijah* and *St. Paul.* He is also remembered for his five symphonies, his violin concerto, and his many works for voice, piano, and organ.

Cast Thy Burden upon the Lord, 110 (Music)
O God, the Eternal Father, 175 (Music)
Hark! the Herald Angels Sing, 209 (Music)

Meredith, Joleen G.

LDS. American, born 1935 in American Fork, Utah. Her musical heritage extends back to her grandfather, William Grant, who was asked to settle in American Fork and take music to the people there. She has composed music since the age of eight. To her credit are many published compositions, including piano solos, choral works, and Primary songs. Her Church service has included membership on the YWMIA General Board. She has made her home in Salt Lake City for the past thirty years.

Where Can I Turn for Peace? 129 (Music)

Merrill, William Pierson

American, 1867–1954. Born in Orange, New Jersey, he was educated at Rutgers College and Union Theological Seminary and became a vigorous and innovative Presbyterian pastor. He served first in Philadelphia, then in Chicago, and then in New York. He published a number of theological works; the best remembered are those in which he preached peace through international Christian brotherhood. He received an honorary degree from Columbia University in 1927.

Rise Up, O Men of God, 323; 324 (Text)

Meyerbeer, Giacomo

German, 1791–1864. He is remembered as an operatic composer who was influenced greatly by Italian and French operatic tastes. He was highly popular in his own time. The operas best remembered today are *Robert le Diable, Les Huguenots,* and *Le Prophete.* Although German by birth, he was chiefly associated with the Paris Opera. (His name is pronounced approximately *JAH ko mo MY er ber.*)

Jesus, Once of Humble Birth, 196 (Music)

Milgrove, Benjamin

English, 1731–1810. He was music leader and organist of the Countess of Huntingdon's Chapel at Bath when he published *Sixteen Hymns* in about 1769.

Lord, We Ask Thee Ere We Part, 153 (Music)

Millard, Harrison

American, 1830–1895. Born in Boston, he joined the Boston Handel and Haydn Society and then pursued further vocal studies in Europe. He taught voice in New York. At the outbreak of the Civil War, he joined the Union forces and was wounded in the Battle of Chickamauga. He was a prolific composer, publishing over three hundred songs, a mass, and an opera.

Abide with Me; 'Tis Eventide, 165 (Music)

Miller, Roger L

LDS. American, born 1937. A native of Idaho Falls, Idaho, he showed early musical talent as a singer, pianist, and organist. He received his bachelor and master of arts degrees from Brigham Young University and his doctorate in musicology from Case Western Reserve University in Cleveland, Ohio. He served as a missionary in Hawaii. He has taught music in public schools, at BYU, and at CWRU. At the University of Chicago he pursued additional graduate study in near eastern languages and civilizations. Later he was an editor of the Scriptures Lexicon for the LDS Church Translation Division. He has been a member of the University of Utah music faculty, the Tabernacle Choir, and the General Music Committee of the Church.

Know This, That Every Soul Is Free, 240 (Music)

Mills, William Gill

LDS. Irish-born American, 1822–1895. A native of Ardglass Down, he came to Utah in 1855, after having received some education at King William's College, Isle of Man. An attorney by profession, he served as justice of the peace several times in Utah and was the second mayor of Gilroy, California. He wrote several hundred poems, including translations from

Latin and Greek, and published widely in periodicals. He was at one time married to Emily Hill (Woodmansee), author of "As Sisters in Zion" (no. 309). He later married Louisa Avelina Sleater.

Arise, O Glorious Zion, 40 (Text)

Mohr, Joseph

Austrian, 1792–1848, born in Salzburg. His mother was a seamstress and his father a soldier. Because of his gifts, a parish priest took an interest in him and saw to his education. He sang in the Salzburg Cathedral Choir and later attended Salzburg University. He was ordained a Catholic priest in 1815.

Silent Night, 204 (Text)

Mönch, Louis F.

LDS. German-born American, 1847–1916. The eleventh of sixteen children in an indigent family, he emigrated with his father to America at age ten. He worked as a tanner but was determined to gain an education. He took night classes in Chicago and eventually entered Bryant Stratton College. He departed by wagon to seek a teaching position in California, but he went no farther than Salt Lake City, Utah; the kindness of the woman who gave him shelter there after he lost goods and wagon in a fire so impressed him that eventually he became a Latter-day Saint. Encouraged by Lorenzo Snow and Franklin D. Richards, he became superintendent of Weber County Schools. After a mission in Germany, he became founder and principal of Weber Stake Academy.

Hark, All Ye Nations! 264 (Text)

Monk, William Henry

English, 1823–1889. Born in London, he was trained as an organist and a music scholar. He held many important organ posts in London. He is chiefly remembered as music editor of *Hymns Ancient and Modern,* a landmark volume in the history of English hymnody.

Abide with Me! 166 (Music)

Montgomery, James

English, 1771–1854. He was born in Ayrshire, Scotland, but lived in England from age six or seven. Through talent and perseverance, this orphan boy established himself as a successful newspaper publisher. Both his parents had been missionaries in the West Indies, and James Montgomery wrote and published many articles against the African slave trade, which was finally abolished in England in 1807. He became famous for his lecturing and poetry, and during the last twenty-one years of his life he received a government pension of two hundred pounds a year. He is the author of the well-known Christmas hymn text "Angels from the Realms of Glory."

A Poor Wayfaring Man of Grief, 29 (Text)
The Lord Is My Shepherd, 108; 316 (Text)
Prayer Is the Soul's Sincere Desire, 145 (Text)

Moody, Michael Finlinson

LDS. American, born 1941 in Payson, Utah. He grew up in Spanish Fork, Utah, and served a mission in France and Switzerland for The Church of Jesus Christ of Latter-day Saints from 1960 to 1963. He received his bachelor and master of arts degrees from Brigham Young University, and in 1972 he received a doctor of musical arts degree from the University of Southern California in Los Angeles. From 1972 to 1977 he was executive secretary of the Church Music Department, and since that time he has served as chairman of the General Music Committee of the Church. He was chairman of the 1985 Hymnbook Executive Committee. He and his wife, Maria Toronto, are parents of seven children and one foster daughter on the Indian Placement Program. He has served as bishop of the Woods Cross Third Ward in Bountiful, Utah.

Testimony, 137 (Music)

Moore, Thomas

Irish, 1779–1852. Born in Dublin, the son of a grocer, he was educated at Trinity College, Dublin. Hymn writing was one of the minor activities of his life, and the text in our hymnal is the only one of his texts in use today. A musician as well as a poet, he made a name for himself as a spokesman for Irish feeling with the publication of his *Irish Melodies.* He was also known for his political satire. The text of the popular ballad "Believe Me, If All Those Endearing Young Charms" is an example of the sentimental appeal of much of his work.

Come, Ye Disconsolate, 115 (Text)

Morton, Mary Ann

LDS. English-born American, 1826–1897. Little is known of her life except that she emigrated to the United States in 1856 and married George Mann.

Sweet Is the Peace the Gospel Brings, 14 (Text)

Murdock, Joseph Stacy

LDS. American, 1822–1899. A native of Massachusetts, he was one of the original Utah pioneers, arriving in 1847 with the Ira Eldridge company. He lived in Salt Lake City until 1856, when he was sent to Carson Valley, Nevada, to buy ranches for a colony of Latter-day Saints. In 1858 he settled in American Fork, Utah. There he was appointed the first bishop of Wasatch County, a position he held for seven years. In 1867 he went to Dixie, Utah, for three years, where he worked raising cotton. The last years of his life were spent in Heber, Utah.

Come, Listen to a Prophet's Voice, 21 (Text)

Murray, James R.

American, 1841–1905. Born in Massachusetts to recently arrived Scottish immigrant parents, he studied music under Lowell Mason, George F. Root, and William B. Bradbury. After the Civil War, during which he served as a Union soldier, he alternated between teaching music in the public schools and working for music publishing houses. He published several Sunday School hymnals during his lifetime.

Thanks for the Sabbath School, 278 (Music)

Nägeli, Hans Georg

Swiss, 1773–1836, born in Zurich. He established a music publishing firm in Switzerland that printed many important first editions. He was a progressive and forward-looking music educator and worked to incorporate the principles of the educational theorist J. H. Pestalozzi into the teaching of music. Many other musicians and composers acknowledged his influence, among them Lowell Mason in the United States.

How Gentle God's Commands, 125; 314 (Music)

Naisbitt, Henry W.

LDS. English-born American, 1826–1908. He grew up in Yorkshire and was reared in a strict Wesleyan (Methodist) home. His mother died when he was only nine. He was a diligent student of the Bible and an avid reader of the great authors of his native England, including Shakespeare, Gray, Milton, Burns, and Byron. In 1850 he was converted to Mormonism after hearing the preaching of Orson Pratt, and he emigrated to Utah in 1854. He returned to England twice to fulfill missions for the Church, serving during one of them as assistant editor of the *Millennial Star.*

This House We Dedicate to Thee, 245 (Text)

Neander, Joachim

German, 1650–1680. Born in Bremen, he led a carefree and light-minded student life until a sermon by a famous pastor caused him to search his soul and alter his life. He was a gifted writer of both texts and music, and his output of some sixty hymns is impressive, considering that he died of tuberculosis at age thirty. Neanderthal man, *Homo neanderthalensis,* is indirectly named after him, because the Neanderthal skeleton was discovered in a valley that had been named in his honor.

Praise to the Lord, the Almighty, 72 (Text)
He Is Risen! 199 (Music)

Neibaur, Alexander

LDS. Alsatian-born American, 1808–1883. Said to be the first Jewish convert to The Church of Jesus Christ of Latter-day Saints, he heard the elders preach in Preston, England, and was baptized in 1838. A scholar and linguist, he taught Greek and Hebrew to the Prophet Joseph Smith. After the Neibaur family arrived in Salt Lake City in 1848, Alexander

Neibaur practiced dentistry. His journal gives eyewitness accounts of many of the most important early events of the Church.

Come, Thou Glorious Day of Promise, 50 (Text contribution)

New Golden Chain, The

This hymnbook was published in New York by Biglow and Main in 1866. It was the first volume to include the tune MONTCLAIR, or MARCHING HOME, written by William Bradbury for the anonymous text "We Are All Enlisted" (no. 250).

We Are All Enlisted, 250 (Text)

Newell, Charlene A.

LDS. American, born 1938 in Price, Utah. She has had a lifelong interest in musical and dramatic performance. She is a graduate of College of Eastern Utah and Brigham Young University, where she studied voice, piano, organ, speech, and drama. She continued her training at BYU–Hawaii, at the New England Conservatory of Music, and through workshops of the Composers' Guild, of which she is a member. Her compositions have earned many awards, and she has published songs for both children and adults. She directs a community children's group, the Song Shoppe, and has held many Church callings. She has taught music in public schools, and she now works as a private music teacher. She and her husband, Robert Newell, have twelve children.

A Key Was Turned in Latter Days, 310 (Music)

Newman, John Henry

English, 1801–1890. Born in London, he received his bachelor of arts degree from Oxford and was ordained a clergyman of the Church of England three years later. He became one of the leaders of the Oxford Movement, also called the Tractarian or High Church Movement. A main goal of this movement was to restore the sacramental nature of the rites of the Church of England, but its detractors accused Newman and his colleagues of blurring the distinction between the Church of England and Roman Catholicism. After much soul-searching and introspection, Newman joined the Roman Catholic church in 1845 and was later made a cardinal. He is one of the great prose stylists of English literature.

Lead, Kindly Light, 97 (Text)

Newton, John

English, 1725–1807, born in London. An inscription at the church of St. Mary Woolnoth, London, was written by John Newton himself to describe the transformation that had come about in his life:

John Newton, Clerk
Once an infidel and libertine,
A servant of slaves in Africa,
Was, by the rich mercy of our Lord
And Saviour Jesus Christ,
Preserved, restored, pardoned,
And appointed to preach the Faith
He had long labored to destroy. . . .

He left the lowest possible type of life as a sailor and slave-trader to become an Anglican clergyman. He wrote the famous hymn text "Amazing Grace" and was a friend and collaborator of William Cowper.

Glorious Things of Thee Are Spoken, 46 (Text)

Nibley, Reid N.

LDS. American, born 1923 in Santa Monica, California. He grew up in southern California and began music study at the age of eight. He received his doctor of musical arts degree from the University of Michigan and was professor of music there for four years. A well-known pianist, he has given concerts throughout the United States, Canada, Europe, Japan, and New Zealand. He was professor of music and artist-in-residence at Brigham Young University for sixteen years before his retirement in 1985. He has published numerous compositions, arrangements, and piano method books. He is married to Marjorie McBride, and they are the parents of six children.

I Know My Father Lives, 302 (Text and music)

Nicholson, James

Irish-born American, 1828–1876. He emigrated to the United States in the early 1850s and lived in Philadelphia for twenty years. He later worked as a post office clerk in Washington, D.C. In his spare time he was active in Sunday School teaching and other religious work.

The Lord Is My Light, 89 (Text)

Nicholson, John

LDS. Scottish-born American, 1839–1909. Born in Roxburgshire to a working-class family, he had little formal schooling. In 1861, after reading a tract given to him by Orson Pratt, he joined The Church of Jesus Christ of Latter-day Saints, serving for the next five years as a local missionary. He emigrated to America in 1866 and worked as a painter and paperhanger after his arrival in Utah. He returned to England on a mission in 1878 and became editor of the *Millennial Star,* and then was employed at the *Deseret News* after he returned to Utah. He was well known for his persuasive articles and fearless oratory.

Come, Follow Me, 116 (Text)
While of These Emblems We Partake, 173; 174 (Text)

Norton, Caroline Sheridan

English, 1808–1877. The granddaughter of the well-known playwright Richard Brinsley Sheridan, she was an important figure in the London social scene of her time and much admired for her beauty and her conversational gifts. An unfortunate marriage brought social and financial problems, and through her writings she spoke out for reform of divorce and child custody laws. Though her contribution to our hymnal is as a composer, she devoted virtually all of her artistic energies to the writing of poetry in the romantic style of Lord Byron.

We Thank Thee, O God, for a Prophet, 19 (Music)

Oakeley, Frederick

English, 1802–1880. Born in Worcestershire, he graduated from Oxford and was ordained a minister of the Church of England. He became a supporter of the Oxford Movement, a group that wished to emphasize the sacramental and formalistic aspects of the Church of England and restore some of the elements of Roman Catholic ritual. Eventually he, like John Henry Newman, converted to Catholicism and became a Catholic priest.

Oh, Come, All Ye Faithful, 202 (Translation)

Oatman, Johnson, Jr.

American, 1856–1922. He was a Methodist Episcopal minister who worked most of his life in New Jersey. His religious poems were immensely popular in revival meetings and songbooks, and during his lifetime he wrote more than five thousand of them.

Count Your Blessings, 241 (Text)

Olson, Ernst William

Swedish-born American, 1870–1958. A native of Finja parish, he emigrated to the United States with his family when he was five years old. They settled first in Nebraska and then moved to Texas. In 1891 he graduated from Augustana College in Illinois and thereafter worked as an editor for Swedish-language publications. He was a bilingual man of letters, noted not only for his contributions as an editor but as a writer and poet as well. In 1926 he received an honorary doctorate from Augustana College. He wrote a history of the Swedish settlers in Illinois and served as editor for various Lutheran hymnals. His translation of "Children of Our Heavenly Father" (no. 299 in our hymnbook) was first published in a Lutheran hymnbook in 1925.

Children of Our Heavenly Father, 299 (Translation)

Onderdonk, Henry Ustic

American, 1789–1858. He obtained his bachelor of arts, master of arts, and doctor of divinity degrees from Columbia College and then traveled to London and Edinburgh, where his studies earned him a medical degree as well. He was ordained rector of St. Ann's Church of Brooklyn, and he also served as coeditor of a hymn collection.

How Wondrous and Great, 267 (Text)

Page, Mary Judd

LDS. Canadian-born American, 1818–1907. She was the wife of John E. Page, who was called in 1838 as a General Authority of the Church.

Ye Who Are Called to Labor, 321 (Text)

Palmer, Horatio Richmond

American, 1834–1907. A native of New York, he showed early musical talent and traveled to Italy and Germany for music study. He returned to establish himself as a teacher, editor, conductor, author, and composer. For many years he conducted the New York City Choral Union, a choir of more than four thousand voices. A Baptist minister, he was founding editor of *Concordia Magazine*, published in Chicago.

Precious Savior, Dear Redeemer, 103 (Text and music)
Master, the Tempest Is Raging, 105 (Music)

Parker, Edwin Pond

American, 1836–1925. Born in Castine, Maine, he was educated at Bowdoin College and Bangor Theological Seminary. He served as pastor of the Central Congregational Church in Hartford, Connecticut, for fifty years. A capable musician, he composed and arranged many hymn tunes in the course of compiling several hymnals.

God, Our Father, Hear Us Pray, 170 (Musical adaptation)

Parker, Horatio William

American, 1863–1919. Born in Auburndale, Massachusetts, he showed early musical talent, and after study in Munich became an organist and choirmaster in Boston and New York City. In 1894 he became the first chairman of the music department at Yale, a position he held until his death. As well as writing hymns, he composed music for organ, choir, and orchestra. He is remembered as an important composer in the history of American music.

Rejoice, the Lord Is King! 66 (Music)

Parry, Edwin F.

LDS. American, 1850–1935. A native of Salt Lake City, Utah, he was the son of John Parry, first leader of the Mormon Tabernacle Choir. His father died when Edwin Parry was only eight years old. In 1896 he was called to England as a missionary, where he served as assistant editor of the *Millennial Star.*

Hail to the Brightness of Zion's Glad Morning, 42 (Music)
Oh, Holy Words of Truth and Love, 271 (Music)

Parry, Joseph

Welsh, 1841–1903. Born in Merthyr Tydfil, he came at age thirteen with his immigrant parents to settle in Pennsylvania, where he continued to work in an iron foundry as he had done in Wales since age ten. His musical talents so impressed his fellow iron-workers that they raised funds to send him to New York to study music. He continued his studies at the Royal Academy of Music in London, with funds coming mainly from Welsh musicians who had heard him perform in competitions in Wales. He conducted a private music school in Danville, Pennsylvania, for two years, but chose to return to Wales. He became professor of music at Welsh University College at Aberystwyth, Wales, and later taught at the University College in Cardiff.

O Home Beloved, 337 (Music)

Partridge, Edward

LDS. American, 1793–1840. A native of Massachusetts, he learned the trade of hatter. He was first a Unitarian and then a Campbellite but became converted to The Church of Jesus Christ of Latter-day Saints in Painesville, Ohio. He was baptized by the Prophet Joseph Smith, who described him as "a pattern of piety, and one of the Lord's great men known by his steadfastness and patient endurance to the end." ("History of Joseph Smith," *Times and Seasons,* 15 Sep. 1843, p. 320.) In 1831 he was made the first Presiding Bishop of the Church, and he held this position until his death in Nauvoo, Illinois. His name appears in many places in the Doctrine and Covenants. (See, for example, D&C 41:9–11.)

Let Zion in Her Beauty Rise, 41 (Text)

Penrose, Charles William

LDS. English-born American, 1832–1925. Born in London, he was baptized a Latter-day Saint at age eighteen and spent seven years in missionary work in England. In 1861 he emigrated with his wife and family to America, settling in Farmington, Utah, then moving to Ogden after he returned from a second period of missionary work in England. He is noted for his work as assistant Church historian, as editor of the *Deseret News,* as a writer of missionary tracts, as a member of the Quorum of the Twelve (1904), and as a Counselor in the First Presidency to President Joseph F. Smith and President Heber J. Grant.

O Ye Mountains High, 34 (Text)
God of Our Fathers, We Come unto Thee, 76 (Text)
Up Awake, Ye Defenders of Zion, 248 (Text)
School Thy Feelings, 336 (Text)

Perkins, William Oscar

American, 1831–1902. Born in Vermont, he pursued his music studies in Boston and later in London and Milan. He made his home in Boston and is remembered as both a teacher and a composer, having published forty collections of songs and anthems. He received a doctor of music degree from Hamilton College in 1879.

Did You Think to Pray? 140 (Music)

Perry, Janice Kapp

LDS. American, born 1938 in Ogden, Utah. She spent her childhood in Oregon and then received her musical training at Brigham Young University. She has held positions in all the Church auxiliaries and has been an active sportswoman. Her list of musical publications includes twelve albums and songbooks, four cantatas, two full-length musicals, and many special presentations for general meetings of the Primary, Young Women, and Relief Society. She and her husband, Douglas C. Perry, are the parents of five children and several foster children. They live in Provo, Utah.

As Sisters in Zion, 309 (Music)

Perry, Lee Tom

LDS. American, born 1951 in Logan, Utah. After serving in the Japan West Mission, he earned a bachelor of science degree in university studies and a master of organizational behavior degree from Brigham Young University. He then continued his studies at Yale University, where he received a doctorate in organizational behavior. He has taught at the Krannert School of Management, Purdue University, and Pennsylvania State University. A member of the faculty of the graduate school of management at BYU, he has written many articles for professional journals. He and his wife, Carolyn Bench, have four children.

As Now We Take the Sacrament, 169 (Text)

Petersen, Hans Henry

LDS. Danish-born American, 1835–1909, born in Slagelse. When he was seventeen years old, he and his parents were baptized into The Church of Jesus Christ of Latter-day Saints. He labored as a missionary in Denmark; it was during this time, as he presided over the Saints in the Copenhagen district, that he began to recognize his musical talents. He organized a choir and took singing lessons. In 1862, he emigrated to America with his parents, five brothers and sisters, and fiancée. After settling in Salt Lake City, he organized a Scandinavian choir and also served in many church and civic positions. He earned his living as a mason and plasterer.

I'm a Pilgrim, I'm a Stranger, 121 (Text)
Secret Prayer, 144 (Text and music)

Pettit, Mildred T.

LDS. American, 1895–1977. Born in Salt Lake City, Utah, she lived in California and Michigan as a child and then attended high school and the Latter-day Saints College in Salt Lake City. After teaching school for several years in Salt Lake City, she married William A. Pettit, who had just completed medical school. She was called to the Primary General Board, where she collaborated with Matilda Watts Cahoon on many programs and songs for the young people of the Church. The family moved to Philadelphia in 1934, where musical studies at the Zeckwer-Hahn Institute rounded out the private musical training she had received from Alexander Schreiner, Frank W. Asper, and others. In 1935 Mildred Pettit and her family moved to southern California, where she spent the remainder of her life.

I Am a Child of God, 301 (Music)
The Light Divine, 305 (Music)

Phelps, William Wines

LDS. American, 1792–1872, born in Hanover, New Jersey. The revelation instructing him to be baptized and to become involved in the publication work of the Church can be read in section 55 of the Doctrine and Covenants. Among his numerous activities important in early Church history, he served as a scribe to the Prophet Joseph Smith and was an editor of the first Latter-day Saint hymnal. Though excommunicated for a two-year period, he was reinstated as a member and crossed the plains to Salt Lake City in 1848. He was one of the first regents of the University of Deseret and a member of the Utah legislature.

The Spirit of God, 2 (Text)
Now Let Us Rejoice, 3 (Text)
Redeemer of Israel, 6 (Text adaptation)
Now We'll Sing with One Accord, 25 (Text)
Praise to the Man, 27 (Text)
Come, All Ye Saints of Zion, 38 (Text)
Glorious Things Are Sung of Zion, 48 (Text)
Adam-ondi-Ahman, 49 (Text)
We're Not Ashamed to Own Our Lord, 57 (Text)
Come, All Ye Saints Who Dwell on Earth, 65 (Text)
Gently Raise the Sacred Strain, 146 (Text)
Come, Let Us Sing an Evening Hymn, 167 (Text)
O God, the Eternal Father, 175 (Text)
Joy to the World, 201 (Text alteration)
If You Could Hie to Kolob, 284 (Text)

Pierpoint, Folliott S.

English, 1835–1917, born in Bath. A graduate of Cambridge University, he had the advantage of a private income that allowed him to study, teach, and write as he wished. He served as headmaster of Somersetshire College for a period of time and occasionally taught classical languages and literature.

For the Beauty of the Earth, 92 (Text)

Pinborough, Jan Underwood

LDS. American, born 1954 in Midland, Texas. She received a bachelor's degree in English and a master's degree in linguistics from Brigham Young University. She became an editor in the Curriculum Department of the Church in 1979, an assistant editor of the *Ensign* in 1983, and an associate editor of the Church's international magazines in 1986. She has published a number of articles in the *Ensign* and in international Latter-day Saint periodicals. She has served as a text specialist for the General Music Committee of the Church. She has also served on Church writing committees responsible for the *Family Home Evening Resource Book* and for Relief Society Cultural Refinement lessons. She and her husband, Thomas Vince Pinborough, have one daughter.

A Key Was Turned in Latter Days, 310 (Text)

Pollard, Josephine

1834–1892. No other information is available concerning Josephine Pollard.

I Have Work Enough to Do, 224 (Text)

Pond, Sylvanus Billings

American, 1792–1871. Born in Milford, Vermont, he became a well-known composer of Sunday School songs. He was also affiliated with the publishing house of Firth, Pond, and Company that published the compositions of Stephen Foster. He was active as a conductor of sacred music in New York, and he edited and published several hymnals.

Joseph Smith's First Prayer, 26 (Music)

Pratt, Parley Parker

LDS. American, 1807–1857, born in Oswego County, New York. Originally a member of the Baptist church, he heard of the Book of Mormon and was led to investigate the Latter-day Saints. He was baptized by Oliver Cowdery and ordained a high priest by Joseph Smith. He served as a missionary numerous times, both in the United States and in England, and his dedication and skill as a preacher were attested to by many. His loyalty to the Church led to imprisonment and finally to martyrdom. He was the first editor of the *Millennial Star,* and he wrote *Voice of Warning* and *Key to the Science of Theology*. His autobiography is among the most important in LDS Church history.

The Morning Breaks, 1 (Text)
Truth Eternal, 4 (Text)
An Angel from on High, 13; 328 (Text)
Come, O Thou King of Kings, 59; 332 (Text)
Father in Heaven, We Do Believe, 180 (Text)
Jesus, Once of Humble Birth, 196 (Text)
Behold Thy Sons and Daughters, Lord, 238 (Text)

Prichard, Rowland Hugh

Welsh, 1811–1887, born near Bala, North Wales. A mill worker, he inherited from his father and grandfather the tradition of the "Welsh bard" and was widely known for his fine voice. He published many fine hymn tunes in his lifetime.

In Humility, Our Savior, 172 (Music)

Psalms of Life, The

This hymnbook, published in Boston, Massachusetts, in 1857, is the earliest known source of the text for "Do What Is Right." It does not give the author's name.

Do What Is Right, 237 (Text)

Pure Diamonds

This hymnbook, published in Cleveland, Ohio, in 1872, is the earliest known source for the text of "We Are Sowing." It does not give the author's name.

We Are Sowing, 216 (Text)

Pyper, George D.

LDS. American, 1860–1943, born in Salt Lake City, Utah. In his capacity as manager of the Salt Lake Theater, 1904–1929, he brought many notable productions to Salt Lake City, as he wrote in *The Romance of an Old Playhouse.* He also wrote *Stories of Latter-day Saint Hymns,* and for twenty-seven years he was associate editor of the *Juvenile Instructor.* He was one of the editors of *Deseret Sunday School Songs* (1909). He served as tour manager for the Mormon Tabernacle Choir and as organizer for many Salt Lake City exhibits and entertainments. In 1918 he was chosen to assist David O. McKay in the General Sunday School superintendency and was called as superintendent in 1934. He played a notable role in civic activities as a member of the first Salt Lake board of education and of the first library board.

Does the Journey Seem Long? 127 (Music)

Raile, Vilate Schofield

LDS. American, 1890–1954. Born in Salt Lake City, Utah, she received her education at Brigham Young University, the University of Utah, Utah State University, and Mills College in Oakland, California. She published many poems; her poem "Pioneers" is a part of the "This Is the Place" monument at the mouth of Emigration Canyon. She was a member of the Primary General Board and helped found the Primary Children's Hospital.

Upon the Cross of Calvary, 184 (Text)

Randall, Naomi W.

LDS. American, born 1908 in North Ogden, Utah. For nearly twenty-eight years she was a member of the Primary General Board and was also first counselor in the General Presidency of the Primary. A lifelong resident of North Ogden, Utah, she has shared her creative talents and love of the cultural arts through church and civic activities. She was a member of the editorial board of the *Children's Friend* and has written children's books and lesson manuals. She is in frequent demand as a speaker for church meetings and conferences. She and her husband, Earl A. Randall, have one daughter.

When Faith Endures, 128 (Text)
I Am a Child of God, 301 (Text)

Rankin, Jeremiah Eames

American, 1828–1904. Born in Thornton, New Hampshire, he was a Congregationalist minister who probably derived the fervor and vigor of his preaching from his Scottish ancestors. He held several different posts as pastor until 1889, when he became president of Howard University, Washington, D.C. He edited a number of volumes of gospel-song hymns.

God Be with You Till We Meet Again, 152 (Text)

Redner, Lewis Henry

American, 1831–1908, born in Philadelphia, Pennsylvania. While serving as organist to a large Episcopal church, he was able to accumulate considerable wealth as a real estate investor. He devoted much of his life to upgrading the music and teaching of the Episcopal Sunday School in Philadelphia and also gave considerable financial support to his church.

O Little Town of Bethlehem, 208 (Music)

Reske, Willy

LDS. German-born American, born 1897 in Königsberg. One of nine children born to a religious family, he was eight years old when his father died. He was baptized a Latter-day Saint in 1922 and emigrated to the United States in 1926. He pursued a career of musical performance and composition, serving for thirty-three years as organist of St. Paul's Evangelical Lutheran Church in New York City. He has composed hundreds of hymns, anthems, and organ pieces. He is married to Martha Louise Wiemer, and they live in New York.

Thy Servants Are Prepared, 261; 329 (Music)
God's Daily Care, 306 (Music)

Richards, G. William

LDS. American, born 1918 in Salt Lake City, Utah. He attended the McCune School of Music, Brigham Young University, the University of California at Berkeley, Columbia University, and Union Theological Seminary School of Sacred Music at Columbia University in New York City. He studied organ, hymnology, conducting, and musicology under many of the country's most eminent teachers. As a missionary, he played recitals in Washington, D.C., and was organist for two years at the Little Tabernacle in the San Francisco World's Fair. He taught music at New York University and was church organist for four years at Carnegie Hall and at the United Nations Chapel. He was a member of the 1985 Hymnbook Executive Committee and also served on the executive committee of the Hymn Society for America for twenty-two years. He and his wife, Claire Dyreng of Manti, Utah, are the parents of four children.

'Twas Witnessed in the Morning Sky, 12 (Text adaptation; music alteration)
From Homes of Saints Glad Songs Arise, 297 (Music)

Rinkhart, Martin

German, 1586–1649. Born in Eilenburg, Saxony, he was a choirboy at St. Thomas Church in Leipzig, where Johann Sebastian Bach was later music director. As archdeacon of Eilenburg during the Thirty Years' War, he was left as the sole clergyman of the crowded city after other clergymen had fled or died. His was the grim task of burying the victims of famine and pestilence, and he sometimes had to read forty or fifty funeral services a day. In addition to hymns, he wrote dramas in commemoration of Martin Luther.

Now Thank We All Our God, 95 (Text)

Roberts, Daniel Crane

American, 1841–1907. Born in Long Island, New York, he was a graduate of Kenyon College. After serving as a Union soldier in the Civil War, he became an Episcopal rector, serving in several different New England states. For many years he was president of the New Hampshire State Historical Society. In 1885 he was honored by Norwich College with the degree of doctor of divinity.

God of Our Fathers, Whose Almighty Hand, 78 (Text)

Robertson, Leroy J.

LDS. American, 1896–1971. Born in Fountain Green, Utah, he became one of the prominent American composers of the twentieth century. The prestigious prizes he won included the Reichhold Award for his *Trilogy* (Symphony No. 2). His numerous works, written in virtually every musical form, have been performed by major artists, including the Utah Symphony, Philadelphia Orchestra, Berlin Philharmonic, and Tabernacle Choir. Though largely self-taught, he studied with George W. Chadwick, Ernest Bloch, and Arnold Shoenberg. His academic degrees culminated in a doctorate from the University of Southern California in 1954. He headed the music departments of the University of Utah and of Brigham Young University. For thirty-six years he was a member of the General Music

Committee of the Church. His best-known composition is probably *Oratorio from the Book of Mormon.*

Let Earth's Inhabitants Rejoice, 53 (Music)
Great King of Heaven, 63 (Music)
On This Day of Joy and Gladness, 64 (Text and music)
God of Our Fathers, Known of Old, 80 (Music)
I'm a Pilgrim, I'm a Stranger, 121 (Music)
Upon the Cross of Calvary, 184 (Music)
We Love Thy House, O God, 247 (Music)
Go, Ye Messengers of Glory, 262 (Music)

Robinson, William O.

LDS. American, 1876–1979. Born in Farmington, Utah, he attended Latter-day Saints College in Salt Lake City, Utah, and also received an honorary degree from Brigham Young College in Logan, Utah. After a mission in Colorado, he studied music under Evan Stephens, John J. McClellan, and others. He also attended the American Conservatory of Music in Chicago. He was chairman of the department of music at Brigham Young College and later was head of music, speech, and drama. He served with the MIA General Board and was known for his work as organizer of many festival celebrations and musical and dramatic productions in Salt Lake City.

Rejoice! A Glorious Sound Is Heard, 257 (Text)

Root, George F.

American, 1820–1895. A native of Massachusetts, he became one of America's best-known composers of popular music, including hymns, ballads, and sentimental songs. He is most famous for his Civil War songs, such as "Tramp, Tramp, Tramp," "Just Before the Battle, Mother," and "The Battle Cry of Freedom." He taught at music schools in New York and Boston, including the Union Theological Seminary.

Hark, All Ye Nations! 264 (Music)
In Our Lovely Deseret, 307 (Music)
School Thy Feelings, 336 (Music)

Rounsefell, Carrie E.

American, 1861–1930. No other information is available concerning Carrie E. Rounsefell.

I'll Go Where You Want Me to Go, 270 (Music)

Rousseau, Jean Jacques

Swiss-French, 1712–1778, born in Geneva. A philosopher and political theorist (and only secondarily a musician), he taught that man in his natural state was unspoiled and happy and that society and its influences were the source of evil. He also believed that the head of state served at the will of the people and was bound to obey their wishes. The controversy aroused by his views aggravated an already erratic life; Jean Jacques Rousseau tended to be deeply suspicious and quarrelsome. Though many patrons took an interest in this brilliant thinker, he often offended them and was forced to support himself through menial jobs. His masterpiece, the *Confessions,* was published after his death.

Lord, Dismiss Us with Thy Blessing, 163 (Music)

Rowe, Ed M.

LDS. American, 1878–1951. Born in Spanish Fork, Utah, he attended Brigham Young Academy and Brigham Young University and became an English instructor at BYU after his graduation. He did graduate work at BYU, the University of Utah, Utah State Agricultural College, the University of Chicago, the University of Wales, and Cornell University. He taught at BYU until his retirement in 1949. He was an authority on the poetry of William Wordsworth and was responsible for the Ed M. Rowe Wordsworth Collection at the BYU library.

O Saints of Zion, 39 (Text)

Rowley, Grietje Terburg

LDS. American, born 1927 in Florida. Grietje (pronounced *GREE chuh*) Terburg Rowley attended the Oberlin Conservatory of Music and received a bachelor of music education degree from the University of Miami in Florida. She joined the Church while teaching school in Hawaii. She then moved to Salt Lake City, Utah. She has played the piano in various Church music callings for over thirty years. Her extensive list of publications includes children's songs, prize-winning Relief Society songs, and piano preludes. She is a member of the Composers' Guild, the Association of Latter-day Media Artists, and National League of American Pen Women.

Be Thou Humble, 130 (Text and music)

Russell, Henry H.

English, 1812–1900. Though his life began and ended in England, he spent many years in the United States, where he made his living as a concert singer. For a time he also served as organist at the First Presbyterian Church in Rochester, New York. He wrote many of the popular songs of his day, including "Woodman Spare That Tree" and "A Life on the Ocean Wave."

Who's on the Lord's Side? 260 (Music)

Sabin, Zara

LDS. American, 1892–1980. Born in Bellwood, Nebraska, she served as a Latter-day Saint missionary in Great Britain and was also a researcher for the Utah Genealogical Society for fifteen years. Her poetry appeared in the *Relief Society Magazine,* the *Improvement Era,* the *Children's Friend,* the *Instructor,* and other Church publications, and her book *So Near My Heart* was published in 1960. She was well known for her writing and was a member of the League of Utah Writers. She was also affiliated with the Daughters of the Utah Pioneers and the Daughters of the American Revolution.

With Humble Heart, 171 (Text)

Sandell-Berg, Caroline V.

Swedish, 1832–1903, born in Smaland. Daughter of a Lutheran pastor, she began to write poetry while still in her teens. As a young woman, she worked as an editor in a Lutheran publishing house. She left a legacy of more than 650 poems.

Children of Our Heavenly Father, 299 (Text)

Sateren, Leland Bernhard

American, born 1913 in Everett, Washington. He received his bachelor of arts degree from Augsburg College in Minneapolis, Minnesota, and his master of arts from the University of Minnesota in 1943. Since 1950 he has been professor of music and director of the Augsburg Choir at Augsburg College, and for twenty-three years he served as chairman of the music department. He is in frequent demand as an adjudicator of festivals and competitions and as a choral workshop leader; he has conducted workshops in Norway and Sweden as well as throughout the United States. He has received honorary doctorates from Gettysburg College in Pennsylvania and Lakeland College in Wisconsin, and King Olav of Norway bestowed the St. Olaf medal upon him in 1971.

Behold, the Mountain of the Lord, 54 (Music)

Schlegel, Katharina Amalia Dorothea von

German, 1697–? It has been conjectured that she was one of the women attached to the ducal court at Cothen, her place of residence, but the details of her life are uncertain.

Be Still, My Soul, 124 (Text)

Schreiner, Alexander

LDS. German-born American, 1901–1987, born in Nurnberg. His family, as converts to Mormonism, left Germany for Salt Lake City, Utah, in 1912. After serving a mission in California, he returned to Europe to study with Louis Vierne and other celebrated organists. He earned bachelor of arts and doctoral degrees from the University of Utah, studying under Leroy

Robertson. In 1924 he was called as Tabernacle organist; he filled this position with distinction until retirement in 1977. He became widely known for articles, compositions, arrangements, recordings, radio performances, and concert tours. He received honorary doctorates from the University of Utah, Brigham Young University, Utah State University, and Westminster College.

Truth Eternal, 4 (Music)
Lead Me into Life Eternal, 45 (Music)
Thy Spirit, Lord, Has Stirred Our Souls, 157 (Music)
While of These Emblems We Partake, 174 (Music)
God Loved Us, So He Sent His Son, 187 (Music)
In Memory of the Crucified, 190 (Music)
Lord, Accept into Thy Kingdom, 236 (Music)
Behold Thy Sons and Daughters, Lord, 238 (Music)
Holy Temples on Mount Zion, 289 (Music)

Schubring, Julius

German, 1806–1889. Born in Dessau, he was a pastor, theologian, philologist, and tutor. He served as rector of St. George's Church in Dessau.

Cast Thy Burden upon the Lord, 110 (Text)

Schütz, Johann Jakob

German, 1640–1690. He practiced law in Frankfurt am Main, the city of his birth, for his entire adult life, and he also published two volumes of religious verse. Though he did not emigrate to the New World, he held a financial interest in the company that purchased a tract of land in Germantown, Pennsylvania, from William Penn in 1683.

Sing Praise to Him, 70 (Text)

Sears, Edmund Hamilton

American, 1810–1876. Born in Sandersfield, Massachusetts, he graduated from Harvard Divinity School and served as a Unitarian minister in several congregations in the Boston area. He published widely on religious subjects and for twelve years was editor of a religious magazine.

It Came upon the Midnight Clear, 207 (Text)

Shaw, Martin Fallas

English, 1875–1958, born in London. Determined from childhood to become a composer, he studied at the Royal College of Music in London and held several important posts as organist and music director. He composed a great deal of church music and is also noted for his work as an editor (he helped edit *The Oxford Book of Carols*) and for his collections of English folk songs. He and his brother Geoffrey were friends and collaborators of Ralph Vaughan Williams, and the three together did much to revive interest in English folk music.

Let the Holy Spirit Guide, 143 (Music)

Shipp, Ellis Reynolds

LDS. American, 1847–1939. Born in Davis County, Iowa, she arrived in the Salt Lake Valley at age five. At eighteen, at the request of Brigham Young, she went to live in the Beehive House and was there educated by Karl G. Maeser. She married Milford Shipp and bore five children, two of whom died; and four polygamous wives joined the household. In 1875 she moved to Philadelphia to attend medical school, graduating with honors despite poor health, scanty finances, and the birth of another child. Returning to Salt Lake City, she practiced medicine and taught nursing for sixty years. She helped found Deseret Hospital, served on the Relief Society General Board, bore four more children, and delivered six thousand babies.

Father, Cheer Our Souls Tonight, 231 (Text)

Shurtleff, Lynn Richard

LDS. American, born 1939 in Vallejo, California. He received his bachelor and master of arts degrees from Brigham Young University, with additional study at Indiana University and in Vienna, Austria. After serving as a missionary in Uruguay, he joined the music faculty of Santa Clara University in California, where he is currently chairman of the music department. His activities as conductor and composer have taken him on nine concert tours of foreign countries. He has received the Ferdinand Grossman Fellowship for study in Europe, the Thomas Terry Grant for composition, and the Santa Clara University Distinguished Faculty Award. He has served as bishop and high councilor. He and his wife Alma Don McArthur have five children.

Father, This Hour Has Been One of Joy, 154 (Music)

Sibelius, Jean

Finnish, 1865–1957, born in Hameenlinna. Though his music does not actually use Finnish folk melodies, it reflects profound feelings of Finnish nationalism and a love of the northern landscapes. Jean (also known as Jan) Sibelius wrote many vocal and chamber music works but is best known for his sweeping orchestral tone poems, including *Finlandia,* and his seven symphonies. In 1897 Finland awarded him a lifetime grant so that he could continue his creative work without financial worry.

Be Still, My Soul, 124 (Music)

Sloan, Edward Lennox

LDS. Irish-born American, 1830–1874. Born into moderate circumstances, he received formal schooling only until age twelve, but he obtained a wide education through extensive reading and memorization. He was the only member of his family to be baptized a Latter-day Saint, and by age eighteen he had been ordained an elder and was pursuing missionary work, first in Ireland and later in England, Scotland, and Wales. His poetry and other writings brought him to the notice of George Q. Cannon, who appointed him assistant editor of the *Millennial Star.* He emigrated in 1863 and became assistant editor of the *Deseret News* and then editor of the *Telegraph.* In 1870 he founded the *Salt Lake Herald.*

For the Strength of the Hills, 35 (Text adaptation)

Smith, John Stafford

English, 1750–1836. He was composer for Covent Garden Theater and conductor of the Academy of Ancient Music.

The Star-Spangled Banner, 340 (Music)

Smith, Joseph Fielding

LDS. American, 1876–1972. He was named after his father, the sixth President of the Church. Blessed with a family heritage of missionary work, Church leadership, and scriptural scholarship, he led a life of industry and dedication in many areas. After serving as a missionary in England, he was ordained a member of the Quorum of the Twelve in 1910 and later became Church historian, publishing *Essentials in Church History* in 1922. He directed the evacuation of all Latter-day Saint missionaries from Europe before World War II. He became President of the Quorum of the Twelve in 1951 and a Counselor in the First Presidency in 1965. He was sustained as tenth President of The Church of Jesus Christ of Latter-day Saints in 1970.

Does the Journey Seem Long? 127 (Text)

Smith, Lanta Wilson

No information is available concerning Lanta Wilson Smith.

Scatter Sunshine, 230 (Text)

Smith, Samuel Francis

American, 1808–1895. Born in Newton Centre, Massachusetts, he graduated from Harvard. He also studied at Andover Theological Seminary and became a Baptist pastor. His interest in missionary work was lifelong: he edited the *Baptist Missionary Magazine,* served as secretary of the Baptist Missionary Union, and toured the mission fields of Asia and Europe. He is also remembered as an editor of *The Psalmist,* an important Baptist hymnal. He was a friend and associate of Lowell Mason.

My Country, 'Tis of Thee, 339 (Text)

Smyth, Adam Craik

LDS. English-born American, 1840–1909. Born in Lancashire, he emigrated to Utah in 1864, though not originally with the motive of associating himself with the Saints. He was taught and baptized after his arrival. He worked as a schoolteacher and music teacher in Salt Lake City and then moved to Manti, where he directed the local choir and became a recorder in the Manti Temple. He organized and produced musical productions in the Salt Lake Theater and was especially fond of the operettas of Gilbert and Sullivan.

Joseph Smith's First Prayer, 26 (Musical adaptation)
Zion Stands with Hills Surrounded, 43 (Music)
Come, Thou Glorious Day of Promise, 50 (Music)
Come Along, Come Along, 244 (Music)

Smyth, Richard

LDS. Irish-born American, 1838–1914. Born in Dublin, a hatter by trade, he joined The Church of Jesus Christ of Latter-day Saints and served as a missionary in the Liverpool area before emigrating to America in 1863. He later served two missions to his native Ireland. His poems and other writings were published in the *Millennial Star* and the *Juvenile Instructor.*

Israel, Israel, God Is Calling, 7 (Text)

Snow, Bernard

LDS. American, 1822–1894. Little is known of his life. He traveled from Vermont to Salt Lake City, Utah, settled there for a while, and later lived in other communities in Utah and Idaho.

God Bless Our Prophet Dear, 24 (Text)

Snow, Eliza Roxcy

LDS. American, 1804–1887. At age twenty-one she had already received recognition as a poet: she had won a prize for a poem on the deaths of Adams and Jefferson. She was baptized a Latter-day Saint in 1835 and helped convert her brother, Lorenzo Snow, who became the fifth President of the Church. She taught school in Kirtland and Nauvoo. She was a key administrative figure in the early history of the Church: she was the first secretary and second General President of the Relief Society, and she also helped organize the Mutual Improvement Association and the Primary. She was the first president of the board of directors of Deseret Hospital.

Awake, Ye Saints of God, Awake! 17 (Text)
Great Is the Lord, 77 (Text)
Though Deepening Trials, 122 (Text)
Again We Meet Around the Board, 186 (Text)
Behold the Great Redeemer Die, 191 (Text)
How Great the Wisdom and the Love, 195 (Text)
The Time Is Far Spent, 266 (Text)
Truth Reflects upon Our Senses, 273 (Text)
O My Father, 292 (Text)
In Our Lovely Deseret, 307 (Text)

Southern Harmony

William Walker (1809–1875) was the son of Welsh parents who had immigrated to America. He became famous as "Singin' Billy" Walker, known throughout the Southern United States for his performances of folk songs and religious music. He collected Southern Appalachian folk hymns and tunes and published a selection of them in *The Southern Harmony and Musical Companion* (usually known as *Southern Harmony*) in Philadelphia in 1835. The collection was immensely popular in the southern United States and went through four editions. It included the tune PROSPECT OF HEAVEN (no. 49).

Adam-ondi-Ahman, 49 (Music)

Steele, Anne

English, 1716–1778. Born in Hampshire, she was the daughter of a lay Baptist minister. She suffered a hip injury as a child and never fully recovered from this accident. A second tragedy was the drowning of her fiancé only a few hours before the wedding ceremony was to have taken place; she remained unmarried for the rest of her life. She wrote 144 hymns and is considered the first woman to hold a significant place in the history of English hymn-text writing.

Great God, to Thee My Evening Song, 164 (Text)

Stephens, Evan

LDS. Welsh-born American, 1854–1930. Born in Pencader, he emigrated at age twelve with his parents to Salt Lake City, Utah, and they settled in the town of Willard. His ambition and musical talent carried him from an obscure boyhood to a place of honor in the history of Latter-day Saint music as conductor, author, and composer. George D. Pyper quoted President Wilford Woodruff on the occasion of the Tabernacle Choir's winning second place, under Evan Stephens' direction, at the Chicago World's Fair in 1893: "A shepherd boy came down from the mountains and is here today to contest in this great competition." (*Stories of Latter-day Saint Hymns,* p. 63.)

What Was Witnessed in the Heavens? 11 (Music)
Awake, Ye Saints of God, Awake! 17 (Music)
The Voice of God Again Is Heard, 18 (Text and music)
We Ever Pray for Thee, 23; 312 (Text; musical adaptation)
Our Mountain Home So Dear, 33 (Music)
For the Strength of the Hills, 35 (Music)
Lo, the Mighty God Appearing! 55 (Music)
Raise Your Voices to the Lord, 61 (Text and music)
Praise Ye the Lord, 74 (Music)
Father, Thy Children to Thee Now Raise, 91 (Text and music)
Ye Simple Souls Who Stray, 118 (Music)
Lean on My Ample Arm, 120 (Music)
In Remembrance of Thy Suffering, 183 (Text and music)
Today, While the Sun Shines, 229 (Music)
Let Us All Press On, 243 (Text and music)
True to the Faith, 254 (Text and music)
See, the Mighty Angel Flying, 330 (Music)
O Home Beloved, 337 (Text)

Stott, Douglas W.

LDS. American, born 1925 in Millard County, Utah. He received his bachelor of arts degree from Brigham Young University and his master of music degree from the University of Michigan. He served a mission in eastern Canada. After teaching voice at the University of Texas, he obtained his doctorate in ancient scripture from BYU in 1970. From 1970 to 1984 he was director of the institute of religion in Columbus, Ohio. He has written curriculum for the LDS Church Educational System, and a recent assignment to direct the development of seminaries and institutes in the West Indies has taken him to Haiti. He has performed frequently as vocal soloist.

Saints, Behold How Great Jehovah, 28 (Text)

Stralsund Gesangbuch

Stralsund is the name of the city in East Germany where the *Erneuerten Gesangbuch* was published in 1665. The second volume of this hymn collection included the tune LOBE DEN HERREN (no. 72). The book's title means "revised" or "renewed" hymnbook.

Praise to the Lord, 72 (Music)

Sullivan, Sir Arthur Seymour

English, 1842–1900. Born in Lambeth, the son of a bandmaster, he showed early musical talent, and scholarships allowed him to study organ and composition. He is well remembered for the operettas he composed in collaboration with W. S. Gilbert, including *H.M.S. Pinafore, The Mikado,* and *Yeoman of the Guard*; the tuneful charm and satirical wit of these and other operettas spread the names of Gilbert and Sullivan throughout the English-speaking world. Sullivan himself always felt, however, that his most significant work was his serious music, including his religious cantatas.

Onward, Christian Soldiers, 246 (Music)

Swain, Joseph

English, 1761–1796. Born in Birmingham, he was an orphan boy apprenticed to an engraver in his early life. After hearing the preaching of John Rippon, he began the serious study of the scriptures and became a Baptist minister.

Redeemer of Israel, 6 (Text)

Sweney, John R.

American, 1837–1899. Born in West Chester, Pennsylvania, he showed an early interest in music. As a boy, he found opportunities to lead music in public school and Sunday School. At nineteen years of age he began more formal study of music, learning piano and violin. After a short period as professor of music at the Pennsylvania Military Academy, he served as a soldier in the Union Army. After the war, he returned to that same school, which later conferred two degrees on him. In addition to conducting vocal groups and bands, he wrote over one thousand religious songs and was known as an enthusiastic conductor of congregational singing at revival meetings.

The Lord Is My Light, 89 (Music)
There Is Sunshine in My Soul Today, 227 (Music)

Tanner, John Sears

LDS. American, born 1950 in Salt Lake City, Utah. He grew up in Pasadena, California, one of thirteen children. After attending Brigham Young University, where he graduated with highest honors, and serving a mission in Brazil, he enrolled in graduate studies at the University of California at Berkeley, where he received a doctorate in English. He has taught at Florida State University and is presently a member of the English faculty at BYU. He has also served as bishop of a student ward. His principal scholarly interest is Milton, Shakespeare, and other writers of the English Renaissance. He is married to Susan Winder, and they are the parents of five children.

Bless Our Fast, We Pray, 138 (Text)

Tate, Nahum

Irish-born English, 1652–1715. He was born in Dublin and received a bachelor of arts degree from Trinity College, Dublin, choosing thereafter to live in England. A dramatist as well as a poet, Tate is best remembered for his adaptations of the plays of Shakespeare. His version of *King Lear,* in which he altered the tragic ending so that Cordelia survives to marry Edgar, was widely performed for many decades. He was named poet laureate of England and wrote the libretto for Henry Purcell's important opera *Dido and Aeneas.*

While Shepherds Watched Their Flocks by Night, 211 (Text)

Taylor, John

LDS. English-born American, 1808–1887, a native of Milnthorpe. He emigrated to Canada in 1832, then moved to the United States in 1838. His long life of service is one of the most remarkable and inspiring in all the history of the Church. He was present at the martyrdom of Joseph Smith and was himself severely wounded; he served as a missionary in England, France, and Germany; he edited *Times and Seasons;* he served as a member of the Utah Territorial Legislature; he organized the Primary Association; and he was a prolific writer and journalist. He was ordained an Apostle in 1838; he was sustained as President of the Quorum of the Twelve Apostles in 1877; and he was sustained as third President of the Church in 1880.

Go, Ye Messengers of Glory, 262 (Text)
Go, Ye Messengers of Heaven, 327 (Text)

Taylor, Thomas Rawson

English, 1807–1835, born near Wakefield. He worked first in a merchant's office and then in a printer's office, but a strong desire to follow a religious vocation led him to begin study at age eighteen for the Congregational ministry. He was assigned to a congregation in Sheffield, but poor health forced him to leave the post after only six months. He died at twenty-eight years of age.

God Is Love, 87; 313 (Text)

Tennyson, Alfred Lord

English, 1809–1892, born in Lincolnshire. Of all Victorian poets, Tennyson was the most important spokesman of his age. His verse reflects the values and conflicts of English Victorianism, stressing the importance of duty and personal strength while exploring the problem of faith and isolation in an increasingly faithless, mechanistic world. In his vast output, important short poems include "Crossing the Bar" and "The Lady of Shalott"; a significant larger work is *Idylls of the King*, based on Arthurian legend. He was created a peer of the realm (thus "Lord Tennyson") and poet laureate of England.

Ring Out, Wild Bells, 215 (Text)

Teschner, Melchior

German (Silesian), 1584–1635, born in Fraustadt. In Frankfurt and Wittenberg he studied theology and philosophy as well as music, thus qualifying himself as both a Lutheran pastor and a musician. He was killed in a Cossack raid; thereafter his son and grandson succeeded him as pastors of his parish. J. S. Bach incorporated the hymn melody included in our hymnbook into several choral works, including the *St. John Passion.*

All Glory, Laud, and Honor, 69 (Music)

Thayne, Emma Lou

LDS. American, born 1924. A native of Salt Lake City, Utah, she earned her bachelor and master of arts degrees from the University of Utah and has taught in the English department of that university for more than three decades. Her extensive publications include ten books as well as poetry and articles in many periodicals, both Church-related and general. Her novel *Never Past the Gate* was a New York Book Club Selection, and she has received major awards from Lambda Delta Sigma, the Association for Mormon Letters, Brigham Young University, and the University of Utah. Her other interests include skiing, hiking, and tennis. She and her husband, Melvin E. Thayne, are the parents of five daughters.

Where Can I Turn for Peace? 129 (Text)

Theodulph of Orleans

760?–821; born in Spain, but lived his adult life in France. A bishop of the Catholic Church, later canonized as a saint, Theodulph was renowned both as a poet and an administrator. In about 781, Charlemagne heard of his abilities and called him to his court, where he astounded the learned gathering with his knowledge and his creative gifts. As bishop of Orleans, he established free schools for poor children in the surrounding villages. During the political unrest that followed the death of Charlemagne, St. Theodulph was deprived of his bishopric and then imprisoned.

All Glory, Laud, and Honor, 69 (Text)

Thesaurus Musicus

This collection, published in London and dated variously from 1740 to 1745, is the source of the hymn tune NATIONAL ANTHEM (United Kingdom) or AMERICA. It also includes a portion of the text for "God Save the King." *Harmonia Angelicana*, published in London in 1743 or 1744, included this tune and text as well. No names of composer or author were given in these sources.

My Country, 'Tis of Thee, 339 (Tune)
God Save the King, 341 (Tune and part of text)

Thomas, Carrie Stockdale

LDS. English-born American, 1848–1931, born in Plymouth. A woman of education and refinement, she emigrated to America in 1864 and one year later was married to Richard K. Thomas. She held leadership positions in Latter-day Saint wards in Salt Lake City, Utah, and attended conventions of the National Council of Women. She was a charter member of the Utah Women's Press Club. She and her husband were the parents of twelve children.

Great King of Heaven, 63 (Text)

Thompson, H. S.

Born about 1852. No other information is available concerning H. S. Thompson.

O Ye Mountains High, 34 (Music)

Thompson, R. Paul

LDS. American, born 1926 in St. George, Utah. He served two years in the United States Navy and then obtained bachelor and master of arts degrees in music from Brigham Young University. He received further training in the education of the blind at BYU, Utah State University, the University of Utah, and San Francisco State University. He has been instructor and principal at the Utah School for the Blind and branch chief of the programs for the severely handicapped for the United States Department of Education. Church service has included a mission in the North Central States, membership on the MIA General Board, and a calling as a Regional Representative. He and his wife, Geniel Parry, have eight children.

Rejoice, Ye Saints of Latter Days, 290 (Music)

Thompson, Robert B.

LDS. English-born American, 1811–1841. He was originally a Methodist preacher. After he emigrated to Canada in 1834 he heard the Latter-day Saint missionaries, accepted their message, and was baptized by Parley P. Pratt in 1836. Shortly thereafter he was ordained an elder by John Taylor. He married Mercy Rachel Fielding and was General Church Recorder from 1840 until his death the following year. He was a close friend and companion of Hyrum and Don Carlos Smith.

See, the Mighty Angel Flying, 330 (Text)

Thompson, Will Lamartine

American, 1847–1909, born in East Liverpool, Ohio. Educated at Mt. Union College, Ohio, he also attended music schools in Boston, Massachusetts, and in Leipzig, Germany. He wrote secular songs, patriotic songs, and gospel songs, and he established a highly successful music publishing firm.

Have I Done Any Good? 223 (Text and music)
Put Your Shoulder to the Wheel, 252 (Text and music)

Tillman, Charles Davis

American, 1861–1943. A native of Alabama, he was the son of a Methodist preacher and gospel singer. He became widely known as a singing evangelist, often appearing with Sam Jones, a Southern Methodist evangelist. He compiled and published many songbooks.

Truth Reflects upon Our Senses, 273 (Music)

Tomer, William Gould

American, 1833–1896. He acquired his musical training through attending singing schools and singing in choirs. After serving in the Pennsylvania infantry during the Civil War, he worked as a federal employee in Washington, D.C., for twenty years. During this time he was also music director for Grace Methodist Episcopal Church. The last years of his life were spent teaching school in New Jersey.

God Be with You Till We Meet Again, 152 (Music)

Toplady, Augustus M.

English, 1740–1778. Born in Surrey, he was educated at Westminster School and at Trinity College, Dublin. Though converted for a while to Methodism, he returned to the Church of England and became a minister. He was a theological opponent of John Wesley, and for many years the two men fought a bitter verbal battle, with Toplady defending the Calvinist doctrine of salvation through election.

Rock of Ages, 111 (Text)

Towner, Daniel Brink

American, 1850–1919. Born in Rome, Pennsylvania, he received his early musical training from his father, who was a singer and music teacher. He served as music director for several Methodist congregations and then joined the famous revivalist preacher Dwight L. Moody in his campaigns. In 1893 he became head of the music department of the Moody Bible Institute in Chicago. He received an honorary doctor of music degree from the University of Tennessee, and by the end of his life had written more than two thousand songs.

Ye Who Are Called to Labor, 321 (Music)

Townsend, Joseph Longking

LDS. American, 1849–1942. Born in Bradford County, Pennsylvania, he was reared on a farm and then pursued his education at the University of Missouri and the Agricultural College of Missouri. He traveled to Salt Lake City, Utah, in search of a climate that would better suit his health, and there he was baptized a Latter-day Saint. He taught penmanship at Morgan's Commercial College and at Brigham Young Academy and was principal of Payson High School. He also taught at Salt Lake City High School. He filled a mission to the southern states. For fifteen years he was proprietor of a drug and mercantile business in Payson, Utah.

The Day Dawn Is Breaking, 52 (Text)
Nearer, Dear Savior, to Thee, 99 (Text)
Reverently and Meekly Now, 185 (Text)
Let Us Oft Speak Kind Words, 232 (Text)
Choose the Right, 239 (Text)
O Thou Rock of Our Salvation, 258 (Text)
Hope of Israel, 259 (Text)
Oh, Holy Words of Truth and Love, 271 (Text)
The Iron Rod, 274 (Text)
Oh, What Songs of the Heart, 286 (Text)

Tucker, F. Bland

American, 1895–1984. Born in Norfolk, Virginia, the son and brother of Episcopalian clergymen, Tucker entered the Episcopalian priesthood after graduation from the University of Virginia and Virginia Theological Seminary and military service in World War I. He served as editor of major hymnals and in 1980 was made a fellow of the Hymn Society of America.

Our Father, by Whose Name, 296 (Text)

Tucker, Henry

Ca. 1863. No other information is available concerning Henry Tucker.

Now Let Us Rejoice, 3 (Music)

Tuckett, Henry A.

LDS. 1852–1918. In *Stories of Our Mormon Hymns* (p. 119), J. Spencer Cornwall informed us that Henry A. Tuckett was a candy maker in Salt Lake City, Utah, who pursued music as a hobby. He taught children's music classes, of which J. Spencer Cornwall was a member.

We Ever Pray for Thee, 23; 312 (Music)
We Are Sowing, 216 (Music)
Choose the Right, 239 (Music)

Tullidge, John Elliot

LDS. English-born American, 1806–1873. He was born in Weymouth into a family that offered many cultural advantages, and when he showed musical talent as a small child, he was given excellent musical training. He received his education at Eton, one of England's finest schools. With his fine tenor voice, he was able to make a living as a singer in London. He moved to Wales to become founder and conductor of the Newport Harmonic Society. His son Edward, later to become a noted Utah historian, was the first to be converted to Mormonism. The entire family emigrated to Utah, and John Tullidge was baptized after a year's time. He was active in Salt Lake City as a performer, composer, arranger, teacher, and music critic. His song "Hail! Young, Beautiful Spring" is said to be the first piece of music printed in the Rocky Mountain region.

An Angel from on High, 13; 328 (Music)
Come, All Ye Saints of Zion, 38 (Music)

Turk, Marie C.

American, twentieth century. Little is known about Marie Turk. Willie Reske, the composer of the music for "God's Daily Care" (no. 306), indicated that she was born and lived in Arizona, that she published several books of poetry and wrote many poems for Lutheran publications, and that she died in the 1950s.

God's Daily Care, 306 (Text)

Turton, William H.

LDS. English, 1856–1938. The identity of William Turton is a matter of some confusion. Our hymnbook lists him as a Latter-day Saint contributor but gives the dates of an English military man, William Henry Turton, who wrote many hymn texts and scholarly works and was not a Latter-day Saint. The first Latter-day Saint hymnbook to print his hymn text was the 1927 hymnal, which gave his middle initial as *B*. The text has a distinctly Latter-day Saint flavor, but Church records do not seem to contain any information regarding a William B. Turton.

O Thou, Before the World Began, 189 (Text)

Tyler, Walter G.

No information is available concerning Walter G. Tyler.

Called to Serve, 249 (Music)

Vaughan Williams, Ralph

English, 1872–1958. Born in Gloucestershire and educated at Cambridge, Vaughan Williams (*Ralph* is pronounced *Rafe*, and *Vaughan* is the first half of a double surname) is considered the most important English composer of his generation. Though he studied with continental composers such as Max Bruch and Maurice Ravel, his compositions reflect the temperament and folk songs of his native England. Folk melodies occur in many of his works (including the popular "Fantasia on Greensleeves"), and he set to music the words of such English poets as George Herbert and A. E. Housman. He made important contributions to English hymnody as a hymnbook editor and hymn arranger.

I Saw a Mighty Angel Fly, 15 (Musical arrangement)
All Creatures of Our God and King, 62 (Musical arrangement)
For All the Saints, 82 (Music)
If You Could Hie to Kolob, 284 (Musical arrangement)

Wade, John Francis

English, 1711?–1786. He lived most of his life at Douai, France, and made his living as a music copyist, producing beautiful manuscripts for Catholic institutions and wealthy Catholic families. He also taught Latin and church music.

Oh, Come, All Ye Faithful, 202 (Text and music)

Walford, William W.

English, 1772–1850. Born in Bath, he was educated at Homerton Academy and became a Congregationalist minister. He served at pastorates in Norfolk, Suffolk, and Uxbridge.

Sweet Hour of Prayer, 142 (Text)

Walker, Charles Lowell

LDS. English-born American, 1832–1904. Born in Bath, he sailed for America in 1849, working in St. Louis and Kentucky to raise money to help his parents emigrate. Arriving in Salt Lake City, Utah, in 1855, he went to work for his brother-in-law, Parley P. Pratt, and endured much hardship during the difficult winters of 1855 and 1856. He became a blacksmith, married, and was becoming comfortably settled when the call came to settle the Dixie Cotton Mission in southern Utah. During the forty years he lived in St. George, he composed scores of poems and songs to lift the hearts of people in those difficult surroundings.

Dearest Children, God Is Near You, 96 (Text)

Wallis, James Hearknett

LDS. English-born American, 1861–1940. Born in London, he was baptized a Latter-day Saint in 1877 and emigrated to Utah in 1881. He filled several missions for the Church. He was ordained a bishop by George Albert Smith and served as bishop of the Vernal First Ward, Uintah Stake.

Come, Ye Children of the Lord, 58 (Text)

Walter, William Henry

American, 1825–1893. A boy of precocious musical skill, born in Newark, New Jersey, he became organist at major New Jersey Protestant churches. His career as organist at several large cathedrals culminated in an appointment as organist at Columbia University, where he received an honorary doctorate in 1864. He published several works pertaining to organ technique and church music.

Rise Up, O Men of God, 324 (Music)

Walton, James G.

English, 1821–1905. We have few facts about his life other than that he was born in Lancashire and edited a book called *Plainsong Music for the Holy Communion Office.*

Faith of Our Fathers, 84 (Music of refrain)

Ward, Samuel Augustus

American, 1847–1903. He studied music with several music teachers in New York City and then began a successful music store in Newark, New Jersey. He became organist at Grace Episcopal Church in Newark, and later founded the Newark Orpheus Club, serving as its conductor for fifteen years.

America the Beautiful, 338 (Music)

Warren, George William

American, 1828–1902, born in Albany, New York. His organ career took him to many of the major churches and cathedrals in New York. He received an honorary doctorate from Racine College, Wisconsin, which he had attended as a young man. His compositions include church music of all types.

God of Our Fathers, Whose Almighty Hand, 78 (Music)

Watkins, Vanja Louise Yorgason

LDS. American, born 1938. Vanja (pronounced *VON yuh*) Watkins attended schools in Ogden, Utah, and received her bachelor and master of arts degrees in music education from Brigham Young University. She then returned to Ogden to become music coordinator for the Ogden City Schools; she was also a television teacher in elementary music. She has taught music education at Brigham Young University, and she has been a stake Primary president and has served on the Primary General Board, the General Music Committee of the Church, and the 1985 Hymnbook Executive Committee. Her compositions are well known to Primary children. She and her husband, Jack B. Watkins, are the parents of five children.

Press Forward, Saints, 81 (Music)
Families Can Be Together Forever, 300 (Music)

Watts, Isaac

English, 1674–1748. Born in Southampton, he was offered a scholarship to become a minister of the Church of England, but he followed the religious principles instilled by his family and became a Congregationalist minister. Other churchmen of his denomination approved only of the singing of psalms, but he found such hymns unsatisfying. He believed that Christians should be able to sing about Christ and Christ-centered topics. He left over six hundred hymns, venturing far beyond the limits of biblical paraphrase. Because of his innovative views and poetic gifts, he is considered the single most important figure in the history of English hymnody.

O God, Our Help in Ages Past, 31 (Text)
Praise Ye the Lord, 74 (Text)
With All the Power of Heart and Tongue, 79 (Text)
Great God, Attend While Zion Sings, 88 (Text)
From All That Dwell below the Skies, 90 (Text)
Come, We That Love the Lord, 119 (Text)
Sweet Is the Work, 147; 317 (Text)
He Died! The Great Redeemer Died, 192 (Text)
Joy to the World, 201 (Text)

Webb, George James

English-born American, 1803–1887, born in Salisbury. He sailed for America in 1830 and made his home there for the rest of his life. For forty years he was organist at the Old South Church in Boston, Massachusetts. He was a friend and colleague of Lowell Mason of the Boston Academy of Music and collaborated with him on a number of important publications.

We Give Thee But Thine Own, 218 (Musical arrangement)

Webbe, Samuel, Sr.

English, 1740–1816, born in London. After serving an apprenticeship to a carpenter, he left that vocation to study music, earning his living as a music copyist while taking organ lessons. He also became fluent in several languages. He served as organist in the Portuguese, Sardinian, and

Spanish embassies in London, and his publications were a significant contribution to Roman Catholic church music.

Come, Ye Disconsolate, 115 (Music)

Weber, Carl Maria von

German, 1786–1826, born in Oldenburg. Considered the founder of German romantic opera, he was a student of Michael Haydn. His operas *Der Freischutz* and *Oberon* are still performed today, and the waltz "Invitation to the Dance" is known worldwide. (His surname is pronounced approximately *VAY ber*.)

Softly Now the Light of Day, 160 (Music)

Welch, James B.

LDS. American, born 1950 in Whittier, California. He grew up in Los Angeles and was encouraged in musical studies by his family. Later, his organ teachers included Parley Belnap, Alexander Schreiner, and Herbert Nanney; he studied at the Mozarteum in Salzburg, Austria, and at Stanford University, where he received his doctorate in music. He has held a Fulbright fellowship for study in Brazil, where previously he had served as a missionary. As a concert and recording organist, he has toured the United States, Europe, and South America. He is an associate of the American Guild of Organists and has served as dean of the Santa Barbara chapter. Presently he is a faculty member at the University of California at Santa Barbara.

Bless Our Fast, We Pray, 138 (Music)

Wells, Emmeline B.

LDS. American, 1828–1921, born in Petersham, Massachusetts. She taught school in Massachusetts, in Nauvoo, and in Winter Quarters; after journeying to Salt Lake City in 1848, she again was a teacher for two years before marrying Daniel H. Wells. One of the remarkable women of early Utah, a fine organizer as well as a writer, she was fifth General President of the Relief Society and editor and publisher of the *Woman's Exponent.* At the request of President Brigham Young, she accepted the assignment of directing the storage of wheat; as a result of this project, two hundred thousand bushels of wheat were available when the United States government asked to purchase them in 1918.

Our Mountain Home So Dear, 33 (Text)

Wesley, Charles

English, 1707–1788. He was born in Lincolnshire. While students at Oxford, he and his brother John gathered together with a group of other young men who were serious about their spiritual studies and moral conduct and founded a "methodist" society. They became the principal leaders of the Methodist church movement, which finally made a formal break from the Church of England and became an important Protestant denomination in both England and America. Charles himself was personally opposed to this separation, however. He is remembered as a tireless preacher as well as the writer of some sixty-five hundred hymns. (See also the discussion of "The Morning Breaks," no. 1.)

Rejoice, the Lord Is King! 66 (Text)
Jesus, Lover of My Soul, 102 (Text)
Ye Simple Souls Who Stray, 118 (Text)
Christ the Lord Is Risen Today, 200 (Text)
Hark! the Herald Angels Sing, 209 (Text)
Come, Let Us Anew, 217 (Text)

Wheelock, Cyrus Hibbard

LDS. American, 1813–1894. A native of New York, he was baptized a Latter-day Saint in 1839. A friend of Joseph Smith, he was one of the last members of the Church to visit Carthage jail before the martyrdom. (See *History of the Church,* 7:99–101.) He filled a mission in Vermont and traveled to England with Parley P. Pratt for additional missionary work. He also served as president of the Northern States Mission.

Ye Elders of Israel, 319 (Text)

Wheelwright, Lorin F.

LDS. American, 1909–1987. Born in Ogden, Utah, he studied piano and organ with Mona Smith, Edward P. Kimball, Alexander Schreiner, and Percy Grainger. He received his bachelor of arts degree from the University of Utah, master of arts from the University of Chicago, and doctorate from Columbia. He taught music at Oswego, New York, and then was music supervisor for the Salt Lake public schools for thirteen years. He was arts manager for the Utah Centennial in 1947, head of the Wheelwright Litho Company for twenty-two years, and a member of the Sunday School General Board for thirteen years. He spent nine years at Brigham Young University as dean of the college of fine arts and communications and assistant to President Dallin H. Oaks.

Oh, May My Soul Commune with Thee, 123 (Text and music)
Help Me Teach with Inspiration, 281 (Text and music)
O Love That Glorifies the Son, 295 (Text and music)

Whitney, Orson Ferguson

LDS. American, 1855–1931. Born in Salt Lake City, Utah, he studied music and oratory and was a student at the University of Deseret. He served as a missionary in the eastern states and in the British Isles and as president of the European Mission. His interests included acting, public speaking, journalism, poetry, history, theology, and politics. He was assistant editor of the *Millennial Star,* publication supervisor of the *Journal of Discourses,* and author of the four-volume *History of Utah.* He was regent and chancellor of the University of Deseret and served in the Utah state senate. In 1902 he was called as assistant Church historian and in 1906 became a member of the Quorum of the Twelve Apostles.

The Wintry Day, Descending to Its Close, 37 (Text)
Savior, Redeemer of My Soul, 112 (Text)

Widtsoe, John Andreas

LDS. Norwegian-born American, 1872–1952, born on the island of Froyen. His mother was left a widow when he was six years old. After her conversion to The Church of Jesus Christ of Latter-day Saints, she sailed with her two young sons to America and settled in Logan, Utah, in 1883. John Widtsoe first attended Brigham Young College in Logan and then enrolled at Harvard University, graduating with highest honors in chemistry in 1894. He earned a doctorate from the University of Goettingen in 1899. He served as president of Utah State Agricultural College and then of the University of Utah. In 1921 he was called to be a member of the Quorum of the Twelve Apostles, and he presided over the European Mission from 1927 to 1933. He wrote thirty books and innumerable articles, tracts, and manuals.

Lead Me into Life Eternal, 45 (Text)
How Long, O Lord Most Holy and True, 126 (Text)

Willes, William

LDS. English-born American, 1814–1890, born in London. Though his father was a tradesman, William obtained a good education and at age twenty-two was put in charge of a boys' school in Cardiff, Wales. As a result of his baptism into The Church of Jesus Christ of Latter-day Saints in 1848, he lost his teaching position. He and Elder Joseph Richards served as Latter-day Saint missionaries in India and Burma, and in 1855 he sailed for America. He was called as a Sabbath School missionary after his arrival in Utah, and he traveled from Sunday School to Sunday School singing songs and telling inspirational stories.

Come Along, Come Along, 244 (Text)
Thanks for the Sabbath School, 278 (Text)

Williams, Aaron

English, 1731–1776. He lived in London and made his living as a teacher, publisher, and engraver of music. He compiled several collections, one of which was reprinted in America.

Come, We That Love the Lord, 119 (Music)

Williams, Peter

Welsh, 1772–1796, born in Carmarthenshire. Converted to Methodism as a boy, he was ordained to the Methodist ministry in 1744 and became prominent in the Methodist revival in Wales. He was controversial in his views and was dismissed from several positions, but he built a chapel on land that belonged to him in Carmarthen and continued to preach there. He published an annotated Bible and a hymnbook in Welsh.

Guide Us, O Thou Great Jehovah, 83 (Translation of first verse)

Williams, Ralph Vaughan

See Vaughan Williams, Ralph.

Williams, Thomas E.

English, died in 1854. No other information is available concerning Thomas E. Williams.

Up, Awake, Ye Defenders of Zion, 248 (Music)

Williams, William

Welsh, 1717–1791, born near Llandovery. He turned from the study of medicine to music and religion and became perhaps the most important figure in Welsh hymnody. Although he was never ordained a clergyman, by the end of his life he had traveled almost one hundred thousand miles throughout Wales as a preacher. He wrote some eight hundred hymns, all in Welsh.

Guide Us, O Thou Great Jehovah, 83 (Text)

Willis, Richard Storrs

American, 1819–1900. He was born in Boston, Massachusetts. After graduating from Yale, he went to Germany where he studied with Felix Mendelssohn, whose biography he later published. He returned to America and became a music critic, working for several different newspapers. He wrote secular as well as religious music and also published books on church music topics.

It Came upon the Midnight Clear, 207 (Music)

Winkworth, Catherine

English, 1829–1878, born in London. Known for her devout nature and her quick mind, she left her mark on English hymnody through her translations of German hymn texts. The two parts of her *Lyra Germanica* appeared in 1855 and 1888, and in 1863 she published the *Chorale Book for England,* for which her musical collaborators were Otto Goldschmidt and William Sterndale Bennett. She became affiliated with the Clifton Association for the Higher Education of Women and devoted much of her life, as both teacher and administrator, to the cause of women's education. She is known today as the foremost translator of German hymn texts into English, and the present Lutheran hymnal includes thirty of her translations.

Praise to the Lord, the Almighty, 72 (Translation)
Now Thank We All Our God, 95 (Translation)

Wingate, Mary B.

Born 1899. No other information is available concerning Mary B. Wingate.

Dear to the Heart of the Shepherd, 221 (Text)

Wolford, Darwin K.

LDS. American, born 1936 in Logan, Utah. After graduation from Utah State University, he received his master of music and doctoral degrees from the University of Utah. He studied organ under Alexander Schreiner and Robert Cundick and composition under Leroy Robertson, Ned Rorem, and John LaMontaine. His compositions and arrangements, which include works for chorus, orchestra, piano, and organ, have been published widely and performed by the Utah Symphony, the Mormon Tabernacle Choir, and many other groups. He served on the General Music Committee of the Church and the 1985 Hymnbook Executive Committee and was responsible for much of the music editing for the 1985 hymnal. He is director of organ studies at Ricks College in Rexburg, Idaho. He and his wife, Julie Lofgren, are the parents of five children.

We Listen to a Prophet's Voice, 22 (Music)
Sons of Michael, He Approaches, 51 (Music)

Woodmansee, Emily Hill

LDS. English-born American, 1836–1906. At age twelve she heard the message of the Latter-day Saint missionaries, and at sixteen she was baptized. With her sister, she emigrated to America in 1856 and pushed a handcart across the plains with the Willie handcart company. In 1857 she was married and had a child, but her husband deserted her. She married Joseph Woodmansee in 1864, and they had four sons and four daughters. After they suffered financial reverses, she entered into business and real estate with great success. Orson F. Whitney called her the "possessor of a poetic as well as a practical mind. . . . Her busy pen has brought forth many meritorious productions." (*History of Utah,* 4:593–94.) She is the author of the Primary song "Let the Little Children Come."

As Sisters in Zion, 309 (Text)

Yorgason, Laurence M.

LDS. American, born 1937 in Ogden, Utah. A student of music from age five, he played the piano, tuba, and string bass. He earned a bachelor's degree in music theory and a master's degree in history from Brigham Young University. He served a mission in Norway. For more than twenty years he has taught in Latter-day Saint seminaries and institutes of religion. He has served in many Church callings, including that of bishop. He is married to Kay Lynne Olsen, and they have six children.

We Meet, Dear Lord, 151 (Music)

Young, John Freeman

American, 1820–1885, born in Kennebec County, Maine. He studied at Wesleyan University in Connecticut. He was converted to the Episcopal Church and thereafter entered the Virginia Theological Seminary, graduating in 1845. He was a vigorous missionary throughout the southern states, and he also laid the foundations for Episcopal missionary work in Cuba. In 1867 he became bishop of the diocese of Florida. Not until 1957 was he discovered to be the translator of "Silent Night."

Silent Night, 204 (Translation)

Photos of Sarah F. Adams, Joseph Addison, Cecil Frances Alexander, Henry Alford, Sabine Baring-Gould, Joseph Barnby, Katharine Lee Bates, Bernard of Clairvaux, Phillips Brooks, William Cowper, Grace Noll Crowell, George W. Doane, Philip Doddridge, John Ellerton, John Fawcett, Thomas Hastings, Annie S. Hawks, Reginald Heber, Edward Hopper, Julia Ward Howe, Thomas Ken, Francis Scott Key, Rudyard Kipling, Henry Wadsworth Longfellow, Robert Lowry, Martin Luther, Henry F. Lyte, Samuel Medley, William Pierson Merrill, Joseph Mohr, Joachim Neander, John Henry Newman, John Newton, Johnson Oatman, Jr., H. R. Palmer, Folliott S. Pierpoint, Jeremiah E. Rankin, Martin Rinkhart, Daniel C. Roberts, Edmund H. Sears, Samuel F. Smith, Alfred Lord Tennyson, Augustus M. Toplady, Isaac Watts, and William Williams are taken from Mildred C. Whittemore, *Hymn Writers of the Christian Church* (Boston: Whittemore Associates, 1963). Used by permission of the publisher.

Photos of Robert B. Baird, Ebenezer Beesley, Wallace F. Bennett, Tracy Y. Cannon, George Careless, John M. Chamberlain, William Clayson, William Clayton, Joseph J. Daynes, Hugh W. Dougall, Alfred M. Durham, Lewis D. Edwards, William Fowler, Ruth May Fox, Thomas C. Griggs, Franz Gruber, Orson Pratt Huish, John Jaques, J. Marinus Jensen, Joel H. Johnson, Edward P. Kimball, Frank I. Kooyman, John J. McClellan, Thomas McIntyre, Annie Pinnock Malin, George Manwaring, Felix Mendelssohn, Henry W. Naisbitt, Charles W. Penrose, Parley P. Pratt, George D. Pyper, W. O. Robinson, Ed M. Rowe, Joseph Fielding Smith, A. C. Smyth, Richard Smyth, Eliza R. Snow, Evan Stephens, John Taylor, Joseph L. Townsend, and Orson F. Whitney are taken from J. Spencer Cornwall, *Stories of Our Mormon Hymns* (Salt Lake City: Deseret Book Company, 1961). Used by permission of the publisher.

Photos of Benjamin Carr, F. Bland Tucker, and Charles Wesley are taken from *The Hymn* 32, no. 1 (January 1981); 35, no. 2 (April 1984); and 35, no. 3 (July 1984), respectively. *The Hymn* is published by the Hymn Society of America. Used by permission of the publisher.

Photos of Joseph Barnby, William Croft, and Orlando Gibbons are taken from Myles Birket Foster, *Anthems and Anthem Composers* (London: Novello and Co., 1901).

The photo of Lowell Mason is taken from *Hymn-Tunes of Lowell Mason, A Biography*, comp. Henry L. Mason (Cambridge, Mass.: University Press, 1944). Used by permission of the publisher.

Photos of Archibald F. Bennett, John Menzies Macfarlane, Edward Partridge, William W. Phelps, Ellis Reynolds Shipp, John E. Tullidge, Emmeline B. Wells, John A. Widtsoe, and Emily H. Woodmansee are used courtesy of the Historical Department of The Church of Jesus Christ of Latter-day Saints, Salt Lake City, Utah.

The photo of George F. Root is taken from the February 1988 issue of the *Music Educators Journal* published by the Music Educators National Conference. Used by permission of the publisher.

Photo in the Introduction of George F. Root, Lowell Mason, and William B. Bradbury is taken from the February 1988 issue of the *Music Educators Journal* published by the Music Educators National Conference. Used by permission of the publisher. Other photos in the Introduction are used courtesy of the Music Department and the Historical Department of The Church of Jesus Christ of Latter-day Saints, Salt Lake City, Utah.

SELECTED REFERENCES

Bailey, Albert Edward. *The Gospel in Hymns*. New York: Charles Scribner's Sons, 1950.

Cornwall, J. Spencer. *Stories of Our Mormon Hymns*. Salt Lake City, Utah: Deseret Book Co., 1975.

Hatch, Verena Ursenbach. "Thoughts on Music and Worship." *Dialogue: A Journal of Mormon Thought* 10 (Spring 1975): 18–20.

Hatch, Verena Ursenbach. *Worship and Music in The Church of Jesus Christ of Latter-day Saints*. Provo, Utah: M. Ephraim Hatch, 1968.

Hauessler, Armin. *The Story of Our Hymns*. St. Louis, Mo.: Eden Publishing House, 1952.

Hicks, Michael. "Poetic Borrowing in Early Mormonism." *Dialogue: A Journal of Mormon Thought* 18 (Spring 1985): 132–42.

Julian, John, ed. *A Dictionary of Hymnology*. 2 vols. 1907. Reprint. New York: Dover Publications, 1957.

Kerr, Phil. *Music in Evangelism*. Glendale, California: Gospel Music Publishers, 1939.

Lubeck, Kathleen. "The New Hymnbook." *Ensign* 15 (September 1985): 7–13.

Lynn, Karen. "Our LDS Hymn Texts: A Look at the Past; Some Thoughts for the Future." *Dialogue: A Journal of Mormon Thought* 10 (Spring 1975): 44–48.

Madsen, Carol C. "Our Heritage of Hymns. *New Era* 5 (November 1975): 10–17.

Maxwell, Bruce David. "Source Book for *Hymns* (1950)." Copyright 1982. Photocopy distribution by the author.

McCutchan, Robert Guy. *Our Hymnody: A Manual of the Methodist Hymnal*. New York: Abingdon Press, 1937.

Moody, Michael F. "Latter-day Saint Hymnbooks, Then and Now." *Ensign* 15 (September 1985): 10–13.

New Grove Dictionary of Music and Musicians. 6th ed. 20 vols. Edited by Stanley Sadie. London: Macmillan, 1980.

Nibley, Reid. "Thoughts on Music in the Church." *Ensign* 2 (February 1972): 13.

Nutter, Charles S., and Tillett, Wilbur F. *The Hymns and Hymn Writers of the Church*. New York: The Methodist Book Concern, 1911.

Osbeck, Kenneth W. *101 Hymn Stories*. Grand Rapids, Mich.: Kregel Publications, 1982.

Packer, Boyd K. "The Arts and the Spirit of the Lord." *Ensign* 6 (August 1976): 60–65.

Pratt, John Barnes. *Present Day Hymns and Why They Were Written*. New York: A. S. Barnes and Co., 1940.

Primary Song Book. Salt Lake City, Utah: Deseret News Press, 1939.

Pyper, George D. *Stories of Latter-day Saint Hymns*. Salt Lake City, Utah: Deseret News Press, 1939.

Reynolds, William J. *Companion to Baptist Hymnal*. Nashville: Broadman Press, 1976.

Robison, Clayne W. "Singing Hymns with New Power." *Ensign* 7 (July 1977): 32–34.

Ronander, Albert C., and Porter, Ethel K. *Guide to the Pilgrim Hymnal*. Philadelphia: United Church Press, 1966.

Schreiner, Alexander. "Guidelines for Writing Latter-day Hymns." *Ensign* 3 (April 1973): 52–58.
Stulken, Marilyn Kay. *Hymnal Companion to the Lutheran Book of Worship*. Philadelphia: Fortress Press, 1981.
Weight, Newell B. "The Birth of Mormon Hymnody." *Dialogue: A Journal of Mormon Thought* 10 (Spring 1975): 40–43.

The *Juvenile Instructor* from 1930 to 1970 contained monthly articles on music and hymns. Specific references for 1961 through 1970 may be found in the *Index to Periodicals of The Church of Jesus Christ of Latter-day Saints, 1961–1970.*

The following items are doctoral dissertations and should be requested through a college or public library's interlibrary loan department:

Macare, Helen Hanks. "The Singing Saints: A Study of the Mormon Hymnal, 1835–1950." Ph.D. disseration, University of California at Los Angeles, 1961.
Moody, Michael Finlinson. "Contemporary Hymnody in the Church of Jesus Christ of Latter-day Saints." Ph.D. dissertation, University of Southern California, 1972.
Weight, Newell Bryan. "An Historical Study of the Origins and Character of the Indigenous Hymn Tunes of the Latter-day Saints." D.M.A. dissertation, University of Southern California, 1961.
Wheelwright, David Sterling. "The Role of Hymnody in the Development of the Latter-day Saint Movement." Ph.D. dissertation, University of Maryland, 1943.
Wilkes, William LeRoy. "Borrowed Music in Mormon Hymnals." Ph.D. dissertation, University of Southern California, 1957.

INDEX